RENAISSANCE MINDS
AND
THEIR FICTIONS

Parmigianino, Self-Portrait in a Convex Mirror. Vienna, Kunsthistorisches Museum.

RENAISSANCE MINDS
AND
THEIR FICTIONS
CUSANUS, SIDNEY,
SHAKESPEARE

Ronald Levao

University of California Press
Berkeley
Los Angeles
London

University of California Press
Berkeley and Los Angeles, California

University of California Press, Ltd.
London, England

Library of Congress Cataloging in Publication Data

Levao, Ronald.
    Renaissance minds and their fictions.

    Includes index.
    1. English literature—Early modern, 1500–1700—
History and criticism. 2. Renaissance. 3. Nicholas,
of Cusa, Cardinal, 1401–1464. 4. Sidney, Philip, Sir,
1554–1586—Criticism and interpretation. 5. Shakespeare, William, 1564–1616—Criticism and interpretation. I. Title.
PR411.L38 1985   820'.9'003   84–8756
ISBN 0–520–05275–7

Printed in the United States of America

1 2 3 4 5 6 7 8 9

For my father and mother, with love

ANSELM OF CANTERBURY,
WHY GOD BECAME MAN

No one paints on water or in air, because no traces
of the pictures would remain. Now when we
present unbelievers with these harmonies you
speak of, as so many pictures of a real event, they
think that this belief of ours is a fiction, and not a
real happening, and so they judge that we are,
as it were, painting on a cloud.

ROLAND BARTHES, *ROLAND BARTHES*
BY ROLAND BARTHES

A *doxa* . . . is postulated intolerable; to free
myself of it, I postulate a paradox; then this
paradox turns bad, becomes a new concretion,
itself becomes a new *doxa*, and I must seek
further for a new paradox.

WILLIAM SHAKESPEARE, *HAMLET*

Is it not monstrous that this player here,
But in a fiction, in a dream of passion,
Could force his soul so to his own conceit
That from her working all his visage wann'd;
Tears in his eyes, distraction in's aspect,
A broken voice, and his whole function suiting
With forms to his conceit? And all for nothing!

CONTENTS

LIST OF ILLUSTRATIONS

PREFACE

The Renaissance, Wallace Ferguson once remarked, is "the most intractable problem child of historiography." This study proposes to explore one source of such unruliness: the volatile mixture of enthusiasm and anxiety with which Renaissance authors regard the mind's craving for figures and fictions. To that end, this book proposes some new approaches to literary and philosophical works, not to present a compendium of Renaissance attitudes or to chart lines of influence, but to show how a cluster of related problems simultaneously animates and haunts diverse texts of the period. I say "haunts" because, though these problems are sometimes acknowledged openly, they are as often felt in subtler ways—in the obstacles or deflections they impose on speculation and in the variety of attempts writers make to exorcise them. Modern critics who are sensitive to Renaissance antinomies have found valuable resources in social and political studies. Intellectual history remains valuable for such study as well, for it enables us to consider patterns of thought not only for the doctrines they represent but also for the pressures they seek to accommodate or contain.

It is with pleasure that I thank Stephen Greenblatt, Paul Alpers, Stephen Orgel, William Bouwsma, and Phillip Damon, who advised and encouraged me during the early stages of my work, and who remain important to me as ideal readers. I also want to thank David Bromwich, Lawrence Danson, David Quint, and Thomas Roche for many acts of kindness and support, as well as numerous colleagues, teachers, and friends at

Princeton, Rutgers, Berkeley, and elsewhere: Joel Altman, John Anson, Christopher Coats, George Dardess, Margaret Doody, Michael Goldman, William Howarth, David Kalstone, William Keach, Alvin Kernan, Ulrich Knoepflmacher, Seth Lerer, Earl Miner, Michael Murrin, Joseph Phillips, Richard Poirier, Barry Qualls, Norman Rabkin, Peggy Rosenthal, and Isadore Traschen. Richard Levao and Robert Platt should have their own sentence.

Grateful acknowledgment is made to *PMLA* for permission to use "Sidney's Feigned Apology" 94 (1974): 223–33, which appears in revised form as chapter 5; to the Arthur J. Banning Press for permission to quote from Jasper Hopkins's *Nicholas of Cusa on Learned Ignorance: A Translation and an Appraisal of "De docta ignorantia"* (1981) and *Nicholas of Cusa's Debate with John Wenck: A Translation and an Appraisal of "De ignota litteratura" and "Apologia doctae ignorantiae"* (1981); and to the National Endowment for the Humanities for a summer stipend supporting a project concerning the assumptions of cultural and intellectual history.

My greatest debt is to my wife, Susan Wolfson, with whom I have been sharing love and sentences for fifteen years. She, more than any, makes the brazen world golden.

ABBREVIATIONS

Apology	Sir Philip Sidney, *An Apology for Poetry*
AS	Sir Philip Sidney, *Astrophil and Stella*
De con.	Nicholas of Cusa, *De coniecturis*
DDI	Nicholas of Cusa, *De docta ignorantia*
GGN	*Gammer Gurton's Needle*
NA	Sir Philip Sidney, *New Arcadia*
OA	Sir Philip Sidney, *Old Arcadia*
PL	*Patrologia latina*, ed. J. P. Migne
Schmitt	*Sancti Anselmi opera omnia*, ed. F. S. Schmitt
ST	St. Thomas Aquinas, *Summa theologica*

INTRODUCTION

The burst of literary creativity in England during the final quarter of the sixteenth century gave rise to a preoccupation with the nature of poetic fictions. This self-consciousness was an intrinsic feature of the creative surge itself and found expression in the works of the age's most brilliant writers, among them Sidney, Spenser, and Shakespeare. My contention is that this twin birth is part of a larger movement in Renaissance thought and letters, one that brought increased attention to bear on both the power and contingency of human constructions—literary and extraliterary—and came ultimately to contribute to a vision of culture, not as structured by eternal categories, but as a distinctly human artifact. One historian has recently suggested that Max Weber's view of man as "an animal suspended in webs of significance he himself has spun" received its first modern coloring in the Renaissance.[1] This study aims to situate the Elizabethan "golden age" of poetic fictions within this emerging attitude by focusing on three case studies of the Renaissance imagination. Before introducing these, it will be useful to draw a broad preliminary sketch of their common historical context.

In the middle of the thirteenth century, St. Bonaventure ascended Mount Alverna in search of spiritual peace, and, like St. Francis before him, witnessed a miraculous vision pointing the way: "I immediately saw that it signified the suspension of our father himself in contemplation and the way by which he came to it."[2] In the following century, Petrarch ascended Mount Ventoux, an act he first attributed to secular curiosity, but which his retrospective account casts as an allegory of the soul's pilgrimage. But so ostentatiously does the author represent himself in the very act of interpreting his experience that he impresses us less with an immediate, objective meaning than with the mind's motions as it surveys possible meanings, embracing some and testing others. The account ends not with Petrarch's often-cited reading of St. Augustine but with a storm in the author's breast and his fear that a shift in his volatile mood might subvert his very intention to record the event.[3]

The instability that Petrarch at once laments and dramatizes is an early instance of a new psychic agitation. Medieval writers often assume a sacramental cosmos that sustains and validates their institutions, signs, and symbols—a framework within which human thought and emotion may find expression. The Renaissance proliferation of numerologies, providential histories, and metaphysical systems—what Angus Fletcher calls "its wild fascination with inconceivable devices of order-in-chaos"[4]—testifies to the survival of those traditional harmonies, as does the work of compilers such as Pierre de la Primaudaye who picture the world as "girt and buckled with bands of concord." But we must ask ourselves whether such texts certify a continuity of attitude or reveal a willed conservatism, a strenuous and self-conscious effort to shore up a profoundly unsettled edifice. We should also consider whether the most distinguished of such texts are merely reactionary. Do "great texts," Dominick LaCapra asks, at times achieve their status because they "both reinforce tradition and subvert it," thus allowing them "to confirm or establish something—a value, a pattern of coherence, a system, a genre—and call it into question"?[5] Signs of instability and questioning are far-reaching and various: the turn of rhetorical humanists away from Scholastic verities; the juxtaposition of incompatible assertions of authority in the Protestant and Catholic Reformations; the fascinations with other worlds in time and space—a joint development of historical consciousness, new-world exploration, astronomical speculation, and skeptical thought. All exert pressure on the ways Renaissance minds shape the world they know and the ways that world shapes them. Responses to such challenges range from the Reformation piety of Luther and Calvin, who condemn "fictitious customs" and "presumptuous imaginations," to a sometimes bizarre playfulness that gives new life to such paradoxes as the *theatrum mundi*, *serio ludere*, and the praise of folly. Tropes uniting play and earnest may be commonplaces in classical and medieval thought, but they are never more startlingly juxtaposed than in the Renaissance when, as Johan Huizinga notes, ideals are "pursued in holy earnest" with "violence, depth, and purity" alongside a world "whose whole mental attitude . . . was one of play."[6] Folly becomes the mark not merely of religious or epistemological modesty, but of a struggle to hold in suspension an enormous number of symbols, beliefs, and quasi beliefs, elements of a world increasingly subject to centrifugal forces.

It is this struggle that motivates the period's most ambitious philosophical and literary performances. The three figures represented in this study—Cusanus, Sidney, and Shakespeare— are often regarded as bearers of central traditions, yet their speculative and imaginative powers also arise from a willingness to confront, and even exploit, the fissures of those traditions.

Cusanus presents the challenges of the Renaissance imagination in the most general, philosophical terms. He has long attracted scholars as a kind of archetypal figure. Historians of philosophy, science, religion, politics, and aesthetic theory rarely establish any direct influence on his contemporaries, but from Ernst Cassirer's endorsement of him as the focal point of the age to Alexandre Koyré's placement of him at the transition from the closed world to the infinite universe to Dorothy Koenigsberger's recent characterization of him as the "artist's philosopher," he has become an embodiment of Renaissance intellectual ferment.[7] Unlike some of the humanists who de-emphasize larger philosophical problems, and unlike the Neoplatonists who often mask the difficulty of their discoveries behind a conservative metaphysic, Cusanus allows us to witness the deformation of traditional modes of conceiving the world and their transformation into new patterns—patterns that highlight the mind's active share in their very production.

This metamorphosis lies at the heart of Renaissance poetics. The abiding critical concern over symbolic heterocosms and the imaginations that create them, first apparent in Italy, repeats many of the preoccupations we find in Cusanus. By education, experience, and inclination, Sir Philip Sidney brings these concerns to Elizabethan literature, together with an ironic and self-conscious perspective on the cultural ideals he seemed to so many of his contemporaries to personify. The *Apology for Poetry*, *Astrophil and Stella*, and the two *Arcadia*s, all probably written within six years, constitute a literary career rivaled in importance by few. For Sidney not only provides a major impetus for literary criticism, sonneteering, and prose fiction, but his works, culminating in the vast *New Arcadia*, shape one of Renaissance England's most engaging, ambitious, yet disturbing visions of the imagination.

It is in the theater that the problem of human invention achieves its fullest expression, especially in the plays of Shakespeare, the focus for the final part of this study. Shakespeare's five earliest histories and *Hamlet* offer a sequence that traces his evolving dramatic representation of the mind's encounter with a radically unsettled external order. A study of comic reconciliations would point perhaps in a somewhat different, though not opposite, direction. It is in history and tragedy, however, that Shakespeare most decisively uncovers the terrible emotional and intellectual hunger that drove his age to seek resolution. Shakespeare's investigations continue, of course, through *The Tempest*, but *Hamlet* is a convenient terminus at the turn of the century. Seventeenth-century texts continue the work of the sixteenth, but seek a new direction, as I plan to show elsewhere.

Two complementary assumptions should be made clear. 1. Periodization, for all its discrepancies, is a key historical category: despite linguistic, social, and religious differences, a fifteenth-century German philosopher and two sixteenth-century English poets illuminate one another and in conjunction reflect the international movement historians call the Renaissance. 2. Texts are elusive. Some literary historians seem more decisively committed to monolithic "world pictures" than their counterparts in intellectual history. The reason may be an urge to chart the meaning of poetic documents, to point their acknowledged complexity and suggestiveness toward some systematic interpretation of reality. The aim in this book is not to deny historical universals or the force of official ideologies but to see world pictures themselves as multivalent human creations. Renaissance thought is not so much a background for poetry nor poetry so much an illustration of doctrine as both are expressions of a common effort to come to terms with a dynamic, and often disorienting, world.

These assumptions make the case study an attractive form of organization. It encourages juxtaposition without making problematic claims for the transmission of shared doctrine. Indeed, part of what makes Cusanus, Sidney, and Shakespeare valuable as case studies is the difficulty of reducing any one of them to the terms of another. The theologian, the aristocratic amateur, and the professional playwright see the world in distinctive ways, and their texts inhabit different realms of discourse. Yet once we explore the ways their texts function—that is, the strategic maneuvers they adopt in inventing and arranging significant metaphor, argument, and theme, as well as the ways in which they seek to elicit response—we discover a range of implication as compelling as that supplied by specific lines of influence. Vital affinities emerge, in fact, at those moments when each of these writers is most fully engaged with his particular mode of vision, for it is then that their divergent points of view bring into focus one common concern: the energies of human feigning—that is, the mind's power to shape schemes of coherence independently of, or in ambiguous relation to, an external given. Indeed, all three writers enact a similar drama: the release of extraordinary ingenuity in a problematic universe. Cusanus's speculations describe the stimulated mind shaping conjectural patterns in a world that lacks fixed points and precise essences; Sidney's typical figure is a poet inventing fictions in a "brazen" world; and Shakespeare's plays concentrate on brilliant, but tragic, figures seeking equilibrium or advantage in the flux of history.

The relations that bring these three writers together in this study can, moreover, be seen in their interlocking concerns. Cusanus's theological and metaphysical framework encourages an epistemological inquiry into human invention; Sidney explicitly develops this question of invention and brings it to bear, not only on poetry itself, but on the dynamics of desire and, more broadly, on questions of justice and power; Shakespeare takes up such political themes and turns them toward an increasingly sophisticated epistemology of human invention, returning us through tragedy to the deepest theological and metaphysical concerns. The exposition, then, is both progressive and circular: each section plays off against the preceding one, until what begins in Cusanus as a framework promoting human inquiry produces on the Shakespearean stage the most unsettling of questions. The progression realizes a tragic potential latent from the start.

This requires some qualification, however, for Renaissance fiction making is not unilaterally devoted to the discovery of psychic distress. Fiction making is a fully ambiguous intellectual resource, releasing as well the constructive energies of reason and fancy in search of a valid or clarifying picture of reality.

The notion of perspective, for instance, proceeds from a recognition of its utter artificiality: artists project a mental grid for the sake of rendering an image "true to nature," but they never forget that this image is no more—and no less—than a consummate illusion. The joy of intellectual mastery is one we must assume was shared on some level by all great artists.[8] But the pleasures of feigning are often linked to the darker possibilities suggested by sixteenth-century usage, an equivocation suggested by its etymology: *fingere*, to shape, fashion, or contrive, is the root of both "fiction" and "figment." Feigning may denote the calculated shaping of a literary fable; it may also indicate a mental error or unreal imagining, even the malicious putting on of deceptive appearances. It is not surprising that the distinction between legitimate and illegitimate feigning should have become a major theoretical topic. Its practical consequences—so often associated with a heightened, or even restless, mental activity—are, however, more difficult to categorize. If some writers praise man's free-ranging creativity, others warn that man places too much trust in his contrivances. "Each man's mind is like a labyrinth," Calvin notes; once its energies begin "wandering about," pernicious idols flow forth "just as waters boil up from a vast full spring."[9]

Cusanus, Sidney, and Shakespeare may be interpreted as tracing a progression from theologically oriented confidence to increasingly anxious probing. I am more interested, however, by the ways in which each is involved in the optimism and the pessimism of the Renaissance. Each discovers a world where the presence of human invention is inescapable, even in the structure of man's desire for stability beyond invention. The paradox is not startling for one acquainted with modern discussions of the ways in which humanity creates symbolic worlds through culture; nor were Renaissance humanists ignorant of the process. But the very conservatism of the Renaissance, its longing to assert an eternal coherence underwriting the human, amplifies the suspicion that ideas of order may themselves be contingent and hypothetical, and ultimately turns that suspicion into a crisis over the status of cultural forms.

It is a long journey from Cusanus's enigmatic speculations about the individual and the cosmos to Hamlet's mysterious confrontation with a time out of joint, but it is one that leads us through some of the most revealing paradoxes of the age and opens to view the restless anxiety that lies behind so much of the brilliance of Renaissance culture.

NICHOLAS OF CUSA
AND THE POETICS
OF CONJECTURE

INTRODUCTION TO PART ONE

"Observe that in this world we walk in the ways of metaphors and enigmas."[1] Written a year before his death, Nicholas of Cusa's advice to a young monk sounds the voice of one who has explored both active and contemplative lives. Canon lawyer, bishop, cardinal, humanist, mathematician, and mystic theologian, Cusanus (1401–64) sought to reconcile all diversity within a unity of truth, to trace all metaphor back to its grounding in ineffable reality. His search, he believed, revealed to him a thread that could guide the mind through the labyrinths of the early modern world.

The task of recovering that thread has led historians into their own interpretative labyrinths. Some see Cusanus as a late-medieval apologist for hierarchy; others, as a dismantler of hierarchies and the herald of a new conception of mind and meaning; still others, as a Janus, facing in two directions. For although his works present us with a good deal of familiar Neoplatonic and Scholastic doctrine, they also send us conflicting signals. At times Cusanus takes classical and medieval traditions to be a series of symbolic approximations of truth, even playing the *bricoleur* who builds a world out of the materials at hand. Yet the mental operations that are meant to figure forth images of union also impress him with their astounding diversity and fecundity. "I think there is not, nor ever was, any perfect man that did not frame some conception of the mind," Cusanus writes in *De idiota* (3.1); "the mind is the bond and measure of all things." Only when we attempt to take stock of such Protagorean sentiments do we discover how difficult it has

3

become to frame the measure of that measure. The mind's store seems boundless; its metaphors and enigmas ostensibly point to a final rest in the highest wisdom, but the very process of their invention significantly alters the map upon which the pilgrimage is imagined to take place.

The next three chapters trace some of the more controversial features of that expansion and revision. Cusanus's mature writings unfold an original insight through a series of confrontations with archetypal paradoxes. The first chapter studies the speculative restlessness of "learned ignorance" and introduces the epistemological dilemmas that distance Cusanus from traditional means of resolution; the second studies some of the origins and implications of Cusanus's attempt to exploit that distance through a positive "conjectural art"; and the third surveys the general consequences of conjecture for all creative human effort, consequences that bring the mind to a broadly poetic understanding of its culture, its God, and itself.[2]

I

LEARNED IGNORANCE

MEDIEVAL CONTEXTS

One of the preoccupations of medieval thought is its insistence on fixing the mind's proper boundaries. Tertullian's attack on philosophical speculation in the early third century is an extreme instance but clearly indicates the issues at stake: "What indeed has Athens to do with Jerusalem?" After Revelation, the dialectic of philosophers is superfluous, "an art so far-fetched in its conjectures [*coactam in coniecturis*], so productive of contentions . . . retracting everything and really treating of nothing."[1] Indulging reason leads only to conjecture and controversy, producing a wealth of "fables" without establishing certainty. Even if speculation were not an open enemy of truth, it must be avoided because of the intellectual restlessness it engenders: "For where shall be the end of seeking? where the stop in believing? where the completion in finding?" The philosopher, Tertullian warns, finds no end; in violating the "boundary" set by God, he forfeits his "resting place."[2]

Echoes of Tertullian's anti-intellectualism sound throughout the Middle Ages. The revival of dialectic in the eleventh century also provoked Peter Damian (1007–72), who spurned Plato as a foolish searcher into, and calculator of, the "hidden things of nature," Pythagoras as one who sought to divide the world "with his mathematician's rod," and Euclid, who grew "round-shouldered from poring over his complex geometrical problems."[3] To Damian, all three proved the intellect not only inadequate but, in its restless and irrelevant hunger for knowledge, a force to be shut in. Those who would follow Christ's command to be perfect (Matt. 5:48) must remember that the mind "must be completely surrounded with this wall of virtue; that which is not permitted to expand in its own surroundings must necessarily be carried above itself."[4]

These sternly cautionary voices continue to the end of the Middle Ages and into early modern Europe. The subtleties of Scholastic and late Scholastic thought provoke a new phase of reaction, a longing for mystical immediacy with God the intense piety of which would suppress not only human intellection but any form of self-affirmation. The anonymous *Theologia Germanica*, later to have an impact on Luther, insists that man's primary sin is any form of egocentricity. Adam's sin was not in eating the apple, but in "his arrogating something to himself, because of his I, Mine, Me, and the like. Had he eaten seven apples, and yet never arrogated anything to himself, he would not have fallen: but as soon as he arrogated something to himself, he fell and would have fallen if he had never bitten into an apple."[5] The only remedy is "true obedience," to be realized in a complete annihilation of the ego: "A man should stand and be so free from himself, that is, from selfhood, I-hood, Me, Mine, and the like, that in all things he should no more seek and regard himself and his own than if he did not exist, and should take as little account of himself as if he were not and another had done all his works."[6] So, too, a contemporary English work, *The Cloud of Unknowing*, warning that mental activity can only estrange us further from God, exhorts us to suppress the "vigorous working of [an] imagination" prone to exploit contemplation as a springboard to action: "Unless you suppress it, it will suppress you!" Even holy thoughts set the mind in motion and must be quelled. True love of God requires that one "crush all knowledge and experience of all forms of created things, and of yourself above all . . . destroy this stark awareness of your own existence."[7]

This alienation—not only from the world, but from the

very workings of the mind—marks one extreme of medieval thought. For boundaries can also delineate an articulated and intelligible cosmos, one that encourages the mind's search for coherence. Both Scripture and Christian Platonism, in suggesting the beauty and harmony of God's handiwork, are powerful examples. Paul's claim that God's invisible nature has been clearly perceived in the things that are made (Rom. 1:20) seemed to many to sanction human speculation, and Boethius pictured Lady Philosophy herself freeing the mind from its "sick anxiety."[8] The most impressive statements of cosmic optimism appear in twelfth-century Platonism, which draws on both classical and biblical sources to praise the dignity of man: "Man holds high his head in contemplation / To show his natural kinship with the skies," writes Bernard Silvestris. Man's creation in God's "image and likeness" (Gen. 1:26) is interpreted as referring explicitly to his expansive intellectual power: "The dignity of our mind is its capacity to know all things."[9]

Historians sometimes treat these manifestations of medieval optimism and pessimism as alternating phases. I am more concerned here with the ways in which thinkers throughout the period seek to negotiate an equilibrium in their attitudes toward the mind's place within the larger structure of reality. For rather than any single school of theology, logic, or metaphysics, it is the effort itself—one that bridges very different forms and subjects of speculation—that is most important for our understanding of Cusanus. Plotinus (205–70) provides the best starting point both because he explicitly traces the motions of the mind and soul within a vast Neoplatonic scheme and because that scheme would, through the agencies of Augustine, Proclus, and the Pseudo-Dionysius, exert an enormous influence on later attitudes, including those of Cusanus. In the collection of treatises later named the *Enneads*, Plotinus pictures all Being emanating from its ineffable source, the One. Each succeeding generation, or "hypostasis," diffuses the Good into multiplicity, ending with the World Soul breathing life into matter: "The heavenly system, moved now in endless motion by the soul that leads it in wisdom, has become a living and a blessed thing; the soul domiciled within, it takes worth where, before the soul, it was stark body—clay and water— or, rather, the blankness of Matter" (5.1.2).[10]

Despite this systematic economy, there appears to be a conflict in Plotinus's thinking about individual souls on earth, for the diffusion of the Good can yield to division; the soul is imprisoned in the body as a punishment for its "self-will," fallen, as in Plato's *Phaedrus*, from the higher realms of Being: "The evil that has overtaken them has its source in self-will, in the entry into the sphere of process, and in the primal differentiation with the desire of self-ownership. They conceived a pleasure in this freedom and largely indulged their own motion; thus they were hurried down the wrong path" (5.1.1). The consequences of self-assertion are anxiety and isolation: "Differentiation has severed it; its vision is no longer set in the Intellectual; it is a partial thing, isolated, weakened, full of care, intent upon the fragment" (4.8.4).[11]

The remedy for Plotinus is not, however, the suppression of self-interest but an encouragement of the mind's present curiosity about itself: "Our general instinct to seek and learn will, in all reason, set us inquiring into the nature of the instrument with which we search" (4.3.1). Self-reflexiveness becomes, in fact, the soul's most significant operation: "Its natural course may be likened to that in which a circle turns not upon some external but on its own centre, the point to which it owes its rise. The soul's movement will be about its source" (6.9.8). The result is not isolation or solipsism, but the discovery of a path to the World Soul and beyond. The soul's desire for its source leads it to its internal point of contact with the Absolute, "a Principle in which all these centres coincide, . . . the centre of all the centres, just as the centres of the great circles of a sphere coincide with that of the sphere to which all belong. Thus we are secure" (6.9.8). Self-interest takes on a new meaning, "self-conversing, the subject is its own object," and in this fusion a higher self includes, and is included in, all Being, no longer fragmentary and full of care.

This security held a strong attraction for St. Augustine (354–430), who drew much of Plotinus's speculation into the orbit of Christian theology. For Augustine, an original contemplative closeness to God was ruined by the Fall, when the soul gave way to its "restlessness," deforming the "image and likeness of God" by "making trial of its own powers." But, like Plotinus, Augustine invokes the mind's self-knowledge as a stage in the search for God. The distortions of the sensory world turn the mind back on itself, where it proves its own existence to itself in the act of doubting: *si fallor, sum*. And when self-realization discovers its own finiteness, the mind seeks the Word of God, the very principle of knowledge whose divine illumination makes all truths visible to the mind and makes cognition possible.[12] Etienne Gilson summarizes the process: "All the Augustinian itineraries of the soul in quest of God are substantially the same: they go from the exterior to the interior, and from the inferior to the superior."[13]

The itinerary itself may demonstrate the mind's vigor. Exegesis, for example, becomes a source of pleasure if we admit, with Augustine, that figurative language, the use of "obscurities and ambiguities," delights us more than does plain language. The mental challenge posed by an enigma, Augustine writes in a famous letter, is exciting and good for the soul's health: the soul "gathers strength by the mere act of passing from the one [corporeal emblem] to the other [spiritual things], and like the flame of a lighted torch, is made by the motion to burn more brightly, and is carried away to rest by intensely glowing love."[14]

For Augustine, however, liberation depends on a more keenly felt sense of self-limitation than it does for Neoplatonists. The soul is ultimately helpless without grace and illumination.[15] Augustine insists on a strict subordination of means to ends: the mind may be used, but not enjoyed for its own sake. He attacks the gratuitous "thirst for knowledge," the mind's restless and sinful self-indulgence.[16] The mind must read itself allegorically, as it were, to search for its own spiritual kernel until it finds the "Interior Teacher," the Word of St. John upon which all words depend, but which is itself beyond words. The end of the quest is silence, a liberation from the "bondage to a sign."[17] Augustine's juxtaposition of human dynamism and insufficiency finds expression in a late letter: "There is in us as it were a learned ignorance [*docta ignorantia*], an ignorance taught by the spirit of God which comes to the help of our weakness."[18]

Nicholas of Cusa would turn this paradoxical formulation into his central metaphor, but not before Dionysius the Pseudo-Areopagite further investigated the necessity of *ignorantia* and silence. It is surely one of the great ironies of intellectual history that Dionysius's *via negativa*, a technique dedicated finally to annihilating the deceptions inherent in human discourse, should itself have been born from, and maintained by, the deceptiveness of language—specifically, authorial masquerade and the ambiguities of interpretation. Dionysius, now more appropriately known as the Pseudo-Dionysius, gained authority by impersonating Dionysius the Areopagite, a figure in Acts of the Apostles who was converted by Paul's sermon against idols: the "representation [of God] by the art and imagination of man" (Acts 17:16–34). Pseudo-Dionysius filters this Pauline text through the medium of Proclus's debatable interpretation of the *Parmenides* as a theological work. The first hypothesis of Plato's dialogue is that the One is not merely beyond mortal knowledge, it is beyond being, so we cannot even say that it "is": "It cannot have a name or be spoken of, nor can there be any knowledge or perception or opinion of it" (141d–42a). If, in the original dialogue, Parmenides offers this hypothesis as one possibility among many, a bit of logical showmanship calculated to dazzle the young Socrates, in the hands of Proclus and Dionysius it becomes a central truth about the possibility of knowing God.[19] But because worship must have some positive content, Dionysius also acknowledges an affirmative way. The mind requires "material figures" before it can rise to the immaterial; for that reason the word of God itself uses "poetic representations of sacred things." Furthermore, Dionysius interprets creation as a kind of "theophany," a manifestation of God, adapting Proclus's Neoplatonic hierarchy to depict the cosmos as a symbolic field from which the mind draws its terms. The mind does not create its symbols, but finds them in the nature of things themselves.[20] Even so, these symbols are radically inadequate. In its search for God, the mind must transcend them, and it is here that the emphasis of Dionysius's *Mystical Theology* lies. The goal is one of total silence, the annihilation of all intellectual activity. We must renounce "all the apprehensions of . . . understanding," "plunging into the Darkness" where "we shall find ourselves reduced not merely to brevity of speech but even to absolute dumbness of both speech and thought."[21]

Dionysian influence, as it winds its way through the Middle Ages, tempers its negativism in many ways. John Scotus Erigena, a Platonist writing in the glow of the ninth-century Carolingian renaissance, is an important example for Cusanus. A translator of Dionysius, he continues the insistence on the negative way as a corrective to affirmative symbol and, like Dionysius before him, turns theological discourse into a kind of writing *sous rature* that predicates terms of God in an infinite degree (for example, God is not "essence" but "superessential"), affirming only to cancel human understanding. But Eriugena also regards man's nature as "[a] hydra, a manifold source of infinite depth," whose mind, by God's enlightenment, becomes a theophany.[22]

Neoplatonism's balancing of negation and affirmation was to be severely challenged by a revival of dialectic in the eleventh century that opened a new era of medieval thought and encouraged a new virtuosity in the exercise of human reason. For dialectic, rather than settling the ambivalence we have been tracing, fueled the controversy. It was now fought with technical sophistication and bitterness between those eager to demonstrate their ingenuity by reasoning through the mysteries of faith and those who found such displays unseemly. The opposing camps are not easy to isolate. Opposition to the supposed rational excess came not only from such stern reactionaries as Peter Damian, but also from a thinker such as Bernard of Clairvaux. Bernard envisioned man's love of God as beginning with man's love of himself for himself alone, but his Augustinian inclinations were so threatened by Abélard's dialectic that he had the former condemned: "He shifts the boundary stones set by our forefathers by bringing under discussion the sublimest questions of Revelation. . . . He presumes to imagine that he can entirely comprehend God by the use of his reason."[23]

The shifting of boundaries is, however, a difficult one for the historian to map. An advocate of man's self-love such as Bernard might attack man's excessive use of reason, but so, too, a self-proclaimed conservative might prove a brilliant explorer of the possibilities of reasoning. St. Anselm (1033–1109) is an example of the latter, and is perhaps the most sensitive register of the questions raised by such possibilities. Concerned by the heretical direction dialectic was taking among Nominalist thinkers, he insisted that his own works never violated patristic, and particularly Augustinian, limits. He is clear, in other words, on the priority of faith. But he is also clear on the virtual necessity of seeking to understand what one believes. For as the monk Boso observes in the dialogue *Cur Deus homo* ("Why God Became Man"), it would be "careless for us, once we are established in the faith, not to aim at understanding what we believe." This attitude informs Anselm's famous *dicta*: "faith seeking understanding" (*fides quaerens intellectum*) and "I believe in order to understand" (*credo ut intelligam*).[24] Yet despite, or perhaps because of, this unambiguous subordination, there is something of the virtuoso performance in his writing. The preface to the *Cur Deus homo* announces that the argument will proceed with "Christ being put out of sight, as if nothing had ever been known of him" (ostensibly because this will make the work a useful reply to unbelievers), and will seek the rational grounds of why God became man.[25] Although the work's reputation rests on its important rethinking of the Atonement, I want to consider here not Anselm's arguments but the attitude he takes toward them.

Anselm is exquisitely aware of his arguments' effects. Investigation may be difficult, he warns in the preface, but the arguments are "appealing because of the usefulness and beauty of the reasoning" (p. 101). When he describes his discussion of the Virgin Birth as a series of paintings on the surface of truth, Boso concurs: "These pictures are very beautiful and reasonable" (2.8, p. 154). Such notes of pleasure are, however, sounded only with an important accompaniment—the reminder that "deeper reasons . . . remain hidden" (1.2, p. 103). In the chapter "How What Is to Be Said Should Be Taken" (1.2), Anselm insists: "I want everything I say to be taken on these terms: that if I say anything that a greater authority does not support, even though I seem to prove it by reason, it is not to be treated as more certain than is warranted by the fact that, at present, I see the question in this way, until God somehow reveals something better to me" (p. 103; cf. p. 132).

This deference to higher authority is both prudent and consistent with Anselm's deeper assumption of faith's priority. But the juxtaposition of virtuosity and deference produces a curious effect: the displays of reason take on a hint of detachability, as if the mind's subtlest arguments were temporary constructions subject to possible revision at any moment. Revision may yield further pleasure, yet the very tentativeness of reason makes it crucial that the soundness and solidity of argument be evident if reason is to be at all effective. As Boso reminds Anselm:

> No one paints on water or in air, because no traces of the pictures would remain. Now when we present unbelievers with these harmonies you speak of, as so many pictures of a real event, they think that this belief of ours is a fiction [*figmentum*], and not a real happening, and so they judge that we are, as it were, painting on a cloud.
>
> (p. 105; *PL* 158, col. 365; Schmitt, 2:51–52)[26]

Anselm remains confident throughout of the value of his reasons. Argument, he advises, is substantial as long as we paint on solid truth (*solidam veritatem*), and not on empty fancies (*fictam vanitatem*) (*PL* 158, col. 406; Schmitt, 2:104).

At the same time, the solidity of faith does not protect these two subtle minds from inner turbulence. The preface of *Cur Deus homo* locates the work's compositional history in an agitated context, beginning with a mysterious and unspecified "great distress of mind—the source and reason of my suffering God knows" and concluding in an uncomfortable rush because of unauthorized copying. Boso, too, knew great distress of mind; Anselm's biographer, Eadmer, tells us that he suffered such "tumults in his thoughts" that "he could scarcely remain sane," a fit of anguish attributed to an attack by the devil, and healed by Anselm's simple advice: "Consulat tibi Deus."[27] Eadmer's most dramatic account of mental anguish attributes Anselm's own suffering to his attempt to achieve his most famous feat of intellectual gymnastics, the "ontological proof" of God's existence in the early *Proslogion*. In the prologue to that work, Anselm calls the search to find a single, short argument a "preoccupation" and an "obsession."[28] Eadmer records that "thinking about it took away his desire for food, drink and sleep, and partly—and this was more grievous to him—because it disturbed the attention which he ought to have paid to

matins and to Divine service at other times . . . he supposed
that this line of thought was a temptation of the devil and he
tried to banish it from his mind. But the more vehemently he
tried to do this, the more this thought pursued him."[29] The
answer came to him suddenly, according to Eadmer, through
divine illumination.

As if to prescribe his own cure, Anselm advises the reader
in the first chapter to hide from turbulent thoughts under the
shelter of contemplation. He then produces an argument that
has been a source of philosophical controversy for nine hundred years.[30] Cast as a response to the fool in Psalms who denies
God's existence, it moves from the idea we have of God as "a
being than which none greater can be thought" to an assertion
that the presence of this idea in the understanding proves God's
existence in reality:

> For if it is actually in the understanding alone, it can be thought of
> as existing also in reality, and this is greater. Therefore, if that than
> which a greater cannot be thought is in the understanding alone,
> this same thing than which a greater cannot be thought is that than
> which a greater can be thought. But obviously this is impossible.
> Without doubt, therefore, there exists, *both in the understanding and
> in reality*, something than which a greater cannot be thought.
>
> (p. 74; emphasis mine)

Put more simply, if this greatest conception existed only in the
mind, we could conceive a greater being: one that also existed
in reality. This would be a contradiction, since the greatest cannot have something greater than it. Therefore, that greatest
something must exist in reality.

This is possibly the most ingenious proof of God's existence
ever devised. It is, at the same time, an astonishing affirmation
of the powers of human reason, of its ability to leap from the
logical to the ontological. Yet, even after his triumph, Anselm
wonders "If thou has found him, why dost thou not perceive
what thou has found?" (p. 83).[31] The mind's eye is dazzled by
the divine light "beyond which there is only nothingness and

falsehood," and Anselm now turns to the language of mysticism: "Thou art not simply that than which a greater cannot be thought; rather, thou art something greater than can be thought." "The eye of my soul . . . is blinded by [God's] glory, it is overcome by its fullness, it is overwhelmed by its immensity, it is bewildered by its greatness" (p. 84).

Anselm's mystical boundaries affect one's response to the brilliant displays within them, evoking that peculiar sense of detachability hinted at in the *Cur Deus homo*. Indeed, it is this kind of problem that Anselm's contemporary foe Gaunilo seizes upon in his criticism of the ontological proof: does this elegant feat of reasoning rest on truth, or is it a figment of human invention? Arguing on behalf of the fool in Psalms, Gaunilo illustrates his rebuttal with the example of a utopia: "They say that there is in the ocean somewhere an island which, because of the difficulty (or rather the impossibility) of finding that which does not exist, some have called the 'Lost Island.' " This island, Gaunilo continues, is said to be the wealthiest and most excellent ever imagined. Would one then seriously argue that because it is the most excellent island imaginable, it must also exist in reality? Of course not, he answers, and anyone who thought the argument effective must either be joking or be an even bigger fool.[32] Dionysius, as we have seen, regarded affirmative theology as a kind of "poetic" representation, one based upon objective symbol. Anselm's longing for a rational basis of faith, Gaunilo suggests, merely leads the mind to subjective fiction.

Anselm's *Reply* insists that the argument, when properly applied by a believer to the greatness of God, embodies the "sure reason of truth." Nonetheless, the complaint impressed him as a worthy dialectical counter, one that needed articulation and refutation, as we know both from his directions to include "the criticism and his reply to it in all future copies of the *Proslogion*" and from his having Boso offer a version of it years later in *Cur Deus homo*.[33]

The optimism of twelfth-century Platonism and the growth of the universities in the thirteenth century testify to the increasing vigor of medieval intellectual life after Anselm. The great Scholastic syntheses sought a new equilibrium in medieval attitudes toward the mind, and so made possible ever-greater mental constructions. Though Scholastic and late-Scholastic ideas have a direct bearing on Cusanus, it suffices for the moment to note that the major thinkers of the thirteenth and fourteenth centuries continued to make adjustments until they found themselves once again facing the fundamental questions that had confronted their predecessors.

Signs of caution appear in Albert the Great (d. 1280), whose enormous range of interests included both science and philosophical reasoning. He defends the latter against anti-intellectuals, whom he characterizes as "brute beasts, blaspheming in matters wherein they are ignorant." Yet he is careful to distance himself from the philosophies he would only compile, not espouse, and gives clear priority to faith over reason.[34] Albert's pupil Thomas Aquinas (ca. 1224–74), perhaps the greatest of systematic thinkers, shows a similar concern. His affirmation of reason requires that he be as circumspect as the earlier Anselm. The mind must recall its proper boundaries lest "the Catholic faith seem to be founded on empty reasonings, and not, as it is, on the most solid teaching of God."[35] Medieval uncertainties, however, would outlast the systems meant to contain them. Aquinas's care seemed insufficient to the more conservative theologians, who resented his Aristotelianism. In 1277 Bishop Tempier condemned a number of Thomist theses together with more explicitly heterodox propositions of the Latin Averroists.

It was once commonplace to regard the condemnation of 1277 as a crisis in medieval thought, after which its rational syntheses broke down into bitter factionalism. Although reports of fourteenth-century corrosion have been greatly exaggerated,[36] the intellectual universe that allowed Anselm to leap from the logical to the ontological had profoundly altered its dimensions by the late thirteenth century. A scant fifty years separate the Franciscans Bonaventure and Peter Auriole, but the epistemological differences between them—the former relying on illumination and divine Ideas to regulate and make certain man's abstractive knowledge, and the latter believing that only individuals are truly known and that universals are merely the products of human conceptualizing—forecast a disturbing volatility of attitudes. By the fourteenth century, new insights into the mind's field of action were purchased at the cost of limiting its understanding of the articles of faith, even though that faith remained the "only way out" of what would become a "tragic epistemological situation."[37]

It is not surprising, then, that Scholastic discourse grew increasingly intricate and self-conscious at this time. Its complexity accounts, in part, for the dramatic renewal of mysticism in the late Middle Ages, even among those well versed in Scholastic thought, a trend that reveals the longing for a more immediate relation to an incomprehensible divinity.[38] Meister Eckhart (1260–1327), a Dominican with Scholastic training, is an important example. Eckhart's intellectualism has often been emphasized. Knowing, for him, characterizes both God and man, and establishes the former as the image of the latter. But the Neoplatonic and mystical elements in Eckhart's thought, already a feature of Scholasticism and now accentuated, help give voice to the desire to burst through conceptual limitations: "The intellect . . . is not content with goodness, nor with wisdom, nor the truth, no, nor even with god himself. . . . It can never rest until it gets to the core of the matter, crashing through to that which is beyond the idea of God and truth, until it reaches the *in principio*, the beginning of beginnings, the origin or source of all goodness and truth."[39] It is this very dynamism that complicates Eckhart's legacy. If there abides in the depths of the individual soul a "spark" or "citadel" or "ground" that unites the soul with God, that spark also impels

the individual toward the mystical paradoxes of Dionysian abnegation: "I could have so vast an intelligence," Eckhart proclaims, "that all the images that all human beings have ever
received and those that are in God himself were comprehended
in my intellect," but that intellect must become as a "virgin."
Man must recognize the "nothingness" of the creature, and
only through "voluntary annihilation" can he find union with
the Godhead.[40] This mystical impulse is perhaps a higher stage
of Eckhart's intellectualism, but it also bears the seeds of a radical anti-intellectualism, one that appears among later German
mystics influenced by Eckhart. And though Eckhart, in his ser-
mons, may well be a "prophet of the individual in religion," as
R. W. Southern calls him,[41] the realization of that prophecy also
includes the *Theologia Germanica* with its resolute assault on all
forms of self-affirmation.

In more than a thousand years of speculation and polemic,
the medieval attempt to fix the mind's proper boundaries returns repeatedly to an awareness of the task's difficulty, a consequence, in large part, of the diversity of medieval thought
itself. Indeed, the issue not only remains unresolved in the
fourteenth and fifteenth centuries, but burns with an energy
born of renewed instability. It is in this uncertain glow that we
may witness a historical transition to the Renaissance.

DE DOCTA IGNORANTIA:
PERSPECTIVES AND PROBLEMS

Nicholas of Cusa's first major speculative work, *De docta igno-*
rantia (Of learned ignorance; 1440), is framed by expressions
of dissatisfaction with previous doctrines and promises something radically new. Cusanus's preface recommends the work
for its "novelty," its "boldness," and most importantly, for the
"wonder" (*admiratio*) it will provoke in the reader.[42] Wonder,
he writes, echoing Aristotle's *Metaphysics*, is the origin of philosophizing (1.2), and the opening of Cusanus's first chapter

amplifies the first proposition of the *Metaphysics*: "All men by nature desire to know." All things have a "natural desire" to exist in their "best manner"; thus the intellect "insatiably desires" the truth as it "surveys all things." As we shall see, Cusanus's authorial performance acts out this movement, for in his effort to shape his vision, he ranges through both the entire created world and intellectual traditions from the Presocratics to his contemporaries.

Few of his predecessors can match this enthusiasm for the mind's diverse energies, and yet the opening chapter of *De docta ignorantia* places its motions in a paradoxical light. After insisting that an "innate sense of judgment" assures us that our desires are "not in vain but able to attain rest in that object which is desired," Cusanus slides into a discussion of rational inquiry. Inquiry always proceeds by comparison, a "proportional tracing" of the uncertain back to "what is taken to be certain." Pythagoras's belief that "all things" are "constituted and understood through the power of numbers" is cited in this context. But even as we seem to be extending our grasp, including more and more under the aegis of "the certain," certainty itself dissolves. "Precise combination" surpasses human reason, we are told, and a new battery of authorities appears: Socrates who "seemed to himself to know nothing except that he did not know," and Solomon, who "maintained that all things are difficult and unexplained in words." Even Aristotle's *Metaphysics*, Cusanus recalls, warns that there is such difficulty in even the most obvious things that we are like "a night owl which is trying to look at the sun."[43] The chapter concludes by turning our very process of reading to argumentative purpose: the goal of our knowledge is the realization of non-knowledge; we are drawn to learn our ignorance.

The opening chapter is thus an example in miniature of Cusanus's dialectic, which time and again yokes the extremes of medieval attitudes toward the mind into complementary phases of affirmation and denial, expansion and contraction, juxtaposing versions of man as prolific genius and man as reduced to silence, a creature of blindness and insight. The unquestioned goal of almost all Cusanus's maneuvers, positive or negative, is theological. The longing for God is the mind's fundamental impulse, the profoundest revelation of its ignorance, and its guarantee that its desires are not in vain. But Cusanus's fascination with the problem of knowledge in important ways complicates the entire range of his thought.[44] For despite the hunger for final rest, his dialectic is as much concerned with perpetuating its own movements as it is with achieving resolution.

The problem of knowledge emerges from the inevitability of ignorance. Precise truth resides only in the infinite, and since there is no proportion between the finite and the infinite, precision is beyond comparison with anything we can reason about. Only truth itself can know truth: "Truth is not something more or something less but is something indivisible. Whatever is not truth cannot measure truth precisely" (1.3). Cusanus's favorite metaphor for the epistemological dilemma is that of a polygon inscribed within a circle:

> The intellect, which is not truth, never comprehends truth so precisely that truth cannot be comprehended infinitely more precisely. For the intellect is to truth as [an inscribed] polygon is to [the inscribing] circle. The more angles the inscribed polygon has the more similar it is to the circle. However, even if the number of its angles is increased ad infinitum, the polygon never becomes equal [to the circle] unless it is resolved into an identity with the circle.
> (1.3)

Incompletion, however, does not teach man to wall in the restless drive of the mind. It is, rather, the justification for carrying reason to its furthest boundary, if indeed that boundary can ever be encountered.

As the metaphor of the circle suggests, Cusanus follows Platonic and Pythagorean traditions by looking to mathematics as reason's most precise and abstract operation. Its "incorruptible certainty" (1.11) makes it an apt medium through which to symbolize the notions of limit and infinity. For example: the curvature of a circle straightens as its size increases. The straight line, then, is the limit of the curve. And if we extend the circle to infinity, the circle will not be curved at all. The point is not that we can achieve infinity, but that, as our minds struggle to approach it, our most precise conceptual distinctions break down and with them our rational complacency. The triangle is subjected to a similar trick: because the shortest distance between any two points is a straight line, the sum of any two sides of a triangle must be larger than the third. But if that third side were extended to infinity, the others would also be infinity. They would all be one line, in fact, for there can be only one infinite line, which actualizes the potency of all finite lines (1.13–14).

These puzzles are ingenious extensions of verbal figures drawn from medieval predecessors, and all illustrate a common point: the *coincidentia oppositorum*. The coincidence of opposites is a powerful metaphor for Cusanus because it violates the Law of Contradiction, the most fundamental of logical laws. The terms we use, Cusanus reminds us, are of particulars and so each marks a distinction. God, however, is beyond all distinction and opposition. Like the infinite line into which all forms collapse, He is the "enfolding of all things, even of contradictories" (1.22). The mind must short-circuit its own categories, tease itself with the prospect of distinct forms breaking down, in order to remind itself that rational naming and distinctions are ultimately inadequate: "In theological matters negations are true and affirmations are inadequate" (1.26).

These exercises share the search for the unifying One in Neoplatonism through the Pseudo-Dionysian *via negativa*, but instead of concluding in abnegation, Cusanus pursues the most vigorous intellectual gymnastics. Even as the mind falls "into darkness" when it seeks to gaze upon God, the very use of mathematics affirms its power. If negation is emphasized—as it is near the end of 1.17: "When I remove from my mind all things which participate in Being, it seems that nothing remains"—it is soon qualified by the something that contemplates nothing, the mind that makes the negation. And so, at the beginning of the succeeding chapter (1.18), we find: "Our insatiable intellect, stimulated by the aforesaid, vigilantly and with very great delight inquires into how it can behold more clearly this participation in the one Maximum."

This dual concentration on the stimulated and delighted human mind and the infinite gulf separating it from its Absolute goal reappears in book 2 of *De docta ignorantia*, which turns from what we can know about God to what we can know about creation. Plotinus, followed by Proclus and Dionysius, bequeathed an elaborate system of emanations locating man and the cosmos within an objective scheme of descent and ascent, procession and return. Cusanus rejects this mediation: a World Soul cannot exist "either separated or separable from things; for if we consider mind according as it is separated from possibility, it is the Divine Mind, which alone is completely actual. Therefore, there cannot be many distinct exemplars" (2.9). Again we find an insistence on the disproportion between the Absolute and the created, or "contracted," world.[45] "God alone is absolute; all other things are contracted. *Nor is there a medium* between the Absolute and the contracted as those imagined who thought that the world-soul is mind existing subsequently to God but prior to the world's contraction" (2.9; emphasis mine).

One consequence of, and, I suspect, motivation for, Cusanus's denial of mediation is his reassignment of many of the World Soul's functions to the human mind. The rejection of distinct exemplars is a crucial instance: Cusanus's attitude toward universals is ambiguous at best and will be considered more closely when we turn to his negotiations with Nominalism and Realism.[46] But his argument, both here and elsewhere, suggests that though universals may exist in particular things, the only actual metaphysical Form is the Form of Forms in the One, and the only universals to which we have cognitive access are those that "exist contractedly in the intellect before the intellect unfolds them by outward signs for them—unfolds them through understanding, which is its operation" (2.6). Later works develop this emphasis. If, for example, Neoplatonists imagine the World Soul as animating the physical world, giving "worth" to "stark body," Cusanus, in *De ludo globi*, imagines the mind fulfilling that function, "wherewith we see how precious is the mind, for without it, everything in creation would be without value. When God wanted to give value to his work, he had to create, besides other things, the intellectual nature."[47] Cassirer is still the great spokesman for the optimism of Cusanus's revision. The denial of Neoplatonic Ideas as "creative forces," Cassirer argues, leads to "a *concrete* subject as the central point . . . for all truly creative activity. And this subject can exist nowhere but in the mind of man."[48]

Cusanus's focus is not merely on the human mind in general but on specific, individual minds. This affects his metaphysics and, perhaps most famously, his cosmology. Here the destabilizing of fixed, traditional structures proceeds from the theme of measurement. The ancients, Cusanus tells us, operated under the grand illusion that they could locate fixed points of reference. There are, however, no "fixed and immovable poles."

> And since we can discern motion only in relation to something fixed, viz., either poles or centers, and since we presuppose these [poles or centers] when we measure motions, we find that as we go about conjecturing, we err with regard to all [measurements]. And we are surprised when we do not find that the stars are in the right position according to the rules of measurement of the ancients, for we suppose that the ancients rightly conceived of centers and poles and measures.
>
> (2.11)

Error does not teach us to stop measuring in a Peter Damian–like rejection of Plato, Pythagoras, and Euclid. Rather, it leads us to inquire into the presuppositions of measurement, and to discover the perspectivism implied in all human observations:

We apprehend motion only through a certain comparison with something fixed. For example, if someone did not know that a body of water was flowing and did not see the shore while he was on a ship in the middle of the water, how would he recognize that the ship was being moved? And because of the fact that it would always seem to each person (whether he were on the earth, the sun, or another star) that he was the "immovable" center, so to speak, and that all other things were moved: assuredly, it would always be the case that if he were on the sun, he would fix a set of poles in relation to himself; if on the earth, another set; on the moon, another; on Mars, another; and so on.

(2.12)

This perspectivism reinforces and complicates Cusanus's interest in the "concrete subject." If all measurement is conditioned by a relative, and hence partial, point of view, the absence of a single, authoritative account of the cosmos liberates human perspective as the measure of all things. And it is the uniqueness of each perspective that justifies individual creativity and originality: "No one [human being] is as another in any respect—neither in sensibility, nor imagination, nor intellect, nor in any activity, whether writing or painting or any art" (2.1).

Cassirer rightly finds in Cusanus a philosophical expression of Renaissance individualism. But the mind's new power and fluidity entail new burdens. Even as he denies it, Cusanus is well aware, for example, of the value of an objective World Soul for Neoplatonism. It is there that Forms are imagined to exist in their purity, and it is to those Forms that the intellect aspires when it would escape the flux of images and shadows in the material world (2.9). The world Cusanus presents, one where the search for empirical as well as theological precision would lead to endless approximation, might provoke a Neoplatonist to cry out for such transcendence. Indeed, Cusanus's very symbol of the ineluctable difference between the measure and the measured—the circle and the polygon—must *itself* yield to an infinite number of more approximate images to represent man's epistemological condition.

This paradox raises some fundamental questions. If Cusanus wishes to apply the insights of learned ignorance to either theology or cosmology, how can he prevent learned ignorance from being swallowed by its own premise? How can he defend it from the charge that it is merely his own point of view? Indeed, one might mischievously note that his metaphor of a man on a ship, making relative measurements while unaware of the currents beneath him, bears an uncomfortable resemblance to Cusanus's account of his own situation when the inspiration for *De docta ignorantia* first came to him: he was on a ship at sea, returning from Constantinople, part of a mission that sought to reunify the Greek and Latin churches.[49]

Cusanus might answer that this is precisely the value of learned ignorance. It is justified in that it recognizes the inevitable partiality of human knowledge. Yet he also demands more for the method that makes the recognition. He insists that learned ignorance is the best, the truest form of inquiry, that thinking makes real progress by it. Inconclusiveness does not deny approximation; we think "more correctly and truly about the Most High as we grope by means of symbolism" (1.12). But if, as Cusanus also insists, the polygon remains forever separate from the circle, might the progress of learned ignorance itself be illusory?[50]

Cusanus makes several kinds of gestures to rescue the mind from this dilemma, to show how symbolic investigation yields effective knowledge. One suggestive argument authorizes learned ignorance because it yields a perspective on other perspectives. Cusanus advises the reader who "want[s] truly to understand . . . the motion of the universe" to imagine as many points of view as possible, and then to "merge these different imaginative pictures." But this exercise leads the finite mind only to further picturing, or to blankness: "You will see . . . that the world and its motion and shape cannot be apprehended. For [the world] will appear as a wheel in a wheel and a sphere in a sphere—having its center and circumference nowhere" (2.11).[51] Nor are Cusanus's efforts to ascend through mathematics less paradoxical. "Mathematicals," although represented as diagrams and puzzles, are proclaimed "very fixed" and "very certain" because they are free from the "continual instability" of "material possibility." But though Cusanus goes on to cite Pythagoras, Augustine, and Boethius, he does not use mathematics as they do. His diagrams do not reveal the structure of Being; they are symbolic inquiries that, like the multiplying polygon, cannot come to a final resolution.[52] Only the assumed presence of the Absolute can stabilize the mind's play and provide the solid ground that supports intellectual gymnastics. If Cusanus insists on God's transcendence, on the radical disproportion between the infinite and the finite, he also maintains God's immanence: "God is in all things in such way that all things are in Him" (2.5). Cusanus's obscurity on this latter point has left him open to charges of pantheism from his day to ours, but his intentions, at least, are orthodox: to fashion a vision of a transcendent God who is also the source of thought and Being, the enfolding (*complicatio*) of all things, as they are His unfolding (*explicatio*). Cusanus takes such theological and metaphysical terms very seriously, but appeals to an ultimate ground can be made within the movements of learned ignorance only by acknowledging their provisional character, by admitting, along with the Pseudo-Dionysius, that "our understanding of God draws near to nothing rather than to something" (1.17).

How, then, does learned ignorance aid the faithful? Can it teach anything beyond an endless series of paradoxes to tease the "insatiable intellect"?[53] As the mind juggles the various ways in which nothing and everything merge in the concept of the "incomprehensible Maximum," its motions come to seem a form of bondage, not merely what Augustine called the "bondage to a sign," but bondage to the endlessness of human signification. At times, Cusanus attempts to arrest motion through doctrinal closure. Cusanus's geometrical puzzles about infinity are an example. After working a few transformations on them, Cusanus promises to continue the search. But because he has drawn his illustrations from prior doctrine (1.12), he can, at any time, resolve his figures into fixed, allegorical patterns. The emphasis then shifts from hypothetical modes of exploration and toward the privileged truths to which these signs supposedly refer. The infinite triangle that is also a straight line, for example, represents the Holy Trinity, because its three sides are also one (1.19). Reason seems to find a resting point, because, as Cusanus has already told us, "maximal Oneness is necessarily, trine . . . maximal Oneness cannot at all be rightly understood unless it is understood to be trine" (1.10).

But, characteristically, Cusanus cannot resist turning a terminal point into a liminal one. Once the "truth of the Trinity" (1.20) becomes the subject of disclosure, rest inevitably yields to motion. The right understanding of One-as-three proves to be dynamic. Invoking Augustine's warning against reductive notions of the Trinity (1.19), Cusanus insists that "in truth . . . neither the name 'trinity' nor our concept of trinity at all befit the Maximum; rather, they fall infinitely short of this maximal and incomprehensible Truth" (1.20). Even the names "Father," "Son," and "Holy Spirit" are based only on a distant likeness to creatures (1.9, 24), for the process of naming the Trinity is analogous to the ways in which the pagans named their gods. When they considered God's kindness, they named Him "Jupiter," His knowledge, "Saturn," His power, "Mars," His love, "Venus," and so on (1.25). So, too, the names of the

Trinity are partial responses, "manner[s] of considering" inferred aspects of Him (1.26).

The dialectical pulse of Cusanus's thinking, then, drives repeatedly toward stability and self-effacement, only to find that the positing of closure, by the nature of positing itself, exposes the hypothetical cast of all human structures. The movement, however, leads Cusanus toward what he holds to be the very center of his faith, an utterly fixed set of religious coordinates that will answer the exigencies of his thought. He may continue to welcome a world where the "difference of religions, sects, and regions . . . scattered throughout the world" perpetually gives rise to "differences of opinions . . . so that what is praiseworthy according to one is reprehensible according to another" (3.1), but as a Christian he also affirms that "if I am not mistaken, you see that [a religion] which does not embrace Christ as mediator and savior, as God and man, as the way, the truth, and the life is not a perfect religion, leading men to the final and most coveted goal of peace" (3.8). Christ is the judge who as "maximal reason" can resolve all diversity because His judgment lies "beyond all time and motion," and beyond all ambiguity as well: "It is not conducted by the weighing of pros and cons, by parallel cases, by discourses and deliberation" (3.10).[54]

The entire structure of De docta ignorantia leads us to Christ as teacher, the Augustinian magister who instructs us not merely in signs, but in the realities behind the signs. The first book, as we have seen, deals with God, the "Absolute Maximum," or rather, with the mind's struggle to invent terms for Him, while the second speculates about the created world, the "contracted maximum." Book 3 is devoted to Jesus, "who is both Absolute Maximum and contracted maximum" (3, prologue). Because He must teach, He cannot only be a judge whose "sentence and judgment" lie beyond all mortal comprehension; the Incarnation becomes a descent into discourse, God's address across the gulf between infinite and finite.

> To instruct our ignorance by an example: When some very excellent teacher wants to disclose to his students his intellectual, mental word (in order that they may feed spiritually upon the conceived truth once it has been shown to them), he causes his mental word to be indued with sound, since it is not disclosable to his students unless he indues it with a perceptible figure. But this cannot be done in any other way than through the natural spirit of the teacher. From the forced air he adapts a vocal figure that befits the mental word. To this figure he unites the word in such way that the sound exists with the word, so that those listening attain to the word by means of the sound. By means of this admittedly very remote likeness we are momentarily elevated in our reflection—elevated beyond that which we can understand . . . since we were unable to perceive [the Word] in any other way than in visible form and in a form similar to ourselves—the Father manifested the Word in accordance with our capability.
>
> (3.5)

The doctrine of accommodation—the theory that Revelation is adapted to the limited capacities of its audience—receives a distinctly rhetorical coloring. And this coloring enforces Cusanus's self-consciousness: as he pictures the teacher giving vocal shape to his mental word, he reminds us of his own role as teacher, one whose examples must rely upon "admittedly very remote likeness" (*remotissima similitudine*). But in order to sustain his ultimate drive toward synthesis, he must also sustain his metaphor; because "Jesus's humanity is as a medium between what is purely absolute and what is purely contracted," He is for us "truth, as temporally contracted to a 'sign' and an 'image,' so to speak, of supertemporal truth" (3.7). The life of Christ becomes a discursive series of such signs, God's figures instructing man in the faith. In the birth of Christ we picture the union of time and eternity. In His death "minimum things coincide with maximum things. For example, maximum humiliation [coincides] with exaltation; the most shameful death of a virtuous man [coincides] with his glorious life, and so on—as Christ's life, suffering and crucifixion manifest all these [points] to us" (3.6).

As Cusanus meditates on the traditional mysteries of the Incarnation, we seem at the same time to be witnessing the apotheosis of his favored metaphor: the coincidence of opposites. The paradox, with the full weight of the entire treatise behind it, proves its value for Christology as all formulations revolve around and are drawn into it. And yet, the paradox also returns us, at the least propitious moment, to the enormous span of possibilities it has accrued by the third book. The coincidence of minimum and maximum recalls to us God as the absolute unity that unites all things. The manifesting of these points also recalls the dynamic potential of the human mind as it attempts to reconcile opposing geometrical forms, enlarging its domain even as it seeks to collapse its distinctions. Finally, the coincidence of opposites has symbolized the limit beyond which the mind cannot go; an illustration not of the divine but of the mystery that prevents the individual from comprehending it, because it is "far and away beyond our understanding, which is fundamentally unable by any rational process to reconcile contradictories." The coincidence of opposites, then, represents the infinite, the finite, the reconciliation of infinite and finite, and the immeasurable gulf between them. It becomes a powerful symbol of the ambiguities of human discourse, not an escape from them.

Cusanus brings the entire force of his faith to bear on settling his final expository problem. Having called upon Christ as the mediator between God and man, Cusanus describes the relation between Christ and man. Each is, in his own way, a locus of all things. First it is man as microcosm: "Human nature . . . enfolds intellectual and sensible nature and encloses all things within itself, so that the ancients were right in calling it a microcosm, or a small world" (3.3). Then it is Christ as *Verbum*: "In the Word, all things [exist]; and every creature [exists] in the supreme and most perfect humanity, which completely unfolds all creatable things. Thus, all fulness dwells in Jesus" (3.4). Belief in Jesus as God and man helps us to picture "human nature . . . elevated unto a union with Maximality"; "In Him the humanity was united to the Word of God" (3.3, 4). Qualifications, however, begin almost immediately: "For since the intellect of Jesus is most perfect and exists in complete actuality, it can be personally subsumed only in the divine intellect, which alone is actually all things. For in all human beings the [respective] intellect is potentially all things; it gradually progresses from potentiality to actuality" (3.4). Such progression, however, would be endless, for "the maximum intellect, since it is the limit of the potentiality of every intellectual nature and exists in complete actuality, cannot at all exist without being intellect in such way that it is also God, who is all in all" (3.4). We are, in fact, returned to the familiar paradox, which Cusanus now repeats "by way of illustration: Assume that a polygon inscribed in a circle were the human nature and the circle were the divine nature" (3.4). Does Christ's humanity, then, by virtue of its very perfection, threaten to vanish beyond the gulf separating the finite from the infinite?[55]

Cusanus's faith remains firm; because "human nature put on immortality . . . all shall arise through Christ," and the saved will be transformed by His glory into adopted sons of God (3.6–8). Nor is Christ's presence less crucial for the mind's pilgrimage in this world. As the closing pages of *De docta ignorantia* remind us, "the intellect's desire does not attain its end" for it has a "temporally insatiable desire." But even as Christ helps us to pass from "virtue to virtue, and from degree to degree," so, too, He guides the mind to its object in "incorruptible truth" (3.12). In the closing letter to Cardinal Julian, Cusanus insists that after years of study, he has found that for one who enters into Jesus, "neither this world nor any writings can cause [him] any difficulty," for "Christ is the end of intellectual desires." Even so, Cusanus's speculative writings continue to evoke a world fraught with difficulty. Within a theological context that insists on the mind's utter inadequacy, a context that demands intellectual surrender and mystical self-annihilation, Cusanus is drawn irresistibly toward the motions of the individual mind and their value. The quieting of intellectual desires is a consummation devoutly to be wished, but Cusanus's works return time and again to the most adventurous epistemological themes, to the mind's seemingly endless explorations.[56]

DE DOCTA IGNORANTIA:
THE BOOK OF THE WORLD

Like his medieval predecessors, Cusanus sometimes makes use of the trope of the universe as a book, written by the finger of God.[57] Why has the text grown so problematic? One possible clue lies in Cusanus's career in the Church. His was an active, tumultuous life dedicated to achieving harmonies that remained forever elusive. Born in 1401, he was raised during the final stages of the Great Schism, when two, and, for a time, three, popes claimed simultaneously to be sole head of the Church. The resolution of the dispute through the Council of Constance held out the promise of higher unity through the conciliar movement, and we get some sense of Cusanus's early optimism in his De concordantia catholica (1433), a lengthy theoretical work on church politics that the young Nicholas, a rising canon lawyer, presented to the Council of Basel. Here we find a vision of diversity harmonized through a hierarchical flow of power from God through creation.[58] The harmony must have sounded increasingly distant as the council grew raucous and divided, splintering into bitter factions.

Cusanus's switch of sympathies from the conciliar to the papal party had immediate intellectual as well as material rewards. The quest for harmony could continue, and it was as part of the papal delegation escorting the Greeks to a unification conference in Italy that Cusanus received his divine "gift" at sea, his inspiration for *De docta ignorantia*. His ecclesiastic triumphs were, however, to expose him to constant turmoil. His elevation to cardinal in 1448 and his installation as bishop of Brixen in 1450, rewards for his effective championing of the papacy in Germany, intensified the enmity of conciliarists still smarting over his political defection, and his efforts at church reform—which more than once put his life in danger—met with mixed results. The man Aeneas Sylvius called the "Hercules of the Eugenians" for his loyalty to Pope Eugenius proved to be a vulnerable hero. Near the end of his life, his friend Aeneas, now Pope Pius II, described him as bursting into tears over his frustrated efforts to achieve reform.[59]

According to Cassirer, Cusanus's political and ecclesiastical career reveals his "tragic error" in underestimating the turbulent forces of his time: "The opposing forces that Cusanus tried to reconcile *intellectually* diverge in his *life*. What he had tried intellectually to bring together into a systematic unity and harmony fell apart in the immediate reality in which he stood." But if, as Cassirer himself argues, Cusanus's philosophy reflects "the entire manifold of the age," we should not be surprised to find in it signs of disturbance that complicate its more optimistic tracings of the order, beauty, and proportion of God's book.[60]

Without racking the traditional trope too far, we can see that the genre of the *liber mundi* has become clouded. Southern's characterization of the twelfth century as a romance, a "search for new experiences and adventures" that transgresses boundaries in its quest for a wider world of "variety and mystery," often matches Cusanus's concept of the fifteenth-century world; he thinks of the mind's quest within it in terms of a cosmographer charting new fields of thought.[61] But even as Renaissance poets and critics would foreground the problematics of literary romance, so Cusanus's attempt to surpass traditional systems of thought would lead him to a vaster and more difficult terrain than he may have expected. His world must have seemed at times too various and mysterious, and the romance endless. We find him turning back to a stabler metaphysic and cosmology to provide hermeneutical keys to creation. Cassirer emphasizes Cusanus's use of Platonic "participation" as a way of asserting the presence of the harmonizing One in the many, and the many in the One. The couple *complicatio/explicatio*, borrowed from the Neoplatonists of twelfth-century Chartres, also attempts to make coherent the diversity of creation as an unfolding of the One, an "explication" of the infinite richness of the Word. If that explication is "privatively infinite" (2.1)—not actually infinite, because only God can be that—then the notion of a *universum* helps to impose a conceptual unity on its boundlessness, so that there can be what one historian calls "a kind of ontological limit for the irrational endlessness of finite relations."[62] Such terms make possible the claim that "all things have a certain comparative relation to one another" even if the relations are "hidden from us and incomprehensible to us" (1.11), and the claim that the "intellect's understanding follows . . . the intelligibility of nature" (2.6).

In order for these terms to provide the interpretive rules Cusanus's thought demands, however, they must be posited *outside* the field of human limitation, something that the premise of learned ignorance makes extremely difficult. Cusanus himself concedes this difficulty, for he warns us early in this work that we should not take his terms literally—not insist, that is, "upon the proper significations of words which cannot be properly adapted to such great intellectual mysteries" (1.2). For that reason, his assurances about the rational coherence of the universe often appear elusive or questionable. In *De docta ignorantia*, we make our rational measurements assuming that all reflect some underlying unity of truth, but "no one understands how God . . . is unfolded through the number of things" (2.3). It may be contingency alone that accounts for the "confusion" and "discord" of things (2.2), whereas it is a thing's likeness to God that grants its oneness, its being "united to the universe" (2.2). But if all creation is radically disproportionate to the Infinite, what is our justification for positing any degree of coherence?

The Cusan romance, then, presents special difficulties for its hero. He finds himself in a world of signs and enigmas, a *viator* searching for his Author. He must have faith that the text in which he finds himself is coherent, for the Author Himself is "the Beginning, the Middle, and the End" that binds together its variety (3.1). But he cannot know the intention behind the text, whether it was written "to make His goodness known" or as an exercise of power, "so that there are those who are compelled and who fear Him and whom He judges" (2.2). If he believes that the visible in some occult way reflects the invisible, he also knows that a reliance on visible signs would entail an infinite regress, "since these signs themselves, in regard to their own being, would likewise require other things through which [to appear], and so on *ad infinitum*" (2.2). He must continue the quest of interpretation, as the titles of Cusanus's works imply (*De quaerendo Deum, De venatione sapientiae*), but only with the knowledge that every interpretation is radically inadequate. Five years after *De docta ignorantia*, Cusanus imagines a brief conversation between a Christian and a pagan where the former rejects every Neoplatonic and mystical concept about God the latter can produce, including those of God as the source of all Being and God as ineffable. Even these will not do, because God is prior to every formulation, and the sheer presence of a concept in the mind guarantees its inadequacy, the need for the quest to continue (*De Deo abscondito*).

At times, Cusanus seems abashed by the book of the world as he transcribes it. The ingenious investigations of reason come to seem too arbitrary, and its goal too distant. It is at such moments that we find a trace of nostalgia for the Anselmian universe, where a virtuoso display of reason, however detachable it threatened to become, could always claim to rest on the solid surface of truth, and where the mind's quest—*fides quae-rens intellectum*—was a more clearly defined genre. More revealing than occasional borrowings from Anselm are Cusanus's attempts to reconstruct something like the assumptions that underlie Anselm's thought. About to present his extraordinary cosmology, where subjects and objects move through boundless space, Cusanus warns that "since it is not possible for the world to be enclosed between a physical center and [a physical] circumference, the world—of which God is the center and the circumference—is not understood" (2.11). Then, after describing the freedom of human subjects to posit their own poles of reference, he concludes: "Hence, the *machina mundi* will have its center everywhere and its circumference nowhere, so to speak; for God, who is everywhere and nowhere, is its circumference and center" (2.12). Modern responses to this argument characterize it in terms ranging from "astonishing" to "bizarre" and "unintelligible,"[63] but it is clear what Cusanus hopes to suggest: an objective foundation for the mind's perception of relativity. The mind can project a center everywhere because the center *is* everywhere.

But despite his ingenuity, Cusanus only demonstrates the unresolvable dilemmas of his thought. In the context of *De docta ignorantia*, the claim that God is the circumference and the center of the cosmos cannot be a literal statement about God or the structure of the universe. It is, rather, another example of the mathematical puzzles in book 1, where finite forms were stretched until opposites merged at infinity. It is only one of our symbolic expressions for a transcendent, yet omnipresent, God as we struggle to break down the distinctions of reason and realize that we can never comprehend Him. Though the passages appear to be guaranteeing the mind's operations through God's presence, in effect they describe the appropriateness of our way of knowing (or not knowing) the world in terms of the way we know (or do not know) God. The unity is neither between ourselves and the world nor between ourselves and God, but between our modes of cognition, whether as astronomers or as mystical theologians.

Unable to create a continuity between reason and an ontological foundation, Cusanus can only literalize his metaphor and use *it* as an absolute justification. He wants to be able to make Anselm's claim of painting on a solid surface of truth, but can support one level of design only with another level of design. Human reason is demonstrated to be equal to itself, just as God, who is truth, is the truth that measures itself. And yet it is this very circularity that leads Cusanus to more strenuous and more important recognitions.

2

CONTROVERSY AND
THE ART OF CONJECTURE

Readers looking to Cusanus for a herald of modernity must come to terms with what appear to be long stretches of the most traditional Neoplatonic and Scholastic exposition. Even when one grants Cassirer's point that the new direction of Cusanus's thought must seek expression in the language of the old, there still remains a large body of material seemingly inconsistent with that direction.[1] One study of the shifts in Cusanus's political thought focuses on such material to argue that Cusanus maintained a belief in a hierarchical cosmos and is thus a more traditional thinker than Cassirer and his successors propose.[2]

Others, however, have found Cusanus's uses of tradition disturbing. Vincent Martin has labeled Cusanus's thought "insidious." "However orthodox his intentions may have been . . . in the end he reduces God to a mere objectification of what is not attainable by human reason," Martin writes. Cusanus, he complains, "destroys both the essence of God and the trinity of the Persons."[3] D. J. B. Hawkins accepts Cusanus's historical importance but does so with irritation:

> Lovers of paradox will find entertainment in Nicholas of Cusa, but to a more prosaic mind these dialectical fireworks are a poor substitute for the sober analytical reasoning of the great thinkers of the thirteenth century. The philosophy of Cusanus is not only astonishing in itself, but it is astonishing that such a system should

39

have been put forward not by some obscure eccentric but by one of the leading European figures of the age.[4]

Similar notes of astonishment and outrage were sounded in Cusanus's own time. The Scholastic theologian Johannes Wenck, rector of the University of Heidelberg, condemned Cusanus as a dangerous innovator who would bring ruin to all knowledge, natural as well as theological, and compared him to those vain and curious speculators attacked by Paul in Romans whose "thinking became futile and their minds dark."[5] Wenck may have had ulterior, political motives; a supporter of the conciliar movement, he resented Cusanus's defection to the papacy. His sense of betrayal, however, extends beyond questions of party loyalty; Cusanus, for him, subverts the fundamental notions that make the world coherent to the Scholastic mind.

Whereas some of Wenck's charges—for example, that of pantheism—may be dismissed as willful or careless misreadings of Cusanus's paradoxes, many reveal the elusive contours of Cusanus's thought with extraordinary clarity. So, too, does the philosophically simpler, but equally important, dispute in which Cusanus engaged a few years later with Vincent of Aggsbach, a mystical "purist." Both debates show the ways in which Cusanus's thought evolved from sometimes tortuous negotiations with the intellectual currents of his time.

Born in an age that heard the conflicting claims of Platonism's metaphysical Realism, Scholasticism's moderate Realism, and various blends of Nominalism and mysticism, Cusanus's thought must be seen as part of the early modern struggle to determine anew the mind's relation to extramental reality. Viewed together, these two controversies propel us into what may seem to be a maelstrom of late-medieval "isms," but for Cusanus such movements proved to be a remarkably rich resource from which, and against which, to shape his attitudes.

THE TWO CONTROVERSIES

How can one debate with Cusanus, Johannes Wenck complains early in his *De ignota litteratura*, when his central strategy is to embrace all contradiction and so abolish the rules of inference? And yet he must be exposed, for here, Wenck charges, is a false prophet who violates the beauty of God's creation, the authority of Holy Scripture, and the truth of Christ's humanity (pp. 21–23, passim). The attack is mounted against ten theses extracted from *De docta ignorantia* together with the pernicious corollaries they engender. Of particular interest here is Wenck's attack on Cusanus's account of knowledge.

The natural world, Wenck reminds us, presents the mind with objects it can grasp and that conform to its capacities. Cusanus threatens to make that world incoherent by violating the first principle of reason, the Law of Contradiction. Wenck's authority is, of course, Aristotle, and he notes with irony the echo of the *Metaphysics* at the start of *De docta ignorantia*. It is only when we turn to the text Wenck cites in his attack— book 4 of the *Metaphysics*—that we realize how profound the irony is.

Aristotle's discussion there may be one of the best glosses we have on the interrelatedness of Cusanus's thought, for it demonstrates how the violation of logic's first principle can generate what are indeed Cusanus's central tenets. The coincidence of opposites, Aristotle warns, makes permissible contradictory accounts of an event, and so denies us any final, objective account (4.5). We are left with Protagoras's sophistic doctrine that man is the measure of all things, a consequence that delights Cusanus as much as it displeases Aristotle. Cusanus's cosmology, as we have seen, insists on the relativity of the human perceiver, and he continues in his subsequent writings to insist on the importance of individual perspectives and the measurements that proceed from them. In his later *De be-*

ryllo (1458), Cusanus will make an explicit defense of Protagoras's notorious doctrine against Aristotle's authority.[6]

A related consequence, Aristotle tells us, is the destruction of substance and essence. If someone can be both man and not-man, as the coincidence of opposites would allow, everything that can be said about him, including the fact that he is a man, becomes an accident; there will be no irreducible essence, no object of scientific knowledge—a crucial issue for Wenck when he considers the problem of "quiddity," as we shall see. And if there are no essential differences, Aristotle continues, we are left with Anaxagoras's doctrine of "all in all" (4.4). Jointly with 1 Corinthians 15:28, Anaxagoras nevertheless inspires one of Cusanus's paradoxical descriptions of creation and its relation to God: all things are in all because all derive their being from God, their "complication."

Not only does the coincidence of opposites render the external world incoherent, dismantling the structure of Being, but it subverts the very structure of thought. Book 4 of the *Metaphysics* tells us that if one "says at the same time both 'yes' and 'no' . . . he makes no judgment but 'thinks' and 'does not think' indifferently." "What difference," Aristotle asks, "will there be between him and a vegetable?" No one really holds such a view, for a man coming to a well or the edge of a precipice guards against falling, proving that he "does not think that falling in is alike good and not good" (4.4). Furthermore, if there were an intermediate between contradictories, the intellectual consequences would be equally absurd, for an infinite regress would be inevitable. As a modern editor summarizes the point: "If there is a term *B* which is neither *A* nor not-*A*, there will be a new term *C* which is neither *B* nor not-*B*," and so on.[7] Every statement we make would cause us to stumble endlessly between affirming and denying. Without an end, our thoughts would follow each other indefinitely, without unity, coherence, or purpose. As Aristotle argues in *De anima*: "All practical purposes of thinking have limits—they all go on for the sake of something outside the process, and all theoretical processes come to a close in the same way as the phrases in speech which express processes and results of thinking. . . . Thinking has more resemblance to a coming to rest or arrest than to movement" (1.3).

Cusanus may imagine a final resting point in faith, but, according to Wenck, learned ignorance, because it subverts all intelligibility, cannot avoid endless and futile wandering. Wenck focuses his attack on *De docta ignorantia* 1.3, where Cusanus introduces the polygon and the circle. Whereas Cusanus's point is that there can be no precise symbol for the Absolute, the principle of incommensurability extends to all efforts to know the world of "more or less": where there is no *praecisio*, all representations imply endless approximation. Wenck quotes: "There cannot be found two or more things which are so similar and equal that they could not be progressively more similar *ad infinitum*. . . . A finite intellect cannot by means of likenesses precisely attain the truth about things, because there always remains a difference between the measure and the measured" (pp. 28–29). Aristotle understood as much, Wenck concedes, but the fact that there always remains a difference between the mind's image and the object "does not destroy knowledge." Wenck finds Cusanus's argument recklessly extreme, especially in its claim that quiddity, the goal of "all philosophers," is unattainable (p. 29; *DDI* 1.3).

Wenck's source of contention is a notion of Scholasticism that grounds both epistemology and metaphysics. Aquinas, following Aristotle, denies mental access to Platonic Ideas as such; there can be nothing in the understanding that was not first in the senses, so man must find forms as they are embodied in material objects. And yet, despite the rejection of Platonic Ideas, Aquinas affirms embodied forms as the proper objects of knowledge. Sense knows only accidents, but "to understand [*intelligere*] means to read what is inside a thing [*intus legere*] . . . the intellect alone penetrates to the interior and to the essence of a thing."⁸ The intellect seeks the "whatness," the "quiddity" of a thing, and so a chain of mental events first transforms sensation into mental phantasms, which are in turn illuminated by the active intellect, revealing the "intelligible species." Possession of the species finally allows us to answer the mind's question, what is it? (*quid sit?*), whose answer is the quiddity or essence of the thing.⁹

Cusanus does on occasion refer to similar notions of "contracted quiddity" or "specific form," and he responds to Wenck by insisting that he does not destroy, but establish, the quiddities of things. Cusanus's discussions of quiddity and essence are apt to shift, however, according to his specific argumentative purposes. If at times created things are described as virtually perfect because filled with fullness of being, at others creation "does not have even as much being as an accident, but is altogether nothing" (*DDI* 2.2–3). Thomas McTighe argues in his studies of Cusanus's metaphysics that for Cusanus the only precise quiddity is the Quiddity of quiddities, the Absolute that is the source of all Being. Finite things have for us no "positive quidditative content," no "essential density." They are what they are only in relation to what they are not, "constituted by negativity."¹⁰ Some note a shift in the later Cusanus toward a more positive sense of the world's indeterminacy as *posse fieri*: creation is charged with the "power-to-become." But this view is still disastrous for the Scholastic theory of truth. The theory requires that the mind be able to judge whether its concept of a thing is in conformity with a fixed reality behind the changing appearance, whether there is an *adaequatio rei et intellectus*:

> The classic theory of truth as *adaequatio rei et intellectus* assumes that the *res*, the *realitas*, is something stable, complete, definitive, motionless; but if we assume that reality or "being itself," the metaphysic, is *fieri*, is multiple or dynamic, subject to continuous

change, the classic conception of the truth can no longer be maintained, for there can be no conformity with something that is not yet complete.[11] It is just such an implication that Wenck is quick to perceive. The intellect has a "natural movement" toward "the quiddity, or truth of things." "But if it were unattainable, then this intellectual movement would be without a *terminus ad quem*. Consequently, there would be no end of motion; and hence the motion would be infinite and in vain. This would be to destroy the intellect's proper operation" (p. 29).

Wenck joins Aristotelian teleology with the injunction of Psalm 45: "Be still and see that I am God"—a command to which he alludes throughout his attack. Here, he declares, is "the legitimate enlistment of all our mental activity": we must "behold with quietude" (p. 21). He is irritated by Cusanus's refusal to be "enclosed by sound doctrines." Not content with human limitation, Cusanus's unrestrained drive for novelty produces not true knowledge but mere fictions: "For just as a feigned [*simulata*] holiness is a double abomination, since it is the feigning [*fictio*] of what does not exist, so this learned ignorance which is feigned [*ficta*] existence of knowledge, has a false appearance of knowledge, and therewith a lack of knowledge" (p. 34). Cusanus, "leaving behind all the beauty and comeliness of creatures, vanishes amid thoughts" (p. 25). The mind, deprived of its *terminus ad quem* and burning with "infernal inflammation" (p. 40), would finally be consumed by the futility of its endless operations.

Cusanus responds to this nightmarish vision of his thought in his *Apologia doctae ignorantiae* (1449). Even granting its polemical aim, this work, a selection and reassertion of claims made by *De docta ignorantia*, is uncharacteristically defensive. Cast as a communication from one enthusiastic disciple to another, it describes the beloved teacher, Cusanus, as rising above petty malice, smiling indulgently while the youth heaps abuse on

Wenck, and doubting that Wenck is worth refuting. Nonetheless, a glance at Wenck's deceitfulness and political motives is
followed by a brief, methodical refutation. Cusanus insists, for
example, that learned ignorance does not destroy knowledge,
but instead makes proper allowances for the beauty of creation
and the affirmative way of worship (p. 11). The work's primary concern, however, is with the mystical vision beyond the
mere "victory of words" (p. 8). The "Aristotelian sect," because it holds the coincidence of opposites to be "heresy," is
imprisoned by its own logic (p. 6). Discursive reason is, of
course, natural to man. Like a hunting dog seeking its prey
through its senses, human logic makes its investigations from
point to point: *discursus est necessario terminatus inter terminus a
quo et ad quem.* But for man there is also a higher way; he can
ascend from the limits of discourse to the *intellectus*, a faculty
where opposites coincide and the partialities of hearing yield
to the immediacy of mental vision (pp. 14–15).

Cusanus reminds his pupil that "a wise, humble, and modest man openly admits how far he is from the summit" (p. 3),
but as in *De docta ignorantia*, modesty grants privilege. Having
admitted his distance from the summit, Cusanus argues "that
learned ignorance elevates someone, in the way that a high
tower does," so that he can look down and judge how near or
far the discursive wanderer is in relation to his goal on the plain
below (p. 16). Yet in relation to his own goal, the visionary
"approaches more closely" only when he finds that the goal
"has moved farther away." As Dionysius said, the worshipper
leaves all things behind and "seems to ascend unto nothing
rather than unto something" (pp. 13, 20). *De docta ignorantia*
had already placed the negative above the affirmative (1.26),
but the *Apologia* elevates it even higher, until it becomes an
authority over thought rather than a consequence of it.

Two years after the reply to Wenck, Cusanus engaged in
another controversy, which led him to stress the other side of
his sympathies. The new attack, by Vincent of Aggsbach, a

Carthusian monk, came from an angle opposite to Wenck's, protesting not against Cusanus's violation of the laws of reason but against his failure to annihilate them. Vincent considered himself a mystical purist. He argued that the true mystical tradition had shown that peace lay only in the full consumption of knowledge in an affective, not an intellectual, assent. His assaults began against the French theologian Jean Gerson, who, he asserted, allowed human intelligence too large a role in mystical experience. Vincent soon found other antagonists, however, including Cusanus and one of his admirers in the monastery at Tegernsee, whose "fictions, imaginations, suppositions, estimations," he said, must never replace "solid doctrine."[12]

The Tegernsee monks sought Cusanus's advice, which appears in his letters to them in the 1450s. Cusanus reasserts the importance of elevation over the sensible world, and warns that there are many who are deceived by a fantastic vision they hold to be true. Nevertheless, he does not think that negative theology is the proper way to enter divine darkness. If all is negated and nothing posited, God will not be found to be, but rather not to be.[13] The point is not radically new: De docta ignorantia conceded the necessity of positive worship. But the urgency with which Cusanus reminds his friends that we can love the good only under the concept of the good, and that pure ignorance, rather than guarding against fantastic visions, only makes it easier for a Satanic angel to deceive the worshipper, suggests a more critical stance in relation to the via negativa.[14] Dionysius compares the exercise to a sculptor's removing superfluous matter to reveal the hidden beauty of his marble, but, Cusanus seems to ask, if all conceptions are inadequate, must we carve until the marble is pulverized? Resisting such annihilation, Cusanus claims that affective ascent is neither learned nor ignorant, because those very terms imply the presence of intellectual power. If one turns to the original Greek of Dionysius, Cusanus insists, one finds that the disjunction of negative and affirmative theologies can be healed by a "copulative theology," a coincidence of opposites that transcends the limitations of either.[15]

Cusanus thus relies on mystical silence to refute Wenck and demands a place for affirmation to answer Vincent. If we keep both these responses in mind, we shall see that the dialectical movement begun by De docta ignorantia widens its circle throughout Cusanus's career, invoking both affirmation and denial but resting in neither. It is just this movement that gives shape to his most remarkable epistemological theme, which he calls the "conjectural art."

CONJECTURE AND ITS
DISCONTENTS

We have seen how De docta ignorantia collapses rational distinctions through a series of mathematical thought experiments. It is, however, equally important to note that Cusanus introduces these puzzles in the imperfect subjunctive in order to signal their hypothetical status: "Dico igitur, si esset linea infinita, illa esset recta, illa esset triangulus, et esset sphaera" (1.11).[16] Though such forms cannot exist within the realm of our experience, by extrapolating from what we do know of finite forms (for example, the curve of a circle straightens as its size increases), we concede what Aristotle calls in the Poetics an "impossible probability." And though the aim is to use thought in order to tease us out of thought, it is the very production of hypothetical forms that assumes prominence in book 2, where Cusanus turns from the Absolute Maximum to creation.[17] Here the mind's inventions are intended not for self-consumption, but for a self-affirming reinterpretation of tradition. The Cusan observer, recognizing the errors of the fixed poles of the ancients, posits his own: "Consider carefully the fact that just as in the eighth sphere the stars are [moved] around conjectural poles, so the earth, the moon, and the planets—as stars—are moved at a distance and with a difference around a pole [which] *we conjecture* to be where the center is believed to be" (2.11; emphasis mine).

Such passages inspire Cassirer's important interpretation of *De docta ignorantia* as a movement from the ontologically determined to the freely hypothetical,[18] and point us toward Cusanus's second major work, *De coniecturis* (1440–44), which continues to develop a positive theory of mental effort against the background of the negative way. The admitted inadequacy of our concepts no longer demands their effacement, but asserts their value *as* conjecture.

Conjecture, for Cusanus, is the best the mind can rationally accomplish. It is not simply a guess awaiting confirmation by more conclusive evidence, in part because it appears to embody truth in some way, but also because all evidence, once apprehended, becomes conjectural. Cusanus fuses these two aspects of conjecture in several formulations in the work, the most striking of which claims a coincidence of positive assertion and otherness: "Coniectura . . . est positiva assertio, in alteritate veritatem, uti est, participans" (*De con.* 1.11). The sense in which positive assertion in otherness can claim to be participating in truth when that very claim must *itself* be made in otherness points the way to further difficulty, but it is more important first to note how the promise of a positive direction for thought functions in *De coniecturis*. It allows Cusanus to locate the play of the mind within a context where the mind's constructions need neither be affirmed as precisely true nor dismissed as merely false. That context allows humanity to continue its insatiable quest for truth through a Renaissance version of the "philosophy of 'as if.'"[19]

Cusanus's attitude may not satisfy Scholastic criteria, but he takes pains to clarify standards of internal coherence. He finds them in mathematics, which (as in *De docta ignorantia*) represents mental precision and so is ideal both for the symbolic projection of thought and as the clearest possible analogy for how

1	2	3	4	5	6	7	8	9	10
1		10			100				1000
1	2	3	4	20	30	40	200	300	400

1. The Natural Progression of Number, from *Opera omnia* 3:17.

thought unfolds. Part of that representation entails the absorption of conservative elements of Cusanus's predecessors, for much of the work pays tribute to tradition as a series of conjectural efforts to come to terms with the mysteries of the One and the many. But now these efforts are conceived *as* a coming to terms, hypothetical patterns that are both inadequate symbols and celebrations of the mind's power to invent them.

It is the celebrative tone that dominates the opening, as Cusanus compares the mind's rational conjectures to God's creation of the real world through the Word (*De con.* 1.1–2). Next, he attempts to picture the generation of conjecture from the mind's unity by demonstrating how number evolves from one. A "natural progression" is sketched in a fourfold development that is repeated three times: one, two, three, and four are added to reach ten, explicating the second unity (ten) from the first (one). The pattern proceeds from the second unity: ten, twenty, thirty, and forty form one hundred, and this third unity joins two hundred, three hundred, and four hundred to complete the process in one thousand (1.3). Cusanus names these mental unities "divine mind," "intelligence," "soul," and "body," allegorizing them, as it were, so that the progression may serve as a hierarchical picture not only of the mind's unfolding but also of the analogous generation of the world's

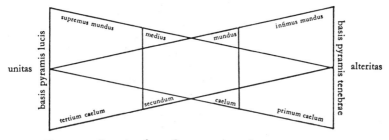

2. *Figura paradigmatica*, from *Opera omnia* 3:46.

body from the One (1.4–8). And this analogy supports, and is supported by, further analogy: the fourfold geometrical progression from point to line to surface to body (1.8).

The second diagram, the *figura paradigmatica* or "figure P," is a fundamental one for the remainder of the work. It is also the one most familiar to modern eyes because of Yeats's use of the same figure as his "gyres" in *A Vision*. Cusanus represents two intersecting pyramids, one of light and one of shadow, whose vertices touch each other's bases at their midpoints. The diagram's range of application, *mutatis mutandis*, is no less broad than that of Yeats's figure, for by picturing the dynamic relation of unity and otherness at the heart of creation, the pyramids can represent indivisibility and divisibility, actuality and potency, masculinity and femininity, soul and body, intellect and sense, or any other opposition that falls under discussion. One descends into the other, while the latter rises to the former, and between them may be imagined the vast fecundity and diversity of the world and of the mind.

The most ambitious conjecture in the work, an architectonic that includes themes from the others, is the *figura universi*. A single large circle surrounds three smaller circles placed vertically down its axis. Within each of these is another set of three smaller circles, and within these still another set of three, so that when completed, the image shows twenty-seven small cir-

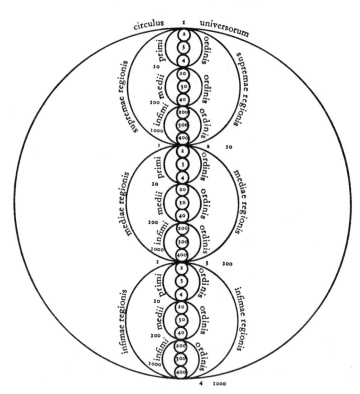

3. *Figura universi*, from *Opera omnia* 3:64.

cles strung like beads, grouped into threes by nine larger circles, which are in turn grouped by three larger circles, and all
included in the "grossest," for a total of forty circles. The diagram allows Cusanus to demonstrate his mastery over intellectual traditions that become for him a repertoire of metaphors
that can be evoked and combined at will. Important doctrines
can be visually grasped and interrelated: the fourfold progression of number, the omnipresent vestiges of the trinity,
"everything in everything" (every specific thing contains
within itself a version of the whole), perhaps even, in the tran-

sition from one to twenty-seven circles, an implied "lambda formula" derived from medieval commentary on the *Timaeus*, the harmony of the World Soul that Plato's Demiurge bases on the squares and cubes of even and odd numbers, ending with the proportion 1:27. Later Renaissance thinkers would admire the inclusiveness and elegance of the figure and adapt it to illustrate their own versions of cosmic harmony.[20]

We must remember, however, that for Cusanus such constructions are not objectively fixed accounts of reality. The Neoplatonic models from which many of their features derive assume an identity between the structure of Being and of thought, hence the power of introspection to lead the soul back to the One.[21] *De coniecturis* is, in part, a criticism of such assumptions, even as it exploits them for its own ends. The same must be said for its number symbolism. Cusanus is always enthusiastic about mathematics, and in a late work goes so far as to regard it as a quasi-mystical force glowing through its proximity to truth. But again we must not be misled. Mathematics does not bridge the gap between finite and infinite; its "precision" refers not to the unattainable *praecisio* of metaphysical truth, but to the precision with which it figures forth the motions of reason, making visible the mental patterns we unfold when we seek to understand anything.[22] What appear to be Neoplatonic hypostases in *De coniecturis* might be better characterized as instances of hypostatization; they are conceptual models treated *as if* substantial.

Part of the point is subversive. Cusanus wants to unsettle the complacency associated not only with Platonism but also with Scholasticism. Aquinas, too, was keenly aware of the difficulty of theology, but an assumed hierarchy of Being allowed him to perceive the excellence of creation as bearing some proportion to the Creator. We can, he thought, invent valid analogies to God. Even if our terms fail to represent His eminence, we may still go beyond metaphor; they "signify the divine substance and are predicated substantially of God" (*Summa theo-*

logica 1.13. 20).[23] Cusan conjecture, by contrast, unsettles the metaphysical ground on which Thomist analogy rests, a point that Johannes Wenck understood. Cusanus's ground is what he calls the "foundation of unattainable precision." It keeps us constantly in motion; reason may never question that three plus two equals five because it does not question its own standards of accuracy (*De con.* 2.1). The foundation of unattainable precision, however, both supports and undermines our criteria, provoking a continuous dialectic of conjecture and discontent.

As in *De docta ignorantia*, then, the constructive dovetails into the destructive. But given the constructive emphasis of the work, we are placed under greater pressure than before to determine how such invention participates in truth. Some readers for that reason look to passages in Cusanus suggesting that conjecture, though not truth itself, is "true as far as it goes." The conjectural art, then, becomes a series of "partial victories of Truth."[24] Others, however, have resisted such claims. Nancy Struever, for example, argues that Cusanus opposes "false reification" by inventing "texts which are complicated tissues of signs." "The creative autonomy of the mind's symbolizing capacity" yields figures that are non-referential, including mathematical figures used "in a most literary way." Wittgenstein becomes a gloss for Cusanus: "It is just because forming images is a voluntary activity that it does not instruct us about the external world." This is not a subjectivist reading, Struever concludes; rather, it focuses on Cusanus's use of the universe of signs for ethical, communal instruction and action.[25]

Struever's argument for Cusanus's "symbolic activity . . . as the site of discovery" is incisive, as is her emphasis on his didacticism; both figure P and the *figura universi* purport to lead beyond themselves to help the reader to attain hidden knowledge (1.9, 13). But Cusanus is not entirely comfortable working within what Struever calls a "self-correcting semiotic medium," even with the proviso that signs do not become idols.[26]

He often reaches for some point of leverage outside the making of symbols for the sake of justifying the mind's penchant for figures. Such moments are most obvious when they are theological, as when Cusanus claims at the end of *De docta ignorantia* that the theme of the coincidence of opposites came to him directly by divine inspiration. Subtler is the pressure we feel in *De coniecturis* to accept something more substantial than an as-if metaphysic to protect conjecture from the dangers of solipsism. When Cusanus tells us that humanity "does not proceed outside itself when it creates, but when it unfolds its power, it reaches to itself alone," it seems we must accept the ontological claims in the same chapter for man as microcosm—a creature who already contains all things "humanly" within himself—in order to justify the mind's fascination with its own inventions (2.14).

Perhaps the surest indication of both the desirability and the difficulty of anchoring conjecture to something outside itself lies in the epistemology of *De coniecturis*. Here Cusanus traces a mental hierarchy from *sensus* to *ratio* to *intellectus*—that is, from the primary and confused material of sensory experience to the shaping of rational order and, finally, to a higher capacity that transcends mere rationality and embraces the coincidence of opposites (1.8). Conjecture appears to be supported by, and suspended between, two poles: on one side, empirical experience, which, according to Karsten Harries, reins in the power of the imagination whose "freedom threatens a loss of contact with reality," leaving man lost "in his own empty constructions";[27] on the other, the *intellectus*, a faculty only hinted at in *De docta ignorantia*, but developed here into Cusanus's most important justification. It is to the *intellectus* that Cusanus appeals, as we have seen, when Wenck charges him with merely "feigning . . . what does not exist." All rational exercise depends upon the *intellectus*: it is both the illuminating unity that descends into rational otherness and the path by which thought may ascend to the ineffable. Its central role, however, proves to be a mixed blessing. The *intellectus*, because it is suprarational, shares with the Absolute a transcendence over the Law of Contradiction, but if it suggests a completed hierarchy, it also reasserts the problem of incommensurability. Cusanus tells us that when in *De docta ignorantia* he referred to God as the coincidence of opposites, he was only speaking "intellectually." God's negation of opposites must be understood as "improportionably simpler" than the fusions of the *intellectus* (1.6). If this is so, the *intellectus*, rather than clarifying the work's enthusiastic premise of an analogy between divine and human fecundity, restates and compounds the worshipper's difficulty with both sides of the comparison: as a suprarational category, it must transcend discourse; but as a human faculty, it bears no proportion to God.

I suggested in chapter 1 that Cusanus is sometimes nostalgic for Anselm's intellectual universe; his appeals to the *intellectus* perhaps express a similar nostalgia for that of the Neoplatonist. They allow him to picture a release from the labyrinth of self-validation by using a version of the Platonic "divided line" to trace a hierarchy whose last step intuitively and nonconjecturally links the mental and the extramental. But the appeals must be understood as the work of conjecture, and it is not surprising to find that Cusanus continues to tinker with the relationship between the *intellectus* and discursive reason in his later works.[28] Indeed, he must, because each level of activity seeks its unity and precision in the level above itself; if the first two levels are not proportional to each other, what does this say about the integrity of the mind? This is one problem that Cusanus does resolve in *De coniecturis*, when the ascent of the *intellectus* to silence is juxtaposed with the necessity of its descent. It may be perched on a high tower in the *Apologia*, but here it must come down to the realm of the senses, even against its desire, in order to be itself most fully (2.16). The quest for truth is inexhaustible (1.4), and so, too, is Cusanus's storehouse of geometrical and verbal figures illustrating the process. All, however, tell similar stories. The higher realm is actualized even as the lower is elevated, and all seek the divine unity "which is infinite life and the truth and rest of intellect" (2.16). But the interpenetration of intellect and sense also recalls to us the energies of reason and imagination generated between them, energies that set into motion the forging of metaphor in this life.

THE NOMINALIST QUESTION

Conjecture does not only mine tradition for its figures; the art itself evolves from medieval antecedents. Attempts to trace its lineage prove somewhat frustrating, however. Some have found in Cusanus echoes of the thirteenth-century Spanish mystic Ramon Lull, who sought to schematize religious and philosophical truths in geometrical forms and to engage the minds of his readers in their complex movements. We know that Lull's "Art" was an important influence on the art of conjecture by virtue of the sheer number of Lull's works present in Cusanus's famous library.[29] But Cusanus regards his own constructions with a different set of assumptions. He is not, like Lull, a philosophical Realist—that is, one who relies upon universals prior to, and independent of, particular things and the mind's understanding of them. Closer in spirit to Cusanus's conjectures are the schemata of the fourteenth-century Nicholas of Oresme, whose work Cusanus probably read while at Padua. Professing to know that he knew nothing, Oresme developed an approach to natural philosophy that Marshall Claggett describes as "essentially conjectural." It proceeds through geometrical fictions or "configurations," which Oresme acknowledges as "feigned" because they exist in the imagination rather than in things.[30] Oresme's configurations are strongly colored by Nominalism, but when we examine Cusanus's conjectures, we find that though they are not Realist, they are not entirely Nominalist either. They operate, rather, in a kind of hybrid realm that attempts to preserve both Lull's and Oresme's assumptions. In order to get further bearings on Cusan conjecture, then, we must see it in relation to the important controversy in medieval thought over the nature of universals. The underlying question of this debate concerns the relation of the ontological and conceptual spheres. It broadly pursues three lines of inquiry: do the terms we use for groups of individuals—for example, "humanity"—refer to a higher Form in which they participate (Realism)? an imbedded essence that the mind abstracts (moderate Realism)? or only to an imposition by the mind, a classification having to do with words, not things (Nominalism)?

A brief survey of the problem is revealing. Boethius, commenting on Porphyry, wondered if species and genera should be understood as "things which are" or as the products of an "empty cogitation of the mind."[31] With the revival of dialectic in the eleventh century, the problem demanded more explicit scrutiny, and was aggravated by the extremism of early Nominalists: universals, they claimed, have no extramental reality; they are mere verbal noises (*flatus vocis*) arbitrarily attached to groups of individuals. Anselm, whose own dialectical subtleties were prodigious, found the Nominalist tendency to be dangerous, even heretical, and in the following century Peter Abélard tried to temper its extremism while preserving some of what it uncovered. Universals are not prior to particulars, Abélard writes, but are acts of the intellect. We impose the name "man" on both Socrates and Plato, but that name does not refer to any essence independent of them, for "no thing is man except a discrete thing." Yet the name is not meaningless, for it refers to their true "status" as men.[32]

Because of the peculiar status of "status," Abélard's position is not clear. The example he gives is ingeniously elusive: "status" is the cause of a common name even as a man's failure to appear in court is the cause of his being lashed, an illustration that insists on the paradoxical causality of absence.[33] There is, however, an evident direction to his compromise: universals are neither independent things nor arbitrary words, but nouns that signify meaningful conceptions about things. William of Ockham developed this compromise further in the fourteenth century. The intellect does not abstract an essence from a thing, as Aquinas held, but, like sense, has direct, intuitive knowledge of individuals, which are the only truly extramental objects. The mind, however, still requires universals for scientific and logical knowledge, and it therefore fashions them as mental artifacts based on perceived resemblances. The theory of the mind's direct intuition of individuals is sometimes cited as a late-medieval "hunger for reality,"[34] but given a tradition that long regarded universals as either metaphysical exemplars marking divine presence or as essences imbedded in the knowable structure of Being, Ockham's position remains a challenge to historians.

Etienne Gilson, who regards Aquinas's moderate Realism as an ideal balance, sees in Ockham the symptom of an "intellectual disease" that alienates man from any knowledge of Being, and whose implications deny "any proof that this world of ours is not a vast phantasmagoria behind which there is no reality to be found."[35] A long scholarly debate has since cleared Ockham of the damning charge of skepticism;[36] he does not mean to say that we know only words, as some of the more extreme Nominalists seem to have held. Nevertheless, all knowledge beyond the particular is mediated through terms that "stand" for things in "suppositions"; we know things only by way of statements about them. Ockham also avoids the classical Scholastic definition of truth as an *adaequatio rei et intellectus*, because for him the forms of discourse do not "reveal a common structure internal to things qua adequated to the mind."[37] There is, in Gordon Leff's tactful phrase, "an asymmetry between truth and being."[38]

If there is a point of origin for this asymmetry, it lies in a problem anterior to that of universals, in Nominalism's atti-

tude toward the very formation of concepts in the mind. Abélard, seeking the source of universals, argues that, unlike the
senses, which require an external body, the understanding can
form its own mental image, "a certain imaginary and fictive
thing, which the mind constructs for itself when it wishes and
as it wishes."[39] The intellect can dispense with these *ficta* if it
has access to substance, but when a particular thing is absent,
or, as in the case of universals, when there is no particular, our
intellect fashions its own thought-objects, which are, strictly
speaking, "non-things," without substance or accident. Abélard admits that it may be abhorrent (*abhorrendum*)[40] for us to
imagine the mind tracing the mediating likenesses of things
through nothing, but for him this is the intellect's special
power; it can operate in a realm populated by its own fictive
constructions. Ockham, in his early discussion of concepts, is
similarly drawn to these ambiguous *ficta*. He suggests, like
Abélard, that they have only a conceptual rather than a real
existence; they are "a kind of mental picture."[41] When Johannes
Wenck a century later threw up his hands at the mental picturing of learned ignorance as a feigned (*ficta*) knowledge of what
does not exist, he may have suspected a Nominalist tendency
in Cusanus, a tendency to which Wenck was strongly opposed.

What exactly are these *ficta*, these "non-things" or "mental
pictures"? Historians of philosophy rightly warn against confusing Nominalist *ficta* with literary or aesthetic fictions, but
we must not allow this distinction to foreclose our own ability
to perceive common likenesses.[42] Both Abélard and Ockham
attempt to clarify the nature of *ficta* by drawing analogies to the
work of an artist. Abélard characterizes the concept as a willed
dream, "like those imaginary cities which are seen in dreams,"
but constructed by the mind "when it wishes and as it wishes."
The remainder of his discussion compares it several times to
the preconceived form an artist shapes in his mind "as the figure . . . of the thing to be formed." Ockham, too, compares
ficta to the "activity of the artist." He warns that they must not

be thought to exist independently of the mind: "Fictions have being in the mind, but they do not exist independently, because in that case they would be real things and so a chimera and a goat-stag and so on would be real things. So some things exist only as thought-objects."[43] Ultimately, however, both Abélard and Ockham reject the analogy because of the unreality it implies. Concepts, Abélard writes, are not "located in empty opinion without the thing, like the following words, chimera and goat-stag which do not give rise to a rational understanding." The mind must look through and beyond its constructions, concentrating not on "a doctrine of these figments, but only through these figments."[44] Ockham, never quite satisfied with the nature of *ficta*, regards them at first only as probable, and later rejects them in favor of a theory of concepts that identifies them with the immediate act of knowing. "A fictive thing," he decides, "hinders the knowledge of the thing . . . if that fictive thing is understood, then the thing outside is not understood."[45]

Cusanus's art of conjecture is not Nominalist per se, but it evolves from a complicated struggle with the issues at the heart of the Realist-Nominalist controversy. *De docta ignorantia* denies our access to extramental universals, but in a single chapter (2.6), it endorses a quasi-Platonic Realism (nature's order requires universals prior to individuals), a quasi Aristotelianism (universals have no independent existence, but do exist in particular things), and a quasi Nominalism (a universal is a rational entity). Commentators sometimes place Cusanus among the Aristotelian Thomists because he does seem to endorse a metaphysic based on moderate Realism.[46] The universe is contracted to genera, genera to species, and species to individuals that actually exist, and though "universals do not exist as actual apart from particulars, nevertheless they are not mere rational entities." But oddly juxtaposed to this metaphysic is a more Nominalist epistemology. The mind does not, as in Aquinas, penetrate to the essence of a thing, to "read what is inside it," for when it abstracts a universal, "the abstraction is a rational entity." This in itself would not create much difficulty were it not for the fact that any claim to an *adaequatio rei et intellectus* is now problematic. Rather, the mind forms "similitudes" of universals, based on universals already contracted in the mind, generating, in fact, a world of similitudes (*mundum . . . similitudinarium*). However Cusanus may imagine the contents of this mental world to be similar to the universals in things, he cannot overcome his own axiom that no two things can be compared without there being an infinity of more similar things.

Cusanus promises in *De docta ignorantia* (2.6) to deal more fully in *De coniecturis* with the question of how the mind abstracts universals, but the issue is overwhelmed in the latter work by his increased interest in the diverse symbolic worlds the mind can produce through number and geometrical form. The most illuminating effort to solve the riddle did not appear for another ten years, when in the third of four dialogues, called collectively *De idiota* (1450), the leading speaker investigates the nature of naming and suggests along the way that all philosophical schools—including Realism and Nominalism—are talking about the same thing from different points of view.

A lowly spoon carver by trade, the *idiota*, or "layman," bases his symbolic investigations on his craft. Because the spoon has no exemplar outside the mind, the artisan fashioning it does not imitate nature. His art, the *idiota* notes somewhat disingenuously, resembles the "infinite art" more than do those of the mimetic sculptor and painter. Once the form appears, he calls the object a "spoon," a name imposed arbitrarily (*impositio nominis fit ad beneplacitum*). And yet the name is not wholly divorced from what the *idiota* mysteriously calls the "natural name united to the form."[47] An attempt to explain leads him to an account of conjecture and universals:

> Because the form in its truth is not found among those things about which reason is conversant, reason *settles on conjecture and opinion*.

Thus genera and species, as they fall under names, are *rational entities*, which reason made to itself out of the concordance and difference of things sensibly perceived. . . . they are similitudes, the sensible things being destroyed, those cannot remain.
(3.2; emphasis mine)[48]

The *idiota* now considers two ways of looking at this mental fashioning of rational entities. First he states the claim of one who finds that "the thing is nothing, but as it falls under a name . . . this enquiry is pleasing to man, because it discourses by motion of reason. This man would deny that forms in themselves and in their truth separated, are otherwise than as they are rational entities, and would make no account of exemplars or Ideas" (3.2). The *idiota* confesses man's self-enjoyment; the very motions of reason please us, for the objects of knowledge are beings of reason. Against this perspective, the *idiota* now juxtaposes the view of philosophers who insist that just as truth precedes an image, so there is "the exemplary and incommunicable truth of forms" behind sensible things; if all men were destroyed, "humanity" would endure (3.2).

What Cusanus has done here is to summarize the art of conjecture until it becomes ambiguous and then divide the account into competing voices. Under the labels *Peripatetic* and *Academic*, he represents "all sects of philosophy": on one side the moderate Realist *cum* Nominalist; on the other a Platonic Realist. All that remains is to recombine them, a task the *idiota* claims is easily done. All schools are reconciled "when the mind lifts itself to infinity," as if antithetical modes of perceiving reality could be fused like the infinite triangles and circles of *De docta ignorantia*. He elaborates. There is only one precise form and that is God, the infinite Form of forms. Peripatetics are right because reason imposes universal names without reference to distinct exemplars, but Academics are also right: the very act of naming is an image of the "one ineffable word" that is the precise name of all things. The tone of faith is reassuring, but the juxtaposition of competing epistemologies with a theology of the infinite remains puzzling: it promises clear resolution based on a premise that is for Cusanus an impossibility—namely, that the rational, finite mind can lift itself to infinity. This dilemma reflects far more than an ingenious, but shaky, syncretism. Cusanus's attempt to harmonize his Nominalist tendencies with opposing schools of thought reveals the challenge his conjectural art presents to any speculative equilibrium. Cusanus shares the Nominalists' recognition of what Struever calls the "active independent power of language" and the "creative use of symbol."[49] And, like the Nominalists, he believes that these constructs are more than mere fictions, that they point to something true outside the imposition. But in order to justify that confidence, Cusanus must leap to a disproportionate, and ultimate, Realism: God becomes the hidden Universal.

Cusanus's attempt to justify human invention through an infinite and ineffable universal continues to have remarkable consequences for the exercise of his own invention, some of which are surveyed in the next chapter. Two general comparisons and contrasts with Nominalism will help summarize the larger issues at stake. Nominalism uncovers a discrepancy in the traditional picture of conceptual and ontological relations, but its response is a rigorous attempt to preserve objective clarity, to prevent a confusion of words and things. The goal of Ockham and Nominalism was not to liberate man's symbolic activity, but to restrain it, to prevent it from filling the world with a maze of futile speculation. Ockham resorts to a traditional methodological tool, now called "Ockham's razor": what can be explained by the assumption of fewer things is vainly explained by the assumption of more things. Here we see the motive behind his rejection of *ficta*: they are so many useless hypotheses, which must be pared away to prevent, in Anton Pegis's terms, "the human intellect from introducing into reality what are only modes of thought."[50]

Cusanus, by contrast, insists that we introduce those modes into the world. True, he often warns us not to be seduced by mere rationality or by fantastic visions. But, rather than slicing back the layers of hypothetical explanations, the conjectural art demands that we produce such explanations, and, as we shall see, allows us to produce them *ad infinitum*. It is only through this production that we can come to terms with a world that would otherwise remain beyond our grasp, and even beyond value. Cusanus shares the belief that Realists have unselfconsciously reified their metaphors, but he makes it increasingly difficult to tell where his own metaphors end and extramental reality begins.

Equally revealing is the contrast between the religious anthropologies of Cusanus and of Nominalism. Nominalist theology, like Cusanus's, emphasizes the disproportion between the finite and the infinite. So awesome is God's absolute power in relation to the contingent world that our relationship to God becomes "contingent and conventional" rather than ontological, still dependable because instituted by God but no longer based on "common natures."[51] The sense of ontological distance restricts our ability to achieve a rational theology, forcing us to depend increasingly on faith and revelation. The restriction, however, finds ample compensation in Nominalist anthropology. In Heiko Oberman's terms, once the supernatural "has receded and become a hemisphere, a dome," the world of experience need no longer be a mere reflection of higher truths. An "autonomous anthropology" can evolve that allows man, as the image and likeness of God, to explain his own freedom and power.[52]

Cusanus begins with the theological premise of infinite disproportion, but his anthropology, however expansive it may become, must refuse the shelter of a "dome." The extreme diversity of conjecture must forever look to the incomprehensible divine harmony to justify the mind's activity. What is surely intended as spiritual encouragement at the same time guarantees epistemological turbulence. The mind, struggling at every moment to reach outside itself, to transcend its otherness from unattainable precision, finds its creative activity in the world forever drawn by the gravitational pull of the Absolute, an unrelenting reminder of its own inadequacy.

This turbulence coexists with Cusanus's assurances of a harmonious participation in the One—assurances that a "fore-taste" of eternal wisdom draws us like children to milk, or like iron to a magnet, and that we experience a progressive "assimilation" to the goal of knowledge. The conjectural art may emerge from medieval traditions—both its content and its attitude toward that content can be understood only in terms of them—but however many threads of Neoplatonism, Scholasticism, mysticism, Realism, and Nominalism crisscross Cusanus's texts, conjecture can neither be identified with, nor justified by, them. If it could be so defended, Wenck's attack would have given Cusanus an opportunity to explain more rigorously how *coniectura* is an approximation of truth and not the restless feigning Wenck decries. As we have seen, however, the *Apologia* turns away the challenge by looking to the cessation of conjecture, confining it within a strict hierarchy where it can be neatly superseded by the *intellectus*.

But however turbulent the flow of conjecture becomes, Cusanus values it too highly to close it off, even to locate its mystical source. The controversy with Vincent and the inventiveness of Cusanus's work bear witness to that. Terms like the *intellectus*, though important to Cusanus, are, finally, momentary resting points: attacked for the instability of his claims, he refines affirmation into the wise passivity of higher silence; attacked for an insufficient commitment to that higher silence, he refines silence into the necessity of mental effort. Within the development of his thought, these maneuvers are more than rhetorical evasions. They allow him, rather, to defer ultimate resolution—precisely because it is "ultimate"—for the sake of concentrating on the diverse, if ambiguous, energies of the conjecturing mind itself. If there is a participation in truth, it must be through the mind's successive acts of composition, decomposition, and recomposition: a participation in, an assimilation to, creative action.

3

PROTEUS AND
THE VISION OF GOD

THE HUMAN GOD
AND THE *IDIOTA*

"Man is God," Cusanus writes in *De coniecturis*, and then qualifies: "He is not absolutely God because he is man; he is therefore a human god" (2.14). Man is potentially a "human beast" as well, but the problem of evil interests Cusanus far less than do visions of expansion: "Just as God does all things for his own sake, in order to be the spiritual beginning and end of all things, so the unfolding of the conceptual world, which proceeds from our mind in comprehending it, is present for the sake of the making mind itself" (*De con.* 1.1). The human god returns in later works, most notably *De beryllo*, where Hermes Trismegistus is praised for calling man a "second god": as God creates real beings and natural forms, so man creates beings of reason and artificial forms (6).

Cusanus's notion of a "human god" seeks to resolve the pronounced antithesis of Aquinas's argument that "to create can be the proper action of God alone," which in turn was a rejection of Peter Lombard's view that God can "communicate to a creature the power of creating" (*ST* 1.45.5). Cusanus does distinguish between human and divine power, nowhere more explicitly than in *De idiota*: God's knowledge creates real beings, whereas man's is only assimilative (3.7). But his distinction between the *vis entificativa* of the former and the *vis assimilativa* of the latter is not as rigid as one might suppose: man's assimilation of the external objects that organize his thought is no mere conformity to a given, but is characterized by originality and self-movement. Cusanus's accounts of both knowing and doing at times anticipate sixteenth-century glorifications of human creativity. *De ludo globi* (1463), like *De idiota*, alludes to mimetic art, but also points to Ptolemy's astrolabe and Orpheus's lyre, artifacts that do not copy external reality but develop from thought itself. In *Cribratio Alchoran* (1461) Cusanus suggests a broad cultural poetic, advising us to gaze upon the beauty and variety of human civilization and its creations: cities, temples, languages, and liberal arts.[1]

Perhaps the most comprehensive view of human inventiveness appears in the four dialogues that make up *De idiota*. The work is contrived to span the entire speculative and cultural field, its dimensions expanding both vertically and horizontally. The first two books, *De sapientia*, explore our relation to divine wisdom and the last, *De staticis experimentis*, encourages a purely empirical investigation of the world through experiments with scales. The central and longest dialogue, *De mente*, scrutinizes the human mind, whose capacities may turn in both directions. In addition to this vertical range, the speakers represent a lateral, cultural inclusiveness: the orator and the philosopher articulate the competing ideals of humanism and Scholasticism, and the *idiota*, while reminding them that wisdom dwells in the highest, also demonstrates the power released by our quest for that wisdom.

This expansiveness reflects one of the central themes of the dialogue: the proliferation of human knowledge. In order to entertain such breadth of inquiry, Cusanus acknowledges and contains familiar counterarguments, including echoes of Pauline warnings against worldly knowledge and the somber warning of Ecclesiastes: "Of making many books there is no end, and much study is a weariness of the flesh" (Eccles. 12:12). But the warnings are directed chiefly against servile adherence to authority. The "opinion of authority," the *idiota* accuses the orator in a flurry of metaphor, has puffed him up, tied him like a horse in a halter, and fed him unnatural food (1). The philosopher is similarly rebuked; authority has so crippled him that he is afraid to speak for fear of making an error (3.1). It is with a shrewdly literary sense that Cusanus depicts the long-robed, pale-faced philosopher as having come to Rome to visit a library dedicated to studies of the mind, and then compensates him for the library's destruction with an edifying conversation with the *idiota*. The *idiota* embodies the intellectual power that generates libraries. His attacks on authority do not signify the author's impatience with the ancients; Cusanus's participation in the humanist search for classical manuscripts is well known. Rather, his layman longs to make knowledge new, to break open the closed finality and completeness of authoritative books by entering the field of human experience anew.

He exploits the immediate circumstance of the dialogues— the Roman forum where merchants meet to weigh and measure—to develop, in the final dialogue, a systematic account of the entire universe, his ingenious play of weights and measures yielding tables for classifying and comparing pulse rates, the value of metals and gems, the quality of crops, the intensity of magnetic and solar energy, the weight of a man's breath and vital spirits, the friendship and enmity of animals, the weight of the earth, and the motions of the stars. There is a redeeming note of playfulness in his seeming monomania; "most of the experiments," notes E. J. Dijksterhuis, "are purely fictitious."[2] But more important than the impracticality, or impossibility, of his experiments is the *idiota*'s vision of a potentially endless library of information, where each discovery makes accessible still further discovery: "Experimental knowledge requires many volumes, for the more there are the easier we may arrive at answers in experiments" (4). The multiplication of volumes reflects his vision of the "book of God" as an endlessly expanding text, infinitely available to human investigation and interpretation.

If *De idiota* extends Cusanus's earlier fascination with the mind's positive constructions in the created world, it goes even further in its vision of the mind's search for God. For here the *idiota* finds a richer fecundity of conjecture than in the empirical sphere, precisely because the Infinite can never be fully explicated. The human mind converts its silent unknowing into infinite discourse, translating the hidden power of the "one unspeakable word" into the "infinite nominability of all names" in a dazzling variety and diversity of expression.[3] Though the *idiota*'s own rhetoric (for example, the "unattainable may be attained unattainably") may cause the orator to balk, behind his enigmatic expressions lies a cultural ideal close to the orator's heart, now projected to infinity: "You can make innumerable similar true propositions and fill all the oratorical volumes, even adding to them without limit, to show how wisdom dwells in the highest" (1).[4]

The cultivation of human discourse is a central value for humanism, not only in the quest for wisdom, but as a display of the self. The Greek émigré George of Trebizond, a friend of Cusanus's who translated the *Parmenides* at the latter's request, broadly praises copious speech for setting forth the reason that would otherwise lie hidden: "Whoever professes to know the extent of the world, the nature of the heavens, their origins and destiny, unless he also adorns and illumines his learning with copiousness of speech, as with so much gold or gems, will seem destitute of any knowledge."[5] Another humanist friend, Aeneas Sylvius Piccolomini, was an early proponent of the generative power of rhetoric.[6] But neither humanist matches the *idiota*'s answer to the orator's request "to tell me, since God is greater than that which can be conceived, how I ought to conceive of Him." The *idiota* replies that he should simply conceive. If you seek a right concept of God, he advises, think of rectitude; if you seek a just concept of God, think of justice.

> You see how easy the difficulty of divine things is, in that it always offers itself to the inquirer in the same way that it is sought. . . .

Every question concerning God presupposes the thing questioned, and what the question presupposes must be answered in every question concerning God. For God, although he cannot be signified, is signified in each signification of terms.

(2)

If, as Cusanus argues in *De Deo abscondito*, the presence of a concept in the mind implies its inadequacy, here its presence also assures its validity. Our questions are answered by echoes of the presuppositions embedded in our questions. The orator suspects that this linguistic reflex might silence all inquiry, since "there cannot be, properly speaking, any question concerning God, since the answer coincides with the question" (2). But for the *idiota*, the very fact that "all theology is a circular course wherein one of God's attributes is verified of the other" (2) generates a continuously expanding, self-reflexive symbolic universe. The *idiota*'s vision of expanding libraries and symbolic forms is, from our perspective, a cultural prophecy: the composition of *De idiota* is contemporaneous with the development of moveable type at Mainz in 1450, which, over the ensuing fifty years, would yield an outpouring of books equal to the entire production of the Middle Ages.

What Cusanus does not foresee, and could not allow himself to consider, is the possibility that this proliferation of discourse, rather than harmonizing around an ineffable center, would intensify the conflicts and hasten the fragmentation he sought so strenuously, both in thought and action, to reconcile or suppress. Indeed, the third dialogue takes as its historical setting the 1450 Jubilee, the glorious sight of diverse people drawn to Rome by the unifying power of faith. It is against this background that the *idiota*, with typical Cusan alertness to conjecture and language, echoes Protagoras by venturing an etymology: "I conjecture [*conicio*] it is called the mind for measuring [*mens a mensurando*]" (3.1). Pliancy and creativity characterize its every operation. It receives the "species" of things because the "arterial spirit"—the subtle intermediary between sense and soul in medieval physiology—is flexible, not like passive wax, but like a wax in which the mind deliberately fashions the likeness of things, even as "the arts of sculpture, painting and carpentry" shape their forms (3.7). At its highest level, the mind operates as if by an "absolute flexibility" infused with intelligence. When the mind seeks to measure things, it makes the point, the line, and the surface, none of which exists in extramental reality (*extra mentem*), but which the mind unfolds. It can measure all things because it is "uncontracted to quantity" and so is a "living measure, measuring by itself, as if a living pair of compasses were to measure by themselves" (3.9). The philosopher praises his simile: the mind, like a compass, extends and contracts to become like determined objects, but is itself of no determined size (3.9).

The indeterminacy of the mind's compass also explains *why* the mind so "avidly" measures all things. It does so to "reach its own measure. For the mind is a living measure which by measuring other things, reaches its own capacity. Therefore, it does all things that it may know itself. But though it seeks the measure of itself in all things, it does not find it; but where all things are one, there is the truth of its precision, because there is its adequate exemplar" (3.9).

The notion that the mind outraces all static self-formulations and so must turn to where "all things are one" is a legacy of the Augustinian tradition. But Cusanus's endorsement of the mind's transformations and its thrust into empirical diversity blends his Augustinianism into a humanist vision of flexibility in a world of diversity, a vision that would soon be crystallized in Pico della Mirandola's praise of man as the miracle of creation.[7] For Pico, man is symbolized by Proteus in the mysteries because he is free from any determined place in the hierarchy of Being. The wise folly the *idiota* teaches, though counseling Christian humility, demands intensity and continual self-exploration; the very search for God ("where all things are one") adds impetus to the mind's restless self-fascination, its longing to measure itself.

This self-fascination, in fact, certifies the dignity of man, even as it seeks its own justification in the mind's likeness to its eternal source:

> In the work that is man, how greatly the power of wisdom shines forth, in its members, in the order of its members, its infused life, the harmony and motion of its organs, and finally, in the rational spirit which is capable of wonderful arts and is, as it were, the seal of wisdom, in which, above all else, as in a close image, eternal wisdom shines forth like the truth in a close similitude!
>
> (*De pace fidei* 4)

What a piece of work is a man! Cusanus sounds to us like an optimistic Hamlet, and, like Hamlet, he might be bounded in a nutshell and count himself a king of infinite space. He sounds so even when the closeness of that divine similitude is less evident. Consider Cusanus's meditation on the Gospel parable of the mustard seed in the early *De quaerendo Deum* (1445): within the potency of the tiny seed lies an entire tree whose branches contain a staggering number of potential seeds, which in turn contain their own trees, and so on to infinity. Not ten worlds, nor a thousand, nor innumerable worlds could contain the power of the seed. Then Cusanus considers the power of the human understanding, which, through its geometrical progressions, not only takes the measure of the seed, but reveals to itself a range beyond this world or an infinity of worlds (3). The purpose of the thought experiment is, of course, the quest for God, compared to whom human beings, and all things, are as "nothing"; but it is only through the infinite potency of our relative nothing that the quest proceeds.

Idiota de mente does not project quite so far, but the mind is no less surely the glory of creation. It has been placed in the world by God to be fruitful and multiply its conjectures so that it may "by its own power" create order and value.[8] We "forge mathematical figures out of the power of the mind" (3.3) while imposing our constructions on the manifold of experience, for the "measure and term of everything is from the mind" (3.9). Cusanus's metaphors emphasize the beholder's share in perception: the mind is a "living law," which as it judges "outward things" looks inward to "read in itself the things that are to be judged"; it is like the pointed angle of a polished, living diamond that looks into its interior to find the "similitudes" of things from which to frame its notions (3.5). The world is only an "explication" of God, but the mind, through its unique self-movement, is a living image of the divine "complication" itself. Cusanus later illustrates its primacy among God's creations with the metaphor of a painter's two self-portraits. Even a close likeness to the model would be inferior to a more distant likeness that could struggle to become closer. The static perfection of the one cannot match the living dynamism of the other, whose capacity for movement and excitement brings it closer to the original creative act (3.13). This sense of dynamic possibility suggests Cusanus as a possible link between theologians such as Bonaventure who conceive of a progressive ascent toward God and Renaissance humanists who stress the mental pliancy that makes man capable of self-fashioning and autonomous action. Man as Proteus grasps the diversity of nature and constructs his own cultural cosmos.[9]

Cusanus seems indeed the ideal humanist—free from the melancholy suffering that plagues his Italian predecessors at the age's very inception. In Boccaccio's interpretation of Prometheus as the hero of human culture, the mythic bearer of civilization's lighted torch upholds the divine spark of consciousness, but his subsequent punishment figures the tormenting anxiety of human thought.[10] Cusanus, according to historians such as Michael Seidlmayer, legitimizes the Renaissance discovery of the individual in a secure metaphysic.[11] But though neither the suffering Prometheus nor the brooding figure of Melancholia darkens Cusanus's pages, his affirmations, as argued in the previous chapter, rest on a most ambiguous metaphysical foundation. The consequences of this ambiguity now make themselves felt in the drive to self-knowledge and mental expansion that *Idiota de mente* represents.

The philosopher has come to Rome to fulfill the Oracle of Delphi's command that the mind "know itself," and the *idiota* concurs: man must frame at least some conception of the mind (3.1). And yet every conception the mind frames about itself will be as inadequate as are its conceptions of the hidden God. The *idiota* leads us to this realization when he reminds us that "every number, and every proportion, and every harmony which proceeds from our minds approaches our mind as poorly as our mind does the infinite mind" (3.7). Once the mind is suspended between its conjectures, which are infinitely below it, and God, who is infinitely above it, the consequences of presenting man as a human god, a second god, are inescapable. Just as God hovers mysteriously and distantly beyond His effects, so, too, the mind hovers remotely beyond *its* constructions and cultural artifacts. There is some element of immanence; the late *De Non Aliud* tells us that the will, wisdom, and power of Trajan are symbolized in Trajan's column, even as the will of God shines in creation (9). But it also tells us that even as God remains ultimately invisible, so though "in municipal buildings, in ships, in artifacts, books, paintings, and countless other things we see the marvelous works of the intellect, nevertheless, we do not make contact with the intellect" (23). We may applaud the mind's brilliant civilizing and aesthetic powers, but we are also aware that the analogy, despite its apparent parallelism, is in fact asymmetrical: only the human god cannot form a proper notion of itself. The *idiota* reminds us in the final chapter of *De mente*: "He who notes . . . that reasons are from the mind, sees that no reason can reach to the measure of the mind. Our mind therefore remains immeasurable, unlimited, and interminable by any reason, which only the uncreated mind measures, terminates, and limits, as the truth does the living image, which is from it, in it and by it" (3.15).

The *idiota*'s topic in this chapter is the mind's immortality: it is invariable, outside of time, and can never fail. Yet it assigns itself a fixed shape only by imagining a leap beyond itself to infinite vision. If this tactic enlists the mind's inexhaustible self-interest in the service of its religious quest, it also guarantees that the oracular command that opens *De mente*—that the mind know itself—will remain as unsatisfiable as the hunger to know the hidden God. The mind as a living compass can never measure itself: "Though it seeks the measure of itself in all things, it does not find it" (3.9). The endless variety of its creations become in effect a series of conjectural approximations in search of an indeterminable self. Indeed, the entire *Idiota de mente* itself, for all its analysis of how the mind works, is also a product of the mind, and must be read as one such conjecture.[12]

The key scriptural text that plays throughout *De idiota*, one Cusanus shares with so many Renaissance advocates of human dignity, is from Genesis: man is made in God's image and likeness (Gen. 1:26). But if the exemplar is the *Deus absconditus*, then the proper identity of the image is itself hidden, a mimesis of mystery. The *idiota* captures the paradox in his echo of Genesis: "Our mind is the image of that infinite entity . . . the first portrait of an unknown king [*ignoti regis prima imago*]" (3.3). The dignity of man becomes a haunting conflation of regal power and amnesia; the mind's images of itself and its creator threaten to become endless reflections of each other, images, that is, of the ever-present desire of the human god for its ever-distant prototype. It is the paradox of this transaction that forms the nucleus of Cusanus's most brilliant attempt at portraiture, a richly imagistic tracing of the movements of his own protean mind: *De visione Dei*.

THE VISION OF GOD: ICON, MIRROR, WALL

De visione Dei (1453) is a meditational guide Cusanus sent to the Benedictine monks at Tegernsee during the mystical controversy with Vincent of Aggsbach. An apparently modest work, it does not openly recommend itself for its novelty or for the wonder it evokes, but rather for the ease of its mystic theology and for the "very simple" method by which it leads to a foretaste of "everlasting bliss." It is the very earnestness of such modesty and piety that allows Cusanus to make an imaginative representation of his speculative pleasures and predicaments. For as long as he is assured that the mind's problematic energies are contained by, are even a part of, spiritual exercise, he can use the meditation to shape a series of ambivalent and self-conscious reflections on his intellectual adventurousness.

As we have seen, Cusanus underscores the necessity of mental action in his advice to Tegernsee. De visione Dei translates this action into aesthetic form. Assuming the necessity of metaphor—"If I strive in human fashion to transport you to things divine I must needs use a comparison of some kind"—he unfolds an increasingly ambitious program. The comparison takes as its point of departure one of "men's works," a portrait whose eyes appear to follow the observer no matter where the latter stands. Cusanus sends along an example of this "painter's subtle art" to mount a small didactic spectacle, engaging the monks as both participants in and spectators of the drama.[13] Cusanus asks the monks first to place the image on the north wall and to face it from various positions. The eyes will appear to each monk to be fixed on him alone: "The imagination of him standing to eastward cannot conceive the gaze of the icon to be turned to any quarter such as west or south." Cusanus then directs a single monk to walk before the image to observe how the eyes seem to follow him, and he multiplies this action by asking several monks to move in different directions under the icon's gaze to note how each will perceive the eyes to be following him alone.

The purpose of this little show is to impress on the meditator's imagination a picture of relative points of view subsumed by the absolute perspective of God. God's vision, Cusanus explains, is not "narrowed down to time and space, to particular objects," but perceives all things at all times. Cusanus's transition from relative to absolute vision requires a vertiginous moment, a disorienting of the individual from the point of view he was initially asked to assume. With a central image that is an optical illusion, Cusanus moves him from a traditional reminder of the unreliability of human perspectives to a more radical self-displacement, the recognition that one's status as an observer is itself illusory; it is the observer who is the observed. Working from his formula of the One present to the many, Cusanus insists that a comparison suggesting God as returning the observer's glance must be reversed because God, as the absolute pattern of vision, is the precondition of every perspective, even as He is the presupposition of every question about Him in *De idiota*. It is the viewer who "returns" the glance in his limited way: "None can see Thee save in so far as Thou grantest a sight of Thyself, nor is that sight aught else than Thy seeing him that seeth Thee."

And yet this understood end does not fully explain Cusanus's means. The first half of the meditation is preoccupied with the illusion, exploiting it to bring to the surface—even to justify—an extreme subjectivism. Interpreting each observer's belief that the icon stares at him alone, Cusanus proclaims: "For Thou, the Absolute Being of all, art as entirely present to all as though Thou hadst no care for any other. And this befalleth because there is none that doth not prefer its own being to all others, and its own mode of being to that of all others . . . none of them can conceive that Thou hast any other care but that it alone should exist" (4).

St. Bernard had already justified self-love as the initial step toward love of God. But Cusanus protracts the phase as if in defiance of traditional warnings against egocentricity. The centrality of the self becomes so essential a part of God's design that the objective orientation of worship diversifies through the worshippers' self-interest: "Man can only judge with human judgment. When a man attributeth a face unto Thee, he doth not seek it beyond the human species, because his judgment, bound up with human nature, in judging transcendeth not its limitation and passivity. In like manner, if a lion were to attribute a face unto Thee, he would think it as a lion's, an ox, as an ox's, and an eagle, as an eagle's" (6). This is a witty conflation of Xenophanes and Ezekiel, recalling on the one hand Xenophanes' ridicule of Homer's anthropomorphic gods—if oxen, horses, or lions could paint, he objects, they would represent the gods as horses, oxen, or lions—and on the other the symbols of Gospel writers derived from Ezekiel 1:10: the lion of St. Mark, the ox of St. Luke, and the eagle of St. John.[14] With subjectivism validated by the Gospels themselves, Cusanus can give intellectual narcissism its most striking expression. God willingly humbles Himself so that man will be enraptured by the image of his own mind: "We embrace our likeness, because we are pictured in the image, and we love ourselves therein" (15). Man does not see himself as a mere "human god" or "second god" here, but feels himself grow into the first God, God the Creator: "In the humility of Thine infinite goodness, O God, Thou dost show Thyself as though Thou wert our creature, that thus Thou mayest draw us unto Thee" (15).

Cusanus reminds his readers, however, that these Faustian visions of human divinity are themselves illusions, gifts of God's endless generosity, and he is careful to accept them with a countering tone of extreme humility, an insistent thankfulness for the gift of egocentricity. Indeed, the meditative tone repeatedly disengages Cusanus from the human limitation he describes, as if protecting him by demonstrating his awareness of humanity's potential illusions. And yet the strenuous balance of engagement and detachment also enhances the meditation's theatrical air. Rather than circumscribing our aesthetic response, the exposure of illusion extends its play to our very reality as observers: the image we see in the mirror of eternity is "not a figure, but the truth, whereof the beholder himself is a figure." We become the tale of ourselves, strutting in our divinity, yet always aware that life's but a walking shadow: "Thou appearest unto me like the shadow following the movement of one that walketh; but 'tis because I am a living shadow and Thou the truth" (15).

Cusanus is spared Macbeth's despair by the presence of that truth; his is a tale told by a different kind of idiot, one underwritten by God's infallible generosity. But the line dividing man's greatness from his annihilation is too thin to prevent a sense of discomfort. The meditator must believe that God loves him more than any other because the icon appears to look at him alone, but the pride of being at the center of God's interest is indissolubly linked to the meditator's absolute dependence on his spectator's attention: "I am because Thou dost look at me, and if Thou didst turn Thy glance from me I should cease to be" (4). Assurances of God's unblinking gaze do not relieve Cusanus of his urgent need to deny his autonomous authorship of the text. Cusanus-as-author must disavow the illusions of power God encourages. Despite his praise of the painter's subtle art, Cusanus translates his own performances into uncompromising denials of self-fashioning. If Cusanus compares himself as a preacher before his congregation to God addressing the world, all praise is referred to the greater Director: God has inspired him with the words the congregation hears, and has given him the face the congregation sees (10). *De visione Dei* exhibits the full range of Cusanus's fondness for farfetched conceits, whose extreme ingenuity forecasts later Renaissance experiments in "metaphysical wit," but each is directly attributed to its divine source: "Thou hast suggested to me an acceptable comparison. . . . Blessed be Thou, o lord my God, who dost feed and nourish me with the milk of comparisons" (11).

Even this caution is insufficient. Time and again the meditation turns against its own premise of the necessity of comparisons: "So long as he [man] formeth any concept thereof, [he] is far from Thy face . . . so long as he seeth aught, it is not what he seeketh" (6); "if anyone should set forth any likeness and say that Thou wert to be imagined as resembling it, I know in like manner that that is no likeness of Thee" (13); "I reject as a delusion any idea occurring to me which seeketh to show Thee as comprehensible" (16). In such a predicament, self-love blends with anxiety. Attempting to conceive of the love of the Trinity, the meditator uses himself as an analogy—"I love myself, I see myself as loveable, and myself to be the natural bond"—only to cry for mercy: "Forgive me that I strive to image forth the unimaginable savor of Thy sweetness. If the sweetness of some fruit unknown may not be pictured through any painting or image, or described by any words, who am I, a miserable sinner, who strives to show Thee, that art beyond showing, and to imagine Thee, the invisible, as visible" (17). God may allow "the blind to speak of light," but he also inspires less sanguine moods: "Thou hast inspired me, Lord . . . to do violence to myself" (9).

What makes *De visione Dei* an impressive work of self-criticism, however, is not merely its desire to cancel itself, but its insistence on representing that desire, on symbolizing the limits of symbolic investigation. The clearest instance of this process is the series of transformations the central image undergoes during the course of the meditation. The original icon, as we have noted, is viewed diversely by diverse viewers, and so becomes a mirror, reflecting the image of each observer. The most decisive alteration transforms the mirror into a wall, blocking our progress. Human reason had seen itself as an image reflected in the mirror of eternity, but it also confronts itself as a sentry blocking the opening through the wall: "I have learnt that the place wherein Thou art found unveiled is girt round with the coincidence of contradictories, and this is the wall of Paradise wherein Thou dost abide. The door whereof is guarded by the most proud spirit of Reason, and, unless he be vanquished, the way in will not lie open" (9). A circuit through the wall of coincidence would provide "sweetest nourishment" by allowing the meditator to act out the mystery of God's enfolding and unfolding—the theme of *complicatio/explicatio*. But within the larger metaphor of spatial progress, it poses a problem: "I go in and go out simultaneously when I perceive how going out is one with going in, and going in with going out." The circuit becomes a figure of frustration in the "wall of absurdity" (*murus absurditatis*), the limit of discursive thought whose coinciding opposites repel any metaphor of progress by equating it with its regressive contrary.

No creature can "scale" the wall, Cusanus continues, but the sheer recognition of impossibility grants an apparently momentary revelation: "I begin to behold thee unveiled, and to enter into the garden of delights! For thou art naught such as can be spoken or imagined, but art infinitely and absolutely exalted high above all such things" (12). The prelude to description (*revelate te inspicere incipio*) leads only to a revenge of spatializing against itself. For God is exalted "high above" the wall, the garden, the effort to enter, all the properties and actions that have made the drama possible. Cusanus longs to experience the rapture of St. Paul, to see what is "beyond revealing," and announces his readiness for a full, mystical episode. Had not Bonaventure transcended symbolic theology in the "apex of the mind"? The mind, he had written, "retreats into itself so that it may look upon God," not merely in a glass darkly, but "in the brightness of the saints" (*Itinerarium mentis in Deum* 1.7; 4.6). But for all Cusanus's claims that *De visione Dei* shows the ease of mystical theology, the author remains straining at the brink of ecstasy (cf. 17, 25). As Karl Jaspers notes of Cusanus's mysticism in general: "this thinking does not lead Cusanus to mystical experience. And yet his own thinking is continually drawing him on to the point where thought itself can go no further, but can only move in dialectical circles, repeat itself in endless variations. His thinking is forever trying to take off and soar into the unthinkable, the ineffable, failing again and again to do so, and rising to a new attempt."[15] The failure of unmediated vision is never catastrophic for Cusanus; for Christ returns blindness to sight. Indeed, the late entry of Christ into the meditation provokes a shower of visual terms: *video* appears nineteen times in chapters 19 and 20. The Son is the "revelation of the Father": "in the absolute Son I behold the absolute Father, for the Son cannot be seen as Son unless the Father be seen" (21; 20). So, too, the Son overcomes the regress of imagery that began with the polygon and the circle in *De docta ignorantia*, as the Son is compared to an "image between which and the exemplar no more perfect image can be interposed" (20). And yet the meditation also makes clear that such revelation does not end *our* imagining. For now the mystery to be conjectured about is not the obscurity of the infinite, but the ineffable union of the infinite and the finite. We cannot comprehend this union for "'tis not possible that Thou [Christ] shouldst be seen this side of the wall" (20). We can, however, imagine it—return, that is, to the world of farfetched metaphor and conceit: suppose, Cusanus ventures, that a man seeks to identify one approaching, but even as his eyes remain focused, his mind becomes "rapt in other thoughts." The eye would not be quickened by the intellect and would not recognize the passerby, though it would not be truly separated from the mind. This, then, is one metaphor for the relationship of Christ's divinity to His humanity: the relationship between man's intellect and his senses when he is daydreaming (22–23).

If *De visione Dei* suggests a theatrical paradigm, the *theatrum mundi* it presents is one that repeatedly reveals to us its ingenuity and its limitations, even as it makes an exit, in this life, impossible. The reality of faith must be assumed behind all mental picturing, and yet this very assumption not only returns us to the inevitability of picturing, but intensifies our appetite for it: "The mind's eye cannot be sated in beholding Thee, Jesu, because Thou art the fulfillment of all beauty the mind can picture, and in this icon I conjecture [*coniitio*] Thy right and marvellous and astounding [*stupidum*] sight, Jesu blessed above all" (22).

In the final chapter (25), Cusanus again gives voice to his "holy yearnings" and gives thanks for God's gifts, which promise full disclosure: "Thou keepest nought secret." Yet he still finds himself asking, "Why then do I delay, why do I not run . . . what restraineth me?" For even as the speaker declares his course "all but finished" and bids the world farewell, as long as he speaks, he remains a human worshipper, shaping and dissolving conjectures about the infinite truth behind an image.

CUSAN POETICS: SOME CONCLUSIONS

The aesthetic dimension of Cusanus's thought has often been noted; one recent study characterizes Cusanus as the "artist's philosopher" of the Renaissance. Though he wrote no separate treatise on art, he shares a community of attitudes with contemporary figures such as Leon Battista Alberti, for whom the task of knowledge is the shaping of harmonies and proportions. Cusanus makes very little distinction between general acts of apprehension and the artist's procedures; the latter appear in his writings as illustrations of the former.[16] Most suggestive is his tireless fascination with perspectivism, from the shipboard observer in De docta ignorantia, to the multiplying perspectives of De visione Dei, to the lens metaphors of the later works, which emphasize the individual's "seeing through" a distinct point of view. Panofsky rightly suggests that Cusanus's conception of space as continuous and infinite, rather than hierarchical and finite, is closely related to the perspective painting of the fifteenth century.[17] All of Cusanus's speculations may, I think, be regarded as perspectival: the mind, a "living compass," orders the deep space of a potentially endless field through its mathematical grids, trusting its orthogonals to converge at an infinitely distant "vanishing point"—that is, the union of all diversity in the *Deus absconditus*. Cusanus's understanding of perspectivism is strikingly comprehensive. At times it suggests the mind's longing to grasp a previously articulated order, as in *De beryllo*'s initial use of its metaphor of a translucent beryl stone; the beryl's concave and convex surfaces render it a lens of coinciding opposites, sharpening our mental vision on distant truths. In the *Compendium* (6), errors of vision are correctable by the "arte perspectiva." But perspectivism also implies for Cusanus the subjective limitations of the observer, as in his comparison of cognition to colored lenses: to red or green glass in *De visione Dei* (6) and again to red glass in *De Non Aliud* (1462). Both works emphasize limitation as a condition of knowledge. In the latter, Cusanus says man must "speculate," but he must do so as one who "sees snow through a red glass, sees the snow, and attributes the redness not to the snow, but to the glass" (9). As early as *De docta ignorantia*, Cusanus is aware that his endorsement of the subjective viewer simultaneously deprivileges his point of view: the universe we measure, he reminds us, would appear very differently to inhabitants of other planets (2.12). Cusanus's perspectivism, then, embraces both what we may for convenience call early Renaissance and Mannerist attitudes. It is an affirmation both of the centrality of the observer and of his potential eccentricity. Indeed, one way of regarding the mind's struggle for transcendence is as an attempt to correct the potential excesses of the eccentric. In *De filiatione Dei*, we are asked to imagine all creatures as differently curved mirrors; it is the role of the living intellect to seek ever-straighter and clearer reflections of truth (3). Had he lived to see it, Parmigianino's *Self-Portrait in a Convex Mirror* would have provided Cusanus with considerable matter for meditation.

Cusanus's medium is not the visual but the verbal, and his aesthetic sense is most suggestive, not in his vision of man as painter or sculptor, but in the implication throughout his work that the discursive hunt for truth approaches the condition of poetry. In the broadest sense, man fulfills the Greek meaning of poet as "maker"; his fashioning of culture and its institutions are, as Giambattista Vico would argue three centuries later, poetic modes of knowledge. And, apart from the drive of learned ignorance for the ineffable, Cusanus anticipates Vico's convertibility of *verum* and *factum*: man can rationally know only what he has made.[18] There is, too, a more specifically literary side to Cusan poetics. Cusanus revels in enigmatic symbol and metaphor, admitting without embarrassment that his comparisons are sometimes farfetched. His aim is to excite wonder, *admiratio*, through his writing, forcing the reader to puzzle over his figures, verbal as well as geometric. In *De coniecturis*, Cusanus assigns these artifacts to the realm of the *verisimile*, and though grounded differently, its operations are in at least one important respect closely akin to poetic "verisimilitude": both fields promote the invention of forms of intelligibility, neither strictly true nor false.[19] For Cusanus and Renaissance poets alike, that very activity is a creative idealizing of the world, an effort that "erects" the mind toward what they hope will be substantial truth.

This assumed teleology frees Cusanus to read all forms of human cognition as kinds of poetic making, placing at the center what many of his predecessors sought to locate at the periphery. In this regard, Cusanus distinguishes himself from those who, when attacking either the irrelevance or inadequacy of a mode of thought, indict it on the grounds of its artifice. So Tertullian brands dialectic as productive of "farfetched conjectures," and Gaunilo parodies Anselm's ontological argument with the mock proof of a utopian island. Nominalism may signal a new concentration on the fictive nature of concepts, but its articulators are careful to exclude the contamination of mere "figments."

What had been irrelevant, or an obstruction to truth, becomes with Cusanus the mind's primary access to truth. Cusanus is not interested in "determining the structure of reality by fixing necessary and stable forms," Eugenio Garin writes. "A truly 'humanistic' standpoint, rather, has to be a poetical one."[20] The conjectural status of thought is not only Cusanus's constant theme; it informs the characteristic style of his writing. He is notoriously difficult to translate or paraphrase; nearly all his major terms are used in a variety of senses and he displays an incurable fondness for the elusive and the paradoxical. Although Jasper Hopkins defends the consistency of Cusanus's thought, he also notes that, despite Cusanus's use of the language of rational argument, his analogies are "illustrative rather than argumentative; they do not try to establish a point but only to render it more plausible." Even when Cusanus most needs a fixed point to stabilize his argument "we remain stranded in the realm of the *as if.*" Locating Cusanus within a stylistic tradition, Hopkins suggests that he at times uses words "to stimulate the imagination rather than to sharpen the understanding. This quasi-poetic use of language—rich as it is with metaphor—is intrinsic to the speculative Neoplatonic tradition."[21]

It is nevertheless important to distinguish Cusan poetics from that of Neoplatonism. The tradition of Dionysius, Erigena, and Eckhart, with its play of symbol and negation, does indeed offer Renaissance writers a self-conscious language of paradox and metaphor. John Colet, the English humanist, learned from Dionysius that affirmative theology portrays truth by "poetic fictions": its symbols are not "altogether fictitious, lest there should be too little authority in a mere fable," but they do create "a sort of stage, and rude show, and indistinct representation" that prepare the way for brighter images of "reality itself."[22] But Neoplatonism generally operates within a more clearly defined arena: its Ideas and hierarchies are treated as an objective, symbolic field from which to draw poetic material and against which to trace human progress. For

Cusanus, that field of reference is *already* a metaphor. Objective reality exists, of course, but our perception of it *as* a symbolic arena forces us to recognize that the work of conjecture has already begun. Cusanus's poetics is therefore more problematic than the Neoplatonists': conjecture proceeds from prior conjecture and leads to subsequent conjecture, a process that relies on an ultimate reality, yet at the same time threatens to cut the mind loose without a point of departure or arrival. Johannes Wenck found this prospect disturbing, even demonic; Cusanus found his open-ended poetics immensely liberating—perhaps, at times, too liberating.

The spirit of "serious play" (*serio ludere*) throughout Cusanus's works reflects a broad Renaissance interest in play as a means of approaching philosophical themes, but his later works carry this interest to ostentatious lengths: speculation seems at times to transform the world into a mere playground for intellectual gymnastics and symbolic games. The most appealing instance of his late playfulness is the ball game of *De ludo globi* (1463), where a spherical ball is indented so that it will display convex and concave surfaces, representing the coincidence of opposites. The ball, when thrown, spirals inward in ever smaller arcs as it loses its "impetus." Because the ball is a human invention guided by human skill, Cusanus asks us to see in its motions a symbol both of the mind's creative freedom, as it spirals within itself to find its center in Christ, and of the infinite diversity of human modes of searching. We can fashion an endless number of possible proportions between convexity and concavity, and the consequent infinity of possible balls with their possible spirals and points of rest suggests to us that all men search in their own way. The fact that no two men ever throw the same ball in precisely the same way also reminds us that all conjecture differently and that their minds trace distinctive trajectories.[23]

Only slightly less ingenious is the spinning top of *De Possest* (1460), where Cusanus brings us to a playground to watch boys playing with this toy. When it spins fast enough, it creates the illusion of being motionless, and so the jargon of the game calls this state being "at rest." The figure of speech becomes a symbol of the coincidence of opposites when the adult steps forward with an intellectual game and asks us to consider the top spinning at an infinite velocity: all points on the circumference would be present at every point at the same time, and so symbolize God as the coincidence of motion and rest. It is difficult to read through these works and not be reminded of Metaphysical poets whose wit exploits the "gap" between their figures' tenors and vehicles. Cusanus's figures revolve around a like notion of "disproportionate likeness" (*similitudo improportionalis*), imaged in the *discordia concors* of their coincidences of opposites.[24]

This free play of conjecture signals both the pleasures of Cusanus's text and Cusanus's own self-enjoyment as writer. The spinning top of *De Possest* is perhaps a somewhat impudent thumbing of the nose at Plato's rejection of an "ingenious objector" who would, by means of a spinning top, demonstrate the coincidence of rest and motion (*Republic* 436d–e). And yet we sometimes find ourselves uncertain about the real point behind the sport. Stranger views of *Cusanus ludens* appear in the numerous language games of the later works, of which the title *De Possest* is one. It fashions a portmanteau name for God by fusing the Aristotelian notions of potency and actuality to signify God as the actuality of all possibility, a conceit that raises both linguistic and conceptual problems.[25] More overtly bizarre is the later meditation in the same work on the word "IN" as an entry into contemplating the Divine. The letter "I" requires a single vertical stroke, and "N" doubles the initial stroke; in so doing, they symbolize both unity and the unfolding, or "explication," of that unity. The double significance of the prefix "IN-" is likewise exploited: because it means either inherence or privation, it symbolizes God's simultaneous immanence and transcendence. Furthermore, the letter "I" is the first letter of *ita* ("so" or "thus"), and "N" the first letter of *non* ("not"), suggesting to Cusanus that "IN" symbolizes the fusion of affirmative and negative theologies.[26] Maurice de Gandillac is right to worry that this kind of gesture may be no more than a "bad play on words";[27] it is difficult to accept such mental doodling as a vehicle for high speculation. But Cusanus seems at times intoxicated by his verbal metamorphoses, and in one of his last works, *De Non Aliud* (1463), he presents his most ambitious language game, naming God the "Not-Other" in order to force the mind to join affirmation and negation. He freely admits the name is only metaphorical, but generates an entire treatise dedicated to the conceit. The name reminds us of God's utter transcendence: all Creation exists in the realm of otherness (*alteritas*), whereas its Creator is "Not-Other." It also symbolizes God's full immanence because He is "not other" than everything that is. Like the tautology of Exodus, I am that I am, the name is self-defining, because the "Not-Other is not other than Not-Other." Because the name signifies itself and all other things, it is more fundamental than the Neoplatonic "One," and is the best conjectural name man can invent, the best, that is, until Cusanus's next work where, inevitably, it is superseded by yet another.

Cusanus tells his listeners in *De Non Aliud* that they should feel free to reject anything he says unless they are "compelled by reason" to accept it, but when we finally reach the list of conclusions at the end of the work and read his riddling Latin: "Nam unitrinum 'non aliud' in uno est unius unitatis unitas et in ente entis entitatis entitas et in magnitudine magnae magnitudinis magnitudo et in quanto quantae quantitatis quantitas et ita de cetera," we may be more inclined to accept the judgment that "at times he [Cusanus] seems to use terms deliriously, almost defying them to be meaningful."[28]

Cusanus exploits the promise of a divine Referent, of an ultimate, if deferred, closure, to play out a "symbolism [that] is never-ending" (*De Possest*). Derived from Scripture and the

Church, religious doctrine has, of course, a place of privilege over ball games, spinning tops, and omnivoyant portraits, but, as we have already seen, there is a compulsiveness to Cusanus's play that cannot allow him to invoke such closure without also submerging its terms in the play of poetic forms. *De coniecturis* reminds us that religion is not fixed: some perspectives may aim higher than others, but considered as a whole, religion is continuously transformed through the flow of history. Doctrine exists in a quasi-Heraclitean flux, or in Cusanus's metaphor, it is like the flowing Rhine, which seems to be one river but is always changing (*De con.* 2.15). In *De pace fidei* (The peace of faith; 1453), a pious Christian, stricken with anxiety over the Turkish atrocities committed at the fall of Constantinople, experiences in a kind of dream vision a heavenly assembly of the world's religions, which discusses the necessity of diverse ritual observances. The hidden God, they assert, has provided various nations with prophets who have legislated religious practices "as if" (*ac si*) they were God's direct laws.[29] In the weakness of their nature, men accept these as immutable truths (1), forgetting that the flow of history inevitably alters all conjecture and interpretation (3). Nor will recourse to scriptural authority halt the process. In *De Non Aliud* Cusanus brings his symbolic transformations to bear on the holy Book itself through a most aggressive exegesis: those who name the Trinity Father, Son, and Holy Spirit may be justified by their "conformity to Scripture," Cusanus advises, but they approach divine mystery "less precisely" than they might; "those who call the Trinity *Unity, Equality,* and *Union* would approach more closely to it *if these terms were found to be inserted in Scripture.* For these are the terms in which 'Not-other' shines forth clearly. . . . Still more simply, the terms 'this,' 'it,' and 'the same' imitate 'Not-other' quite clearly and precisely" (5; emphasis mine).[30] If *De visione Dei* echoes Paul's warning to "put off the old man of presumption and put on the new man of humility" (21), in the opening pages of *De ludo globi* and *De*

Non Aliud, it is the boldness of the hunt itself, the prospect of new forays into the world of image, paradox, and metaphor—the very poetry of conjecture—that makes the aging cardinal "seem to grow young."

There remains, nonetheless, a powerful, antithetical current in Cusanus's thought. The permissible distance between signs and what they signify fluctuates, exposing an uncertainty about the proper range of flexibility. The ecumenical *De pace fidei*, a dream vision of a heavenly conference, insists on the importance of diversity, but also argues, through the voice of the *Verbum*, that because the truth is one, errors might be "eliminated" (*extirpentur*) and the "diversity of religion . . . reduced to one orthodox faith" (3). Cusanus's St. Paul, too, equivocates: he professes to be unconcerned by the inability of some to accept the sacraments of baptism, marriage, and even the eucharist; when a Tartar speaker tells him that the devouring of Christ's body and blood seems "most abominable," Paul responds that "as sensible signs of the truth of belief these things that have been instituted and received as signs are capable of change, not so the thing signified" (16). But he alters his emphasis in the succeeding chapter: the believer must act as a believer when possible and accept such signs (17). A heavenly colloquy is, of course, entitled to switch between eternal and temporal perspectives on such matters, but the hint of another motive appears in an early letter, written at about the time of *De coniecturis*, in which Cusanus calls the visible Church an *ecclesia coniecturalis* whose "signs" are conjectural, and yet uses the language of learned ignorance to justify the Pope's nearly absolute authority within it. For here diversity faces its diabolical counterpart, what Cusanus calls the "crime" of schism; flexibility, the source of pleasure, becomes a cause for alarm.[31]

If it is human weakness that mistakes the fluid for the immutable, the fluid itself may provoke demands for strict obedience—not only in relation to doctrine, but in every area of inquiry. In *De beryllo* Cusanus praises the world of stimulating diversity as "an admirable revelation of the divine intellect" to the inquisitive mind, yet elsewhere calls for a faith that will "overcome the world in such a way that those things which are of this world are held down and trampled underfoot."[32] Such equivocations extend to the mind's creative responses to the world. Cusanus cites the arts to show that man is a second God, but also warns that the arts, though they make life more joyous, and even more virtuous, cannot ultimately "serve the spirit." Only religion can so serve, because it is founded "on divine authority and revelation, to bring man to obedience."[33] The same man who pictured an endless number of intellectual trajectories in De ludo globi and who envisioned the mind's potency as surpassing an infinity of worlds in De quaerendo Deum also exhorts us in a voice like that of Tertullian or Peter Damian: "So long as the mind indulges without restraint in vain knowledge it no more finds the object of its natural desire than does a man who cohabits with every whore"; we must submit to a faith that will "hold captive the intellect that thus it may be victorious and virtuous"; the wise folly of the idiota may promote endless opportunities for investigation and discourse, but a still wiser folly, Cusanus at times suggests, is that of the believer who becomes "as a fool and a slave who renounces the freedom of his reason and willingly lets himself be taken captive" by a faith that not only governs, but finally annuls, rational activity.[34]

This preoccupation with obedience, one recent student of Cusanus argues, "stands out as a foreign body in his thought as if to call attention to an irreducible inconsistency or a dangerous psychological insecurity."[35] That insecurity is perhaps more domestic than foreign, recurring throughout his life and thought, from his early defection to the papacy to his final speculations. For while he craves the stimulation of creative diversity in a virtually boundless cosmos, he also finds himself longing for the stricter direction he may have witnessed, for example, during his visit to his Benedictine admirers at Tegernsee. Their *Rule* anticipates the mind's restlessness, and prescribes obedience, even in the face of "difficulties and contradictions," as the only means to inner stability.[36] If the oft-repeated tradition that the young Cusanus was first schooled by the Brethren of Common Life is true, we may even imagine him reaching back through the sophisticated legal, scientific, and philosophical learning he acquired at the Universities of Heidelberg, Padua, and Cologne, and back through his subsequent fascination with the perspectivism of learned ignorance, to the simpler piety of Thomas à Kempis's *Imitatio Christi*, composed at Deventer during the probable years of young Nicholas's stay there: "Restrain an inordinate desire for knowledge in which is found much anxiety and deception"; "it is much safer to obey than to rule. . . . So do not place too much reliance on . . . your own views" (1.2, 9).

Cusanus's desire to reconcile the opposing impulses of his thought finds expression in what Edmond Vansteenberghe calls his spiritual testament: his final treatise, *De apice theoriae*, completed shortly before his death in 1464.[37] Here Cusanus speaks with renewed assurance: having sought God in obscurity, he tells us, he now emphasizes the clarity and brightness of the goal. A "simple vision" (*simplex visio*) of God may still be incomprehensible, but the mind's ability to see beyond the comprehensible affirms its own power. That this human power is an image of, and will be protected by, a greater power is figured in the new conjectural name Cusanus has found for God. No longer the "One," nor "Possest," nor even "Non Aliud," He is now *posse ipsum*: "Power Itself." "The power of the mind . . . is unlimited on this side of Power Itself" (p. 125), Cusanus proclaims in a statement that returns us to Cassirer's vision of Cusanus as the "great optimist" of the Renaissance, one who "dared to encompass the whole world." Cusanus's final effort of transcendence seems now to validate the mind's expansive capacities for language, artistic and cultural creativity, scientific knowledge, and mystic vision, his search for, to borrow a phrase from *De visione Dei*, "all beauty the mind can picture." The quest that begins as a species of romance has, then, a projected end in a divinely comic resolution. But its motions never defuse its tragic potential. Even as Cusanus draws toward the increasingly positive conception of *posse ipsum*, his late works also renew his interest in Proclus and the Pseudo-Dionysius and their premise of an infinite gulf between God and human understanding. Cusanus cannot quiet the voice that insists that all positive conceptions, even *posse ipsum*, are conjectural. Nor can he resolve the paradox that the inner impetus, the very strength of mind that is our glory and drives us toward our goal, must inevitably fall short of its mark. The image of the mind's centrality and authority, in which Cassirer sees a reawakening of the Pelagian spirit in the Renaissance,[38] escapes eccentricity and reversal only through Power Itself, the goal of all pious longing that becomes not only a *Deus ex machina* to extricate man from his endless cycles of conjecture, but also a *deus absconditus* that is pictured, finally, in the most transparent, and disturbing, of Renaissance projections: the apotheosis of the mind's hunger for autonomy and power.

Nancy Struever locates Cusanus in a broad historical movement whose Nominalism and humanism emphasize the problematic nature of discourse and symbol. Though this emphasis increases attention to illusionism and makes the world's contours less certain, she rightly warns, we must not assume this to be a sign of pessimism. "To associate this aesthetic insight with subjectivism or solipsism is to associate it with the difficulties, not the creativity, with the isolation rather than the fluidity, mobility, *disponibilità* which is characteristic of the Renaissance."[39] The Renaissance would be less paradoxical if we could take either its joy or its pessimism as a resting point, but in the world Cusanus explores, fluidity and isolation, expansiveness and subjectivity, affirmation and anxiety are the poles of a dialectic that cannot be resolved. In the creative activity of the Renaissance, the following chapters argue, these opposites grow inseparable.

PART TWO

SIR PHILIP SIDNEY
AND POETIC
FICTIONS

INTRODUCTION TO PART TWO

Eugenio Garin proposes that a "humanistic" philosophy "has to be a poetical one," and I would add this corollary: poetry and poetics function as important speculative instruments in a humanistic culture.[1] Indeed, a large proportion of the writers who strike us as central to an understanding of Renaissance thought—Petrarch, More, Erasmus, Montaigne, Bruno—are also major figures in the history of the literary imagination. The second part of this study explores this relationship by reading literary texts as embodiments of the speculative challenges of the period. It begins by arguing that many of Cusanus's most powerful themes—the mind's fecundity, the problem of justifying human invention, the dialectic between such invention and perceptions of world order—find their subtlest expression in the age's fictions and its critical attitudes toward those fictions. Italy is the source of much of this inquiry, but by the late sixteenth century, England was also an arena of heightened activity. No English writer better exemplifies the poetic self-consciousness of the Renaissance than Sir Philip Sidney (1554–86). Not only does he bring to bear a complex tradition of critical thought from the Continent, but his major works are preoccupied by the implications of their own making.

In recent years important studies have called attention to the social and political dimensions of Sidney's self-consciousness. Where he was once thought the picture of an ideal Elizabethan—a likely model for Shakespeare's "courtier's, soldier's, scholar's, eye, tongue, sword, / The expectancy and rose of the fair state"—we have come to see him more as a frustrated and defensive young aristocrat who longed for an active life, but whose aggressive championing of the Protestant cause on the Continent and explosive self-assertion at home led to his estrangement from the more cautious Elizabethan court. His life shows a radical disproportion of energy to outlet, for he was never, in Fulke Greville's terms, "possessed of any fit stage of eminence to act upon."[2] It is, however, not without deliberate calculation and an alert sense of irony that Sidney scans the dilemmas of the courtier and soldier through the lens of the "scholar's eye." The Elizabethan aristocrat is also the Renaissance intellectual and poet.

The image of Sidney the intellectual is, of course, an old one: Thomas Moffett reverently describes the three-year-old Philip praying to the moon "as if he had . . . compassed the heavens with his mind"; Greville remembers the schoolboy who directed all play to the enriching of his mind.[3] Modern biographers and critics note that Sidney's broad reading of ancient and modern authors was supplemented by personal acquaintance with the leading European and English intellectuals of his day: Peter Ramus, Philippe Duplessis-Mornay, Hubert Languet, Justus Lipsius, Johann Sturm, John Dee, Giordano Bruno (incidentally, a great admirer of Cusanus's). How formative an influence any of them was on Sidney, and how much any of them tells us about Sidney's philosophical complexion, is open to debate. Languet was Sidney's close and affectionate companion, but he was a different sort of creature. Bruno and Dee may have been no more to Sidney than fascinating diversions. Important, perhaps, is Duplessis-Mornay, a Huguenot whose theological treatise *De la vérité de la religion chrétienne* Sidney began to translate. Here Sidney would have found numerous Christian, Neoplatonic, and Hermetic topics that were also deeply suggestive in Cusanus's meditations. Man must confess "his knowledge is but ignoraunce," Mornay insists: he seeks to know God, but knowledge requires proportion, and "betweene the Creature and the Creator there is none at all"; all creatures picture God in their own image, and if beasts could paint they would counterfeit Him "by a shape like themselves"; man himself "planteth, buyldeth, paynteth, and weaveth a thousande divers workes," but other minds, and even his own, remain a mystery to him.[4] Even here, however, seeming lines of transmission may be deceptive. Sidney's mind is as mercurial as it is assimilative, and it is perhaps inevitable that his wide-ranging curiosity should have been refracted into so many plausible portraits: the Calvinist, the Ramist, the Neoplatonist, the Neoclassicist. Sidney's intellectual character, I argue here, is represented less by informing traditions than by his own practices as poet and critic. It is through these roles that he most deeply explores both the cultural world by which he is defined and the agile efforts of the fiction-making mind to take the measure of that world. Though Sidney sometimes thought that his role as poet was the "unelected vocation" of his "idlest times," the subterfuges and deviations of his art remain the most valuable embodiment we have of his speculative energies.

Yet the attempt to define Sidney as poet and critic risks reproducing the problem of defining Sidney's intellectual orientation. First, is it even possible to characterize Sidney's critical perspective or its value as a piece of original theorizing? His most explicit theoretical statement, the *Apology for Poetry*, seems so derivative, and at times contradictory, that scholars have often had to resort to Sidney's predecessors and near-contemporaries in order to piece together a coherent program. One consequence has been a devaluing of the *Apology* as a work in its own right: "There is not an essential principle in [the *Apology*] which cannot be traced back to some Italian treatise on the poetic art"; Sidney is "not so much a thinker as a persuasive advocate of other men's thought."[5] A second problem is that of the relationship of his own writings to one another. What continuity is there between the apparently didactic *Apology* on the one hand and *Astrophil and Stella* and the two *Arcadias* on the other—works that, for all their ethical concerns, are so often preoccupied with a retreat from the active life, with erotic desire, and with fantastic excess? A common critical strategy has been to abstract a normative doctrine from the rhetorical play of the *Apology* to chart the "true" moral orientation of the other works. The following chapters propose a different view. The *Apology* deserves to be studied less as a restatement of Renaissance commonplaces, however witty and urbane, than as a revelation of the underlying tensions of Renaissance poetics—tensions that parallel Cusanus's problematic discoveries in significant ways. Nor should the *Apology* be seized on as a key to unlock the other texts. Sidney's works all share a community of interests and so illuminate one another, but each fashions its own theoretical and poetic perspective. The *Apology* does so explicitly, whereas the others do so implicitly, their common activity culminating in the *New Arcadia*, Sidney's most ambitious and profoundly unsettling poetic fiction.[6]

4

ITALIAN RENAISSANCE CRITICISM

CRITICAL METAPHYSICS:
THE HETEROCOSM AND
THE FIXED POINT

"The first problem of Renaissance criticism," Joel Spingarn begins his groundbreaking study, "was the justification of imaginative literature."[1] The history of ideas abounds with examples of what literature had to be justified against; works of the imagination have always provoked a special anxiety. "The Author of truth loves no falsehood," writes Tertullian; "all that is feigned is adultery in His sight." Even those who embrace a more liberal sense of the mind's capacities regard the poetic imagination as disturbingly unreal and a source of gratuitous agitation. Peter Abélard took joy in the exercise of intellect and understood both the role of *ficta* in human conceptualizing and the use of allegorical myth to justify the reading of Platonic philosophy. Nevertheless, he warns against the deceptions of poetic fictions and the "pernicious elation of the mind" they can engender. Aquinas, who was no enemy of the poets, insists on the different uses of figurative language by poets and theologians. The theologian's analogies follow the objective structure of Being; the poet's figures follow a contrary course: "The science of poetry is concerned with things which, because of their lack of truth, cannot be comprehended by reason; reason must therefore be beguiled by certain similarities. But theology is concerned with the suprarational, hence the symbolical method is common to them both. Theology is the highest of all sciences, but poetry is the lowest."[2]

The *locus classicus* for the devaluing of poetry that Renaissance critics had to confront was, of course, Plato's banishment of the poets from his Republic. He is the great combatant in the "ancient quarrel between philosophy and poetry" (*Rep.* 607b) with his double charge that poetic fictions agitate us with their immorality and delude us with mere appearances. If some find encylopedic learning in Homer, so much the worse. The poet not only feigns knowledge, but feigns universal knowledge, and so reduces everything to unreality. Just as anyone holding a mirror can revolve it to reflect the entire world, so, too, the artist presents the illusion of unlimited virtuosity and knowledge; but rather than leading us to the Forms behind phenomena, he only estranges us from the truly real (*Rep.* 596d–e). Implicit in Plato's attack is a misgiving that motivates virtually all such assaults: the fear of uncontrolled subjectivity and relativism. An artist may represent an object from any perspective, his Socrates explains, because "you may look at a bed or any other object from straight in front or slantwise or at any angle" (*Rep.* 598a); the artist only presents us with numberless phantasms of things, their contingent appearances rather than their true natures. "Things are not relative to individuals," we hear in the *Protagoras*; they do not fluctuate "according to our fancy."[3]

The Platonic legacy does allow artists a qualified place, but only if we are willing to distinguish between legitimate and illegitimate image makers. Responding to his own moral and epistemological objections, Plato suggests a twofold criterion. He grants moral credit to the "severer poet and storyteller who will imitate the style of the virtuous only" (*Rep.* 398a–b), but his second objection is less easily resolved. Though it is clear that the artist who accommodates individual perspectives through illusionistic distortions should be stigmatized as "fantastic," there is also an icastic branch of image making that draws closer to the original model, a making of likeness (*ei-kon*), not semblance (*phantasma*) (*Sophist* 235a–236c, 264b–268d). Plato does not intend this late icastic/fantastic distinction to validate mimetic arts; he means rather to snare the elusive sophist whose discourse fashions deceptive images. As we shall see here and in later chapters, however, the distinction was to play an important role in Renaissance defenses. It would be seconded, too, by promises of transcendence made possible by the revisionism of Neoplatonic hierarchies. For Plotinus, matter assumes the role of false artist, the universal trickster: "It is no more than the image and phantasm of Mass . . . but a passing trick making trickery of all that seems to be present in it, phantasms within a phantasm; it is like a mirror showing things as in itself when they are really elsewhere" (*Enneads* 3.6.7). The arts, by contrast, can penetrate upward, through the levels of being; they give "no bare reproduction of the thing seen but go back to the Ideas from which nature derives" (5.8.1)—in effect circumventing the "phantasm" of the merely material. It is not surprising that, by the second half of the sixteenth century, Aristotle's ambiguous characterization of poetry as "more philosophical than history" (*Poetics* 1451b) was being Neoplatonized to shape an impressive, if historically suspect, bulwark of justification.[4]

It is here, according to Rosemond Tuve's important *Elizabethan and Metaphysical Imagery*, that the Renaissance poet takes his stand. Thanks to "the pervasiveness of Platonic and Neo-Platonic conceptions of reality," together with analogous schools of thought, the poet "simply has no nervousness about dealing overtly with universals."[5] Grounded on "ontological presuppositions" and oriented by an objective "hierarchy of values," he could be confident that "all metaphor, and perhaps other tropes" are free from the specters of subjectivism and relativism: "These agreements truly exist, to be seen by any discerning mind; they obtain logically, *are discovered, not conjectured*" (emphasis mine).[6]

But is this sense of metaphysical well-being as pervasive as Tuve proposes, or does its very expression hint at a broader distress, against which its optimistic claims are asserted? Before turning to issues of explicit critical theory, it will be helpful to approach the "conceptions of reality" embodied in Renaissance Neoplatonism by comparing the thought of its chief representative, Marsilio Ficino (1433–99), to what we have already seen at work in the speculation of Nicholas of Cusa.

Many of the distinctive turns of Cusanus's thought reappear in Florentine Neoplatonism, even though evidence for direct influence is scanty. Man is again at the center of creation, intellectually synthesizing contraries and demonstrating his infinite potential. Paul Oskar Kristeller notes that for Ficino the true act of thought is thought's awareness of itself; insofar as this awareness is endlessly repeatable, it is called "infinite reflection." As in Cusanus's speculation, the mind's taste of its own potential spurs its self-expansion. The mind "draws a line above the heavens beyond any limit in all directions,"[7] and so affirms its sense of autonomy: "through the reason we are entirely our own law."[8] Such expansiveness again becomes a background to claims for human creativity. Men, Ficino writes in his *Platonic Theology*, "are the inventors of innumerable arts," and through them "produce by themselves whatever nature itself produces, as if we were not slaves, but the rivals of nature."[9] The evidence of paintings, sculpture, buildings, and cities demonstrates our power to construct a symbolic heterocosm, a counterreality that rivals God's creation.[10] Ficino invokes the mechanical marvel of Archimedes' "heaven of brass in which all the movements of the seven planets could be truly performed as in the heavens." Man, then, becomes a "kind of god":

> Now, since man has observed the order of the heavens, when they move, whither they proceed and with what measures, and what they produce, who could deny that man possesses as it were almost the same genius as the Author of the heavens? And who could deny that man could somehow also make the heavens, could he only

obtain the instruments and the heavenly material, since even now he makes them, though of a different material, but still with a very similar order.

Whatever material limitations man faces are subordinated to Ficino's enthusiasm for the "great analogy" between divine and human artists. Like Cusanus, Ficino loosens Aquinas's restriction of creativity to God by emphasizing the godlike power of man's conception.[11] Whereas Ficino's comments on aesthetic theory are only scattered through his works, the implications of Florentine Neoplatonism come into focus in the thought of Cristoforo Landino:

> And the Greeks say "poet" from the verb "piin," which is midway between creating, which is peculiar to God when out of nothing He bringeth anything forth into being, and making, which pertaineth to men when they compose with matter and form. For which cause albeit the feigning of the poet is not wholly of nought, yet it departeth from making and draweth near unto creating.[12]

But Neoplatonists allow man this power only at the cost of retreating to a more conservative context. Consider, for example, the mind's encounter with infinity. To the question "What prevents the mind . . . from wandering around endlessly?" Ficino typically answers, "the mind would be disposed in vain to an infinite progression, if there were not found an infinite limit."[13] When we find a *terminus infinitus* in Cusanus (e.g., the *terminus interminus* in *De visione Dei* or *De principio*), it refers both to the guiding light of an unending end and to a paradoxical coincidence of opposites that reminds us of the conjectural nature of any term we create and of the necessity of continuing the act of creation. But for Ficino the term signifies a fixed point toward which the mind ascends, and from which it reconstructs an objective, hierarchical cosmos.

It is, in fact, this longing for a fixed cosmos that distinguishes the Florentine Platonists from Cusanus. For them, man can rival nature only with the aid of a realm of distinct exemplars above and behind nature for his support. Gone is Cusa's relativistic universe where man is the measure of all things, creating his own hypothetical points of reference. Astronomical relativism is stabilized through reference to an external fixed point. "The Sun," Ficino writes, "determines definite spaces in the heavens." "Thus the astronomers find and measure the motions of the planets by the motions of the Sun, which is already determined."[14] Speculation, too, despite its endless self-returnings, grows cautious about mental autonomy as Ficino returns to the Scholastic account of truth as external correspondence, an "*adaequatio rei et intellectus*."[15]

Neoplatonism's elaborately fixed and insistently objective edifices may legitimize the spirit of intellectual adventure, but its conservatism has a profound influence on its aesthetic theory. Whereas Cusanus's artist takes his own forms of thought as his model, crystallizing in his work a symbol of his "inner motions," Ficino's aspires to a more fully articulated metaphysical justification; as Kristeller points out, the act of making metaphors is "not merely suggested by thinking, but also corresponds to a real relationship existing among objects. . . . In Ficino's metaphors there is evidently a new, ontological element."[16] We see this ontological imperative, for example, in *De sole*, where, in a kind of *serio ludere*, Ficino uses the sun as a metaphor for God. Though he says he "sports divinely" rather than argues dogmatically, his play is nonetheless far from Cusanus's ball game and ingenious optical perspectives; the metaphor is objectively true: "Look at the heaven, please, oh citizen of the celestial fatherland, at the heaven which was made orderly and manifest by God for the purpose of making that clear. . . . The sun will give you signs; who would dare to call the sun false?"[17] Neoplatonism found the medieval allegorical tradition very congenial to its program, and welcomed the presence of deeper and more stable truths beneath the surface of texts. Pico, for example, defends the pursuit of "remote similes" in his allegorical reading of Genesis because the levels

of being are "bound together . . . by a certain harmonious kinship of nature."[18] The doctrine of inspiration, perhaps Neoplatonism's most famous tenet, is dedicated to similar ends. "Vain
imagination deceives you, you love what you dream," Ficino
warns. Poetic furor, however, "separates the good horse, that
is reason and opinion, from the bad horse, from confused fancy
and sense desire"; it is, in fact, the first of a series of furors that
leads "the mind back to the Unity itself." As Kristeller summarizes, "the true poet does not follow the arbitrary impulse
of his human thoughts, but is inspired by God."[19]

These metaphysical and religious assurances seem comfort-
ing, but further comparison with Cusanus shows how much
they are expressions of a distinct *need* to be comforted, attempts to manage darker misgivings. We read, for example, in
Ficino's "Five Questions Concerning the Mind": "If it [reason]
chooses to obey the senses, it always makes a conjecture [*machi-
natur*] about something; it invents new delights; it continually
seeks further, I know not what." According to Cusanus, the
mind is placed in the sensory world so that its conjectures
might be fruitful and multiply; but for Ficino, such worldly
engagement leads to restlessness and frustration. Even when
reason dominates the senses, Ficino worries, we may be
trapped by our own philosophizing, searching "eagerly for the
reasons and causes of things," only to find that "reason is always uncertain, vacillating and distressed."[20]

We have already noted the instability of Cusanus's affirmations, but we have noted, too, his joyousness and daring. Ficino, for all his praise of human dignity, has a more fragile
sense of human possibility. Man plays, Ficino writes in his *Platonic Theology*, to "expel the hidden and perpetual sadness" of
life, but "in the middle of our pleasant games we sometimes
sigh, and having played the games we part all the sadder." Freedom yields to anxiety and alienation: "Anxiety of this sort is
peculiar to man, since it arises from the characteristic powers
of the human soul . . . man alone in this present condition of

life never relaxes, he alone in this place is not content." In perhaps his most chilling depiction of the disorientation of worldly experience, Ficino continues:

> During the whole time the sublime Soul lives in this base body, our mind, as though it were ill, is thrown into a continual disquiet—here and there, up and down—and is always asleep and delirious; and the individual movements, actions, passion of men are nothing but vertigos of the sick, dreams of the sleeping, deliriums of the insane, so that Euripides rightly called this life the dream of a shadow. But while all are deceived, usually those are less deceived who at some time, as happens occasionally during sleep, become suspicious and say to themselves: "Perhaps those things are not true which now appear to us; perhaps we are now dreaming."[21]

The supposed pervasiveness of "ontological presuppositions" in Renaissance poetics must be seen in relation to Neoplatonic pessimism as well as to its optimism. Promises of awakening from the dream of historical experience carry with them a terrifying vision of that experience. Erwin Panofsky has shown, furthermore, that Ficino's justifications of human creativity are similarly linked to deep anxieties. Men of genius are born under Saturn, according to Ficino, and are therefore most susceptible to melancholy. And though melancholy is at times identified with divine furor or with poetic sensitivity, it is also dangerously close to a crippling insanity. In Panofsky's terms, melancholics "are marked by a peculiar excitability which either over-stimulates or cripples their thoughts and emotions and may, if not controlled, cause raving madness or imbecility; they walk, as it were, on a narrow ridge between two abysses."[22] Indeed, Ficino devoted his medical and astrological skills to controlling what he feared to be the harmful influences of Saturn in his own life, to prevent the "infinite reflection" that should lead the mind to Unity from becoming a vicious circle, trapping it within itself. Man's worst fate is to be trapped in subjective fantasy: it is a punishment Ficino finds appropriate for the damned, who, snared by their imaginings while alive, find after death that they are under the "domination of furious imagination." The impure soul, Kristeller summarizes, would be "continually tormented and terrified by the images of its own phantasy . . . the sick imagination persecuted by its own products."[23]

Neoplatonic inspiration, illuminated universals, and fixed hierarchies may promise metaphysical bearings for Renaissance poetics, then, but we should also be prepared to consider them not merely as assumptions but also as forms of wish-fulfillment, idealized projections whose function is to stabilize psychological and historical flux. That its metaphysical terms are culturally significant is beyond doubt; but that their protection is not as absolute as they promise is clear if we recall not only Ficino's melancholy terrors, but the obsessive efforts of the age's greatest literary Platonist, Torquato Tasso, to justify his poetic heterocosm, efforts that intensified his tragic fits of insanity.[24]

ALLEGORY, RHETORIC, AND THE FORMS OF RESTRAINT

The quest of Renaissance criticism for an objectively fixed metaphysical foundation begins long before Ficino. The first major Renaissance defense of poetry, books 14 and 15 of Boccaccio's encyclopedia of pagan mythology, *Genealogia deorum gentilium* (*Genealogy of the Gods*; ca. 1340s–1370s), looks to a solid ground of religious, moral, and historical truth to uphold the value of poetic fictions.[25]

The work is a monument to the endurance of medieval attitudes toward allegory, and yet its entire context hinges on a problematic exercise of the imagination. Boccaccio confesses, in his preface, to the enormous interpretive dilemma facing him, which is nothing less than the imaginative reconstruction of a shattered cultural cosmos. He must gather "fragments of a mighty wreck strewn on some vast shore . . . relics scattered through almost infinite volumes, shrunk with age, half-consumed, well-nigh a blank." The key to a nearly lost pattern of coherence lies in allegory, and yet the search for that deeper meaning itself reveals still further sources of difficulty:

> To arrange the members in any order, I must proceed to tear the hidden significations from their tough sheathing, and I promise to do so, though not to the last detail of the authors' original intentions. Who in our day can penetrate the hearts of the Ancients? Who can bring to light and life again minds long since removed in death? Who can elicit their meaning? A divine task that—not human! The Ancients departed in the way of all flesh, leaving behind them their literature and their famous names for posterity to interpret according to their own judgment. But as many minds, so many opinions. What wonder? There are the words of Holy Writ, clear, definite, charged with unalterable truth, though often thinly veiled in figurative language. Yet they are frequently distorted into as many meanings as there are readers.
>
> (p. 11)

There is, even in reading the most privileged of texts—Holy Writ—an inevitably subjective aspect to interpretation, a distortion into "as many meanings as there are readers." If this is the case with clear, definite, unalterable truth, then it is inescapably so with fragmented human myths.[26]

Boccaccio nevertheless assumes as virtually self-evident that "men learned in nearly every doctrine" would not "spend time and labor merely telling stories which are untrue" (p. 6) and after thirteen books of exhaustive, and often ingenious, scholarship and interpretation he concludes with a defense of poetic fictions in general. The defense takes up Aquinas's argument in the previous century that the theologian's figures indicate a realm above reason, the poet's a realm below. Boccaccio responds by reviving a still older claim: the poet is himself a theologian.[27] Any gap between poetry and truth is bridged by invoking the absolute source, poetry's "springing from God's bosom": "While other arts are matters of science and formula and technique, poetry depends solely upon an inborn faculty, is evoked by a purely mental activity, and is infused with a strange supernal inspiration" (p. 41). Poetry is, then, "stable and fixed . . . founded upon things eternal . . . unshaken by any possible change" (p. 25). Boccaccio constructs his defense on this ground. Poetic fictions are not arbitrary figments of the imagination, he argues, but are polysemous: beneath the fictional surface lie the deeper truths of allegory. "Some men have thought that the learned poet merely invents shallow tales, and is therefore not only useless, but a positive harm. This is because they read discursively and, of course, derive no profit from the story. Now this work of mine removes the veil from these inventions, [and] shows that poets were really men of wisdom" (p. 104–5). The unveiling of allegorical meanings, however, leaves unexplained an antithetical impulse. For Boccaccio finds himself fascinated by the fictional surface itself, admiring the ingenious invention so much that the surface, at times, takes on an autonomous value: "Artistic embellishment acquires value though it is of no practical use whatever" (p. 104). He marvels at the intensity of poetic language, where things are "so vividly set forth that the very objects will seem actually present in the tiny letters of the written poem" (p. 80).

Boccaccio senses the problematic nature of such fascinations and feels called upon to justify them. Even after insisting that poetry and oratory are distinct uses of language, he imagines fiction as a rhetorical address to the reader, which, like the fable Menenius told the Roman plebs, persuades men to virtuous action (p. 50). Now rhetoric also leads us away from the surface, pointing to the reader rather than to the verbal structures themselves. But it values the techniques by which one elicits ethical responses and allows the critic to justify the more immediate workings of fiction.

Allegory and rhetoric, then, might be joined in a comprehensive defense, at once grounding fiction in deeper truth and directing its moral import outward:

> This poetry . . . is a sort of fervid and exquisite invention, with
> fervid expression in speech or writing, of that which the mind has
> invented. It proceeds from the bosom of God, and few, I find, are
> the souls in whom this gift is born; indeed so wonderful a gift it is
> that true poets have always been the rarest of men. This fervor of
> poesy is sublime in its effects: it impels the soul to a longing for
> utterance; it brings forth strange and unheard-of creations of the
> mind; it arranges these meditations in a fixed order, adorns the
> whole composition with unusual interweaving of words and
> thoughts; and thus it veils truth in a fair and fitting garment of
> fiction. Further, if in any case the invention so requires, it can arm
> kings, marshal them for war, launch whole fleets from their docks,
> nay counterfeit sky, land, sea, adorn young maidens with flowery
> garlands, portray human character in its various phases, awake the
> idle, stimulate the dull, restrain the rash, subdue the criminal, and
> distinguish excellent men with their proper meed of praise: these,
> and many other such, are the effects of poetry.
>
> (pp. 39–40)

Boccaccio here seems to present us with his entire argument in
miniature, tracing poetic fictions from their source in divine
inspiration—an external gift provoking an inner motion—to
their practical effects: awakening the idle and restraining the
rash—arguments that Renaissance humanists were to draw repeatedly from Cicero's *De oratore*, where the orator can "arouse
a listless nation" and "curb its unbridled impetuosity."[28]

But there remains a slippery *tertium quid*, never clearer than
in such discussions as the above: the poet's creativity, his ability
to fashion a new world. Before his rhetoric can work on us, we
must first pass through the "strange and unheard-of creations
of the mind," with an "unusual interweaving of words and
thoughts." The path should be clear, for Boccaccio assures us
that the creations are arranged in a "fixed order," that the interweaving fashions a "fair and fitting garment." The way
proves, however, to be somewhat labyrinthine. When we arrive at what seem to be poetry's salubrious effects, the syntax
(a series of infinitives in the Latin) makes it impossible to locate
where the effects are.[29] Are the awakened and the restrained the

poem's readers, or are they part of the invention, together with the armed kings who are marshalled for war within the poem? Engrossed in his description of fiction-making itself, Boccaccio expands the rhetorical concept of *inventio* until it suggests not merely the finding of useful matter, but the creation of a heterocosm with its own kings and fleets, a new sky, land, and sea.[30] It is an impressive moment, but one that leaves us wondering where the boundary of fiction lies, where we make the transition back from the fictive to the real.

Poets, Boccaccio later tells us, do indeed "rouse the reader's mind to higher feelings" (15.1), but the didactic argument requires clearer articulation of how the fictive world of "human character in its various phases" is at once distinct from, and an influence on, the reader's. Assurances of inspiration and allegory protect Boccaccio, at least here, from an abiding concern with fiction's potential self-referentiality, but the defense remains curiously unresolved.[31] Consider, for example, what might be taken as his *propositio*: "Fiction is a form of discourse, which, under guise of invention, illustrates or proves an idea; and, as its superficial aspect is removed, the meaning of the author is clear. If, then, sense is revealed from under the veil of fiction, the composition of fiction is not idle nonsense" (p. 48). And yet the preface to the *Genealogy*, as we have already seen, threatens the vision of a clear, broad, symbolic plane of meaning on historical grounds; the late books confess to intrinsic difficulty as Boccaccio advises "those who would appreciate poetry, and unwind its difficult involutions. You must read, you must persevere, you must sit up nights, you must inquire, and exert the utmost power of your mind. If one way does not lead to the desired meaning, take another; if obstacles arise, then still another, until, if your strength holds out, you will find that clear which at first looked dark" (p. 62). Boccaccio introduces these remarks with a series of quotations from St. Augustine on the benefits of obscurity (pp. 60–61), but if one follows Boccaccio's own procedure, the clarity a reader achieves at the end of exhausting struggle returns him to the ambiguity latent within the poet's originating *inventio*: the twilight boundary between objective discovery and projection; allegory as it is fashioned in the *Genealogy* becomes as much a sign of the imagination at play as a grounded justification of that play.[32]

My point is not that Boccaccio asks us to be skeptical of finding deep foundations for poetic fictions. The sheer vastness of his enterprise, however peculiar that enterprise may sometimes seem, testifies to the vigor of his belief. Nevertheless, the final apologia of the *Genealogy* is valuable to us, not only for its constructive achievement, but also for its indications at the very inception of Renaissance criticism of the difficulties facing those who would justify imaginative fictions. As the fictive surface presents itself as more than a veil to be penetrated, evidence less of inspired truth than of autonomous human making, the task grows increasingly tortuous.[33]

Allegorical defenses of literature coexist in the Renaissance with other, seemingly antithetical, traditions. An adjustment of Boccaccio's emphasis in the direction of rhetoric was an attractive one, satisfying both the need to attend to the surface and the humanist demand for studies directed toward useful and ethical action. The emphasis had the weight of its own tradition, from Cicero's claim that poetry and rhetoric are the closest of neighbors to the absorption of poetics into rhetoric in the medieval scheme of the seven liberal arts. The effect of this conflation can be felt in the first major commentary on Aristotle's *Poetics* in 1548, which, after locating poetry's special area of discourse in the "false and the fabulous," proceeds to transform the work from one concerned with "internal and structural relationship" to one concerned with producing an effect on the reader, a "moral persuasion to action or inaction."[34] Later Antonio Minturno would transfer Cicero's "teach, delight, and move" from the office of the orator to that of the poet, and would be followed by Julius Caesar Scaliger and, in England, by Sidney.

Rhetorical and allegorical models interact in various ways. Landino, for example, regards the *Aeneid*'s surface as a rhetorical incitement to moral behavior in the active life and its underlying meaning as Platonic allegory.[35] But, despite Landino's two-pronged defense and a Renaissance tendency to idealize rhetorical categories, rhetoric does not merge evenly with metaphysics. The Renaissance pursuit of eloquence, as numerous intellectual historians have shown, endorses human flexibility, exploiting rather than transcending the flux of experience, and thereby posing an implicit challenge to metaphysics. Eloquence, rather than authorizing language through universals and fixed hierarchies, assumes the remoteness of timeless certainties and exploits instead the specifics of rhetorical occasion and the contingencies of a pluralistic world.[36]

Rhetoric, of course, has its own restrictions. Aristotle tells us in his comparison of rhetoric and dialectic that just as the latter "does not construct syllogisms out of haphazard materials, such as the fancies of crazy people, but out of materials that call for discussion," so, too, rhetoric "draws upon regular subjects of debate" (*Rhetoric* 1.2). But Renaissance poetics is peculiarly sensitive to troubling instabilities at the heart of the rhetorical tradition. Without a metaphysical "anchor," the pull of practical concerns—probability, the reliance on "accepted opinions" for the stirring of an audience's emotions, and the rhetorical exercise of arguing opposite sides of a question—can swing the rhetorician's art toward the restless versatility, subjectivism, and relativism that poetry's attackers condemned. Coluccio Salutati warns that both poetry and oratory must be stabilized by philosophical wisdom: "The ocean of eloquence becomes infinite and impassable if you lose sight of truth. True things are firm, clearly bounded, such that he who follows them is always on solid ground."[37]

The issue becomes crucial for literary criticism, because

rhetoric's attraction for poetry lies in large measure upon its liberation of nonrational materials. When Boccaccio wondered at the vivid objects that "seem actually present in the tiny letters of the poem," he was both alluding to and enacting *enargia*, the power of figurative language to, in Aristotle's terms, "set things before the eyes." Quintilian provides an important classical analysis:

> There are certain experiences which the Greeks call phantasiae, and the Romans visions, whereby things absent are presented to our imagination with such extreme vividness that they seem actually to be before our very eyes. It is the man who is really sensitive to such impressions who will have the greatest power over the emotions. . . . When the mind is unoccupied or is absorbed by fantastic hopes or daydreams, we are haunted by these visions. . . . Surely, then, it may be possible to turn this form of hallucination to some profit.[38]

The search for profit entails a special risk. The use of fantasy is "the most efficacious way of moving or delighting or teaching," writes Danielle Barbaro in *Della eloquenza* (1557), but it is also "dangerous." For we also see those who "go about . . . building air castles and are so intent on their thoughts that everyone believes them to be frenzied and mad."[39] The faculty exploited by the most eloquent of men, the moral persuader of the many, if abused drifts dangerously close to the madness that can trap him in his own mind. The rhetorician finds here an ironic parallel to the metaphysician; the exploitation of fantasy confronts him with the very anxieties suffered by the melancholy Neoplatonist.

The "age of criticism" finds itself concerned with the search for an equilibrium that would enable both an exploitation and a restraint of the problematic energies that poetic fictions call forth. Metaphysics continues to be useful; a conflation of the Idea and the artist's preconceived mental design allows Platonists such as Agnolo Segni to rely upon an objective realm of exemplars, the "most perfect nature of things existing outside things and outside of the human mind" to distinguish between legitimate and illegitimate fictions—that is, between fabling that produces a mere "tissue of falsehood" and that which "by means of its lies lets us contemplate and recognize truth."[40] Poets and critics could also modulate metaphysical terms into moral ones, as in epic theory, which elevates (or reduces) poetic heroes to the status of universals, "perfect exemplars" of virtues.[41] So, too, the revival of Aristotle's *Poetics*, which, ironically, was to subvert metaphysical defenses, could, as we have already seen, give impetus to the idealizing of poetic fictions. But the defensiveness of such attitudes toward poetry is also apparent. The Platonist Lodovico Ricchieri tells us that man's internal drive for knowledge is first stimulated by "poetic fiction . . . especially since it remains unexpressed and vague and seems always to suggest some other matter." That vagueness and suggestiveness must be monitored by fixing the nature of the "other matter." The philosopher, Ricchieri warns, must stand by to

> administer an antidote, having explained by allegory the outer cloaks of the fables and having used the curative power of their precepts, by which means (as if by a brake) the enticements of the pleasures are restrained and at the same time the violence of the passions is diminished—which, excited for the most part by reading as by a living example placed before it, forces itself upon the very reason and after having trod upon it succeeds in extending its dominion even farther.

Allegory is here less a fulfillment of fiction than a brake against its accelerating pleasures. The fables seem very distant from the universals they should illuminate; if they are a medicine of cherries, they are also a dangerous amphetamine that can so overstimulate the reader that his reason would be overthrown without the antidote of allegory.[42]

The efficacy of that antidote, furthermore, is by no means assured. Uncertainty over the problem of universals, which assumed so important a role in Cusanus's intellectual life, did not leave poetic theory untouched. Girolamo Fracastoro's Platonism, Hathaway notes, has the air of playacting; the descent of inspiration and the ascent to universals assume a hypothetical, even arbitrary, note.[43] Other Renaissance critics take a quasi-Nominalist attitude toward reality even as they echo Neoplatonic and Platonic-Aristotelian justifications. Universals, writes Benedetto Varchi, are "merely concepts created by our minds . . . apprehended only by the intellect, whereas particulars being real things, are known by the senses."[44]

The distancing of metaphysics encouraged this-worldly, didactic models for justifying fictions, but the necessity of restraint remains as urgent as ever. Fictions must be credible if they are to work on the reader: Leonardo Bruni, after praising poetic creations in 1405, admits that when he recognizes a fiction as fiction, he may "pay attention to the genius of the poet, but the matter itself I know to be a fiction, and thus it leaves no moral impression."[45] Horatian critics, responsible in large measure for the rhetorical cast of critical thought, turned accordingly to the opening of the *Ars poetica*, where Horace warns against monstrous figments, such as a woman with a fish's tail, which make a work laughable since they portray only "idle imaginings shaped like the dreams of a sick man." Drawing a distinction between the *res* and *verba* of a work, the subject matter and the verbal surface, the Horatians claimed that Horace's opening lines referred to the *res*, which ought to exhibit a strict "correspondence between the things imitated in art and things in nature." This fit neatly with the more famous Horatian formula that a work should give either pleasure or profit or both. The more serious *res* was then assigned the task of conveying moral profit, as well as proving the writer's wisdom, as if the more purely aesthetic side of expression, the *verba*, could not be trusted with such a task.[46]

Standards of credibility and verisimilitude close one problem only to expose another. Boccaccio defends poets from the charge that they are liars and deceivers by noting that their work generally "bears not only no close resemblance to literal truth, but no resemblance at all" (*Genealogy*, p. 63). But when we come to such sixteenth-century claims as Francesco Robortello's that "in the lies used by poetic art, false elements are taken as true and from them true conclusions are derived" and Paolo Beni's that "in poetry the highest praise is in deceiving the eyes and minds and in making the auditors mistake the false for the true," we are made uncomfortably aware of the paradoxicality of teaching through illusions. Despite appeals to didactic efficacy, we are closer to the tricks of sleight-of-hand than to the rhetorician's proof by enthymeme and example, and far from Tuve's ideal of poetic agreements that "truly exist . . . they obtain logically." Indeed, the logical interests of critics often revolve around the use of "paralogisms," sophistical pseudoarguments that, according to Aristotle, Homer brought to the art of poetry by "teaching the other poets how lies should be told."[47]

If verisimilitude proves to be treacherous, another standard was available in the normative canon of the art itself. Julius Caesar Scaliger endorses the bold Neoplatonic claims for the poet as a "maker" who, in depicting another nature, "transforms himself into a second deity," because Scaliger can rely on literary conservatism to dictate the kind of second nature the poet will make. His guide is the purified nature of Virgil's *Aeneid*; the "Virgilian Idea," an exemplar that offers a proper model for the poet's work, fulfills the function of the Platonic Form.[48]

But the literary tradition could be an unreliable guide, for even the exalted Virgil seemed given at times to fantastic excess.[49] The problems of tradition emerge with particular force in the continuing fascination with medieval romance, which culminated in the writing of *Orlando Furioso* (1516), a work that became a focus for critical anxieties about the proper boundaries of feigning and illusion. The poem set off a storm of controversy not only over its kaleidoscopic multiplicity of plots, but over what appears to be an unrestrained torrent of fantasy—a flying horse, a magical shield, a ring that grants invisibility, an enchanted palace, a trip to the moon. A liberal critic such as Giraldi Cinthio might invoke the tradition itself to defend the work: if literary history teaches us any necessary truth about the laws of poetry, it is that they change. Skillful poets have never felt it necessary to "restrain their liberty within the bounds set by their predecessors." Rules spring, not from fixed precepts, but from the poetic maker himself and his apparently impossible fictions.[50]

Conservative critics likewise concede the need for the marvelous and for variety to evoke *admiratio*, but the overt fictionalizing of Ariosto's romance seemed finally to have gone too far. Minturno's attack, fifteen years after Cinthio's defense, demonstrates a continuing nervousness about poetic freedom. Romance writers, Minturno charges, "fill up their pages with dreams," foolishly assuming that because they write about errant knights, their "poetry should be errant." Two hundred years after Boccaccio's *Genealogia* inaugurated Renaissance criticism, the longing for an objective and fixed poetic foundation persists: the laws of poetry change only in their accidents, not in their essence, Minturno insists, because "the truth is always one, and that which is once true must of necessity be true always."[51]

ARROGANCE AND INSECURITY

The preceding discussion has emphasized some of the ways in which a myriad of critical formulations in the Italian Renaissance sought to regulate the poetic imagination by defining its proper relation to truth and responsible action. The second half of the sixteenth century saw such efforts take on increased sophistication and urgency, impelled both by the religious anxieties of the Counter Reformation and by theorizing and controversies in literary academies and universities. I conclude this chapter with a closer look at some of the issues that surfaced in this over-heated intellectual atmosphere, particularly in the works of three very distinct and important literary figures— Lodovico Castelvetro, Jacopo Mazzoni, and Torquato Tasso[52] —for it is in these years that the tensions that play through Renaissance meditations on fiction making emerge in their clearest form and give fullest expression to criticism's deepening epistemological drama.

Castelvetro's readers have often pointed out that his *Poetica d'Aristotele vulgarizzata et sposta* (1570) is not so much a translation of and commentary on the *Poetics* as an opportunity for Castelvetro to expound his own poetic notions. Not only does Aristotle receive rough treatment at his hands, but so, too, do most of the traditional apologists for poetry. There can be no appeal to metaphysics; as Baxter Hathaway summarizes: "When the poet creates Ideas he has no way of assuring himself and others what he has concocted has real being and is not merely a chimera."[53] For Castelvetro, the theory of divine inspiration is the result of the "ignorance of the common people" and has been fostered by the "vainglory of the poets." Plato's furor must have been intended as a joke (pp. 310–11). Nor does allegory come off any better. One should leave hidden truths to philosophers and scientists. If there is any veiling of truth in poetic fictions, the veil is for pornographic purposes; an audience can enjoy "things that pertain to carnal delights, as the secret parts of the body, lascivious connections." We would be overcome by shame if seen enjoying such things in public, but the dramatist gives us "a veil by means of which we are able to give the appearance of laughing at something else" (p. 314).

Nor, Castelvetro insists, does poetry have any moral utility or lessons to teach. Its sole function is to "delight and recreate the minds of the crude multitude and of the common people" (p. 307). The poet is not a moral teacher, but an entertainer; not a prophet, but an exhibitionist, a show-off of his creative talents. The art of history is a necessary prelude to the art of poetry, but the poet must not merely copy history: if too much were given, he could not show his "keenness in intellect" (p. 305). History, rather, is an obstacle that allows epic and tragic poets to demonstrate their brilliance in overcoming it. Poetic greatness emerges not from objective grounding, but from the "need of superhuman ingenuity" to display originality while imitating the given and the need to transcend "such things" as "anyone can imagine for himself . . . without much cleverness of intellect" (pp. 321–23). In contrast to Scaliger's worship of Virgil, Castelvetro makes originality the essential task: "The imitation necessary to poetry not only neither follows the example given by others, nor makes the same thing as has already been made . . . but it makes something quite original and entirely different from what has been done up to that day."[54]

But alongside this exuberance is a peculiar suspicion about the status of a poet's work, an uncertainty that provokes a retreat to objective reality that at times degenerates to an absurd literalness. The tragedian, for example, must match the duration of his play to the duration of the event represented: "It is not possible to make the audience suppose that several days and nights have passed when they have the evidence of their senses that only a few hours have gone by" (p. 310, n. 15). Though Castelvetro wants to distinguish the truth of history from the verisimilitude of poetry, at times the criterion of verisimilitude comes very close to truth itself, as if Castelvetro were inching his way back to find a firmer footing: "Verisimilitude depends on truth," he writes, "and the thing representing entirely on the thing represented." As H. B. Charlton comments, the line between truth of fact and creative imitation is blurred, and more recently Hathaway has remarked that it is often hard to tell whether Castelvetro is a realist (in the modern sense) or a fantasist; at one moment he praises the poet's clever inventions, his imagining of the "marvelous," and at the next attacks poets who are guilty of "diminishing our faith in their creations and showing that these are but imagined."[55]

Only the comic poet invents pure fiction, because "he cannot be rebuked by history or fame as a falsifier" (p. 320). Those who seek loftier themes are, ironically, far more restricted:

> We cannot create a king, who never existed, by our imagination, nor can we attribute actions to such a king; indeed we cannot even attribute to a really historic king actions which he never performed: for history would give us the lie. . . . For if it is permitted to create kings who never existed, and to give them fictitious actions, it will also be permitted to create new mountains, new rivers, new lakes, new seas, new peoples, new kingdoms, and to transport old rivers into other districts, and, in short, it will be permitted to create a new world and to transform the old one.[56]

Castelvetro, then, upsets the careful balancing of Boccaccio, the Neoplatonists, and Scaliger, an equilibrium that would be so urgently sought after again by Tasso. He insists on freeing fiction from the external ties of inspiration, allegory, didacticism, and traditional models of imitation, but discovers at the very moment of liberation that he must compromise its creativity as well. We find the fiction maker trapped in a desperate situation, faced by an unimaginative audience that will not allow him the liberty of his invention. The moment they perceive the unreality of his work, it will be "just as if they had had a jewel and thinking it good, had rejoiced, but finding it artificial, had been cast into sorrow."[57] His only function is to entertain an audience that rejects him the moment it realizes what he is doing.

If Castelvetro shows a deep uncertainty about the nature of poetic freedom, Jacopo Mazzoni surveys the problem with philosophical and encyclopedic thoroughness. As Hathaway's masterful scholarship has shown, Mazzoni's defense of Dante in *Della difesa della Commedia di Dante* (first three books, 1587) and his brief earlier defense constitute the "most fully developed system of literary aesthetics in the Renaissance,"[58] and though these documents lead us in a decidedly different direction than does Castelvetro's *Poetica*, they reveal, finally, further dimensions of the same dilemma.

Following Aristotle, Mazzoni regards all arts as imitations; what distinguishes poetry is that its objects have "no being or use except from imitation and in imitation." The imitated object is not located in the external world, but is a fabrication of the poet's mind, created for the sake of the poem: "When we concluded above that the image is the object of the imitative arts we did not mean the sort of image that comes into being without human artistic activity . . . but that which has its origin from our art, which usually springs from our phantasy and our intellect by means of our choice and will" (p. 360). Mazzoni lists four species of poetic imitation within a system that neither anchors fictions to metaphysical Ideas and the truths of nature nor excludes the possibility of imitation of truth. It frees the poet, rather, from the very *criterion* of truth. Mazzoni's views are influenced by Aristotle's distinctions in *De anima*: "Imagining lies within our power whenever we wish (e.g., we can call up a picture as in the practice of mnemonics by the use of mental images), but in forming opinions we are not free: we cannot escape the alternatives of falsehood and truth" (*De anima* 3.3). The details of Mazzoni's faculty psychology vary (as we saw above, he elsewhere grants the intellect a role in creating these images or "idols"); what is more important is his characterization of poetry as mental construction, the making of "fictions which we of ourselves are able to feign" (p. 387). Poetry *may* conform to truth, of course, as when geography is accurately depicted, but such facts are usable only *after* they have become images in the mind. Correspondence is not to an external *res*, for the mental object is itself "an adequate object of human imitation" (p. 360). The poet frames his object to fit his intellectual needs, and not the other way around. Fitness is not "objective decorum," but a condition that the object itself must satisfy as it is fabricated by "our phantasy and our intellect by means of our choice and will."

Mazzoni's idols recall Abélard's Nominalist universal, a "certain imaginary and fictive thing, which the mind constructs for itself . . . like those imaginary cities which are seen in dreams," but Mazzoni's sense of the mind's disjunction from objective Being is more radical.[59] The revival of Pyrrhonian skepticism, with its insistence on reserving judgment on truth and falsity, figures prominently in his critical attitude. He protects the poet's fantastic activity by placing it under the aegis of "sophistic, since it has no regard for the truth . . . that which treated of all things rhetorically" (p. 367). Mazzoni seems to be at the opposite pole to Castelvetro; our inventions cannot be given the lie, he writes, as long as we locate them in "strange and remote" lands. Here "the feigning of new countries, new peoples, and new kingdoms, and the alternating and falsifying of the source and course of rivers, the site of countries, and the quality of other things in nature, are in our opinion wholly proper and fitting to the poet" (p. 389).

Declarations of propriety only defer the inevitable question, however. How do we justify these strange and remote kingdoms? Mazzoni's encyclopedic approach draws him into discussion of inspiration and allegory, but because his emphasis lies, as Hathaway argues, in a "this-worldly, poetic handling of the universe . . . rather than toward an Augustinian, Neoplatonic cosmos," his system is vulnerable to such attacks as that of the Aristotelian Bellisario Bulgarini: dreams and idols are "vain" and cannot serve as the basis of poetic imitation; "the foundation, or, as we mean to say, the true form which is the essence of a metaphor is not some power of our mind, but rather the similitude and conformity which is found between diverse things."[60]

Mazzoni, in other words, finds himself in a position analogous to that of Cusanus when attacked by the Scholastic Wenck. But because of his this-worldly orientation, he cannot dismiss the "Aristotelian sect" with an appeal to mystical silence. He shapes, rather, a convoluted defense, claiming at one moment that the mental operations that create the idols truly exist, and so ground the process, and at the next that all other sciences are unknowable, and that life is a dream.[61] But as we have seen throughout Renaissance criticism, the more autonomous and potentially arbitrary the fictional surface becomes, the more insistent grows the need to regulate it and refer it to something outside itself. Mazzoni's criticism is no exception, and we find in it a desire to reconnect the playful fictional world to the realm of serious activity.

Mazzoni attempts this reconciliation by following the lead of both Plato and Aristotle, locating recreation under the architectonic science of politics, which operates by what he calls the "civil faculty." Just as medicine deals with illness as well as health, so the civil faculty "professes to understand not alone the right ordering of human actions, but also the right ordering of the cessation of these operations" (p. 373). Considered in itself, poetry "should be thought of as play," with only pleasure as its end. But because play is regulated by the civil faculty, its utility can extend beyond itself: "the cessation of activity . . . should dispose and prepare men in such a way that they are more apt and more zealous for activity." If left to "itself alone, free and untrammelled by all laws," Mazzoni admits, poetry would deserve censure. But "regulated and qualified by the civil faculty," its "legality" is assured. Poetry is still sophistic, but it is "praiseworthy sophistic" with "utility as its end" (pp. 373–78).

The integration, however, is hardly complete, and we find conflicting definitions of poetry standing side by side. Mazzoni insists that "poetry is capable of three definitions according as it is considered in three different manners." It may be purely an imitation of self-created idols, or mental play for the sake of delight, or an instrument of profit and virtue. Each of these definitions has its own set of authorities to support it, and Mazzoni advocates that we use each set separately as we pass through the definitions (pp. 384–85). He may demand the submission of sophistic to the civil faculty, but his manner of presenting the demand is itself strongly tinged with sophistic. Poetry never fully abandons its self-referentiality, for this is finally what sets it apart from every other art: the historian aims at "leaving behind a memory of the truth," but the poet seeks to "leave behind a simulacrum . . . in the respect that it is a simulacrum."[62]

Tasso found this emphasis disturbing, and in *Discorsi del poema eroico*, he denied Mazzoni's claim that ancient philosophers "praise this disorder of the intellect in certain things, when it was directed to a proper end" (p. 369).[63] The poet is not a sophist, Tasso insists, "not a phantastic imitator, as Mazzoni held"; so too is "Robortello . . . greatly mistaken when he assigns the false to poems as their matter, since . . . the false is the matter of the sophist, who works with what is not" (pp. 28, 32). It is important to remember that Tasso's reaction against what appeared to him to be extreme imaginative license reflects his own intense engagement with the marvelous and the romantic. For his theoretical concern with Mazzoni's idols and with Ariosto's romance fantasy is informed by a self-conscious struggle with his own great epic, the *Gerusalemme liberata*.[64]

Tasso's two major theoretical statements, the *Discorsi dell'arte poetica* (ca. 1570, published in 1587), and the *Discorsi del poema eroico* (published in 1594), painstakingly plot the ontological, religious, and temporal coordinates of the legitimate imaginative cosmos he ultimately hoped his own work presented. The truly noble poet, Tasso argues, must base his plot on history, for the merely fictive cannot move us; moreover, the necessary fusion of the marvelous and the restraint of the verisimilar requires a specifically Christian or Hebrew history, for pagan supernaturalism yields only "vain idols"; yet the poet's freedom of feigning requires that his subject be not in itself sacred and unalterable, and be located in the historical middle distance, neither too obscurely remote nor too easily given the lie by being too modern and familiar (book 2, passim).

The aesthetic ideal toward which all these negotiations are working is to contain, but not suppress, the energies of poetic fantasy and romance within an Aristotelian unity of action, to span the range of the Renaissance imagination within a stable and harmonious Ficinian universe. The epic poet, Tasso writes in an often quoted passage of the 1594 *Discorsi*, can create a heterocosm as diverse as creation itself. Just as God's masterpiece, the world, is filled with stars, birds, fish, rivers, woods, and mountains, and yet is one, "its form and essence one, and one the bond that links its many parts and ties them together in discordant concord," so too

> the great poet (who is called divine for no other reason than that as he resembles the supreme Artificer in his workings he comes to participate in his divinity) can form a poem in which, as in a little world, one may read here of armies assembling, here of battles on land or sea, here of conquests of cities, skirmishes and duels, here of jousts, here descriptions of hunger and thirst, here tempests, fires, prodigies, there of celestial and infernal councils, there seditions, there discord, wanderings, adventures, enchantments, deeds of cruelty, daring, courtesy, generosity, there the fortunes of love, now happy, now sad, now joyous, now pitiful. Yet the poem that contains so great a variety of matters none the less should be one, one in form and soul; and all these things should be so combined that each concerns the other, corresponds to the other, and so depends on the other necessarily or verisimilarly that removing any one part or changing its place would destroy the whole. And if that is true, the art of composing a poem resembles the play of the universe, which is composed of contraries, as that of music is.
>
> (p. 78)

The heterocosm embraces the extremes of action and passion, of discord and enchantment, but all must be contained by the unity of plot: "*hoc opus, hic labor est*" (p. 78).

Tasso's theoretical assertions of harmony are themselves attempts to contain potentially subversive critical insights. The craving for *varietas*, what Scaliger calls "the greatest of poetic virtues," was perhaps "not so necessary in the times of Virgil and Homer"; "our era has found it most pleasing" because of "jaded" and "refined" tastes (p. 77). The Renaissance poet, then, must be exceptionally scrupulous of his poetic teleology, the end or goal (*"il fine"*) toward which all multiplicity must tend, and without which his world would be infected by endless futility: "multiplicity produces indeterminacy, and this progression could go on *ad infinitum*, unless art fixed and prescribed limits" (p. 67). If the poet insists on following the example of explorers who have gone beyond the Pillars of Hercules, he must remember that they have managed "the sea's inconstancy by the constancy of things celestial"; he, too, must always keep the "object itself" in mind, "the truth, which never changes and disappears from the mind's eye" (p. 57). Like Cusanus, whose *homo cosmographicus* charts the potential infinity of conjecture by calling on a unifying *intellectus*, Tasso seeks to justify human inventions by promising to transcend them. He likens the poet to a mystical theologian by invoking the Platonic and Pseudo-Dionysian elevation of an "indivisible mind" above the "divisible," discursive reason. The former carries us beyond mere demonstration, through images of universal truth, to "the contemplation of divine things" (pp. 31–32).

But the goal of the Christian Platonist can come to seem alarmingly distant. The final book of the *Discorsi del poema eroico* opens with tones of a Nominalist, even skeptical, crisis of confidence:

> Any treatment of forms, my illustrious lord, involves great obscurity and difficulty. For if we take the forms as separate entities, what the philosophers have called ideas, we may easily decide either that they do not exist or that they are of no use to our human devices and mortal doings. And if we are not thus persuaded, we may feel constrained at least by the opposite argument to abandon

so lofty a matter of contemplation. Even in contemplating the forms of matter, we encounter tremendous difficulty; for matter is a source of uncertainty and obscurity, so that ancient philosophers compared it to the dark unfathomed deep. But if we separate them in imagination we get involved in falsehoods, or if not actually in falsehoods still our contemplation is directed to no sound purpose.

(p. 171)

The seeker for the Idea grows sensitive to the burden of matter, that Plotinian flux of phantasms that threatens the validity of his very images of transcendence. Whether we find in this passage evidence of tragic disjunction, or the prelude to bracing and courageous discipline,[65] we cannot help but recall Tasso's agonizing uncertainty about the orthodoxy of his own *Gerusalemme liberata*, an anxiety that could not be stilled, even by his own allegorical "key," until he had more completely suppressed his poetic freedom. Nor can we forget the suffering of the poet-theologian of imaginative truth, confined as insane at Sant' Anna and tormented by nightmares of hell and hallucinations of the Virgin, of persecution, and of the "shouts of men . . . and mocking laughter and various animal voices . . . and noises of inanimate things."[66]

Tasso's struggle with poetic and mental instability, what one critic calls his "schizophrenic involvement in the intellectual crisis of his time,"[67] was in large part a consequence of the pressures of the Counter-Reformation. But it also serves to dramatize an aesthetic and philosophical dilemma that confronted Renaissance writers throughout the period: an increasing awareness of the mind's power and freedom to create fictional worlds that outstrips its ability to justify them. Critics and poets produced many strategies to defer or contain their unease, but the dilemma emerged with unnerving clarity in the later Renaissance. As Panofsky summarizes its impact on creative possibility: "In the free but therefore unstable atmosphere created by the developments during the second half of the sixteenth century, the artistic mind began to react to reality with simultaneous arrogance and insecurity."[68] It is this atmosphere, I argue in the remainder of this section, that permeates Sir Philip Sidney's major works as well.

5

SIDNEY'S FEIGNED *APOLOGY*

Any attempt to discuss Sidney's theory of poetic fictions proves to be something of a paradox, since *An Apology for Poetry* opens with a warning not to take theories too seriously. There Sidney compares himself to his master in horsemanship, John Pietro Pugliano, who, not content to teach his young students the practical side of his profession, "sought to enrich [their] minds with the contemplations therein." So mighty does his art appear, thanks to the light of self-love, that "if I had not been a piece of a logician before I came to him, I think he would have persuaded me to have wished myself a horse" (p. 95).[1] Following his master, Sidney opens with a theoretical justification of his own vocation, poetry, but with such a precedent, the reader may wonder if Sidney will persuade him to wish himself a poem (which is, in fact, where Sidney's Astrophil ends up in Sonnet 45 of *Astrophil and Stella*).

The paradoxical opening of the *Apology* sets the tone for the rest of the work, which is filled with contradictions and shifts of emphasis. Its studied carelessness and playfulness are in marked contrast to the intense engagement of a Minturno or a Tasso, yet it is through these gestures that Sidney makes his most suggestive critical probings. What those probings reveal can be maddeningly elusive. Readers have often mistaken his intellectual affinities because of the oblique and self-conscious way in which he echoes traditional philosophical and critical attitudes, or have felt compelled to sketch in the lines of coherence they assume must underlie the argument. The result has been a series of alternative maps to Sidney's many fascinations:

the nature of poetic invention and imitation, of moving through delight, of the distinction between legitimate and illegitimate fictions. These issues were indeed important to Sidney and became increasingly so over the short course of his poetic career. A closer look at his performances both here and in his other major works, however, reveals no single theoretical affinity or formulation, but rather an effort to come to terms with the deepest tensions of Renaissance poetics, as well as Sidney's kinship with the most penetrating and original thought of his time.

THE FORE-CONCEIT

Sidney's purpose seems familiar enough: to justify poetic fictions against the charge that they are unreal and irresponsible fantasies. For the sake of clarity, I begin by dividing my examination into two parts, following the line drawn by Sidney's own argument:

> Any understanding knoweth the skill of the artificer standeth in that *Idea* or fore-conceit of the work, and not in the work itself. And that the poet hath that *Idea* is manifest, by delivering them forth in such excellency as he hath imagined them. Which delivering forth also is not wholly imaginative, as we are wont to say by them that build castles in the air; but so far substantially it worketh, not only to make a Cyrus, which had been but a particular excellency as Nature might have done, but to bestow a Cyrus upon the world to make many Cyruses, if they will learn aright why and how that maker made him.
>
> (p. 101)

What is striking about this defense of poetic invention is that Sidney seeks to justify poetry by turning toward the two extremes it mediates, first to its source in the poet's "Idea" and then to the moral effect it has on the reader's world; it becomes a conduit of the ideal into the actual. To understand how Sidney puts his argument together, we must take a closer look at these two extremes and their relations.

First, what is the Idea, or "fore-conceit"? Modern critics often point to it as an example of Renaissance Neoplatonism and/or Augustinianism. Sidney's poet sets his mind on the Ideas beyond phenomenal appearance; the consequent poetic image "proliferates meanings which the discursive reason cannot hope to encompass."[2]

The *Apology* does entertain echoes of Neoplatonism, or at least the claims Neoplatonism had made possible. After reviewing the arts of man and deciding that all follow the "works of nature" as their object, Sidney follows Landino and Scaliger in setting the poet apart as a free creator:

> Only the poet, disdaining to be tied to any such subjection, lifted up with the vigour of his own invention, doth grow in effect into another nature, in making things either better than Nature bringeth forth, or, quite anew, forms such as never were in Nature, as the Heroes, Demigods, Cyclops, Chimeras, Furies, and such like: so as he goeth hand in hand with Nature, not enclosed within the narrow warrant of her gifts, but freely ranging only within the zodiac of his own wit.
>
> Nature never set forth the earth in so rich tapestry as divers poets have done; neither with pleasant rivers, fruitful sweet-smelling flowers, nor whatsoever else may make the too much loved earth more lovely. Her world is brazen, the poets only deliver a golden.
>
> (p. 100)

The motive for connecting this golden world to Platonic Ideas, or to Augustinian illumination that grants "an apprehension of the reality of things," is succinctly stated by Panofsky in his discussion of the sixteenth-century revival of Neoplatonism:

> The Idea was reinvested with its apriori and metaphysical character . . . the autocratic human mind, now conscious of its own spontaneity, believed that it could maintain this spontaneity in the face of sensory experience only by legitimizing the former *sub specie divinitatis*; the dignity of genius, now explicitly recognized and emphasized, is justified by its origin in God.[3]

Italian critics, as we have seen, often turned to such justifications, and Sidney seems to need them as well. Like the Neoplatonists before him, he praises the poet as a creator "freely
ranging only within the zodiac of his own wit," independent
of nature and of any given subject matter. The poet does not
derive "conceit out of a matter, but maketh matter for a conceit" (p. 120). In the *Apology*, however, Sidney tends to regard
the protection the Platonic-Augustinian argument would afford as part of a voice that he self-consciously affects, and a
voice he asks us to think about critically.

Sidney's discussion of poetic inspiration, for example, is deliberately tangled and ambivalent. He starts by examining the
Roman term for poet, *vates*: he translates this "heavenly" title
as "diviner, forseer, or prophet" and says that the Romans attributed the power of prophecy to Virgil. Sidney then gives us
two contradictory reactions to this information. First he condemns the Romans for their "vain and godless superstition"
(p. 98), and then he tells us they were "altogether not without
ground." He softens his criticisms because "that same exquisite
observing of number and measure in words, and that high
flying liberty of conceit proper to the poet, did seem to have
some divine force in it" (p. 99). The poet, then, is not really
inspired; his heavenly and divine nature is at best metaphorical.
It is an illusion, but an understandable one, based on verbal
artifice and the "high flying liberty of conceit." The irony is
clear: inspiration is not the *cause* of the poet's conceit but the
effect that the conceit has on the reader.[4]

Where Sidney does mention poets who were truly inspired
by God (David, Solomon, et al.), he is careful to set them apart
from "right poets," his subject.[5] He makes so many motions
in distinguishing these right poets from philosophical and historical poets (those who follow a "proposed subject" instead
of their own "invention") that another distinction is easily
missed.[6] It can, however, be deduced easily enough, and it is
equally important to his argument. Sidney is interested in a

poetic grounded in the human mind, and inspiration would compromise its autonomy. As Sidney tells us later, Plato in his *Ion* "attributeth unto Poesy more than myself do, namely, to be a very inspiring of a divine force, far above man's wit" (p. 130).

Sidney's use of metaphysics can be deceptive. Though he uses its terms to praise the poet's creativity, he then dismisses them before they can compromise the mind's autonomy. The same pattern recurs immediately after the *vates* discussion, when Sidney turns to the word *poet*: "It cometh of this word *poiein*, which is 'to make.'" Sidney's use of Greek etymology, like Landino's, serves as an occasion to honor the poet, and Sidney follows with the previously quoted celebration of poetry's golden world and the poet's creation of a new nature. Sidney then defends his claims:

> Neither let it be deemed too saucy a comparison to balance the highest point of man's wit with the efficacy of Nature; but rather give right honour to the heavenly Maker of that maker, who having made man to His own likeness, set him beyond and over all the works of that second nature: which in nothing he showeth so much as in Poetry, when with the force of a divine breath he bringeth things forth far surpassing her doings, with no small argument to the incredulous of that first accursed fall of Adam: since our erected wit maketh us know what perfection is, and yet our infected will keepeth us from reaching unto it.
>
> (p. 101)

Man's position is a gift of God, and he is fitted into a hierarchical series of makers, beginning with God, who surpasses him, and concluding with nature, which he surpasses. But if the gift explains man's capacity, it does not control his use of it, nor bind it to the fixed order of things. After his ironic reading of the superstitious *vates* argument, Sidney invokes the poet's "divine breath" with a self-conscious sense of its status as metaphor, referring to man's own efforts as he brings forth his own creations, echoing only obliquely Scaliger's claim that man "transforms himself into a second deity."[7] Nor is there a clear graduation from the mind's operations to a transcendental source. Sidney's "highest point of man's wit" is *not* a mystical *apex mentis* directly sparked by the divine. It is the faculty that creates fictions, the faculty that creates another nature and so reveals our divinity to ourselves. In order to demonstrate "erected wit," we must be "lifted up with the vigour of [our] own invention" (p. 100). We know our Ideas, not by tracing them back to an eternal Logos, but by making them "manifest, by delivering them forth in such excellency as [we have] imagined them" (p. 101).

Furthermore, the above quotation on the hierarchy of makers is a defense of one possible metaphor—an attempt to show that it is not "too saucy." After his magnificent praise of the erected wit, Sidney tells us that "these arguments will by few be understood, and by fewer granted. Thus much (I hope) will be given me, that the Greeks with some probability of reason gave him the name above all names of learning" (p. 101). He pulls us up with a reminder that the passage is something of an indulgence, a voice he has assumed in order to sound out certain attractive, if abstruse, arguments. He is not concerned with proving their validity, and he neither affirms nor denies them to those who will not grant them. He is satisfied, rather, with showing that the Greek name displays "some probability of reason." Indeed, the argument for the poet as maker is not so much a justification of the wit as a demonstration of it. It is a bold "comparison," which, according to Aristotle and Renaissance rhetoricians, is a prime way of exhibiting wit.[8]

Sidney's discussion of the fore-conceit, or Idea, then, may remind us of Neoplatonic art theory, but its orientation is closer to Cusanus's art of conjecture. The mind's highest capacity, like Cusanus's *intellectus*, may suggest an intuitive leap to a higher unity, but it always return us to the mind's active fashioning. The metaphysical terms of the *Apology*, like the elaborate schemata of *De coniecturis*, must be pictured as lying within, rather than outside of, the sphere of human making.

MANY CYRUSES

If the poet is "lifted up with the vigour of his own invention," so, too, is the reader. Poetry, as its humanist defenders often tell us, is the best teacher, the "first light-giver to ignorance," and the first study to show us the "pleasure in the exercises of the mind" (pp. 96, 98). The separation of the Idea from a fixed ontology, moreover, makes poetry a special kind of exercise. In a fascinating article, A. E. Malloch argues that, for Sidney, it is only in poetry that reason finds an object properly proportioned to its capacities. But Malloch sees this in a Thomist light: the fallen world is deficient, whereas poetry's golden world reveals a "fullness of being" that fully actualizes the act of cognition.[9] I would argue, on the contrary, that the poetic object is best proportioned to our reason because that object is a projection of our reason. Jacopo Mazzoni made this very argument in Italy only a few years after the *Apology* was written. The object of poetic imitation is one that is consciously framed to fit the poet's intellectual needs.[10]

The more autonomous the poet's Idea becomes, however, the more insistent the need to attach it to something outside itself. And if a metaphysical foundation is problematic, then a practical and ethical application becomes all-important. The function of poetry is to reform the will, as well as to perfect the wit, since "no learning is so good as that which teacheth and moveth to virtue" (p. 123). Using a suggestive pun, Sidney writes: "The poet . . . doth draw the mind more effectually than any other art doth" (p. 115). The poet both depicts the mind and leads it to action. And this brings us to the second part of Sidney's theory, that poetry is justified not only by the brilliance of the Idea but by the way it works in the world, bestowing a "Cyrus upon the world to make many Cyruses."

Sidney echoes the rhetorical interpretation of poetry, and following Minturno's transference of Cicero's "teach, delight, and move" from the orator to the poet, he writes that poets "imitate both to delight and teach: and delight to move men to take that goodness in hand" (p. 103). Poetry's rhetorical address to the reader, however, is shaped by Sidney's radical conception of the poet's Idea, and the result is a discussion of didacticism that brings to the surface the intrinsic difficulties of such justifications.

Sidney approaches this discussion by pretending to moderate a dispute between the educative claims of philosophy and history, only to carry the prize away for poetry. A philosopher claims that by teaching what virtue is, his discipline makes clear "how it extendeth itself out of the limits of a man's own little world to the government of families, and maintaining of public societies" (p. 105). Sidney objects that the philosopher never extends himself. He is trapped within the closed world of his fellow philosophers: "The philosopher teacheth, but he teacheth obscurely, so as the learned only can understand him; that is to say, he teacheth them that are already taught" (p. 109). Sidney later parodies the circularity of such discourse: "Nay truly, learned men have learnedly thought that where once reason hath so much overmastered passion as that the mind hath a free desire to do well, the inward light each mind hath in itself is as good as a philosopher's book; seeing in nature we know it is well to do well" (p. 113). The learned learnedly discuss how it is well to do well, but their terms only point to themselves: "Happy is that man who may understand him, and more happy that can apply what he doth understand" (p. 107). The same charge reappears indirectly, if a bit more cruelly, during a later discussion of love: "Some of my masters the philosophers spent a good deal of their lamp-oil in setting forth the excellency of it" (p. 125). Lamp oil, Sidney suggests, is all a philosopher usually "spends" in love. The philosopher fails in teaching and seduction because his definitions "lie dark before the imaginative and judging power, if they be not illuminated or figured forth by the speaking picture of poesy" (p. 107).

If philosophy gives us reason devoid of external application, history poses an opposite extreme, for it is circumscribed by the world of experience, one devoid of any perceivable rationality. The historian is "bound to tell things as things were" and "cannot be liberal . . . of a perfect pattern" (p. 110):

> The historian, being captived to the truth of a foolish world, is many times a terror from well-doing, and an encouragement to unbridled wickedness.
>
> For see we not valiant Miltiades rot in his fetters? the just Phocion and the accomplished Socrates put to death like traitors? the cruel Severus live prosperously?
>
> (pp. 111–12)

Not only is the historian's world one of moral chaos, but history, in recording it, lacks logical coherence. His example "draweth no necessary consequence," and so he follows the logic of "because it rained yesterday, therefore it should rain to-day" (pp. 107, 110). The historian cannot understand the nature of examples and how the mind uses them,

> but if he know an example only informs a conjectured likelihood, and so go by reason, the poet doth so far exceed him as he is to frame his example to that which is most reasonable . . . where the historian in his bare *was* . . . must tell events whereof he can yield no cause; or, if he do, it must be poetical.
>
> (p. 110)

The poet knows that the mind must work through conjectures, that examples can lead only to "a conjectured likelihood." Thus the poet is freed from imitating things as they have been, the "bare *was*," and may concentrate, instead, on the modes of understanding themselves, the lines of connection or consequence the mind attempts to draw in making sense out of the world. His examples are framed according "to that which is most reasonable," rather than any external *res*. It is of small importance that the historian can boast that he brings us "images of true matters, such as indeed were done, and not such as fantastically or falsely may be suggested to have been done" (p. 109), for he knows better "how this world goeth than how his own wit runneth" (p. 105). The poet, by contrast, having no law but wit, can frame examples into purified types of moral ideals: "If the poet do his part aright, he will show you in Tantalus, Atreus, and such like, nothing that is not to be shunned; in Cyrus, Aeneas, Ulysses, each thing to be followed" (p. 110).

The argument, as Sidney notes, is based on Aristotle: poetry is more philosophical than history because it deals "with *Katholou* . . . the universal consideration" (p. 109). Italian critics often fortified Aristotle's universal by associating it with Platonic exemplars, and it is sometimes suggested that Sidney follows their lead. The golden reshaping of the world, like the "Idea" argument, does echo Neoplatonic claims. Ficino writes, for example: "What, then, does the intellect seek if not to transform all things into itself by depicting all things in the intellect according to the nature of the intellect? . . . the universe, in a certain manner, should become intellect."[11] But again, Sidney both appeals to metaphysical claims and refuses their protection. After his ridiculing of philosophers, we cannot leap so adroitly to fixed and timeless exemplars. Nor did Aristotle, as Sidney's cagey circularity suggests: Aristotle's "reason . . . is most full of reason." A closer philosophical analogue to Sidney's "universal consideration" is the Cusan conjecture. The latter, as we have seen, is the mind's response to the unknowable, whether the hidden God or a world without apprehensible quiddities and fixed points; the mind turns to its purest forms of thought, usually mathematics, and projects them outward in a display of its own fecundity. Sidney's "highest point of man's wit" may not produce mathematical forms, but its poetic fictions fulfill a parallel function: the poet's wit is lifted up with the vigor of its own invention.[12] The poet faces a brazen world of moral disorder, which snares the historian in its senselessness, but delivers back a golden world, another nature structured by his mind.

Sidney's justification for such invention is not ontological authority but didactic efficacy. If we look back to the Idea/Cyrus passage, we can see how insistently Sidney attempts to join his golden world and didacticism in a bond of dialectical necessity. The poet's fiction, his delivering of the Idea, is "not wholly imaginative, as we are wont to say by them that build castles in the air; but so far substantially it worketh, not only to make a Cyrus, which had been but a particular excellency as Nature might have done, but to bestow a Cyrus upon the world, to make many Cyruses" (p. 101). Moreover, the poet's effect on the world is as important to the poet as it is to the world he affects. It is the only way he can grant substance to his creations, the only way he can be sure they are not a sign of his estrangement. Like Danielle Barbaro and others, Sidney cautions that eloquent fantasies must be carefully directed to prevent the teacher of the many from becoming the frenzied and solitary builder of "castles in the air."[13]

At crucial junctures in the *Apology*, where Sidney would have found a metaphysical argument most useful, we find, instead, claims for didactic efficacy. Forrest Robinson, in keeping with his argument that the poet has access to absolute patterns, suggests that the fore-conceit is a preverbal mental diagram, which, because of its participation in absolute truth, serves as a universal frame to insure a uniform response in all readers.[14] But when Sidney comes to discuss how this frame works, he tells us simply that when readers of poesy are "looking for fiction, they shall use the narration but as an imaginative ground-plot of a profitable invention" (p. 124). Sidney does not claim that there is any true or universal Idea embodied by, or hidden in, the ground-plot. "Invention" carries its full ambiguity here,[15] and we cannot tell whether the reader comes upon a preestablished meaning or fashions his own, any more than we can be certain that one man's conjectures in Cusanus's universe are the same as another's. All we know is that the "invention" ought to be "profitable." We are not guaranteed a fixed unity between speaker and hearer; the most interpretation can aim for is some ethical utility.

A similar development appears in the icastic/fantastic opposition, so important for Renaissance criticism. As William Rossky has shown, the fear of imaginative distortion was a powerful theme in Renaissance England, and English texts are filled with admonitions to control the imagination.[16] In George Puttenham's *Arte of English Poesie* (1589), a sophisticated understanding of the contingency of cultural norms is chastened by the demand that the mind be fitted to objective truth. Puttenham warns against the "evill and vicious disposition of the braine," which can distort the judgment with "busie and disordered phantasies." Our concepts can become like "false glasses and shew thinges otherwise than they be in deede." Despite his earlier echoes of Sidney that the poet "contrives out of his owne braine" without "any foreine copie or example," Puttenham insists that the orderly imagination must represent things "according to their very truth. If otherwise, then doth it breede Chimeres and monsters in mans imaginations and not only in his imaginations but also in his ordinarie actions and life which ensues." The useful life must be "illuminated with the brightest irradiations of knowledge and of the veritie and due proportion of things."[17]

Sidney, by contrast, avoids such Augustinian metaphysics. More decisively committed to poetic feigning, he welcomes the mind's ability to create such new forms "as never were in Nature, as the Heroes, Demigods, Cyclops, Chimeras, Furies" (p. 100). For him, the icastic/fantastic dichotomy is not an issue of metaphysics but of ethics: "For I will not deny but that man's wit may make Poesy, which should be *eikastike*, which some learned have defined, 'figuring forth good things,' to be *phantastike*, which doth contrariwise infect the fancy with unworthy objects" (p. 125). There is no question here of approximating an image to an external model, of a faithful likeness being opposed to a mere semblance. For Sidney, as for Mazzoni (who places the fantastic over the icastic), this approximation has become too restrictive. But instead of reversing the distinction, Sidney redefines it: "good" and "unworthy" are purely ethical. Thomas Wright was to warn his English audience in 1605 that the distorted imagination "putteth greene spectacles before the eyes of the witte, to make it see nothing but greene."[18] But for Sidney, as for Cusanus, one can never take away the spectacles. All cognition implies some filtering or refraction; we can only hope to control the lenses we use.

But what is the basis of this control? Sidney admits that man's wit can produce irresponsible poetry, and hopes by this admission to answer those who see poetry as a corrupting influence: we should "not say that Poetry abuseth man's wit, but that man's wit abuseth Poetry" (p. 125). Shifting the blame closes one problem, but it opens a larger one. For poetry depends on the wit, it is born in the fore-conceit, and the poet follows no law but wit. Without a direct argument of inspiration or illumination, how can we be sure the light-giving poet himself has the proper light? What is the foundation for his claims? Some critics, borrowing from the rhetorical tradition, argue that the good poet must also be a good man, but this only begs the question.

Sidney's double justification—through the fore-conceit and through didacticism—proves to be doubly problematic. Both are traditionally founded on metaphysics, but Sidney wants to justify poetry without recourse to such support. The poetic "Idea" points to perfection by pointing back to itself; like Cusanus's conjectures, it justifies itself by repeating the act of creation. The other side of the argument, the attempt to translate poetic effects into moral ones, is pursued with perhaps even greater urgency. Sidney would very much like to present poetry as an instrument of the moral, active life, but the very process of making the argument exposes its gaps; indeed, it appears to face a dilemma similar to that of the Idea. Wimsatt alerts us to the problem:

> Sidney, like most of those who have maintained that poetry is (and ought to be) moral, has not been able to resolve an ambiguity of the word ought as used in the formula. Is this a poetic "ought," or is it in fact only a moral "ought"? In the second sense, "ought to be moral" is a tautology—since moral is what all our works ought to be.[19]

The easiest way out for Sidney would have been to repeat Boccaccio's claims for the unity of poetry and theology, or to claim some metaphysical universal at work, as did many who propped up their interpretation of Aristotle's "ought" as a moral term. As Sidney's argument stands, it verges on telling us that poetry ought to be what it ought to be, and like the moral philosophers he parodies, Sidney finds his terms pointing back to themselves.

THE POET NOTHING AFFIRMS

One of the reasons there is such difficulty on both sides of the justification is the paradoxical nature of the poetic fictions that lie between them. Unlike some rhetorical critics who argue that the poet derives true conclusions from false elements, Sidney tells us that the poet

> nothing affirms, and therefore never lieth. For, as I take it, to lie is to affirm that to be true which is false; so as the other artists, and especially the historian, affirming many things can, in the cloudy knowledge of mankind, hardly escape from many lies. But the poet (as I said before) never affirmeth. The poet never maketh any circles about your imagination to conjure you to believe for true what he writes.
>
> (pp. 123–24)

Insisting on the fictional nature of poetry, Sidney argues that its essential feature is the poet's "feigning," "not rhyming and versing" (p. 103).[20] Poetry inhabits a special realm of discourse, one that, like Mazzoni's idols, eludes the strict laws of verification. While Sidney's claim is not unique in the Renaissance, the route by which he arrives at his claim, and the consequences he draws from it, have an important effect on the way we read the *Apology* as a whole and lead us to a more general sense of what all discourse implies for Sidney.

As he explores conventional categories and their limits, Sidney's procedure again resembles that of Cusanus, who is forever testing the coincidence of opposites by attempting to reconcile curvature and straightness, potentiality and actuality. Cusanus also submits personifications of competing cultural ideals—the philosopher and the humanist orator—to the scrutiny of the conjecturing *idiota*, a craftsman who creates forms that never were in nature. Sidney does not deal with the same kinds of puzzles, but his poetic fictions are likewise the result of a coincidence of opposites. The poet fuses the two extremes of the philosopher and the historian as he "coupleth the general notion with the particular example." Poetry is clearly *not* an Aristotelian mean between them, as some Italian theorists reckoned it on a scale of abstractions.[21] Sidney includes both extremes within the synthesis, which gives rise to a distinct mode of discourse, one that he claims surpasses the limits of its rivals. It is, in a sense, more abstract than metaphysics, because it is completely free from nature, unlike the "metaphysic, though it be in the second and abstract notions, and therefore be counted supernatural, yet doth he indeed build upon the depth of Nature" (p. 100). At the same time, it is more concrete than history, since its speaking pictures and shining images are able to instruct and move men immediately.

Neither Sidney nor Cusanus argues for the final sufficiency of conjecture or fiction, but both suggest that all human attempts to make sense out of the world must deal with the conditions of human apprehension. Cusanus tells us in *De docta ignorantia* that previous philosophers erred in their understanding of the nature of things because of their adherence to the illusion that their systems precisely represented some fixed structure. The doctrine of learned ignorance does not free men from the dilemma of representation but brings them to recognize its inevitability, allowing them to manipulate it consciously. The conjectural art, then, becomes a way of rejecting the constraints of both affirmative and negative ways. Sidney continually suggests such paradoxes; indeed, having released the "right poet" from the burden of affirming, he drives the paradox even further than does Cusanus. Poetry is only a special instance of the fictionality that pervades all discourse. The most casual observation shows that other disciplines use fictions to enhance their effectiveness: lawyers use such fictitious names as "John a Stile" and "John a Noakes" in their cases for the sake of making "their picture the more lively," and chess players call a piece of wood a bishop. So, too, historians, despite their claims of truthfulness, still give "many particularities of battles, which no man could affirm" and invent "long orations," which historical figures never pronounced (p. 97).

In a profounder sense, any attempt at rational communication leads to fiction making. Our only choice is whether or not to acknowledge the pretense. So the historian is described as "loaden with old mouse-eaten records, authorising himself (for the most part) upon other histories, whose greatest authorities are built upon the notable foundation of hearsay." Any art that purports to rest on the foundation of external verities finds that its support quickly disintegrates. Even those who go beyond books to nature find themselves in this vertiginous plight: "There is no art delivered to mankind that hath not the works of Nature for his principal object, without which they could not consist, and on which they so depend, as they become actors and players, as it were, of what Nature will have set forth" (pp. 99–100). They pretend to "follow nature" but find themselves on a stage, their words turned into players' lines, their deeds transformed into mere theatrics.

A. C. Hamilton has argued that Sidney's paradox is borrowed from Agrippa's skeptical attack on the vanity of human studies.[22] However much we attribute to Agrippa's influence, whether on the basis of his mocking tone or of his argument that nothing can be affirmed, it is clear that Sidney carries the skeptical argument to its conclusion, that our only access to reality is through fiction and conjecture. As Montaigne writes: "Have I not seen this divine saying in Plato, that Nature is nothing but an aenigmaticall poesie? As a man might say, an overshadowed and darke picture, inter-shining with an infinit varietie of false lights, to exercise our conjecture . . . philosophy is nothing else but a sophisticated poesie."[23] Sidney would object, however, that the only real "poesie" is poetic making itself. It is the greatest of the arts because it is the only one to realize that it is not anchored to a fixed and objective truth. Like Cusanus, Sidney does not let this realization force him back to a passive fideism: the poet recognizes the necessity of conjecture and so boldly sets about inventing his own.

This claim inevitably doubles back to affect the status of the *Apology*. If the only choice is between those who naively entertain fictions and those who act their own, then Sidney, as the speaker of the *Apology*, makes it clear that he thinks of himself as one of the latter.

At the beginning of the *Apology*, Sidney tells us that he is following the example of John Pietro Pugliano, the master horseman and self-promoter, and that in order to defend his own craft, poetry, he needs "to bring some more available proofs." He is alluding to Aristotle's definition of rhetoric as the "faculty of observing in any given case, the available means of persuasion," and so is signaling us that he is about to adopt the role of rhetorician. Kenneth Myrick's book on Sidney helps us to see how self-conscious an actor Sidney is, as he closely models his work after the "judicial oration in behalf of an accused client." Furthermore, Sidney seems to remind us continually of the role he is playing. As Myrick demonstrates, Sidney not only follows the seven-part form of an oration as he found it described by Thomas Wilson but does so in elaborate detail, following the recommended subject matter and style for each section and even marking the transitions between them with conspicuous phrases.[24]

This is a fitting role for Sidney, considering the highly rhetorical role he imagines for poetry. But the paradox thickens when we realize that Sidney is playing not only the rhetorician but the poet as well. He tells us at the start that he has slipped into the title of poet, and he often demonstrates the appropriateness of that title in the *Apology*. After describing poetry as "feigning notable images of virtues, vices, or what else," Sidney proceeds to feign notable images of the poet's competitors, including the moral philosophers, whom he envisions approaching him "with a sullen gravity," and the historian, staggering under a load of mouse-eaten records. Before they have a chance to speak, Sidney gives us a notable image of them as hypocrites and buffoons and, in the process, characterizes himself as one who acts out his own theories.

Sidney leads us to recognize his arguments for his craft as examples of his craft by showing us that they are in the same realm of discourse, the realm of feigned images and self-conscious conjectures. I have already mentioned the discussion of the poet as maker as a kind of conjecture. Later, during a crucial argument with those who claim that fictions are mere daydreams or toys, Sidney counters, "If to a slight conjecture a conjecture may be opposed, truly it may seem, that as by him [Homer] their learned men took almost their first light of knowledge, so their active men received their first motions of courage" (p. 127).

There are, of course, advantages to adopting this role. Sidney can demonstrate the persuasive force of poetry even as he describes it. And by treating his arguments as conjectures, he can arrange a variety of them without strict regard for consistency. He presents us with "something for everyone," aiming different claims at different readers, hoping that all will find something to serve as "an imaginative ground-plot of a profitable invention." We often find, in fact, running counter to what I have described as the central theory, the testing of more conservative possibilities, aimed at those who may be unhappy with the more daring claims for the poet's creativity. We can see this, for example, in the notion of poetic "fitness."[25]

Early in the *Apology*, when praising the poet's creativity, Sidney argues for the peculiar "reverse adequation" found in critics such as Mazzoni. The mind does not fit its concepts to externals but, rather, invents forms to fit its own faculties. Poets are like painters, who, "having no law but wit, bestow that in colours upon you which is fittest for the eye to see" (p. 102). If verse is used in poetry, so much the better, because of the "fitness it hath for memory" (p. 122). But later, when discussing stage productions, Sidney moves far away from the freedom of Mazzoni's idols and closer to the unimaginative literalness of Castelvetro. Unity of place is essential because no audience could believe a rapid change of location. Playwrights are attacked for being too "liberal" with time as well. There must be a correspondence between the imitation and the action imitated. The play should be "fitted to the time it set forth" (p. 134).

These reversals are not restricted to specific questions of dramaturgy. At one moment the poets are free of the works of nature, not enclosed by its "narrow warrant"; at another, they must rely on the "force truth hath in nature," and their proper effects are endangered if the matter is "disproportioned to ourselves and nature" (p. 136). We may even suspect that Sidney is allowing himself to act out his own ambivalence about the poet's "high flying liberty of conceit." Late in the *Apology*, Sidney tells us that "the highest-flying wit [must] have a Daedalus to guide him," and that this Daedalus has three wings, "Art, Imitation, and Exercise": "Exercise indeed we do, but that very fore-backwardly: for where we should exercise to know, we exercise as having known; and so is our brain delivered of much matter which never was begotten by knowledge" (p. 133). Sidney more strictly regulates the poet with a firmer objective orientation. The next sentence, in fact, complains, "For there being two principal parts—matter to be expressed by words and words to express the matter—in neither we use Art or Imitation rightly" (p. 133). Sidney does not openly contradict his earlier idealistic claim that the poet "bringeth his own stuff, and doth not learn a conceit out of a matter, but maketh matter for a conceit" (p. 120), but he is clearly suggesting a safer *res/verba* distinction, as used by the Horatian critics to direct poetry outward.[26]

Sidney can take these liberties because of the manifestly conjectural nature of the *Apology*.[27] But his retreat to more conservative themes does not solve his dilemmas; rather, their conjectural status serves only to remind us of those dilemmas. The claim that poetry neither affirms nor denies may not be unique in the Renaissance, but the suggestion that one's own defense of poetry follows the same pattern forces into question the very possibility of making such a defense.

Sidney's theory requires that he take an affirmative stand somewhere, that he find some first premise from which to deduce his conclusions. Sidney himself makes this need explicit by reducing his argument to a syllogism:

> If it be, as I affirm, that no learning is so good as that which teacheth and moveth to virtue, and that none can both teach and move thereto so much as Poetry, then is the conclusion manifest that ink and paper cannot be to a more profitable purpose employed.
>
> (p. 123)

Sidney makes this statement just after he has given a lesson in logic to the poet-haters, laughing at their argument that "doth (as they say) but *petere principium*" (p. 123). But immediately after his own argument, he undermines the clause on which the entire syllogism rests, "I affirm." For it is here that he chooses to place the already-quoted passage on how the poet "never affirmeth," unlike the others who, "affirming many things, can, in the cloudy knowledge of mankind, hardly escape from many lies" (p. 124). Even as he points out the logical mistakes of his opponents, Sidney seems to be deliberately committing his own, making *any* first premise impossible and so exposing himself to an inevitable infinite regress. To put the matter more simply, if the best the mind can accomplish is conjecture, then its justification is also a conjecture.

Sidney reminds us of this problem in the *peroratio*, or conclusion:

> I conjure you all that have had the evil luck to read this ink-wasting toy of mine, . . . to believe, with Aristotle, that they were the ancient treasurers of the Grecians' divinity; to believe, with Bembus, that they were first bringers-in of all civility; to believe, with Scaliger, that no philosopher's precepts can sooner make you an honest man than the reading of Virgil; to believe, with Clauserus, the translator of Cornutus, that it pleased the heavenly Deity, by Hesiod and Homer, under the veil of fables, to give us all knowledge, Logic, Rhetoric, Philosophy natural and moral, and *quid non?*; to believe, with me, that there are many mysteries contained in Poetry, which of purpose were written darkly, lest by profane wits it should be abused; to believe, with Landino, that they are so beloved of the gods that whatsoever they write proceeds of divine fury; lastly, to believe themselves, when they tell you they will make you immortal by their verses.
>
> (pp. 141–42)

The facetious tone is unmistakable from opening self-deprecation to insistence that we believe the love poet's favorite seduction line. But we also find a summary listing of nearly all the arguments made in the *Apology*, now paraded without distinction. We are conjured to believe arguments that Sidney has made essential—namely, for poetry as a civilizing force and for its didactic efficacy—as well as those he has rejected, such as Landino's claims for poetry as an emanation of divine fury, and those he has deliberately minimized or ignored, such as the view of poetry as a veil of allegory or as a mystery for the initiated. All are brought out like actors at the end of a play, taking their bows.

Sidney cannot expect that his readers will believe so many conflicting points of view, and the lack of distinction among them hurts their credibility. Even his insistence that we do believe them, when he "conjure[s us] . . . to believe," is a self-parody, teasing us with verbal echoes of a previous denial: "The poet never maketh any circles about your imagination, to conjure you to believe for true what he writes."

Myrick, who gives an excellent survey of Sidney's rhetorical strategies, argues that this kind of playfulness adds to the *Apology*'s persuasiveness. It is a sign of Sidney's *sprezzatura*, a "courtly grace which conceals a sober purpose."[28] Sidney does praise the courtier who finds a style "fittest to nature" and who "doth according to art, though not by art," and contrasts him to the pedant who uses "art to show art, and not to hide art" (p. 139). But Sidney is not that courtier. Little is hidden by the style of the *Apology*. His adopted role is announced as an adopted role, and nearly all his persuasive tricks and witty anecdotes are relished as persuasive tricks and demonstrations of wit. We rarely lose sight of the self-conscious fashioning of the *Apology* and cannot forget that Sidney is, in Myrick's terms, a "literary craftsman" constructing a "literary artifact."

It would be tempting to conclude that the *Apology* acts out its own argument, that the work itself moves us through images and fictions while praising the power of poetry to move us through images and fictions. But if this were so, there would be no real argument to act out, only a fiction that neither affirms nor denies, taking as its subject still other fictions. The *Apology* requires another *Apology* to justify it, and so on without end. What the *Apology* does act out are the tensions characteristic of the most adventurous Renaissance thought, whether they appear in the texts of an Elizabethan courtier, an Italian critic, or a German philosopher.

Sidney's friend Hubert Languet had little patience with such protracted ambiguities, and Sidney enjoyed teasing him about it. In his correspondence with the older humanist, Sidney praises the joys of mental exercise: "I am never less a prey to melancholy than when I am earnestly applying the feeble powers of my mind to some high and difficult object."[29] Languet approves of his enthusiasm, but warns him not to spend too much time on studies that do not lead directly to a life of action. He recommends Cicero's letters "not only for the beauty of the Latin but also for the very important matter they contain."[30] But he is guarded about those who practice a double-translation method, turning Latin into a modern language and then closing the book to translate it back again. This exercise in style is considered useful by some, but it smacks too much of what Languet later calls "literary leisure." Sidney responds:

> I intend to follow your advice about composition, thus: I shall first take one of Cicero's letters and turn it into French; then from French into English, and so once more by a sort of perpetual motion . . . it shall come round into Latin again. Perhaps, too, I shall improve myself in Italian by the same exercise.[31]

Like Languet, Sidney wants to direct his learning outward, to energize the will through the wit. As a prospective man of action, Sidney endorses the teleology of mental effort: "It is not *gnosis* but *praxis* must be the fruit." That such a transition can be made is confidently, even aggressively, proclaimed in the *Apology*. But for Sidney, there always seems to be another game to be played by the wit, yet another circuit to be made by its self-circling energies, before it can make that transition.[32]

6

ASTROPHIL'S POETICS

Sidney's sonnet sequence *Astrophil and Stella* presents us with a speaker who has two loves: his distant mistress and his own ingenuity. This double devotion is reflected in the split in critical thinking between those who see the sequence of poems as directed toward an external goal, and those who claim it is a mode of self-scrutiny, a turning inward to the speaker's own wit. Theodore Spencer's important article almost forty years ago argued that Sidney's poetry does both, echoing the "rhythm of thought" for the sake of capturing "this reality, this depth, this pungency."[1] Spencer's synthesis was soon challenged from both sides. C. S. Lewis restricted priority to the subject, insisting that the sequence is a "prolonged lyrical meditation," where "external events" merely "provide themes for the meditation."[2] David Kalstone extends his argument by pointing out that the external plot of the sequence is so conventional, the reader pays his closest attention to the "nimble movements of Astrophel's mind." Astrophil is a "Protean figure" who "seems to be calling attention to his own shifting attitudes."[3] Arguments for objective priority sought to counter this emphasis, not by returning to Spencer's "this reality," but by invoking the rhetorical nature of Astrophil's poems. His *end* is objective, the seduction of Stella, a goal Neil Rudenstine argues "is an objective one: not self-exploration and self-expression as ends in themselves, but the expression of personal feeling for the purposes of rhetorical persuasion."[4]

The critical polarity mirrors an essential and enabling tension in the sequence itself. *Astrophil and Stella* presents the typical Petrarchan configuration—a courtly poet-lover and his distant beloved—in order to focus on the problematic relation between the most self-regarding of speakers and the unattainable object of his desire. The result is a poetic fiction whose versatility and critical self-consciousness surpass anything previously accomplished in Elizabethan poetry. Indeed, Sidney exploits an important feature of sonnet writing that reaches back to Petrarch: a reflexive awareness about the making of poetic fictions.[5] It is that critical dimension that I want to emphasize in this chapter; even as Sidney's most sustained essay of literary criticism engages the processes of poetry, so his great lyric sequence is in important ways a work of criticism. I refer not only to the dozen or so sonnets that deal specifically with problems of style.[6] The sequence as a whole may be read as a counterpart to the *Apology*, for it maps a hypothetical zodiac of the wit, ranging from the joys of poetic invention to the anxieties of poetic collapse.

ASTROPHIL'S IDEA

Sidney's Astrophil introduces himself to us with a brilliant rendering of imaginative self-absorption:

> LOVING in truth, and faine in verse my love to show,
> That the deare She might take some pleasure of my paine:
> Pleasure might cause her reade, reading might make her know,
> Knowledge might pitie winne, and pitie grace obtaine,
>   I sought fit words to paint the blackest face of woe,
> Studying inventions fine, her wits to entertaine:
> Oft turning others' leaves, to see if thence would flow
> Some fresh and fruitfull showers upon my sunne-burn'd braine.
>   But words came halting forth, wanting Invention's stay,
> Invention, Nature's child, fled step-dame Studie's blowes,
> And others' feete still seem'd but strangers in my way.
> Thus great with child to speake, and helplesse in my throwes,
>   Biting my trewand pen, beating my selfe for spite,
>   "Foole," said my Muse to me, "looke in thy heart and write."

The *Apology* may warn that love poets fail through the staleness of their artifice, "coldly . . . apply[ing] fiery speeches" so that their poems lack "forcibleness or *energia*" (p. 138), but this poem has no lack of imaginative heat. The amplitude of its alexandrines, the exuberant, almost gratuitous, displays of wit, and the colloquial bluntness of the Muse banishing tedious predecessors make it one of Sidney's triumphs. And yet it lavishes its energies on itself, on picturing the very process of writing as a struggle against the threat of imaginative failure. The first quatrain proclaims a poetic teleology, the employment of verse as a conduit joining subjective desire and objective fulfillment, yet the outward movement toward "grace" is immediately stalled in the second. The search for proper models of imitation leads to "halting" and helplessness, indeed, to a circling back to the searcher himself. The would-be seducer finds *himself* pregnant—struggling to give birth to the poem— while the chastising Muse awakens him from his reverie only by demanding that he turn his attention yet more purposefully toward his own center, to the image of Stella in his heart.

The speaker first appears before us, then, in his dual role of lover and poet, figured in the punning presence of "feign" within "faine" in the poem's opening line.[7] The realms of fiction and desire must overlap if the poet would "show" his love in verse, transforming love in the very act of revealing it, in order to use its image as a vehicle for actual erotic conquest. The succeeding lines continue to perplex these concerns: impelled by loving, the lover deepens his preoccupation with critical issues. Aristotle's *Poetics* is his *Ars amatoria*. If Aristotle notes that representations of painful and unpleasant things are enjoyable (*Poetics* 1448b), Astrophil hopes a show of love will encourage Stella to "take some pleasure of my pain" (1.2). The logic that follows sets in motion a "marching figure": pleasure leads to reading, reading to knowledge, knowledge to pity, and pity to grace, fulfilling in the space of a single, elaborate rhetorical figure the *Apology*'s program of teaching, delighting, and moving: "To be moved to do that which we know, or to be moved with desire to know, *hoc opus, hic labor est*" (*Apology*, p. 113). Theory gives rise, however, not to execution, but to further elaborations of method. Where does the poet find "fit" terms? What relation does imitation bear to originality? The poem's *energia* springs from its speaker's fascination with these questions: the Rube Goldbergesque mechanics of the first quatrain, the poet's sunburned brain, the childlike Invention fleeing Study's blows, the tripping over "other's feete" are all vivid and comic literalizations of his critical preoccupations.

The persuasion of "the deare She" remains the objective goal, but the entertainments of method—both for the speaker and for us—are never far from center stage. Indeed, the Muse's command in the closing line returns us to the opening paradox of faining and feigning; it is simultaneously a call to sincerity and an activation of the poet's creative faculties.[8] Stella's image is a conceptualized Stella, an analogue to the *Apology*'s Idea or fore-conceit. However Astrophil may reject "poore *Petrarch's* long deceased woes" (15.7), it is that Petrarchan relation between Laura and the poetic laurel that informs his claims; the amatory goal is internalized as the source of poetic genius. Stella is the "ground of all poetical invention" as Ringler phrases it, which allows Astrophil both to flatter her as his sole inspiration—"all the Map of my state I display, / When trembling voice brings forth that I do Stella love" (6.13–14)—and to exult in the vast reaches of psychic territory his love will lead him to figure forth.[9]

It is that territory that Astrophil invokes in sonnet 35:

> WHAT may words say, or what may words not say,
> Where truth it selfe must speake like flatterie?
> Within what bounds can one his liking stay,
> Where Nature doth with infinite agree?
>   What *Nestor's* counsell can my flames alay,
> Since Reason's selfe doth blow the cole in me?
> And ah what hope, that hope should once see day,

Where *Cupid* is sworne page to Chastity?
Honour is honour'd, that thou doest possesse
    Him as thy slave, and now long needy Fame
    Doth even grow rich, naming my *Stella's* name.
Wit learnes in thee perfection to expresse,
    Not thou by praise, but praise in thee is raisde:
    It is a praise to praise, when thou art praisde.

Astrophil's protestations of sincerity—his concern that truth sounds too much like flattery—are at once a witty (and soon to be outrageous) compliment and a means of turning his attention back on his own creative act. Amorous devotion performs the function of the quasi-Platonism of the *Apology*, where the "erected wit maketh us know what perfection is" (p. 101). Praising Stella provokes the poet's free ranging: "Within what bounds can one his liking stay, / Where Nature doth with infinite agree?" "Liking" as affection in line 3 plays against "like" as likening (compare "like" in line 2); there is no limit either to emotion or comparison making. This is the most ambitious of conceits because it is a conceit that would justify all others, an erotic translation of the theological puzzles that so exercise thinkers like Cusanus: Stella's glory is treated as if it were infinite, and so she is at once beyond all finite utterance and is the inspiration for limitless metaphors about her. She sets in motion the unending dialectic of negative and affirmative love-theologies: "What may words say, or what may words not say" (1.1). At once beyond all terms and the ground of all terms, she cannot truly be honored or praised; rather, honor is honored and praise is praised by the mere fact of being predicated of her. Even as language threatens to collapse into paradoxical self-reference in the final line ("a praise to praise, when thou art praisde"), the one privileged name in the verbal universe revives it and opens it toward infinity.[10]

Astrophil, it is true, thumbs his nose at idealizing poets throughout the sequence, echoing the *Apology*'s rejection of inspiration "far above man's wit" (*Apology*, p. 130)—"Let daintie wits crie on the Sisters nine, / That bravely maskt, their fancies may be told" (*Astrophil and Stella*, sonnet 3)—and later reduces the "Poets' furie," as C. S. Lewis remarks, to the quacking of a duck: "But (God wot) wot not what they meane by it" (sonnet 74).[11] Nonetheless, the love theology of sonnet 35 is important; as in the *Apology*, Platonic idealism becomes a metaphor for human fecundity, even as Sidney dismisses its metaphysical pretensions. And again, this denial of metaphysics leaves the mind's proliferating fancies in a most ambiguous position. Neoplatonic love psychology points the inner image toward higher truths, but in sonnet 35, fusion gives way to disjunction. Teasing suggestions of a unifying circuit in lines 6 and 8 as Reason blows desire's coals and Cupid ascends to chastity encircle the hopeless speaker in line 7, who is left facing the gap between his increasing desire and a retreating object.

It is, in fact, the experience of disjunction that becomes central to the sequence as Astrophil maps his state, a disjunction figured not merely in his lamented distance from Stella, but in his distrust of accustomed social and cultural contexts, particularly those modes of discourse that would rationalize or mediate desire. Once the Muse speaks in the opening sonnet, he dismisses in rapid succession traditional love psychology (sonnet 2), poetic predecessors (sonnet 3), the chastisements of Virtue (sonnets 4 and 5), and traditional poetic tropes (sonnet 6). He seems at times to step before us as a poetic embodiment of the Burckhardtian individual, emerging from the corporate, generalizing categories of the past.[12] The fact that Astrophil also exploits convention, as has often been noted, does not cancel the point: his successive denials and affirmations force us to be constantly alert to the potentially arbitrary nature of convention and to his ingenious manipulations of it.

Yet even as we attend to this self being shaped in and against language, we are disturbed by the anxious expressions of regret that seem to compromise its declarations of autonomy. Astrophil admits to self-deception and tells us he is painting his hell in sonnet 2; he is exhausted by the internal struggle of will and wit in sonnet 4. The experience of loving releases his poetic ingenuity, but only by disrupting the smooth course of his life, turning the familiar and the stable into the alien and the fragmentary. He has only the "remnant" of his wit and laments his "partiall lot" and "lost libertie" (sonnet 2). He accuses himself of fantastic self-indulgence: "My youth doth waste, my knowledge brings forth toyes, / My wit doth strive those passions to defend" (sonnet 18). He rues the defeat of his "Great expectation" (sonnet 21), and fears, less a struggle between the erected wit and the infected will, than the transformation of wit itself into an agent of desire: "My best wits still their own disgrace invent" (sonnet 19). Indeed, his ingenious sophistries throughout the sequence demonstrate this transformation; reason, as Hamlet would say, panders will: "Reason thou kneel'dst, and offeredst straight to prove / By reasons good, good reason her to love" (sonnet 10). The faculty that should stand outside of and direct the self-in-action is increasingly implicated in the windings of desire, as if caught in a circular trap: "My young mind marde, whom Love doth windlas so" (sonnet 21).

It is, however, this very struggle—the drama of Astrophil's uncertainty—that most fully establishes the speaker's interiority. David Kalstone and Robert Montgomery provide excellent characterizations. Astrophil performs a "series of rather troubled and self-conscious gestures," writes Kalstone. His "role is one of sustained alertness" that never allows us "to rest with an attitude, a gesture"; he "appears to be involved in perpetual conflict, perpetual motion." For Montgomery, the sequence "defines itself as a dramatic, immediate expression of a mind in the act of thinking and feeling; the verse is psychologically vital and internally revealing. . . . Behind the style of the sequence . . . is a spirit driven by skepticism."[13] Astrophil's skeptical self-consciousness is never more in evidence than when he turns his very interiority, the mounting pressure of subjective experience, into yet another of his dramatized poses. In response to a friend's warning that desire leads to a dissolution of self ("Desire / Doth plunge my wel-form'd soule even in the mire / Of sinfull thoughts"; sonnet 14, lines 6–8), Astrophil mythologizes himself as a suffering Prometheus ("who first stale downe the fire") whose tormenting love signals the fashioning of a yet greater self ("maners frame," "staid with truth," "readie of wit," and so on). But the most conspicuous feature of the self that is fashioned is that it seems always in the process of *being* fashioned. Its energies seek expression in the poems' ever-changing rhetorical texture, which records the transformation of a poetic Proteus, by turns imploring, teasing, tormented, sarcastic, impudent, aggressive, and guilt-ridden.

It is this agitated and dynamic sense of self that informs the poet-lover's perceptions and which Sidney unleashes on the world of social, ethical, and aesthetic norms. In sonnet 5, Astrophil confronts the tenets of Christian humanism, in which he is undoubtedly educated:

> It is most true, that eyes are form'd to serve
> The inward light: and that the heavenly part
> Ought to be king, from whose rules who do swerve,
> Rebels to Nature, strive for their owne smart.
>   It is most true, what we call *Cupid's* dart,
> An image is, which for our selves we carve;
> And, fooles, adore in temple of our hart,
> Till that good God make Church and Churchman starve.
>   True, that true Beautie Vertue is indeed,
> Whereof this Beautie can be but a shade,
> Which elements with mortall mixture breed:
> True, that on earth we are but pilgrims made,
>   And should in soule up to our countrey move:
>   True, and yet true that I must *Stella* love.

The poem first sketches a coherent network of truths and analogies that provide a clear moral hierarchy of human activity, a system that yokes right reason's inner light to heaven and king-ship and denies a place to the questionable activity in which the speaker is now engaged: the idolatry of self-carved images. As Tasso reminds Mazzoni, so Astrophil reminds himself: "An idol," according to St. Paul, "is nothing."

And yet, the ascent from the shadows in the sestet is halted by one further, and irreconcilable, truth: "I must *Stella* love." Kalstone notes the "accelerated repetition of 'true' (twice in the octave, five times in the sestet)" that questions the status of the poem's many truths as "Sidney toys with the word's meaning." The first thirteen lines present what appears to be a seamless world-view until the presence of an anomaly unsettles it. The final line does not destroy the paradigm, but its perspective sets the rest at an angle, forcing us to regard the poem's previous truths *as* a paradigm, still self-consistent but no longer all-en-compassing. "True, and yet true" uncovers a fissure in Astro-phil's universe, which widens in sonnet 71 when Stella herself, the "fairest booke of Nature," comes to embody the world of ethical norms. The unstable coexistence of abstract and per-sonal truth implied by "and" in sonnet 5 gives way to the vio-lence of "but" when Stella seeks to "bend love to good": " 'But ah,' Desire still cries, 'give me some food' " (sonnet 71, line 14), which threatens "to bring a carefully created structure toppling to the ground."[14]

While Astrophil's wit is most conspicuous in its discovery of gaps and discontinuities, it also assumes a constructive role. Astrophil cultivates a stance of isolation in order to shape a new perspective on his former associates.[15] He presents himself in "abstracted guise" in sonnet 27 and shrewdly exploits that dis-tance to view his fellow courtiers as "them that would make speech of speech," gossips dedicated to a world of *verba non res*. They return in sonnet 30 as "busie wits" who babble endlessly about the political affairs of the day. Courtly ladies fare no bet-ter, becoming "chatring Pies" who cannot understand him be-cause he does not playact according to prescribed codes of behavior (sonnet 54). This distinction Astrophil draws between himself and the others is close to the spirit of the *Apology*; not between a realist and fantasists, but between those who unthinkingly live in a fictive world and the one who self-consciously, and wittily, forges his own.[16] Astrophil turns the world into a metaphor of his passion, a screen against which to project amatory conceits. Accounts of public events and history are rewritten as love stories. Tales of Russia become a simile for his state of mind: "Like slave-born *Muscovite*, / I call it praise to suffer Tyrannie" (sonnet 2, lines 10–11); the Turkish invasions explain why Cupid left Greece and took refuge in Astrophil's heart (sonnet 8); the notorious Edward IV becomes England's greatest monarch because he lost "his Crowne, rather then faile his Love" (sonnet 75, line 14). Even the natural world is transfigured. In the sequence's most famous sonnet, the pale, silent moon becomes a melancholy lover, climbing the skies with "sad steps" (sonnet 31, line 1).[17]

This projection of the self onto the world would assert the potency of feigning against the hopelessness of faining; witty self-indulgence becomes Astrophil's preoccupation, as if its very suppleness and ingenuity granted him control over his world. In sonnet 51, he characterizes a friend's moral disapproval as "grave conceits" and shuts him off by invoking poetic decorum: serious matter is "unsuited" to the "sweet comedie" of love. In sonnet 67, he reads Stella's ambiguous glance as Stella's "eye speech," a "fair text," using the "blushing notes" in her "margine" to bolster his hope. Reading others as if they were texts can, however, work both ways, and in sonnets 28 and 104, Astrophil tries to thwart or minimize other interpreters. The former rejects "allegorie's curious frame," because some would find a subject other than love in his utterance, whereas the latter scornfully admits allegory because those who with "moral notes my hid meaning tears" have only unveiled the obvious, "that I / Do *Stella* love."

The most spectacular effort of literary mastery in the sequence is Astrophil's attempt to move Stella through self-metamorphosis.

> STELLA oft sees the verie face of wo
> Painted in my beclowded stormie face:
> But cannot skill to pitie my disgrace,
> Not though thereof the cause her selfe she know:
> Yet hearing late a fable, which did show
> Of Lovers never knowne, a grievous case,
> Pitie thereof gate in her breast such place
> That, from that sea deriv'd, teares' spring did flow.
> Alas, if Fancy drawne by imag'd things,
> Though false, yet with free scope more grace doth breed
> Then servant's wracke, where new doubts honor brings;
> Then thinke my deare, that you in me do reed
> Of Lover's ruine some sad Tragedie:
> I am not I, pitie the tale of me.
>
> (sonnet 45)

From the opening lines the winding together of emotion and artifice is apparent: "the verie face of wo / Painted in my beclowded stormie face" pretends to be our starting point in actuality but its self-conscious emblematizing and slight hint of a mixed metaphor already forecast the direction of Astrophil's thought. Finding Stella more affected by fables than by his own suffering, Astrophil borrows a page from the *Apology*. The tyrannical mistress may be reached even as the tyrannical Alexander Phaeraeus of the *Apology* was moved; the latter could murder without pity but fled a tragic stage play in tears (*Apology*, p. 118).[18] Stella weeps at "a fable which did show / Of Lovers never knowne, a grievous case." Because her fancy is drawn by "imag'd things, / Though false," Astrophil asserts his own "free scope" by becoming a feigned version of himself: a tale of "Lover's ruine some sad Tragedie."[19]

The ultimate goal may be seduction, yet there is a slightly giddy, even reckless, fascination on Astrophil's part with how far he can carry the paradox of literary courtship. He would be the exultant magician free not only of determined human postures but of reality itself, turning himself into an endless poem. Indeed, he invites Stella, and us, into the infinity of his wit, for if one accepts the offer to read the tale of him, it is to the sonnet sequence itself that one must turn, where, in sonnet 45 one finds the offer to read the tale of him, the sequence *Astrophil and Stella*, and so on without end. This virtuoso performance, however, sounds a darker note. For the final invitation—"I am not I, pitie the tale of me"—forecasts degeneration as well as freedom. "I am not I" subverts the grand Renaissance analogy of the poet and the creating God by pronouncing the uncreating word; "I am that I am" (Exod. 3:14) is parodied through negation. Pressed further and further to find a contrivance that will draw Stella's attention and finally set in motion the first sonnet's marching figure, Astrophil flirts with the act of self-annihilation.

HOC OPUS, HIC LABOR EST

Self-annihilation, at this point, is still only an act, and we would be in good company if we emphasized the joys of feigning embodied thus far. Sidney's sequence not only provoked the craze of sonneteering of the late sixteenth century, but also inspired a new fascination with poetic ingenuity. Michael Drayton is a case in point. His first poetic work grimly assures the reader that he will not be troubled by "devises of mine owne invention, as carieng [carrying] an overweening of mine owne wit." He will read no "Poetical fiction. . . . Not of Vanitie, but of Veritie; not of Tales, but of Truethes."[20] Within three years (1594) Drayton produced a sonnet sequence that begins by invoking the "Divine Syr Phillip" as his inspiration to seek originality ("I am no Pickpurse of anothers wit," he declares in a line ironically lifted from Sir Philip's sonnet 74), and by the

1619 edition of *Idea*, Drayton's speaker introduces himself in the prefatory "To the Reader" as if he were Proteus himself:

> (A Libertine) fantastickly I sing:
> My Verse is the true image of my Mind,
> Ever in motion, still desiring change;
> And as thus to Varietie inclin'd,
> So in all Humors sportively I range.

But while Astrophil would raise ingenuity to seeming omnipotence, fashioning his own erotic golden world, that exuberance never escapes its origin in a severe sense of strain. Astrophil may jettison Platonic metaphysics, but he finds himself psychologically enacting its erotic myth. For the dynamics of Eros, as Plato taught the Renaissance, are the consequence of its mixed parentage; it is the offspring of Plenty (itself the son of Invention or Cunning) and Poverty (*Symposium* 203b). Like the philosopher who finds himself between learning and ignorance, love finds itself always scheming and always lacking (*Symposium* 203e). So, too, is Astrophil, in that intermediary state, drawn to an erotic goal "whose presence absence, absence presence is" (sonnet 60), an uncertain terminus that not only provokes the fluctuations of hope and frustration, but also the sequence's critical dimension. If the *Apology* can free the poet from the charge of building mere "castles in the air" (*Apology*, p. 101) only through his power to move, Stella's absent presence and present absence forces the poet, even as he mounts his witty experiments in *energia*, to question the possibility of poetic efficacy, indeed, of any external thrust whatever:

> COME let me write, "And to what end?" To ease
> A burthned hart. "How can words ease, which are
> The glasses of thy dayly vexing care?"
> Oft cruell fights well pictured forth do please.

"Art not asham'd to publish thy disease?"
  Nay, that may breed my fame, it is so rare:
"But will not wise men thinke thy words fond ware?"
Then be they close, and so none shall displease.
  "What idler thing, then speake and not be hard?"
What harder thing then smart, and not to speake?
Peace, foolish wit, with wit my wit is mard.
Thus write I while I doubt to write, and wreake
  My harmes on Ink's poore losse, perhaps some find
  Stella's great powrs, that so confuse my mind.

                              (sonnet 34)

The sonnet totters between poetry as the means to an outward "end" and poetry as self-enclosure. The act of writing
first unburdens the heart but only to confront it with images
("glasses") of its own cares. Astrophil defensively returns to
the Aristotelian allusion of the first sonnet—poetic representation can make the painful pleasant to behold—and then attempts to spring outward with the hope of poetic fame. But
this movement is also countered by the desire to keep the
poems "close." The dialogue form of the sonnet likewise
echoes this ambivalent movement, creating for a time the illusion of some other voice in Astrophil's world, until the final
line "Peace, foolish wit, with wit my wit is mard" locates the
debate within the self-circling motions of the speaker's mind.

    Sonnet 34 nonetheless ends by turning outward, with the
mind's own confusion, evidenced by the entire poem, standing
as a public symbol of Stella's "great powrs." Sonnet 35 then
enlists the tension between affirmation and negation in the service of poetic proliferation, as we have seen. But both sonnets
are surrounded by dream visions that puzzle and torment the
speaker. In sonnet 32, Morpheus is a "Poet" who shapes Stella's
image from the contents of the dreamer's heart; in sonnet 39,
Astrophil attempts to bribe sleep to release him from his "civill
warres," only to find that the greatest treasure he possesses is
the source of his agitation, "*Stella's* image." Sonnet 38 is a

haunting parody of the zodiac of the wit as dominated by an inaccessible dream:

> THIS night while sleepe begins with heavy wings
> To hatch mine eyes, and that unbitted thought
> Doth fall to stray, and my chiefe powres are brought
> To leave the scepter of all subject things,
> The first that straight my fancie's error brings
> Unto my mind, is *Stella's* image, wrought
> By *Love's* owne selfe, but with so curious drought,
> That she, me thinks, not onely shines but sings.
> I start, looke, hearke, but what in closde up sence
> Was held, in opend sense it flies away,
> Leaving me nought but wailing eloquence:
> I, seeing better sights in sight's decay,
> Cald it anew, and wooed sleepe againe:
> But him her host that unkind guest had slaine.

The mind's freedom, its leaving "the scepter of all subject things," is purchased at the cost of intellectual coherence ("unbitted," "fall to stray," "fancie's error"). A speaking picture appears, which both "shines" and "sings," only to startle the dreamer into so intense an alertness that the condition that made the image possible is destroyed: "what in closde up sence / Was held, in opend sense it flies away." Autonomy becomes an illusion fostered by isolation; the opening of sense leaves the speaker with only "wailing eloquence."

The only true release would be through actual seduction, but Astrophil returns repeatedly to the realization that his poetry is *not* persuading Stella. No matter how sweetly he utters forth the conceits of the mind, Astrophil's goal remains irrevocably distant. In sonnet 44, he complains, "My words I know do well set forth my mind, / . . . Such smart may pitie claime of any hart," but his affective program has broken down: "She heares, yet I no pitty find." Perhaps the fault lies with the hearer?

> I much do guesse, yet find no truth save this,
> That when the breath of my complaints doth tuch
> Those daintie dores unto the Court of blisse,
> The heav'nly nature of that place is such,
>   That once come there, the sobs of mine annoyes
>   Are metamorphosd straight to tunes of joyes.

The elaborate compliment of the conceit also presents an epistemological impasse. Astrophil sees the world through the "lens of love," as Kalstone aptly puts it; will Stella in turn filter all communication, remaking it in her terms? Astrophil has rejected the public world to make her his only audience. Now he may be without even that.

The middle sonnets grow increasingly agitated, stretching the limits of persuasion. Astrophil's quest for *energia* grows desperate, becoming a kind of verbal rape, which would mimic rather than invite sexual action. Woe seeks "thorowest words" and schemes to "find *Stella* alone," for in her unpreparedness her soul's "dainty rind, / Should soon be pierc'd with sharpnesse of the mone" (sonnet 57). Stella proves to be more than a match for Astrophil, parrying his thrust by singing his woeful song as if it were an impersonal court ditty. Sonnet 58 reports the consequence: the force of Astrophil's complaint is reflected back at him. The humanist dream of the orator-as-Hercules, a hero leading his captivated audience in verbal chains, becomes a figure of self-entrapment, of a would-be conqueror caught in his own contrivance:[21]

> DOUBT there hath bene, when with his golden chaine
>   The Oratour so farre men's harts doth bind,
>   That no pace else their guided steps can find,
> But as he them more short or slacke doth raine,
> Whether with words this soveraignty he gaine,
>   Cloth'd with fine tropes, with strongest reasons lin'd,
>   Or else pronouncing grace, wherewith his mind
> Prints his owne lively forme in rudest braine.
>   Now judge by this: in piercing phrases late,
>   Th' anatomy of all my woes I wrate,

> *Stella's* sweete breath the same to me did reed.
> O voice, ô face, maugre my speeche's might,
> Which wooed wo, most ravishing delight
> Even those sad words even in sad me did breed.

He professes delight at the sound of her voice, but must worry, too, that the only mind truly moved by his "fine tropes" and "strongest reasons" is his own.

After sonnet 61, where Stella demands Astrophil forbear all "selfnesse," a series of external events hurries the courtship to its crisis. Stella confesses she loves, but only virtuously (sonnet 62); Astrophil catches her stealing a glance at him (sonnet 66); and he steals a kiss from her as she sleeps (song ii, following 72), the latter event occasioning a series of self-conscious *baiser* poems and a renewed verbal swagger (sonnets 75–78). Yet external events are again mingled with signs of a strained ingenuity. Stella's emphatic refusal, "Lest once should not be heard, twise said, No, No," occasions a linguistic juggling act bordering on self-parody, as Astrophil invokes the muse of "Grammer rules" to proclaim "in one speech two Negatives affirme" (sonnet 63). Astrophil retreats to willful self-deception when he insists on interpreting her stolen glance as a sign of affection and addresses Hope as a textual commentator, the accuracy of whose gloss is irrelevant:

> Her eye's-speech is translated thus by thee:
>   But failst thou not in phrase so heav'nly hie?
> Looke on againe, the faire text better trie:
> . . . .
> Well, how so thou interpret the contents,
> I am resolv'd thy errour to maintaine,
> Rather than by more truth to get more paine.
>   (sonnet 67)

Armed with false premises, Astrophil finally acts, and for a moment the erotic promises to overtake the poetic ("Cease eager Muse . . . / Wise silence is best musicke unto blisse," sonnet 70, lines 12–14). But when an ambiguous assignation and a

moment of uncertain intimacy (sonnets 84, 85, song iv) lead to
a sharp reversal of fortune (sonnet 86, song v), the sequence
reaches its peculiarly muted crisis in song viii:

> In a grove most rich of shade,
> Where birds wanton musicke made,
> May then yong his pide weedes showing,
> New perfumed with flowers fresh growing,
>
> *Astrophil* and *Stella* sweete,
> Did for mutuall comfort meete,
> Both within themselves oppressed,
> But each in the other blessed.
>
> (lines 1–8)

The song signals its importance by being the only one of a
hundred and nineteen poems to be written in the third person—that is, from a rhetorical stance outside of Astrophil's explicitly subjective point of view. According to Richard Young,
"The lovers are seen from a completely objective point of view,
as if at a distance, and from this objective point of view they
appear in a new intimacy; the distinction Astrophil constantly
is forced to make between 'I' and 'she' is eliminated in the 'they'
of the song."[22] Young's reading is attractive, but its attractive-
ness may obscure a further dimension of the song. The scene's
lushness and comfort, the very goldenness of the moment, is
not so much a release from the sequence's drama as a rhetorical
voice within the drama. Song viii is not an objective view but
a subjective effort to create the *illusion* of perspective and distance. All is composed by Astrophil's will: the fusing of the "I"
and "you" into "they" may be subtler than the two negatives
becoming affirmative in sonnet 63, but it, too, bears the mark
of a strenuous effort to reshape a recalcitrant world. Astrophil's
longing for reciprocity finds emblematic form in "their eyes
by love directed / Enterchangeably reflected" (lines 15–16),
and even within this temporary golden world, the notes of desire and ironic self-reference are heard: after an elegant plea for

love, Astrophil's "hands in their speech, faine / Would have made tongue's language plaine" (lines 65–66). The pictured intimacy functions as well as a turning away from a moment too unbearable to verbalize *in propria persona*: the recognition of futility. If Astrophil sought to become "the tale of me" to woo Stella in sonnet 45, here he fictionalizes himself for his own protection. By song's end, however, both the distanced Astrophil and the observing Astrophil recoil from the same blow: "Therewithall away she went / Leaving him so passion rent, / With what she had done and spoken, / That therwith my song is broken" (lines 101–4). The final line carries the force of the rejection from the distanced lover to the singer. Narrator and persona are rejoined through the knowledge that rejection is irreversible, that it stands beyond the reach of all fictions and witty transformations.

"MAZEFULL SOLITARINESSE": THE FINAL SONNETS

Astrophil makes fitful efforts in the final sonnets to regroup his poetic forces through some return to the poetic Idea, as in sonnet 88, where he defies "traytour absence" with the strength of "inward sight." The late sonnets, however, are preoccupied with loss. Sonnet 89 smothers sonnet 88's "inward sight" with its claustrophobic line endings, an alternation of "night" and "day" that traps the speaker in a monotonous cycle where the "horrors of silent night" find no relief, for "no night is more darke then is my day." Efforts to assert any continuity between his "inward sight" and that of Stella, who is by now the only other mind he acknowledges, end only in frustration, or inadequate resolution. Song x asks:

O deare life, when shall it be,
That mine eyes thine eyes may see?
And in them thy mind discover,
Whether absence have had force

> Thy remembrance to divorce,
> From the image of thy lover?

He sends forth a personification of Thought to reconnoiter, but Thought itself can do no more than provide a masturbatory fantasy:

> There unseene thou maist be bold,
> Those faire wonders to behold,
> Which in them my hopes do cary.
> Thought see thou no place forbeare,
> Enter bravely every where,
> . . . .
> Opening rubies, pearles deviding.

But though Astrophil's fantasy is one of mutual pleasure—

> With glad moning passed anguish,
> We change eyes, and hart for hart,
> Each to other do imparte,
> Joying till joy makes us languish

—his release is solitary and confused, the double entendres joyless:

> O my thoughts my thoughts surcease,
> Thy delights my woes increase,
> My life melts with too much thinking;
> Thinke no more but die in me.

So, too, melts the poet's brilliant inventiveness as the sequence lapses into a series of unrelieved and conventional complaints about the pain of love. Richard Young suggests that the loss of his unique personality marks a positive discovery: "By the end of the sequence, through his relation to Stella, Astrophil has been made aware of the nature of love as the Petrarchan universal: he has discovered himself as part of the convention, which, by virtue of his participation in it, has acquired permanent validity."[23] Astrophil's intelligence is indeed subsumed into the literary convention against which it had defined itself.

But the Platonic cast of Young's remarks—"universal," "participation," "permanent validity"—is misleading. The final sonnets, rather than raising Astrophil above self-affirmation, drive him beneath it, into passivity and solipsism. The enabling tension between subject and object is lost; the poetry, which only recently was threatened by a surfeit of joy (sonnet 70), now collapses inward as the later sonnets parody the outward thrust of the earlier ones. In sonnet 94, Astrophil looks once again for an inner image, but "inbent eyes / Can scarce discern the shape of mine owne paine." The expansiveness of sonnet 35 is negated: the promise of endless proliferation when praise is praised and honor honored yields to a circling back into solitude and darkness: grief "growest more wretched then thy nature beares, / By being placed in such a wretch as I."

If there is any "participation" of mind in a larger context, it is in the experience of darkness:

> Thought with good cause thou likest so well the night,
>   Since kind or chance gives both one liverie,
>   Both sadly blacke, both blackly darkned be,
> Night bard from Sun, thou from thy owne sunne's light;
> Silence in both displaies his sullen might,
>   Slow heavinesse in both holds one degree,
>   That full of doubts, thou of perplexity;
> Thy teares expresse night's native moisture right.
> In both a mazefull solitarinesse:
> In night of sprites the gastly powers stur,
> In thee or sprites or sprited gastlinesse:
> But, but (alas) night's side the ods hath fur,
>   For that at length yet doth invite some rest,
>   Thou though still tired, yet still doost it detest.
>   (sonnet 96)

The world of thought is silent, perplexed, and lost in "mazefull solitarinesse"; like the night it is dark, silent, sullen, moist, and plagued by spirits. And yet, the final three lines undo the hope of even this union; Night can offer rest, but thought is doomed to wander, hammering out versions of the same theme.

Astrophil's symptoms clearly indicate melancholy, the occupational hazard of lovers and poets.[24] Indeed, he becomes a meeting place for two strains of the disorder. Having sought to fuse sexual longing and poetic creation, he falls victim both to the topos of the sighing lover, and Renaissance anxieties about creative minds caught up within, and undone by, their own agitated and fevered state.[25] Trapped by the motions of his "blind braine" (sonnet 97, line 13), he recalls his initial program, "to paint the blackest face of woe" in order to move his beloved (sonnet 1, line 5), but he has now become his own, and only, spectator, regarding the image of his sorrows: "the blacke horrors of the silent night, / Paint woe's black face so lively to my sight" (sonnet 98, lines 9–10). The sequence ends without relief or resolution:

> When sorrow (using mine owne fier's might)
>   Melts downe his lead into my boyling brest,
>   Through that darke fornace to my hart opprest,
> There shines a joy from thee my only light;
> But soone as thought of thee breeds my delight,
>   And my yong soule flutters to thee his nest,
>   Most rude dispaire my daily unbidden guest,
> Clips streight my wings, streight wraps me in his night,
>   And makes me then bow downe my head, and say,
> Ah what doth *Phoebus'* gold that wretch availe,
> Whom iron doores do keepe from use of day?
> So strangely (alas) thy works in me prevaile,
>   That in my woes for thee thou art my joy,
>   And in my joyes for thee my only annoy.
>
> (sonnet 108)

Astrophil ends where he began, with Stella's inner image, but now it has been fixed into an inescapable cycle of joy and despair, rising fancy and sinking failure. The infectious excitement that caught Drayton's ear now hardens into the kind of grimness we hear in the late sonnets of Fulke Greville's *Caelica*:

> In night, when colors all to black are cast,
> Distinction lost or gone down with the light,
> The eye a watch to inward senses placed,

Not seeing, yet still having power of sight,
Gives vain alarums to the inward sense,
Where fear, stirred up with witty tyranny,
Confounds all powers, and thorough self-offense,
Doth forge and raise impossibility.

Such, as in thick depriving darknesses,
Proper reflections of the error be,
And images of self-confusednesses,
Which hurt imaginations only see,
  And from this nothing seen, tells news of devils,
  Which but expressions be of inward evils.

(*Caelica*, sonnet 100)[26]

Astrophil's late complaints (cf. sonnet 99) may well have served
as Greville's model. Indeed, his final vision of self-entrapment
is, in some ways, more unnerving than the latter's puritanical
self-scrutiny. Greville is able to end his sonnet, and his sequence, with some statement of certainty; he finds a platform
from which the agonized speaking voice can make moral sense
of its situation. "Desire's Idolatries," "Poets feigning wit," and
"ambition infinite" (*Caelica*, sonnets 105, 107) are rejected and
the concluding poem ends with a plea to "sweet *Iesus*" to
"yeeld the sinne her euerlasting doome" (*Caelica*, sonnet 109).
Sidney's sequence ends only with the fact of paralysis: "In my
woes for thee thou art my joy, / And in my joyes for thee my
only annoy."[27] Not only does the chiasmus enforce a sense of
futility, but the very flatness of the lover's paradox has become
a wall beyond which Astrophil's poetry can no longer range.
His nimble and self-conscious mind has frozen into an image
of his sorrows; no longer the intelligence behind the making
of fictions, he has simply become "the tale of me."

The ending of *Astrophil and Stella* has long presented itself as a
challenge, and it is not surprising that some editors used to
"correct" it by splicing on two of Sidney's *Certain Sonnets*, calling them numbers 109 and 110. Both are poems of transcendence, as their first lines fully attest: "Thou blind man's marke,
thou foole's selfe chosen snare," and "Leave me o Love, which

reachest but to dust." Not only do these two poems free Astrophil from his psychological paralysis, but they also tidy up the questionable morality of his sensual and adulterous desires. The first gives him a moral ground on which to stand, while the second, a marvelous poem in its own way, forecasts his spiritual ascent to a greater Love that unites the inner life to the highest Good:

> Then farewell world, thy uttermost I see,
> Eternal Love maintaine thy life in me.

The emendation has been emphatically discredited,[28] but this has created for some critics a yet greater problem: how could Sidney, translator of Psalms and author of the apparently didactic *Apology*, have devoted so many poems to carnal love and an ultimately unredeemed protagonist? One strategy has been to read the sequence as a bitter warning against idolatrous love and poetry. Proceeding from a proper distinction between Sidney the poet and Astrophil the fictive persona, these critics regard the poems as an ironic attack on their cupidinous speaker. By allowing his sinful passion to overcome his better judgment, Astrophil turns his back on God and morality, and so finally suffers the fate he deserves.[29]

Astrophil's questionable morality is indeed an issue; Astrophil himself makes it one, and his numerous rejections and evasions are not always appealing (see sonnet 91). But while Astrophil may be plagued by his folly, he is neither as pathetic nor as vicious as some have tried to make him. Sidney is alert to ethical questions, but employs them as part of a different kind of drama. What he has created in Astrophil is not a poetic "object lesson," but an embodiment in English verse of a poetic "subject"—complex, passionate, self-conscious, caught up, perhaps, in its own egotistical drives and self-deluding fictions, but also aware in the end that it is doing so. It is an achievement that would not be surpassed until Shakespeare's *Richard II*. Astrophil is not Sidney's autobiographical alter ego, but neither is he wholly other. For it is in Astrophil's ingenuity and agility that Sidney presents to us a hypothetical image of his creative powers, no more but also no less important to him than the image of the didactic poet fashioned by the *Apology*. The tragic curve of the sequence is also a part of that image, even as the regressive paradoxes of the *Apology* are a part of its image. For the sequence also embodies a profound uncertainty about the full consequences of Sidney's "unelected profession," an uncertainty he was unable, or unwilling, to resolve.

INTRODUCTION TO
CHAPTERS 7 AND 8:
SIDNEY'S TWO *ARCADIAS*

In all these creatures of his making, his intent, and scope was, to turn the barren Philosophy precepts into pregnant Images of life . . . his purpose was to limn out such exact pictures, of every posture in the minde, that any man being forced, in the straines of this life, to pass through any straights, or latitudes of good, or ill fortune might (as in a glasse) see how to set a good countenance upon all the discountenances of adversitie, and a stay upon the exorbitant smilings of chance.

Fulke Greville, *The Life of the
Renowned Sir Philip Sidney*

He never lets a casual observation pass without perplexing it with an endless running commentary. . . . [The *Arcadia*] is spun with great labour out of the author's brains and hangs like a huge cobweb over the face of nature! . . . He cannot let his imagination or that of the reader dwell for a moment on the beauty or power of the real object. He thinks nothing done, unless it is his doing. . . . The moving spring of his mind is . . . dry, literal unceasing craving after intellectual excitement. . . . In a word (and not to speak it profanely) the *Arcadia* is a riddle, a rebus, an acrostic in folio.

William Hazlitt, "Lectures on the
Dramatic Literature of the
Age of Elizabeth"

Literary historians have been more willing to endorse Greville's high-minded view of the *Arcadia* than Hazlitt's seeming Romantic incomprehension of Elizabethan formal artifice. For Greville, Sidney's prose epic transforms the pastoral worlds of Jacopo Sannazaro and Jorge Montemayor into a program for moral survival in a treacherous world; it is a didactic encyclopedia representing "every posture of the mind," with "moral Images and Examples (as directing threads) to guide every man through the confused Labyrinth of his own desires and life." How apposite this seems, compared to Hazlitt's petulant dismissal of it as "one of the greatest monuments to the abuse of intellectual power upon record."[1] Yet Sidney's own description of the work in a letter to his sister sounds closer to Hazlitt's than to Greville's. The *Arcadia*, he writes, is an "idle work of mine, which I fear (like the spider's web) will be thought fitter to be swept away than worn to any other purpose," the creation of a "young head, not so well stayed as I would it were (and shall be when God will), having many, many fancies begotten in it, if it had not been in some way delivered, would have grown a monster, and more sorry might I be that they came in than that they got out."[2] Far from providing "directing threads," the *Arcadia* itself threatens to become a labyrinth.

Social and compositional contexts may be invoked to explain Sidney's self-disparagement. Sidney's remarks are part of the courtier's ironic social style, a sophisticated nonchalance "wherein," writes Greville, "men commonly (to keep above their workes) seeme to make toies of the utmost they can doe."[3] In terms of composition, Sidney's letter may refer to an earlier version of the work—now called the *Old Arcadia*—even though first printed with the *New* in 1590. For the original version, lost as a separate text until 1907, does seem on first inspection to be a lesser thing, in Sidney's phrase "an idle work," while the second weaves heroic action into the original narrative, producing an epic as Sidney would have understood the form from Antonio Minturno. Such contexts, however, complicate rather than explain his remarks. Elizabethan courtiers may be masters of self-presentation, refracting political ambition into the more acceptable language of play and artifice, but Sidney repeatedly alerts us to the conflicts, rather than the accommodations, of courtly performance. The defensive ironies of *sprezzatura* receive a further twist from Sidney; his characterization of his "head" as "having many, many fancies begotten in it" is less an act of self-distancing than an inclusion of his own mental state in his most enduring thematic preoccupation. Nor is the reworked *Arcadia* the mark of a head more "well stayed." The first version is in its own way ambitious and meticulously crafted, even if its genre is curiously elusive. The second, the broadest-ranging of all Sidney's literary efforts, strains to present itself as a didactic epic filled with notable images, and yet it is here that the ambiguities of Sidney's poetic find their fullest expression. The *New Arcadia* never seeks the rich density of analogy that characterizes a work such as *The Faerie Queene*, but is in its own way an epic exploration of the human imagination, from the mazes of a solitary lover to an entire culture's patterns of coherence. What establishes the importance of both versions for the Renaissance is not so much their didactic programs as the intense awareness they foster about all efforts of human making, even if that awareness finally drives Sidney to abandon poetic fiction altogether.[4]

7

THE *OLD ARCADIA*

THE MENTAL LANDSCAPE

Sidney's first major literary effort projects an imaginary world dedicated to a testing of the various roles of the imagination, from its rudimentary place in a hierarchical faculty psychology to its share in the production of the broadest cultural codes. For while the *Old Arcadia* raises social, political, and psychological themes, all revolve around the fundamental thematic opposition of all Sidney's works: the tensed relationship between public action and human fictions. To enter Arcadia is, in other words, to enter poetics.

The work's deliberateness is felt in its immediate concentration on the volatility of the imagination, as if posing its central problem. Two sets of characters—Arcadia's ducal family and two heroic princes—come under the domination of "fancies" and "errors," and so retreat from the world of history, politics, and adventure to a small pastoral lodge.[1] Duke Basilius, anxious about his future happiness, receives an obscure oracular message threatening the loss of his daughters, the paradoxical committing of adultery with his own wife, and foreign domination of his state. He responds by giving up his leadership of a world of apparently ideal mental stability, one whose citizens follow "the course of nature" and "good laws," and whose "very shepherds . . . had their fancies opened to . . . high conceits" thanks to the presence of the Muses (*OA*, p. 4). Basilius's eccentric folly is emphasized both by his disapproving counselor and by the narrator, but the duke is interested only in the "confirmation of fancies," not the "correcting of errors," and responds to all advice with "dukely sophistries to deceive himself" (*OA*, pp. 6, 9). Prince Pyrocles makes an analogous retreat, turning from his heroic path when, in an Arcadian gallery, he spies a "picture, newly made by an excellent artificer, which contained the duke and duchess with their younger daughter Philoclea" (*OA*, p. 11). He is wounded by the image of the beloved, and while the narrator is more sympathetic to his plight than to Basilius's, his ironic view of this traditional entrapment by image is made clear by his parodic glance at the Neoplatonic *icones symbolicae*, visual stimuli that supposedly provoke ever-widening speculation: "arguing with himself came of a further thought; and the more he argued, the more his thought increased" (*OA*, p. 12).[2] Indeed, Pyrocles turns easily to the voice of the Neoplatonic *vita contempliva* to rationalize his lovesickness, a voice that also forecasts the *Apology*'s free-ranging poetic wit: "The workings of the mind, I find, much more infinite . . . in such contemplations" (*OA*, p. 14).

Both retreats encounter resistance from the voice of prudence. Basilius hears it from his counselor Philanax, who reminds him that "wisdom and virtue . . . be such guides as cannot fail. . . . it is most certain no destiny nor influence whatsoever can bring man's wit to a higher point than wisdom and goodness" (*OA*, p. 7); Pyrocles is similarly lectured by his older cousin Musidorus, who invokes the well-trained mind that changes its course only "upon well grounded and well weighed causes." The terms of his reproach anticipate the Neoplatonic-Neoclassical division some critics have found in the *Apology*.[3] The self is a work of art, but a decorous one: "Even the very countenance and behaviour of such a man doth show forth images of the same constancy by maintaining a right harmony betwixt it and the inward good" (*OA*, p. 13); if Pyrocles' behavior is not "fit," the effect will be as if an "ill player should mar the last act of his tragedy" (*OA*, p. 19).

This resistance to fantastic excess raises moral issues, which become increasingly urgent as the work progresses. But as is so often the case in Sidney's work, proper advice is too easily said. Its assured tone ignores a premise of the *Arcadia*: "There is nothing so certain as our continual uncertainty" (*OA*, p. 5). The initial function of such advice is not so much that of orienting our moral perspective as of emphasizing the disruptive energies put into play.[4] Unlike Ariostan romance, the *Arcadia* presents neither magic shields nor flying horses; apart from an occasional giant or monster, its "marvels" are entirely psychological. Indeed, the release of imagination becomes a virtual metaphysical principle in Arcadia, a spirit moving through the landscape to transform its characters. The sanity of Philanax will be severely compromised by the story's end, and Musidorus's moral and aesthetic distance evaporates almost immediately. He may decry the ludicrous unreality of Pyrocles' plan to disguise himself as the Amazon "Cleophila" in order to gain access to the sequestered Philoclea—"Is it possible that this is Pyrocles. . . . Or is it, indeed, some Amazon Cleophila that hath counterfeited the face of my friend in this sort to vex me?" (*OA*, p. 18)—but he soon finds himself very much a part of the world of feigning and faining. For after helping to dress his cousin, while making sly references to the sexual perverseness of image makers and image lovers (*OA*, p. 27), he catches sight of Philoclea's older sister, Pamela, and enters the Arcadian lodge in an indecorous disguise of his own as Dorus, a shepherd.

The princes' entry into the ducal family's pastoral retreat sets in motion "a very stage-play of love," in which the promptings of desire provoke imaginative extremes: Basilius cannot see through Pyrocles' disguise and is immediately infatuated by "her," his head filled with "absurd follies. . . . intermixed imaginations" (*OA*, p. 45); the guileless Philoclea is also fooled, but finds herself drawn toward the mysterious and powerful woman and tormented by "unquiet imaginations" (*OA*, p. 54); Gynecia sees through the disguise, only to find herself a competitor with both her husband and her daughter for the love of the transvestite hero. Nor is the hero himself exempt. In one of the work's many interspersed poems, Pyrocles seeks release by weeping into a brook, sighing about his secret woes and writing verses in the sandy banks. But release becomes reflex as he beholds "in wat'ry glass my watered eyes" and hears the rebounding echo of his laments. His poem merely displays to him the story of his woe—a figure, perhaps, for the very poem we have been reading (*OA*, p. 118).

David Kalstone suggests that even while the lovers are caught in this "unbreakable circle of desire," their highly patterned verse makes them seem "masters of their griefs."[5] Yet it is a mastery that often seems "wholly imaginative, as we are wont to say by them that build castles in the air" *(Apology*, p. 101). Even the name "Cleophila" suggests that the lover has become the image of the beloved, Philoclea, and Sidney carries the conceit one step farther by having Pyrocles for a time make his formal declarations of love to his own mental images: "Often would she [Cleophila] speak to the image of Philoclea (which lived and ruled in the highest of her inward parts), and use vehement oaths and protestations unto her" (*OA*, p. 212). So entranced are the lovers by their own woes that at times they can scarcely distinguish the sound of their own minds from the evidence of other minds. When Gynecia hears a mournful love song, she is certain that "such griefs could serve fitly for nothing but her own fortune," only to find, to her "dull amazement," that the singer is Pyrocles, source of her suffering (*OA*, p. 94). The confusion is reciprocal: hearing in a darkened cave the sound of "moanful melody," Pyrocles wonders what singer is "so well acquainted with me, that can make so lively a portraiture of my miseries?" (*OA*, p. 181). The singer proves to be his amorous enemy, Gynecia.

The small pastoral lodge, then, is crowded with self-absorbed, intersecting fantasies; as the narrator comments at the end of a hectic day, "each party, full fraught with diversely working fancies, made their pillows weak props of their over-loaden heads" (*OA*, p. 214). If, as Sidney tells his sister, his is a head having "many, many fancies begotten in it," he creates the world of the *Old Arcadia*, in important ways, in his own image.

SUBJECTS OF A POET'S CUNNING

When Musidorus first reproaches Pyrocles for his refusal to leave Arcadia, he is met with praise of the place as a "heavenly dwelling" where the grass "excel[s] . . . emeralds" and flowers "require a man's wit to know, and his life to express." Musi-dorus "marvel[s]" at his "excessive praises," but has little dif-ficulty identifying the voice:

> . . . I think you will make me see that the vigour of your wit can show itself in any subject; or else you feed sometimes your solitari-ness with the conceits of the poets whose liberal pens can as easily travel over mountains as molehills, and so (like well disposed men) set up everything to the highest note—especially when they put such words in the mouth of one of these fantastical mind-infected people that children and musicians call lovers.
>
> (*OA*, pp. 16–17)

Pyrocles aligns himself with the interior rather than the frame of Musidorus's comparison: "I be not so much the poet, the freedom of whose pen can exercise itself in anything, as even that very miserable subject of his cunning" (*OA*, p. 17). It is the older Musidorus who first discovers what Pyrocles will come to know: these voices are not mutually exclusive.

A world filled with hyperactive imaginations is also filled with opportunity for one who can manipulate the fancies of others, assuming not only rhetorical mastery of inner grief, but the mastering hand of the poet. Musidorus, for example, dis-poses of Pamela's rustic guardians—Dametas, Miso, and their daughter Mopsa—by shaping fictions that will activate the rul-ing fantasy of each, whether covetousness, jealousy, or idle curiosity, and sends each on his or her way with "an image in his fancy" (*OA*, p. 188). He also piques Pamela's interest with his poetic skills, but does so here by calling attention to his technique. Feigning love to Mopsa within Pamela's hearing, he manages his lofty "matter" and "manner" to show a "very unlikely proportion" to his object (*OA*, p. 100), counting on his deliberate breach of decorum to invite her close "scanning of him" for a "second meaning" (*OA*, p. 99). Musidorus then enacts Astrophil's paradox, telling her "the tale of me": a princely Musidorus, it seems, for the sake of love once took on the very estate of the humble Dorus, teller of his tale. Shipwrecked with a young friend in Arcadia, this prince found himself "enchanted," "entangled" in a "maze of longing" for the duke's eldest daughter, and donned a shepherd's costume to approach her. Patent self-reference forestalls an infinite regression of disguised princes telling tales of disguised princes. It is clear that he "meant the tale by himself," as both narrative "veil" and disguise become transparent (*OA*, pp. 105–6).

Pyrocles, the originator of the masquerades, also fashions intentional structures out of the stuff of fantasy, and so develops from being the mere "miserable subject" of a poet's cunning into a poetic maker supervising his own plot: Cleophila "had now a kind of confused conceit. . . . as a painter doth at the first but show a rude proportion of the thing he imitates, which after with more curious hand he draws to the representing each lineament, so had her thoughts (beating about it continually) received into them a ground plot of her device" (*OA*, p. 215). The plot disposes of Philoclea's amorous parents by arranging for simultaneous assignations with both in a darkened cave, thus leaving Gynecia preoccupied by the "picture of her approaching contentment" and Basilius "fuller of livelier fancies than many years before he had been" (*OA*, p. 227).

Despite their ingenuity, or because of it, both princes face unexpected obstacles. Their beloveds are dazzled, and more than a little dismayed, by the web of fictions spun by their suitors; neither can be sure where the fancies end and the reality begins. Musidorus's tale of himself leaves Pamela rejoicing over his noble station, but doubt soon arises: "Who dare place his heart in so great places dare frame his head to as great feignings?" (*OA*, p. 106). If Pamela suspects him of political and sexual opportunism, Musidorus fails to allay her doubts; finding that he has "given alarum to her imagination," he sings "to hold her the longer in them." His contrivance is effective, but Pamela finds herself being swept along too quickly, and abruptly closes off this stage of the seduction; the young prince has temporarily outsmarted himself.

Pyrocles, too, is momentarily thwarted. He has already confessed his identity and his love, and after deceiving the duke and duchess, surprises Philoclea in her bedchamber, only to find that she, resentful over some feigned sleights he was forced to perform at her expense, is a few levels of deception behind him. Nonetheless, he hopes to point to the *res* beyond the maze of *verba*: "For, in truth, there may most words be spent where there is some probability to breed of both sides conjectural allegations; but in so perfect a thing as my love is for you, as it suffers no question so it seems to receive injury by any addition of words unto it" (*OA*, p. 233). Setting his sights on the highest perspective, he calls upon "the almighty powers, whom I invoke to be the triers of my innocency" (*OA*, p. 234). But Philoclea, like Pamela before her, is suspicious of a man who can so easily frame his head to such "great feignings": "Have you yet another sleight to play; or do you think to deceive me in Pyrocles' form, as you have done in Cleophila's? Or rather, now you have betrayed me in both those, is there some third sex left you into which you can transform yourself . . . ?" Pyrocles the poet and lover seems to her Pyrocles the villainous Proteus, whose cunning, having already violated the sexual law of contradiction, can be bounded only by complete skepticism: "My only defence shall be belief of nothing" (*OA*, pp. 234–35).[6]

The sisters relent, but their uncertainties remain part of a larger system of warning signals in the text. The characters in this fluid, metamorphic world find it increasingly easy to juggle terms, to justify any course of action by simply redefining what is authentic. Basilius attempts to seduce Cleophila by dismissing ethical norms as "imaginative rules," mere figments "whose truth stands but upon opinion." Similarly, as Pyrocles slips into Philoclea's bedroom, "All the great estate of his father seemed unto him but a trifling pomp, whose good stands in other men's conceits" (*OA*, p. 228). Gynecia, the most complex figure in the original work, suggests the tragic possibilities of such a world. She sees the better, but follows the worse: "There appeared unto the eyes of her judgment the evils she was like to run into . . . she saw the terrors of her own conscience" (*OA*, p. 91). Like the others, she seeks refuge in sophistical metamorphoses—"O virtue . . . thou wert never but a vain name and no essential thing" (*OA*, p. 91)—but she cannot so easily delude herself. In her, the urge to reshape the world after one's own desire is exposed as a menace to self and others. She suffers from the full horrors of the imagination, a terrifying nightmare of sexual frustration and death (*OA*, p. 117), against which she struggles by threatening to rewrite the "stage play of Love" in a darker genre: "I will not be the only actor of this tragedy! . . . I will end my miseries with a notable example of revenge" (*OA*, p. 184).

Imaginative excess spreads out from the pastoral center like an intellectual disease. A group of Phagonian townsmen, drunk in celebration of Basilius's birthday, fill their ruler's "absented manner of living" with wild notions about his retirement until, "the very unbridled use of words having increased fire to their minds," they produce "far-fetched constructions" that threaten their political order. Like those within the lodge, they begin to see the authentic as a contrivance, no longer "astonished with vain titles that have their forces but in our forces" (*OA*, p. 127). Their rebellious assault on the pastoral lodges is halted only by Pyrocles' momentary reversion to the active life, with a strong arm and persuasive oratory. Despite the narrator's aristocratic disdain of the rebels—"Cleophila did quickly make them perceive that one eagle is worth a great number of kites" (*OA*, p. 124)—the episode provokes a special nervousness. Not only does it remind us of the vulnerability of all social and political structures, and the necessity of force—defined as "well doing"—in sustaining them, it transforms the image of "well doing" itself. If we hear in Pyrocles' address the voice of a humanist orator defending the "holy name of your natural duke" to the "many-headed multitude" (*OA*, pp. 130–31), we are not allowed to forget that that voice emanates from a speaker in drag whose *ethos* is an ironic fraud—"O Arcadians, that a woman should give public counsel to men . . . a woman may well speak to such men who have forgotten all manly government" (*OA*, p. 129)—and whose homily against disobedience is directed toward private ends.[7] When Basilius, alarmed by the near rebellion, soon afterward "determines to leave the solitary life," Pyrocles blocks his move, fearing the "many eyes" of the "public place" will see through his disguise (*OA*, p. 178). If we continue to enjoy tracing Pyrocles' "daily changing labyrinth" (*OA*, p. 178), we also feel a growing tension in the work between delight and dismay, between pleasurable masquerade and unsavory egotistical manipulation.

THE PROBLEMS OF JUDGMENT

To maintain a sense of moral balance in this world of cunning artificers, we must sooner or later make some judgment about the princes' behavior. There are moral categories throughout Sidney's text: characters invoke them in long speeches; symbolic events imply them; a chatty narrator continually offers them; and tuneful shepherds and disguised aristocrats sing them in a dazzling variety of verse forms in the eclogues separating the five books or "Acts." And yet Sidney characteristically presents them in skewed or ambiguous contexts. If the

characters' speeches are a rich storehouse of ethical commonplaces, it is a storehouse divided against itself; as many have
noted, these speeches are paired in debates that, at best, explore
the terms without coming to clear resolutions.[8] At times, in
fact, these debates primarily seem interested in a free play of
rhetorical counters. The initial debate between Pyrocles and
Musidorus is a case in point. Its ostensible topic, the relative
merits of active and contemplative lives, is a central, abiding
concern for Sidney and humanists in general, yet the princes
seem oddly disengaged from the problem itself. Pyrocles pretends to measure the value of retirement against that of action,
but suddenly he stops, "like a man unsatisfied in himself" (*OA*,
p. 15), and shifts to praise of the pleasant place. Musidorus
suffers "new doubts" because he is called upon to invent a new
rebuttal:

> For, having in the beginning of Pyrocles' speech which de-
> fended his solitariness framed in his mind a reply against it in the
> praise of honourable action (in showing that such kind of contem-
> plation is but a glorious title to idleness; that in action a man did
> not only better himself but benefit others; that the gods would not
> have delivered a soul into the body which hath arms and legs (only
> instruments of doing) but that it were intended the mind should
> employ them; and that the mind should best know his own good
> or evil by practice; which knowledge was the only way to increase
> the one and correct the other; besides many other better arguments
> which the plentifulness of the matter yielded to the sharpness of
> his wit), when he found Pyrocles leave that, and fall to such an
> affected praising of the place, he left it likewise.
>
> (*OA*, p. 16)

We know that Musidorus has been trained in the active life and
must assume his genuine commitment to it, but it is the curious
formality of that training that becomes dominant: his first concern is with his rhetorical arsenal; his second, to keep pace with
his cousin's turns of mind. If the latter's arguments are merely
signs of the "vigour of your wit" as the former charges (*OA*,
p. 17), the former's are also signs of the "sharpness of his wit"

(*OA*, p. 16), an improvised arrangement of received maxims stored in the mind (even as they are stored in the parentheses above) and whose efficacy is soon challenged by Musidorus's falling in love.[9]

We may feel more confident with the symbolic and iconographic hints that lie beyond the characters' witty constructions. Consider, for example, the sudden attack of a lion and a bear near the end of the first book (*OA*, pp. 46ff.). Here we find an elegant conflation of meanings, and as the princes spring into action, so, too, do our interpretive faculties. Does not the sudden interruption suggest the fragility of the artificial retreat? the predatory violence of the beasts the lustfulness of the princes? the deaths of the beasts the necessity of restraining desire?[10] And yet, these signals seem at odds with a narrative that insistently attends to a different dimension, to Pyrocles' delight when Philoclea first shrinks against him for protection, to the billowing up of Philoclea's "light nymphlike apparel" as she flees, so that "much of those beauties she would at another time have willingly hidden were presented to the eye of the twice-wounded Cleophila [Pyrocles]; which made Cleophila not follow her over hastily lest she should too soon deprive herself of that pleasure" (*OA*, pp. 47–48). When the narrator steps back from the event, it is not to moralize but to enjoy the "sport" of Philoclea's flight from a now-imaginary fear, Pyrocles' voyeuristic delight, and Gynecia's following close behind in amorous pursuit of the disguised prince. The symbolic images may remain with us, but we cannot help feeling a little awkward in the face of a narrator who asks us to sympathize because we, too, have "feelingly known" the power of love (*OA*, p. 49).

The narrator, in fact, becomes a primary agent of our disequilibrium. If at times he functions as Sidney's epic voice, transcending the speeches and the action to offer moral and political commentary, at other times he is amused, ironic, and indulgent; he feels "compassion" for the characters' "passion"

(*OA*, p. 27) and invites us to join in a moral holiday. His most daring moment of sympathy is at the work's erotic center, Pyrocles' sexual consummation with Philoclea at the end of book 3, when he moves from erotic blazon, to sophisticated irony, to tenderness at the thought of the "due bliss of these poor lovers" (*OA*, p. 243).[11]

If the narrator's perspective is so inconstant, where are we to turn to get our bearings? Our best hope would seem to be those intermissions in the story itself, the eclogues between the books that appear like islands in the shifting narrative stream. But they prove to be floating islands at best. At times amatory and imaginative excess is openly flogged: "Poor painters oft with silly poets join / To fill the world with strange but vain conceits" sings Dicus in his attack on Cupid in the first eclogues, and he returns in the second to brand Musidorus's love a "sick man's frenzy" (*OA*, pp. 65, 140). Another shepherd moralist, Geron, sternly warns Philisides (Sidney's nominal self-projection) to "bind / This tyrant love; or rather do suppress / Those rebel thoughts" (*OA*, p. 73). But Geron's moral uprightness is presented as the egotism of a joyless pedant, whose age "having taken from him both the thoughts and fruits of that passion, wished all the world proportioned to himself" (*OA*, p. 64). Dicus's attack is also deflected by a prose tale in the eclogues of princess Erona, who would "deface and pull down" all the images of Cupid in her country because the "pictures and images were superstitiously adored" (*OA*, p. 67), for which she is punished by an obsessive love for the base Antiphilus. If the tale warns against the dangers of idolatry, it also warns of the futility of suppressing the erotic imagination. Nor does the princes' enthusiastic idealism offer a solution. Musidorus invokes the "high erection" of the lover's wit in the first eclogues and in the second borrows his younger cousin's conceited praise of "solitariness" and "Contemplation . . . / Bounded with no limits" (*OA*, p. 166; cf. pp. 14–15), while Pyrocles professes limitless devotion to a love described, by turns, as a "sacred muse," a "saint," a "goddess," and an "Idea" (*OA*, p. 83). Yet these Neoplatonic aspirations run athwart the narrator's terse remarks about Basilius, which immediately follow their first effusions and apply equally to them: "Any man . . . knows love is better than a pair of spectacles to make everything seem greater which is seen through it" (*OA*, p. 88). The subjective lovers, unlike the subjective moralists, are at least capable of fitful self-awareness. Pyrocles in one song bids his muse sing heroic fables, "the fall of old Thebes . . . the death of Hector," instead of the mere solipsism of a lover's complaint: "The singer is the song's theme / . . . / Nor eye receives due object" (*OA*, pp. 163–64). But if we attempt to follow this thread back to objective value in the heroic life, a life Histor keeps before us in his prose narratives in the first two eclogues, we find ourselves returned to our point of departure. For his tales begin with Erona's assault on Cupid's images; to rebel against love's idolatry can be as disastrous as to reject the active life.

Rather than transcending the narrative dilemmas, the eclogues crystallize them, and as the plot thickens, the songs darken. Plangus in the second group sounds a tragic note in the natural theater, singing of "wretched human-kind" as "Balls to the stars, and thralls to Fortune's reign / . . . Like players placed to fill a filthy stage" (*OA*, p. 147). A glimmer of traditional harmonies returns with the pastoral marriage of Lalus and Kala in the third group, where Dicus cheerfully sings the "war of thoughts is swallowed up in peace" and Geron instructs Histor on man's harmonizing with nature through lawful procreation (*OA*, pp. 245, 262). But peace lasts scarcely longer than the length of an epithalamion. For here Philisides also sings his "Ister bank," the group's most intriguing poem. It begins by crediting "Old Languet" with teaching how best to please the heavens with "jump concord between our wit and will" (*OA*, p. 255), but its theme is political discord and its origin in the ambiguous versatility of human consciousness.[12]

Although Geron is outraged by Philisides' song (*OA*, pp. 259–60), its melancholy tone dominates the fourth and final eclogues. Here Strephon and Klaius sing their famous double sestina, "Ye goat-herd gods," an intricate lament for the loss of Urania that transforms the harmonious pastoral world into a vision of entrapment, terror, and violence, evolving finally into a hymn to wretchedness (*OA*, pp. 328–30); Philisides tells of the interruption of his life (a near reflection of Sidney's, *OA*, pp. 334–35) as if it marked the collapse of a once fixed and comprehensible cosmos (*OA*, pp. 336–37); and Agelastus laments, "Death is our home, life is but a delusion" (*OA*, p. 348). The comic structure of the *Old Arcadia* ultimately relieves us of the weight of such voices, but they also remind us that the vision of "lamps of heav'nly fire to fixed motion bound, / The ever turning spheres, the never moving ground" (*OA*, p. 336) is one very distant from human experience.[13]

The *Old Arcadia*, then, is a work that conspicuously reminds us of traditional harmonies, but spares us the necessity, or denies us the comfort, of ready application. If one reader extracts a "broad inclusive system of symbolism" to measure the princes' fall from "neo-platonic purity" to sensual degradation, another can invoke a similar Neoplatonic system to demonstrate the princes' rising toward heroic purity.[14] The point is not that moral formulae are only driftwood sculptures pieced together out of cultural fragments, but that the experience of reading the *Old Arcadia* often leaves us uncertain as to whether we are approximating a valid perspective on its events or merely adding to its maze of conjectural constructions.

Sidney's first major fiction is not so much a mirror that reflects opportunities for moral judgments as one that makes us self-conscious about our attempts to assume a moral posture. The irony would be less intriguing if the work were only a dispassionate analysis of ethical ambiguity. But it escalates its demands on our moral capacities even as it frustrates them: Musidorus's attempted rape of Pamela as he flees Arcadia with its heir apparent (*OA*, pp. 201–2), and both princes' willingness to use force, even to mount an armed attack on Arcadia, to achieve their goals "though it were the death of both of her [Philoclea's] parents" (*OA*, p. 216), are surely intended to disturb us. The plot reaches its crisis in book 4 as Gynecia, in her illusory meeting with Pyrocles, brings what she believes to be an aphrodisiac but is apparently a deadly poison. When Basilius drinks it and collapses, Arcadia must face the sudden death of its sovereign, and Gynecia the experience of moral vertigo: "O bottomless pit of sorrows in which I cannot contain myself . . . still falling and yet by the infiniteness of it never fallen!" (*OA*, p. 279). Judgment, however problematic, is now unavoidable.

THE FURTHEST REACH
OF REASON

The concluding movement of the *Old Arcadia* is a search for moral, psychological, and political equilibrium through the finality of authoritative judgment. For now it is not merely the sophistical speeches that tremble, in Richard Lanham's phrase, like a "house of cards"; the entire state totters "like a falling steeple, the parts whereof (as windows, stones, and pinnacles) were well, but the whole mass ruinous" (*OA*, p. 320). The unsettled populace appears ready to explode in a riot of fantasy, "hearkening on every rumour, suspecting everything, condemning them whom before they honoured, making strange and impossible tales of the duke's death . . . all agreeing in the universal names of liking or misliking, but of what in especial points infinitely disagreeing" (*OA*, p. 320). Nor is the many-headed multitude the only party affected by "an extreme medley of diversified thoughts" (*OA*, p. 320). The crumbling state becomes a breeding ground for diverging political theorists, whose further disfiguring of Arcadian culture is prevented only by their own limitations as "discoursing" rather than "active" types, more interested in "imagination than practice"

(*OA*, p. 321). But more pragmatic manipulators are not far behind (*OA*, pp. 321ff.). The opportunistic Timautus attempts to seize the moment, and while he is put down by the regent Philanax, we find small relief in that quarter. The work's first spokesman against irresponsible fancy, Philanax now finds his own mind torn by "a strange medley betwixt pity and revenge, betwixt liking and abhorring" (*OA*, p. 301). Persuaded by his own conspiracy theory, he refuses to soften even to Philoclea, renewing "the image of his dead master in his fancy, and using that for the spurs on his revengeful choler" (*OA*, p. 305) until his obsessive "imagining" produces in him a "raving melancholy" (*OA*, pp. 359–60).

The only antidote for imaginative and social chaos is the ambitious externalizing of judgment in a final trial scene. Before turning to the presiding judge, I want to consider the renewed challenges judgment must face; for whereas events demand a broad drive toward final clarification, that drive is itself embodied in a series of incompatible points of view.[15] Gynecia's is the most extreme. "Closely imprisoned," she is "left more freely to suffer the firebrands of her own thoughts," which shape a psychologized hell, "especially when it grew dark and had nothing left by her but a little lamp, whose small light to a perplexed mind might rather yield fearful shadows than any assured sight. . . . Then she would imagine she saw strange sights, and that she heard the cries of hellish ghosts," together with images of her own mutilation and death (*OA*, pp. 366–67). Conscience-stricken, she would quiet her agonies by assuming complete guilt: "I, and only I . . . brought death to him and loss to Arcadia" (*OA*, p. 382). Philanax assumes the role of prosecutor and promises an antithetical vision, the penetration of all the veils of illusion. He warns the judge not to "imagine . . . some tragedy invented of the extremity of wickedness," for he will deliver a "just recital of a wickedness indeed committed" (*OA*, p. 386). Though he has himself earlier indulged in such dramatizing (*OA*, p. 360), he now insists that aesthetic shaping must be abandoned. Imaginative license becomes for him the symbol of moral and political turmoil. He proclaims in his oration against Pyrocles:

> This man, whom to begin withal I know not how to name, since being come into this country unaccompanied like a lost pilgrim, from a man grew a woman, from a woman a ravisher of women, thence a prisoner, and now a prince; but this Timopyrus [a new disguise Pyrocles assumes for the trial], this Cleophila, this what you will (for any shape or title he can take upon him that hath no restraint of shame), having understood the solitary life my late master lived, and considering how open he had laid himself to any traitorous attempt, for the first mask of his falsehood disguised himself like a woman.
>
> (*OA*, p. 387)

Philoclea's earlier nervousness is grimly moralized in Philanax's own paranoiac fiction; Pyrocles becomes a protean monster who can take on "any shape or title," the priest of a demonic mystery cult of falsehood: "a cave hereby was chosen for the temple of his devotions, a cave of such darkness as did prognosticate he meant to please the infernal powers; for there this accursed caitiff upon the altar of falsehood sacrificed the life of the virtuous Basilius" (*OA*, pp. 387–88). Metaphors of magic soon yield to those of theater and poetry. Musidorus's early teasing of the amorous Pyrocles, accusing him of possessing the "conceits of poets whose liberal pens can as easily travel over mountains as molehills" (*OA*, pp. 16–17), returns in darker tones: "Was all this play for nothing? Or if it had an end, what end but the end of my dear master? Shall we doubt . . . such changes and traverses as a quiet poet could scarce fill a poem withall, were directed to any less scope than to this monstrous murder?" (*OA*, p. 389).

The nobler sentiments of the princes offer only minor relief, for the heroes, in part, lend substance to Philanax's hysterical distortions. Attempting to turn the trial into theater, the princes don new disguises to protect their true identities, while invoking the privileges of rank, complete with gorgeous attire—Pyrocles in white velvet with "great buttons of diamonds," Musidorus in purple satin with a "Persian tiara all set down with rows of so rich rubies" (*OA*, p. 376). More than a little irony deflates Pyrocles' claim that his "truth is simple and naked" (*OA*, p. 392). Philanax's "tale" may be a "cunning" artifice that has "mingled truths with falsehoods, surmises with certainties" as Pyrocles charges (*OA*, pp. 391–92), but his own account is scarcely "the thread to guide you in the labyrinth" (*OA*, p. 393).[16]

True judgment requires an outsider's perspective, one both geographically and intellectually detached from the Arcadian world of fantasy. The "fittest instrument" for that point of view is Euarchus, the visiting philosopher-king of Macedonia who serves as judge. His is a mind that guards against illusion: "his thoughts true to themselves, [he] was neither beguiled with the painted gloss of pleasure nor dazzled with the false light of ambition. This made the line of his actions straight and always like itself" (*OA*, pp. 357–58). Euarchus is not merely the sober rationalist; he is the consummate civic humanist, transforming the private retreat into a public arena for debate.[17] Nor is he ignorant of the paradoxes that complicate the humanist ethic. His own mind is immune to "painted gloss," and he knows how to appeal to, even pander to, the nonrational, imaginative needs of his audience:

> For Euarchus did wisely consider the people to be naturally taken with exterior shows far more than with inward consideration of the material points; and therefore in this new entry into so entangled a matter he would leave nothing which might be either an armour or ornament unto him; and in these pompous ceremonies he well knew a secret of government much to consist.
>
> (*OA*, p. 375)

The private stage play of love becomes the public stage play of power, an antique image of Renaissance courtly magnificence.

Sidney is careful, furthermore, to legitimize Euarchus's
"shows." His motive is strictly ethical, to gather the energies
of an audience whose "many circles of imaginations can hardly
be enclosed in one point" (*OA*, p. 363) and to direct them toward a fundamental humanist insight: the complementary recognitions of human limitation and human sufficiency, the belief that man, for all his epistemological shortcomings, is
capable of significant moral action.[18]

> . . . I am to require you not to have an overshooting expectation
> of me. . . . remember I am a man; that is to say, a creature whose
> reason is often darkened with error. . . . lay your hearts void of
> foretaken opinions, else whatsoever I do or say will be measured
> by a wrong rule, like them that have the yellow jaundice, every-
> thing seeming yellow unto them.
>
> (*OA*, p. 365)

Euarchus's candor enhances his promise as a judge. By confessing his own limitations, he would make the Arcadians self-conscious of their own; he cannot purge them of their need for
exterior shows, but hopes to control eccentric excess, the dis-
torting lens of extreme subjectivism. The "reward" he promises is a return to stable law together with access to genuine,
because virtuous, power.

Yet even as Sidney legitimizes Euarchus, he engineers a
growing anticipatory tension, for we know one detail Euarchus does not: the accused princes are his own son and nephew,
whom he has not seen since their childhood. We understand
from the beginning that the judge himself will ultimately be
tried. Indeed, we conduct this trial in our minds throughout
the scene, for we find ourselves alternately fascinated and repelled by Euarchus's cold brilliance. His competence and virtue
first draw our admiration. Listening to Gynecia's melancholy
and fantastic confession, he holds himself aloof from tragic images and rhetorical figures, attending "more the manifest proof
. . . than anything relenting to those tragical phrases of hers

(apter to stir a vulgar pity than his mind which hated evil in what colours soever he found it)" (*OA*, pp. 382–83). During the other orations, he shows "no motions either at the one's or other's speech, letting pass the flowers of rhetoric and only marking whither their reasons tended" (*OA*, p. 403). His own discourse moves crisply from the general to the particular as he considers the meaning of the law and exposes the fallacies of others' arguments. His theme is logical and moral clarity: the issues must not be confounded "no more than good and evil are to be mingled"; the punishment must in "no way exceed the proportion of the trespass" (*OA*, p. 405). And clarity is possible only by imposing boundaries. If the world is a stage where ethical human conduct is enacted, there must be a brake on the fancies that have brought the state to the brink of disaster. The mind's motions must be restricted, and Euarchus becomes a Daedalus lecturing a nation of Icaruses as he explains "how to judge well":

> And that must undoubtedly be done, *not by a free discourse* of reason and skill of philosophy, but *must be tied to the laws* of Greece and municipal statutes of this dukedom. For although out of them these came, and to them must indeed refer their offspring, yet because philosophical discourses stand in the general consideration of things, they leave to every man a scope of his own interpretation; where the laws, applying themselves to the necessary use, *fold us within assured bounds*, which once broken, *man's nature infinitely rangeth*.
>
> (*OA*, p. 404; emphasis mine)

"Free discourse" gives rise to laws ("out of them these came"), but it inevitably subverts them. The power of judgment must finally turn back against the mind's own fecundity. For "philosophical discourses" here imply not the dry abstractions attacked in the *Apology*, but the mind's infinite ranging. The zodiac of the wit, with its endless transformations, cannot remain our home.[19]

It is with such restrictions in mind that Euarchus first ranks the "probable" testimony ("Certainly as in equality of conjectures we are not to take hold of the worst" [*OA*, p. 405]), and then plots rigorous demarcations isolating evil deeds from good ones and fixing their proper punishments. Musidorus may cry that "laws are not made like lime twigs or nets" (*OA*, p. 402), but it is the precariousness, not the inflexibility, of cultural systems that concerns Euarchus. A "show of conveniency" might satisfy the human longing for festive comedy by arranging a double marriage of the attractive young couples, but this would leave unchecked those disturbing impositions of the will that the flux of events always encourages among the princely and the egotistical: "If that unbridled desire which is entitled love [were condoned] . . . he that steals might allege the love of money, he that murders the love of revenge, he that rebels the love of greatness, as the adulterer the love of a woman." The survival of "public society" demands the restraint of "young men, strong men, and rich men who shall ever find private conveniences how to palliate . . . committed disorders" (*OA*, pp. 406–7).

The trial scene thus becomes, for some critics, a "ritual catharsis under the rational control of Euarchus's law and order . . . as truth emerges it comes clothed in brighter and brighter lights." Even Richard Lanham, the sharpest commentator on the work's rhetorical slyness, settles on Euarchus as "the undeniable ethical touchstone of the romance"; under his control, "rape, rebellion and murder are finally given their right names. Reason has asserted itself."[20] But others have found the transition from release to clarification to be unbearable; the effect of Euarchus's judgments as they toll throughout the scene is less one of illumination than of suffocation. Gynecia is sentenced to be buried alive with Basilius; Philoclea to be kept a lifelong "prisoner among certain women of religion like the vestal nuns"; Pyrocles and Musidorus, while cleared of murder, are sentenced to death for ravishing the princesses, the former to be thrown from a high tower and the latter to be decapitated by Dametas. Basilius's folly may have turned the state upside down, hiding away his daughters and elevating the unworthy and buffoonish Dametas to power, but Euarchus's reassertion of order threatens to produce no less monstrous inversions.[21]

The sudden revelation by a stranger that Euarchus has sentenced his own son and nephew—news so shocking that even the raving Philanax is "mollified"—does not alter the man "whose thoughts are always true to themselves." "What . . . I have said hath been out of my assured persuasion what justice itself and your just laws require. . . . I weighed the matter which you committed into my hands with my most unpartial and furthest reach of reason" (*OA*, p. 411). Euarchus passes his own test of disinterestedness, but only at the cost of discovering where the furthest reach of reason may lead. If Gynecia has brought death into Arcadia, so too has Euarchus, who despite a flood of emotion, can only cling to his unyielding ethic in the face of painful and baffling experience:

> Let my grey hairs be laid in the dust with sorrow. Let the small remnant of my life be to me an inward and outward desolation, and to the world a gazing stock of wretched misery. But never, never, let sacred rightfulness fall. . . . No, no, Pyrocles and Musidorus, I prefer you much before my life, but I prefer justice as far before you.
>
> (*OA*, p. 411)

In a world filled with articulate discourse, whether fancifully excessive or scrupulously reasoned, only the inarticulate groaning of a waking fool rescues the characters, and us, from an unbearable conclusion. The poison drunk by Basilius proves to have been only a powerful sleeping potion, and his sudden awakening with a "great voice of groaning" redeems all.

REACHING FURTHER

It is characteristic of Sidney that the final sequence of judgment and forgiveness should be the source of the *Old Arcadia*'s most vexing interpretive problems. Euarchus's resolutions are both just and intolerable; Basilius's universal clemency both a relief and the beginning of a new round of fiction making (*OA*, p. 416).[22] In a world where "nothing is so certain as our continual uncertainty," we have been lured into believing that a perspective is possible outside what Musidorus calls the "charmed circle," only to find its circumference is more inclusive than we thought.

What could have led Sidney, one of the finest products of English humanism, to plot so disorienting a conclusion? A. C. Hamilton speculates that he was "exorcising his private nightmare"; Euarchus is thus a fictive embodiment of Sidney's stern father, whose disapproval of Philip's retreat at Wilton is both evoked and defused in the comic resolution.[23] That nightmare is, I would add, public as well as private, its implications cultural as well as autobiographical. The best foil for the last movement of the *Old Arcadia* is Spenser's House of Alma (*The Faerie Queene*, bk. 2, canto 9), where in an allegory of the human body we encounter "Phantastes" in the mind's first chamber. This creature appears to have been born under the sign of "*Saturne*," "full of melancholy," with "sharpe staring eyes, / That mad or foolish seemd" (2.9.52) and a "working wit, / That neuer idle was, ne once could rest a whit" (2.9.49). Spenser's picture of the imagination is matched by his portrayal of its inventions: the chamber presents "Infinite shapes . . . / Some such as in the world were neuer yit . . . / Such as in idle fantasies doe flit: Infernall hags, *Centaurs*, feendes, *Hippodames*, / Apes, Lions, Aegles, Owles, fooles, louers, children, Dames" (2.9.50), together with the sound of buzzing flies:

> All those were idle thoughts and fantasies,
> Deuices, dreames, opinions vnsound,

Shewes, visions, sooth-sayes, and prophesies;
And all that fained is, as leasings, tales, and lies.

(2.9.51)

The chaos of imaginative energy Phantastes represents is a necessary prelude to the next mental chamber, where we find pictures

Of Magistrates, of courts, of tribunals,
Of commen wealthes, of states, of pollicy,
Of lawes, of iudgements, and of decretals;
All artes, all science, all Philosophy

(2.9.53)

The passage from one chamber to the next, A. Bartlett Giamatti points out, figures the movement from "the individual imagination to that of institutions, from fantasy to civility; youth to maturity. . . . In this chamber of civil fullness the chaotic energy of imagination's den is ordered and arranged. This is the world of 'artifice,' those things—systems, institutions, codes, conventions—by which we live and which we call civilization."[24] The *Old Arcadia* promises an even more decisive subduing of fantastic excess to the objective clarity of judgment, law, and civic duty; the trial scene would bind Proteus and expel him from Arcadia as the Other. The surprise resolution, however, frustrates that enterprise by collapsing rational judgment into the realm it has judged, the realm of the partial, the contingent, even the dangerously excessive. It is Proteus's answer to his detractors: *et in Arcadia ego*; civilized norms are never free from the ambiguities of human *poiesis*.

Euarchus had proclaimed his wisdom to be "an essential and not an opinionate thing" (*OA*, pp. 361–62), and Sidney's conclusion has set readers to scanning the text for surer signs of essence. David Kalstone argues that the resolution is the "result of comic accident," but others have insisted on precisely the opposite to accident; a larger purpose guides all coincidence: the essence of essences, the hand of Providence.[25] Indeed, after his daring sympathy with the lovers at the end of book 3, the narrator opens book 4 with stern reminders of "everlasting justice," "our faults," "our shame," and "our repentance" (*OA*, p. 265), and though the radical shift in tone makes us reluctant to privilege what may be only a momentary, or even parodic, stance, the precise ironies of the plot's final unfolding seem to uphold his claims for a "great constellation," a "strange and secret . . . justice" governing all (*OA*, pp. 272, 385).

But even providentialism does not provide us with a fixed interpretive point. Elizabeth Dipple regards the happy ending as a "cynical *deus ex machina*,"[26] while those who do find it a fitting solution disagree radically about what it means. Jon S. Lawry, for example, calls Basilius's awakening a "resurrection" that signals the "corrective confluence of human reason and divine design," reaffirming the "rational order of the cosmos"; Franco Marenco sees the conclusion as a fitting end to a "gloomy, almost desperate book" that demonstrates the miserable futility of all human powers and institutions: "Nothing remains strongly in Arcadia; not wise government, not chastity, not faith, not physical or moral strength."[27] While I share the reluctance of most readers to accept Marenco's bleak interpretation, it strikes me as no more partial than Lawry's "golden laugh . . . as gentle as it is serenely confident."[28] Sidney has not dismantled the humanist's universe, but he has radically altered the light in which we see it. Euarchus's careful balance has become at once more indulgent and more tense, more open to joy and wit, yet also more deeply anxious, releasing the kind of sophisticated laughter made possible, and necessary, by a fluid and problematic world.

The one providential guide we can invoke with genuine certainty in the *Old Arcadia* is the one who first engineers a perfect scene of tragic recognition, as Aristotle describes it (*Poetics* 1453b–1454a), and then the "comic accident" that reverses it— namely, the very human god who calls the Arcadian world into being on the "loose sheets of paper" he sends to his sister. Pyrocles and the entire cast of characters are, as that young prince indicates, subjects of a poet's cunning: Philip Sidney's. The impious oracle who glimpses the future at the start reveals his riddling plot summary, and the narrator's amazement at the fortuitous fallings out of events is Sidneyan self-advertisement for his skill in weaving the threads of his complicated narrative into what proves to be, in retrospect, the causal matrix of a five-act Terentian comedy.[29] However dizzying the events may have become, we are able to look back at the whole as superbly crafted, a balanced form that rescues Arcadia from chaos even as it sets its characters free. The work begins in praise of Arcadia, a land "ever had in singular reputation" (*OA*, p. 4) and ends with a last glance at reputation: Gynecia becomes "the perfect mirror of all wifely love . . . so uncertain are mortal judgments, the same person most infamous and most famous, and neither justly" (*OA*, p. 416). The conclusion affirms neither human perfection nor human depravity and does not rest in notable images of virtue and vice. It leaves us, rather, with the uncertain pleasures of a world perceived *sub specie fictionis.*[30]

The *Old Arcadia* is Sidney's first major survey of his poetic powers, and its conclusion is at once astonishing and poised as only a brilliantly fashioned paradox can be. But Sidney was, by the work's end, already suspicious that its poise might have been too easily won, for in the final sentence he invokes a broader imaginative world, an expanding series of untold narratives—"comical adventures," "wonderful chances," "extreme affection," and "poor hopes"—that, he suggests, "may awake some other spirit to exercise his pen" (*OA*, p. 417). It is Sidney's challenge to himself, which he will attempt to meet in the *New Arcadia.*

8

THE *NEW ARCADIA*

FROM *OLD* TO *NEW*

Sidney populates the *Old Arcadia* with characters who try to organize the world after their hearts and minds, but who find at the end of all their scheming that they are trapped by their own ingenuity. At such moments, the characters can only appeal to a higher perspective as their own deep plots do pall. When Musidorus's elopement with Pamela is foiled by a band of ruffians, he cries, "Alas, how contrary an end have all the inclinations of my mind taken! . . . I invoke that universal and only wisdom (which examining the depth of hearts, hath not his judgements fixed upon the event) to bear testimony with me" (*OA*, p. 311). So, too, Pyrocles, discovered in bed with Philoclea, presumes to cast aside the "vain shadow of discourse" by reading Jove's "unsearchable mind," and it is, ironically, only Philoclea's "well conceived and sweetly pronounced speeches" that can prevent him from executing the suicide he believes Jove sanctions (*OA*, pp. 291–97).

Imprisoned in the fifth and final book, the princes make the *Old Arcadia*'s most urgent effort to search for a larger pattern of coherence. To Pyrocles' momentary doubt that "the heavens ever held a just proportion," Musidorus responds: "O blame not the heavens, sweet Pyrocles . . . as their course never alters, so is there nothing done by the unreachable ruler of them, but hath an everlasting reason for it" (*OA*, p. 371). Not to be outdone in "the sweet mysteries of philosophy," Pyrocles seconds his cousin's optimism with speculation on the afterlife: when the mind is no longer darkened by the body's prison, "returning to the life of all things, where all infinite knowledge is, it cannot but be a right intelligence . . . though void of imagining to itself anything, but even grown like to his creator, hath all things with a spiritual knowledge before it" (*OA*, p. 373). This elevation from mere "imagining" to the very origin of thought—the "vital power of that very intelligence"—is scarcely the speculative triumph the princes proclaim. As Lanham has noted, Musidorus is a little too confident that their earthly lives, the source of Arcadia's political chaos, have already "achieved the causes of their hither coming," and a little too breezy in his condemnation of "baser minds too much delighted with the kennel of this life." And Pyrocles is too quick to call "all the gods to witness . . . the inward honour, essential pleasure, and living life I have enjoyed in the presence of the faultless Philoclea" (*OA*, p. 372). Should Musidorus make equal claims for his love of Pamela, he adds, "we shall have a debate in the other world" (*OA*, p. 372). We are scarcely surprised when the ascent to the realms of *intellectus* is forgotten in the succeeding trial scene, with its complex theatricality and rhetorical cross fire.[1]

But if transcendent vision is never truly available in the *Old Arcadia*, the longing for such vision remains a psychological fact, and it is with an expression of that longing that Sidney opens his revised *Arcadia*. The shepherds Strephon and Claius revisit the scene of their beloved Urania's last appearance, lamenting their lost love in terms loaded—even overloaded—with philosophical and religious significances; her very name suggests at once the Neoplatonic Venus Urania, goddess of Heavenly Beauty, and the Muse of Christian poetry and astronomy.[2] The shepherds' love reverberates with suggestions of Platonic furor, theological analogy, and intellectual elevation. "Over-busie Remembrance, Remembrance, restlesse Remembrance" commands them to the place, and the place commands them to remember more, giving "newe heate to the feaver" (*NA*, pp. 5–6), an opening derived from Montemayor that in this context intimates deeper forms of *anamnesis*. The goal of their longing, moreover, is beyond finite comprehension; just as the sun's dazzling beauty is better seen in its reflection on the waters, so, too, Urania's "sun-stayning excellencie" is better sought for in her effects. And where better than in their own minds, which have been raised above the "ordinary levell of the worlde" through their love, until "great clearkes do not disdaine our conference" (*NA*, p. 7)? Indeed, they confess that "the desire to seeme worthie in her eyes made us when others were sleeping, to sit vewing the course of heavens" (*NA*, pp. 7–8). There is no better emblem for their state than the Neoplatonic image for the mind's penetration to higher truths; Urania has "given eyes unto *Cupid*" (*NA*, p. 8).

Ficinian vision, however, is still far out of reach; as if to remind us that we are in the realm of "continual disquiet," the narrative explodes in a welter of cruel events. Musidorus is washed up on shore, the victim of a shipwreck (and of human treachery), and the two shepherds must restrain him from suicidally casting himself back into the sea when he discovers he has lost Pyrocles. Scouting the wreck for survivors,

> they saw a sight full of piteous strangenes: a ship, or rather the carkas of the shippe, or rather some few bones of the carkas, hulling there, part broken, part burned, part drowned: death having used more then one dart to that destruction. About it floted great store of very rich thinges, and many chestes which might promise no lesse. And amidst the precious things were a number of dead bodies, which likewise did not onely testifie both elements violence, but that the chiefe violence was growen of humane inhumanitie: for their bodies were ful of grisly wounds, & their bloud had (as it were) filled the wrinckles of the seas visage: which it seemed the sea woulde not wash away, that it might witnes it is not alwaies his fault, when we condemne his crueltie.
>
> (*NA*, pp. 9–10)

The striking juxtaposition of Urania-worship and "humane inhumanitie," the imagistic transformation of the sea as reflector of the golden face of the sun to the sea as a face, itself wrinkled and crusted with blood, suggests to E. M. W. Tillyard the distance "between the idea of man's 'erected wit' and the pitiful spectacle of what in crude fact man has made of man."³ Sidney is indeed playing off contrasts; but his program is less schematic than Tillyard allows.

Both "erected wit" and "pitiful spectacle" are rhetorically ambiguous. The shepherds' minds have been brought to a hyperactive state, but the heavenly orientation is less than certain despite their interest in astronomy. Their ostentatious use of hyperbole and the peculiar discrepancies in Sidney's overall treatment of Urania in his works strongly imply that we should regard the shepherds' vision with some sense of irony; so, too, does the mixture of admiration and amusement they evoke from a prominent Arcadian: "It is a sporte to heare howe they impute to love, whiche hath indewed their thoughts (saie they) with suche a strength" (*NA*, p. 27).⁴ The initial idealism is questioned more deeply by Sidney's choice of speakers: Strephon and Claius ("writhe" and "weep") are imported from the *Old Arcadia*, where their most notable contribution is the double sestina picturing a claustrophobic world of anxiety and loss. True, they are transformed in the process of revision from melancholy gentlemen posing as shepherds to genuine shepherds, but their love continues to complicate transcendence with torment: Strephon is "hopelesse" and "dolefull" and Claius pictures their rapture in terms of entrapment and deadly threat. They are "held by that racking steward, Remembraunce"; "As well may sheepe forget to feare when they spie woolves, as wee can misse such fancies" (*NA*, p. 7). Nor is the shipwreck a "crude fact" that explodes a golden moment; it is as much a moment of rapt fascination as anything that precedes it. As Myrick superbly characterizes its elaborate artifice, the scene evinces an authorial mind "only too alert" whose "tendency [is] to dazzle the reader with dexterity."⁵ The transformation of event into conceit—the sea that would not wash its face to exonerate itself of exaggerated charges of cruelty—is subtly balanced by a complementary movement—the ship becoming the carcass of a ship, then the bones of the carcass, a deepening conceit suddenly literalized in the image of human corpses "ful of grisly wounds." A didactic point about human cruelty is surely made, but it is difficult to assess whether it is the goal of, or serves as an excuse for, the extraordinary flood of ingenuity.[6] Rather than sketching a comprehensive pattern, the opening of the *New Arcadia* jolts us with a display of the kinds of moral and imaginative extremes that will be released in a fiction forever rising and sinking from melancholy to exaltation to despair to renewed efforts of comprehension.

In Sidney's revision the heroic task is the achievement of some form of mastery in an increasingly volatile world. The effort already begins with the shepherds' survey of the wreck: "They came so neere as their eies were ful masters of the object." The young princes will likewise attempt to order events in their minds, to become, in Kalstone's phrase, "*read*ers of their experience."[7] And yet the *New Arcadia* returns to the problematics of the *Old* not with a heightened perspective, but with a mounting torrent of images that ultimately challenges any mastery, whether by protagonist, poet, or reader. Unlike the characters of the *Old Arcadia*, who seek resolution by curbing the mind's restlessness, whether in Pyrocles' vision of the afterlife, or Euarchus's civic folding of the mind "within assured bounds," Sidney pushes invention to its furthest reaches, determined to explore the implications of fiction making and the world it represents through the strenuous activity of the imagination itself.

If, as Myrick argues, Strephon and Claius's opening is an epic invocation to the Muse, it is profoundly appropriate to these explorations. *Urania abscondita* symbolizes a world where human longing must confront the gulf separating it from guaranteed fixed points. What would become a crisis of confidence for Tasso in his *Discorsi del poema eroico* as he doubts his access to eternal forms is the driving force behind Sidney's work. For the characteristic motion of his epic will be not so much upward as outward, its field of action stretching from shepherds to shipwreck, from metaphysics to murder.

"A DELIGHT TO PLAY WITH IT SELFE"

Once the shipwreck has been left behind, the most notable feature of the new Arcadian landscape is a stream of didactic images figuring forth restraint and proper pleasure, as if relieving and reorienting us after the narrative's traumatic birth. A stable social hierarchy is imaged in the "proud . . . stately trees" and "humble vallies" content with their "base estate." A spacious, countrified Utopia appears where houses are decently separated yet close enough for "mutual succour: a shew, as it were of accompanable solitariness, & of a civil wildnes" (*NA*, pp. 13–14). Even the animals have elegantly ordered fancies, the nightingales turning anguish into ornament as they strive "one with the other which coulde in most dainty variety recount their wrong-caused sorow" and lambs sound their "bleting oratory" (*NA*, p. 13). Musidorus's first lodging seems to place us at the Arcadian moral center. The noble Kalander's "great house" is "an honorable representing of a firme statelines," whose structure is "rather directed to the use of the guest, then to the eye of the Artificer" (*NA*, p. 15). There could be no saner place for Musidorus to recover his health. "Handsome without curiositie," Kalander's house does indulge a few frisks of the imagination, but all are self-correcting. A reflecting pond replicates the garden "in shaddowes," a white marble Venus's blue veining becomes the body's veins, and an astonishingly illusionistic painting of Atalanta seems itself to run, but all is governed by the garden's larger aesthetic, so "wel arrayed" that "it seemed that arte therein would needes be delightfull by counterfaiting his enemie error, and making order in confusion" (*NA*, pp. 17–18).

These pictures do not hold their shape for long. Basilius, promoted from duke to king of Arcadia, has already made his retreat, despite Philanax's warnings against "curiositie" and "fansies" (*NA*, p. 24). Nor is Basilius the only curious Arcadian. Kalander, wonderfully generous but incurably garrulous, can narrate the details because he has read a confidential letter to Basilius, a letter copied by his son, whom he blames for "curiositie," but that he cannot resist reading either (*NA*, p. 23). The people, as in the original *Arcadia*, are now buzzing with rumors, the nobility already rising in envy against Philanax, who rules in Basilius's stead, and the shepherds, whose elevated wits have them versifying from an early age, are "under hidden formes uttering such matters, as otherwise they durst not deale with" (*NA*, pp. 26–28). As the pressures of political dissention swell, exploding into prominence in the final book, they are matched by the refurbished intrigues of the love plot. Once the princes are reunited, fall in love, and slip into their disguises, the stage play of love begins again with "such intricatenes" that a player can "see no way to lead him out of the maze" (*NA*, p. 94).

There is, to be sure, a deliberate heightening of the characters. Sidney will not allow his princes to ravish their loves; their heroic qualities, as well as the princesses' virtues, are more firmly pronounced. But the wooing of near exemplars produces increasingly baroque and convoluted courtships. If Pamela has grown into an imposing figure, the consequence for Musidorus is that he not only must tell the tale of himself, but must playact a series of noble roles to draw her attention, appearing "like my selfe" by pretending to assume "the part of a King in a Tragedie" one day, and by playing the role of Paris on another (*NA*, pp. 165, 180). So, too, must this prince, disguised as a shepherd disguised as prince, prove his courtly grace, dancing the "Matachine daunce in armour" with "gracefull dexteritie." If his performances are designed to reveal his noble origins, they also make conspicuous the artifices of his courtliness as he thrills his love not only with the depth of his passion but with his ingenuity: "I thinke no day past," Pamela marvels, "when by some one invention he would appeare unto me to testifie his love" (*NA*, p. 180). The ludic spirit fills the pastoral retreat as never before; the lodge becomes Basilius's playground with its "artificiall inventions": a "waterworke" produces rainbows, artificial birds deceive both the eye and ear, and a water-driven table, which Basilius controls for "sport," turns itself and those seated at it round and round (*NA*, p. 92). In this giddy world, Pyrocles and Philoclea are again infatuated by each other. Philoclea is stricken through a curious exercise in imitation: so admirable is the Amazon before her that she copies her every gesture, stolen glances and furtive sighs included, until "(. . . ere she were aware) she accepted . . . not only the signe, but the passion signified" (*NA*, p. 170). Pyrocles, already stricken by Philoclea's portrait, allows himself to drift from reality to fantasy as he turns his eyes and mind into a gallery of images: "Sometimes my eyes would lay themselves open to receive all the dartes she did throwe, sometimes cloze up with admiration, as if with a contrary fancie, they woulde preserve the riches of that sight they had gotten, or cast my lidde as curtaines over the image of beautie, her presence had painted in them" (*NA*, pp. 92–93).

Perhaps the most peculiar instance of increased fancifulness in the *New Arcadia* is the elaborate game of interpretive hide-and-seek Sidney himself plays with us. At times we are comfortable identifying the moral significance of the narrative's symbolic images and allusions: Actaeon, for example, means concupiscence; Phaeton suggests presumption. A critic inclined to privilege the Neoplatonic patterns of the *Old Arcadia* will find the *New* even "more Platonic."[8] But Sidney's pleasure in twisting and qualifying his patterns also escalates. Consider Pyrocles' Amazonian disguise. He takes the name "Zelmane," rather than "Cleophila," to honor a self-sacrificing admirer from an earlier heroic adventure, and Tillyard reads the "symbolic significance" of the transvestitism as "disinfect[ing], as it were, the queer complications of events . . . this disguise occasions." Indeed, for Tillyard the action must be "kept in the more abstract realm dictated by [its] emblematic nature" to prevent our perceiving it as "ridiculously improbable and slightly disgusting."⁹ But while the disguise has new, heroic overtones, it continually pulls us down from the abstract realm; the Amazon's feminine beauties are lovingly described before we are told who is under the charming costume, and the symbolic device she wears teases us with its mutually exclusive possibilities: an image of Hercules dressed as a woman by Omphale's command, with the "worde in Greeke, but thus to be interpreted, *Never more valiant*" (*NA*, p. 76). How, Sidney seems to challenge us, will you interpret that which I have thus interpreted: never more valiant than now, or valiant nevermore?¹⁰

The attempt to interpret images, to master them, can become a bewildering shuffling of significances, which may account in part for Hazlitt's exasperated cry that "the *Arcadia* is a riddle, a rebus, an acrostic in folio." Perhaps the best example of Sidney indulging this kind of game emerges near the midpoint of his revision, in book 2, chapter 11. The following events take place: Pamela's guardian Mopsa falls asleep and Musidorus attempts to seize "that occasion" to declare his love, only to be fended off. The two princesses then bathe in the river Ladon, where they are observed by Zelmane, who composes an erotic blazon celebrating Philoclea's body, but then finds a rival suitor and voyeur in the noble Amphialus, and wounds him. The chapter is crowded with allusive clues. When Musidorus tries to act while "this dragon sleepes, that keepes the golden fruite" (*NA*, p. 215), we are tempted to make something of the allusion to the dragon Ladon killed by Hercules in fetching the golden apples of the Hesperides. It was at the Arcadian river Ladon, moreover, that Hercules performed another of his twelve labors, capturing the golden hind. The river Ladon is also the scene of Pan's attempt to ravish Syrinx, which, Ovid tells us, was frustrated when the nymph was metamorphosed into a handful of reeds; Pan's disappointed sigh over them gave birth to the pan pipe and pastoral music. Again we are teased into drawing some connection, for Zelmane in sexual frustration finds an outlet in song, a blazon ironically attributed to "divine fury" (*NA*, p. 218). And once we recall that Ovid puts the tale of Pan and Syrinx itself into the mouth of Mercury as he lulls the monstrous guardian Argus to sleep to rescue Io, we find ourselves casting back to the sleeping guardian, Mopsa, the chapter's starting point.[11]

The better versed we are in classical myth and fable, the more labyrinthine our responses are liable to be. The princesses are, after all, bathing nude in a "priveleged" place where "upon pain of death . . . nobody durst presume to come hither," certainly alluding to Actaeon and Diana, whose painted image hangs in Kalander's picture gallery (*NA*, p. 18); Amphialus and his spaniel complete the picture by suggesting Actaeon and his hounds. But Amphialus, attacked by Zelmane, is stabbed in the thigh, much to Zelmane's repentant dismay, and so becomes not a stag but, perhaps, Adonis, while Zelmane in rapid succession plays wistful Pan, peeping Actaeon, wrathful Diana, attacking hounds, goring boar, and, possibly, sorrowful Venus. If Sidney's mind appears to be, in Myrick's terms, "only too alert," his writing produces a congruent effect on his readers. We are stimulated not merely by the discovery of allusive clues, but by their overabundance; they proliferate like the reflections of the princesses in the Ladon as they strike the water "with their hands, the water (making lines in his face) seemed to smile at such beating, and with twentie bubbles, not to be content to have the picture of their face in large upon him, but he would in ech of those bubbles set forth the miniature of them" (*NA*, p. 218). It is at such moments that Sidney most fully indulges in the pleasures of the text, itself represented emblematically in the course of the Ladon, "not running forth right, but almost continually winding, as if the lower streames would returne to their spring, or that the River had a delight to play with it selfe" (NA, p. 216).[12]

The New Arcadia, it has sometimes been suggested, was revised with the Apology in mind, its heroicizing following the sense of purpose that critical document displays. But where are we to find the sober Daedalus to guide us? He is, in fact, implied by this scene, in the very description of the Ladon, which is another Ovidian echo, this time of Ovid's simile for Daedalus's Cretan maze:

> Daedalus renowmed in that lande
> For fine devise and workmanship in building, went in hand
> To make it. He confounds his worke with sodaine stops and
>   stayes,
> And with the great uncertaintie of sundrie winding wayes
> Leades in and out, and to and fro, at divers doores astray.
> And as with trickling streame the Brooke Maeander seemes to
>   play
> In Phrygia, and with doubtfull race runnes counter to and fro,
> And meeting with himselfe doth looke if all his streame or no
> Come after, and retiring eft cleane backward to his spring
> And marching eft to open Sea as streight as any string,
> Indenteth with reversed streame: even so of winding wayes
> Unnumerable Daedalus within his worke convayes.
> Yea scarce himselfe could find the meanes to winde himselfe
>   well out:
> So busie and so intricate the house was all about.
>   (Metamorphoses 8.159–68)[13]

Daedalus, Sidney would remind us, is not only the teacher of restraint, but the architect of labyrinths. The confluence of the Ladon and the Maeander carries us a long way from the lucid order of Kalander's great house.

Sidney's habitual turning from sobriety to irony and sportive paradox does not mean he would jettison the moral dimensions of fiction; it marks, rather, his impatience with the merely schematic, the easy confidence in fixed interpretive coordinates. The literary pleasures in which the *New Arcadia* indulges also allow Sidney to set up a more ambitious critical laboratory than he did with the *Old*. When the Arcadian narrative turns back on itself, it does so not only in sport, but in earnest, to reflect on the vulnerability of poetic images, their possible defacement or detachment from genuine moral concerns.

Two episodes in the first book consider the possibility of healing a breach between image and ideal. The story of Argalus and Parthenia, a tale of violence, separation, and wish-fulfillment, explicitly presents its heroine as the notable pattern of virtue, "one, that to praise well, one must first set downe with himselfe, what it is to be excellent: for so she is" (*NA*, p. 32). She is sadistically disfigured by her rejected suitor and flees from her true love, Argalus, despite his "having her faire image in his heart" and his maintenance of the "trueth of love (which still held the first face in his memorie) . . . inward worthines shining through the foulest mistes" (*NA*, pp. 34, 35). Argalus, in turn, widens the gulf between them when, seeking revenge, he is captured by the rebellious Helots in Laconia. But here the catastrophic is quickly mended by the world of epic romance, which both rejoins lovers and reunites image and truth. The princes' valor preserves and releases Argalus, and Parthenia returns miraculously healed. She completes the thematic pattern by pretending to be Parthenia's cousin; Argalus rejects what he believes to be a mere image—"It was *Parthenias* selfe I loved . . . no likenes" (*NA*, p. 50)—only to find he has passed the test: the image is what it seems. All rejoice at the wonderful event, celebrating the marriage "with al conceipts that might deliver delight to mens fancies" (*NA*, p. 54).

But by the end of book 1, we read the comic, if bizarre, tale of Phalantus and Artesia. Theirs is a love based entirely on the disjunction of surface and meaning, of sign and significance. Phalantus had been a bored young courtier who decided to play the role of a lover, "taking love uppon him like a fashion" (*NA*, p. 98). He meets his match in Artesia, who since youth has been taught by her aunt Cecropia that "there is no wisdome but in including heaven & earth in ones self: and that love, courtesie, gratefulnesse, friendship, and all other vertues are rather to be taken on, then taken in ones selfe" (*NA*, p. 98). If ever there was a rupture between *verba* and *res*, it is in this courtship. Phalantus becomes her servant "for tongue-delight," his love a rhetorical display rivaling that of the god of oratory's: "He with cheerefull lookes would speake sorrowfull words, using the phrase of his affection in so high a stile, that *Mercurie* would not have wooed *Venus* with more magnificent Eloquence." The crafty Artesia, however, snares him with his own wit:

> She tooke the advauntage one daye uppon *Phalantus* unconscionable praysinges of her, and certaine cast-awaie vowes, howe much he would doo for her sake, to arrest his woord assoone as it was out of his mouth, and by the vertue thereof to charge him to goe with her thorow all the courts of *Greece*, & with the chalenge now made, to give her beauty the principality over all other. *Phalantus* was entrapped, and saw round about him, but could not get out.
>
> (*NA*, p. 99)

The challenge takes an appropriate form: a jousting for painted images: "the defendant should bring his mistresse picture" to be "set by the image of *Artesia*," with the winner keeping "both the honors and the pictures" (*NA*, p. 97).

Sidney was himself a participant in at least four Accession Day tournaments, those allegorical and chivalric performances that assumed so important a role in Elizabethan political life.[14] It is the fantastic quality of tournaments that Sidney now emphasizes, the very arbitrariness with which their symbols may be juggled. Phalantus, an expert with the lance, has remained undefeated, collecting an impressive gallery of portraits through victories Sidney compares to the sophist's: "(As many times it happens) that a good pleader makes a bad cause to prevaile; so hath his Lawnce brought captives to the triumph of *Artesias* beauty" (*NA*, p. 100). He has won a "forced false testimonie to *Artesias* excellencie." Here the dominant metaphor of the episode also makes the solution a simple one: a better jouster to defeat Phalantus and end the charade. Pyrocles performs the task, and his victory asks to be taken as another realignment of image and idea, of external show and intrinsic meaning. If there is some residual irony—Pyrocles has by now passed through two false identities and now assumes the disingenuous disguise of the "ill apparelled Knight"—we may still endorse him as champion; he brings no picture to stake but insists that "her liveliest picture (if you could see it) is in my hart" (*NA*, p. 110). But we are still only in book 1; Sidney will take us much further than this.

"NOTABLE IMAGES OF VIRTUE, VICE, AND WHAT ELSE"

Both tales, of Argalus and Parthenia and of Phalantus and Artesia, remind us of the importance of heroic action in the revised *Arcadia*. From the moment we see Pyrocles riding the broken mast with his sword held aloft in the opening shipwreck scene, we know that tales of heroic valor will assume a new prominence. They are Sidney's most conspicuous additions, providing important action in the first book, generating an intricately woven series of retrospective narratives in the second, and completely engulfing the original love plot in the political rebellion and agonizing captivity episode of the third.[15]

Heroic adventures consistently ask questions about the proper uses of feigning. Musidorus's assault on the Helots in book 1, for example, depends on a stratagem he had gleaned from history books: he turns his forces into a kind of acting company. "All the men there," he determines, "shoulde dresse themselves like the poorest sorte of the people in *Arcadia*, having no banners, but bloudie shirtes hanged upon long staves," while a select group are disguised as prisoners in chains, which "were made with such arte, that though they seemed strong and fast, he that ware them might easily loose them" (*NA*, pp. 40, 41). All "being performed," they gain entrance to the enemy town when a "cunning fellow" under the "maske" of simplicity, using a "Rhetorike as weeded out all flowers of Rhetorike," persuades the rebel Helots that they are sympathetic rebels from Arcadia.

Once the love plot has been well established in book 2, heroic action returns in the ambitiously plotted series of retrospective narratives inaugurated by Musidorus's thinly veiled autobiography. What had been an ingenious bit of seduction in the original becomes both an outline of the protagonists' heroic education and a progressive complication of Sidney's own critical inquiry. The princes' education begins with the profit and delight of stories and images:

> For almost before they could perfectly speake, they began to receave conceits not unworthy of the best speakers: excellent devises being used, to make even their sports profitable; images of battailes, & fortifications being then delivered to their memory, which after, their stronger judgements might dispens, the delight of tales being converted to the knowledge of al the stories of worthy Princes, both to move them to do nobly, & teach them how to do nobly.
>
> (*NA*, pp. 189–90)

Having been moved to learn, they next hunger for "the practise of those vertues, which they before learned" (*NA*, p. 191), and determine to set sail to join Euarchus at Byzantium. The course from *gnosis* to *praxis*, however, never did run smooth. Their harmonious world, represented in the sea's "smooth and shining face," proves to be treacherous. Once they have set sail, its "guilden shewe" is transformed into a "mournefull stage for a Tragedie to be plaied on"; they are blown upon a rock, which did "closely dissemble his cruel mind" beneath the "outragious waves" (*NA*, pp. 192–93). Here is a test the princes pass splendidly, displaying "the rule of vertue, not to abandon ones selfe" (*NA*, p. 194), the proper foundation for their adventures in

Asia Minor. The very terms of the testing, moreover, a personification of nature as a malicious and deceiving artificer,
serves as a thematic overture, for the princes will confront a
world of diseased imaginations and the spectrum of vices such
disease fosters.

The heroic righting of wrongs is cast in terms of the war
between the icastic and the fantastic. In Phrygia, they confront
a "Prince of a melancholy constitution both of bodie and mind;
wickedly sad, ever musing of horrible matters" (*NA*, p. 196).
A darker version of Basilius, he will listen only to those who
confirm his distorted, private visions, living in "tode-like re-
tyrednesse, and closenesse of minde" (*NA*, p. 196). His plans
for a public execution of Musidorus drive Pyrocles to demonstrate the contrivances of a healthy mind: costuming himself
as the executioner's servant complete with makeup—"having
his beautie hidden by many foule spots he artificially put upon
his face" (*NA*, p. 199)—he daringly rescues his cousin. After
the melancholy tyrant is killed and a new government erected
in his place, the princes discover a new version of mental im-
balance in the king of Pontus, who considers every friend "but
a playfellow," only to kill him when he grows bored. His beheading of the princes' loyal servants provokes further reformation, another tyrant toppled and a virtuous government
established.

These early adventures encourage the princes, and us, with
the adequacy of their heroism and their mastery of the "ethic
and politic consideration" (*Apology*, p. 104). They continue to
root out the vicious and the fantastic, making the world safe
for moral intelligibility: "good governours" are established,
"giants and monsters" subdued (*NA*, p. 206). Their ambitions
broaden; if imitation begets emulation, as critics have long suspected, the princes prove the point with their determination to
overgo the stories of their youth, "thinking it not so worthy,
to be brought to heroycall effects by fortune, or necessitie (like
Ulysses and *Aeneas*) as by ones owne choice, and working"

(*NA*, p. 206). The quest for autonomy, however, immediately complicates their world; their foes become not merely the mad but the cunning, as if forcing them to confront a parody of their own self-fashioning. The third adventure introduces the bastard Plexirtus, who has displaced his legitimate half brother and has blinded his father, the king of Paphlagonia. The tale is notable as the source of the Gloucester subplot in *Lear*, including a particularly unnerving portrait of its villain. Plexirtus, whose name suggests the twistings of his character, is an irresistible playactor. He is a Machiavel in the pursuit of power, employing "poysonous hypocrisie, desperate fraude, smoothe malice, hidden ambition, & smiling envie" (*NA*, p. 209), and a sophist who exploits his audience's virtues: "the exercise of craft conformed him to all turnings of sleights, that though no man had lesse goodnes in his soul then he, no man could better find the places whence arguments might grow of goodnesse to another" (*NA*, pp. 212–13). When his back is to the wall, he plays to his brother's pity by turning his despair into theater, a performance beyond even the narrator's imaginative talents: "With a rope about his necke, barefooted, [he] came to offer himselfe. . . . how artificially he could set out the torments of his owne conscience . . . I am not cunning inough to be able to expresse" (*NA*, p. 213).

Plexirtus introduces us to a more complicated sense of the perverse imagination. He cannot be jousted with like Phalantus or overthrown like the melancholy tyrant. He may be defeated, but his containment, like that of Spenser's Blatant Beast, is temporary; he will return to haunt us. As if seeking a moment's respite, the narrative returns us to the lovers in the Arcadian present, but the twists of fancy are kept before us, for the Ladon episode, discussed above, now appears. Hints of a growing concern about imagery surface when the tale-telling resumes. Relocated from the original *Arcadia* are the tale of Erona's futile effort to end the idolatry of Cupid's "pictures & images" and the poem condemning painters and poets for "fill[ing] the world with strange but vaine conceits" (*NA*, pp. 232, 239). The latter is now Miso's unthinking libel against Cupid, and outrages the amorous Pyrocles. Yet when he takes over the narrative chores, he, too, reveals a curious ambivalence about images as he tells of his decision to test his resources apart from his older cousin:

> I would needs goe alone . . . desirous to do something without the company of the incomparable Prince *Musidorus*, because in my hart I acknowledge that I owed more to his presence, then to any thing in my self, whatsoever before I had done. . . . He taught me by word, and best by example, giving me in him so lively an Image of vertue, as ignorance could not cast such mist over mine eyes . . . which made me indeed find in my selfe such a kind of depending upon him, as without him I found a weakenesse, and mistrustfulnes of my selfe, as one strayed from his best strength, when at any time I mist him.
>
> (*NA*, pp. 263–64)

The aggressive optimism with which the two princes departed from the models of Ulysses and Aeneas becomes a more troubled and solitary response; Pyrocles is at once grateful for, yet feels his "selfe" compromised by, the images that fill his mind.

In Sidney's world, however, images are inescapable. No event seems complete unless it is also theatricalized or represented in some way. When Pyrocles kills a monster, it is "to so great admiration of many (who from a safe place might looke on) that there was order given, to have the fight, both by sculpture and picture, celebrated in most parts of *Asia*" (*NA*, p. 301). After a later separation (reported earlier thanks to the digressive narrative), Musidorus finds his cousin's "fame flourishing, his monument engraved in Marble, and yet more durable in mens memories" (*NA*, p. 74). Images are inevitable because the world is always starved for more; one's only course after receiving them is to offer one's own to others.

There is nothing overtly sinister about such transactions. Heroic images are the staple of a didactic epic, and clearly drawn "notable images" are inevitably mixed with subtler moral implications. One critic describes these tales as a "miniature *Mirrour for Magistrates*," and another argues that their "larger purpose . . . is to serve the reader even as stories of princes served them"—that is, to set virtuous examples before the reader's eyes.[16] But even as the princes grow restive under the restriction of stories, so, too, the reader is forced to recognize the ironic constraints of grandly heroic images. Pyrocles may inspire noble sculpture and pictures, but the celebration of them requires a willful forgetting of their ambiguous genesis; Pyrocles killed the monster to protect the vicious Plexirtus: "My vertue had been imployed to save a worse monster then I killed" (*NA*, p. 301).

Heroic images, and the human imagination itself, are progressively strained as the retrospective narrative continues; the very efficacy of heroism seems to falter as the products of human fantasy become increasingly bizarre. The world of adventure seems to be populated by the species *homo ludens* run out of control. Dido's ruinous love for Pamphilus begins as a game, but she becomes like "them I have seene play at the ball, growe extremely earnest, who shoulde have the ball, and yet every one knew it was but a ball" (*NA*, p. 267). The lusty Andromana ("man crazy" is Walter Davis's no-nonsense translation) has an insatiable appetite for erotic sport and imprisons both princes, wishing them, as Pyrocles puts it, to be as fish "to bite at her bait" or to act "as if we should have played a request at Tennis betweene us: and often wishing that she might be the angle, where the lines of our friendshippe might meet" (*NA*, p. 279). One more fantastical tyrant is always ready to act out "whatsoever pleased his fansie" and so make "his kingdom his teniscourt" (*NA*, p. 330). There is, to be sure, an oasis of sanity in the description of Queen Helen's court and its proper use of play; her people are ready for the sternest tests, for "by continuall martiall exercises without bloud, she made them perfect in that bloudy art. Her sportes were such as caried riches of

Knowledge upon the streame of Delight" (*NA*, p. 283). But it is very much an oasis; we learn of these sports because her knights have come to the yearly jousts held in honor of the perverse Andromana. Whatever pictures come to us from this world are as likely to carry images of sadism and confusion as knowledge and delight. A disappointed suitor gives way not to sonneteering but to mass slaughter, as if he wrote "the sonets of his Love, in the bloud, & tuned them in the cries of [his beloved's] subjects" (*NA*, p. 233). He may be stopped, but the heroic qualities on which we have depended, the worthy forms of the icastic, are also tormented and stretched out of shape. The worthy Plangus finds Andromana has turned his kingly father against him and his every noble impulse, "the liberty of his mind, the high flying of his thoughts," is "translated into the language of suspition" (*NA*, pp. 246–47). He escapes his father's court and finds heroic outlet elsewhere, only to be further tormented by a cruelly ironic world until all consolations of Providence and Reason seem to him a "Poets fiction" (*NA*, p. 230). The protagonists, too, are vulnerable. The epic models they thought to supersede return in the form of horrifying parody when Pyrocles meets Dido and Pamphilus, the ruthless seducer she calls her "false *Aeneas*" (*NA*, p. 268). Dido has joined forces with other betrayed women and is about to castrate and gouge out the eyes of her former suitor when Pyrocles rescues him. There is hope of release into loftier matter through a chivalric combat with Anaxius, but it, too, becomes a heroic nightmare when Pyrocles must flee and endure the humiliating jeers of the spectators in order to rescue Dido from the now-vengeful Pamphilus and his henchmen, who are intent on raping and murdering her before her father's eyes. Further intervention places Pyrocles in the clutches of Dido's miserly father, who would sell him to his enemies, and the false Aeneas finds a more fitting mate in a false Lavinia named Baccha, "the most impudentlie unchaste woman of all *Asia*" (*NA*, p. 290). The grotesque is seconded by the ambiguous. Virtuous deeds may be performed for vicious motives, as when Plangus's father punishes malefactors out of hatred for his innocent son (NA, p. 277), or vice performed with virtuous intentions, as when the princes are tricked into killing Tiridates in an act that looks very much like "abominable treason" (NA, p. 236). The virtuous may even knowingly protect the vicious: Pyrocles is compelled to defend Plexirtus because of his virtuous daughter's dying wish (NA, p. 298). The triumph of the icastic over the fantastic is never more in doubt than when the princes end their Asian tour by naively allowing Plexirtus to arrange their sea passage to Greece, putting themselves into the hands of a captain who would "kill God him selfe" (NA, p. 304). They are saved from assassination only by an outbreak of mutiny, which evokes images not of heroism but of "the narrownesse of the place, the darknesse of the time, and the uncertainty in such a tumult" (NA, p. 305).

An influential account of the retrospective series is Nancy Rothwax Lindheim's, which traces its calculated progression. Early adventures are comprehensible within the "boundaries" of a learned "system of values," but the narrative gradually moves beyond that "security" into an "ambiguous, unclassifiable world." The princes are thus forced to descend from objective "aloofness" into the flux of relativistic experience.[17] Lindheim, furthermore, sees a coherent didactic program at work, a progressive unfolding from the simple to the complex to serve as an "initiation into the full complexities of moral life." But once we return to the main narrative, we find scant evidence of new flexibility or moral insight; what persists from the retrospect, rather, are its warped and fantastic images. After Gynecia's terrifying dream of sexual frustration and death, the narrative explodes into a grotesquely sadistic comedy, the *New Arcadia*'s expanded version of the Phagonian revolt:

> Among the rebels there was a dapper fellowe, a tayler by occupation, who fetching his courage onelie from their going back, began

to bow his knees, & very fencer-like to draw neere to *Zelmane*. But as he came within her distance, turning his swerd very nicely about his crown, *Basilius*, with a side blow, strake of his nose. He (being a suiter to a seimsters daughter, and therefore not a little grieved for such a disgrace) stouped downe, because he had hard, that if it were fresh put to, it would cleave on againe. But as his hand was on the grounde to bring his nose to his head, *Zelmane* with a blow, sent his head to his nose. That saw a butcher, a butcherlie chuffe indeed (who that day was sworn brother to him in a cup of wine) & lifted up a great leaver, calling *Zelmane* all the vile names of a butcherly eloquence. But she (letting slippe the blowe of the leaver) hitte him so surely on the side of his face, that she lefte nothing but the nether jawe, where the tongue still wagged, as willing to say more, if his masters remembrance had served. O (said a miller that was halfe dronke) see the lucke of a good fellow, and with that word, ran with a pitchforke at *Dorus*: but the nimblenes of the wine caried his head so fast, that it made it over-runne his feet, so that he fell withall, just betwene the legs of *Dorus*: who setting his foote on his neck (though he offered two milche kine, and foure fatte hogs for his life) thrust his sword quite through, from one eare to the other; which toke it very unkindlie, to feele such newes before they heard of them, in stead of hearing, to be put to such feeling.

(*NA*, pp. 312–13)

Granted that Sidney had few, if any, democratic sympathies, and that chronicles often tell of cruelty to those of lower birth, it is still difficult not to be appalled by the callous humor and brutality that masquerade as ideal heroism in this passage.[18] No physical or rhetorical quarter is spared the louts who would fashion themselves into the image of their betters, including a tailor who ludicrously aspires to swordsmanship, a butcher who displays "butcherly eloquence," men who even in death achieve only the most distastefully mock heroic: the drunken miller "vomits his soul out in wine and blood" (*NA*, p. 213). And yet the violence of the passage savages not only the rebels but its own discourse. Heroic valor and courtly wit degenerate into sadistic slapstick as hands and noses are chopped off in balanced clauses and the slitting of a throat becomes a merry jest about rhetorical effect running backwards: the miller's ears feel the news before hearing it, rather than hearing the news to feel it. If Sidney thought to protect the aristocracy's exclusive rights to heroic action, or to imitate the grimly ingenious scenes of slaughter in the *Iliad* and the *Aeneid*, he did so with the most subversive results. This is hardly an instance of painful events made pleasurable by imitation (one of Sidney's favorite Aristotelian notions); rather, the disgusting is elevated to a self-consciously aesthetic form, and by its very incongruity renders that form ludicrous, even oppressive.

The flippant cruelty of the passage is, I think, a sign that Sidney's literary experiment has gotten out of hand. He had hoped to enrich the genre of the heroic poem with the ambiguous energies that inform all his works, to animate the didactic by means of a densely imagined rendering of human experience. But he finds himself at this point increasingly frustrated with the unpredictable world his imagination has represented, a world that does not so much educate his heroes as threaten to render them obsolete. For the heroic personality, as Sidney would have understood it from Renaissance criticism, is a static embodiment of ethical universals; if one hears "tales of Hercules, Achilles, Cyrus, and Aeneas," one "must needs hear the right description of wisdom, valour, and justice" (*Apology*, pp. 113–14).[19] The *Old Arcadia* maintained an ironic and poised distance from such abstractions by turning fixed categories of perception into rhetorical chess pieces and conjectures. Though the *New Arcadia*, as we have seen, is premised on such distance and playfulness, it ultimately longs for a more ambitious coordination of universals and the flux of experience, and the strain grows apparent. The blind king of Paphlagonia virtually bursts from his conflicting responses to a world of extreme contrasts, "his hart broken with unkindnes & affliction, stretched so farre beyond his limits with this excesse of comfort" (*NA*, p. 212). Characters with more complicated inner lives begin to appear: the self-divided Gynecia of the original is joined by the amplified roles of Plangus and Erona and the new creation of the tragic Amphialus. But the protagonists themselves, more than ever notable exemplars, find it increasingly difficult to discover a genuine outlet for their heroic energies. Sidney's frustrated attempt to match vigorous action with its adequate object is reflected more directly in the final victim of the carnage. He, too, is a lowly townsman with a somewhat literal sense of his craft, yet he, like his creator, is a maker of images, eager to picture high and notable representations in the most lively way, only to find himself crippled by his intense engagement with his project:

> That blow astonished quite a poore painter, who stood by with a pike in his handes. This painter was to counterfette the skirmishing betwene the *Centaures* and *Lapithes*, and had bene very desirous to see some notable wounds, to be able the more lively to expresse them; and this morning (being caried by the stream of this companie) the foolish felow was even delighted to see the effect of blowes. But this last, (hapning neere him) so amazed him, that he stood still, while *Dorus* (with a turne of his sword) strake of both his hands. And so the painter returned, well skilled in wounds, but with never a hand to performe his skill.
>
> (*NA*, p. 313)[20]

CAPTIVITY AND
THE GOLDEN WORLD

The *New Arcadia*'s third book marks Sidney's final attempt to stabilize his fictive world by projecting its ambiguities into extreme moral opposites, what Jon Lawry terms "an almost Manichean struggle."[21] The original narrative line is discarded, and in its place the still-disguised Pyrocles and the two princesses are taken captive by the anarchic forces of the imagination, now embodied in Cecropia, an Elizabethan's nightmare of a willful female ruler.

She is the meeting place for all the work's visions of disorder—metaphysical, political, sexual, and poetic—and has, from the beginning, lurked behind the scenes as Arcadia's evil genius. What had been a "chance" attack by a lion and a bear in the *Old Arcadia* becomes a Cecropian plot in the *New*; the Phagonian revolt is no longer merely the result of mob drunkenness, but springs from her diseased wit, stirred up by her agents. Even Phalantus's strange tournament of images is partly her doing: it was she who taught Artesia to include "heaven and earth in ones self" (*NA*, p. 98). Egocentrism is all her joy, and she reaches out to others only to infect them with self-absorption. The quintessential Machiavel, she represents the dark side of the princes' drive for autonomy through the "law of vertue"; her world is ruled by blind Fortune, against which she struggles with amoral will and ingenuity. The widow of Basilius's brother, she praises the latter's "vertue" because together they laid plots to seize the Arcadian throne, and now her hopes lie in their son, Amphialus, whom she instructs, "what is done for your sake (how evill soever to others) to you is vertue" (*NA*, pp. 363–64). The triple kidnapping is her attempt to set his self-assertion in motion, part of a master plot to force a marriage with Philoclea and so enhance his claim to the throne.

In this rebellion, the political subversive becomes a demonic poet, and her co-conspirators are practiced in the art of verbal illusion. She stirs the Phagonian revolt through Clinias, one who "oft had used to be an actor in Tragedies, where he had learned, besides a slidingnesse of language, acquaintance with many passions, and to frame his face to beare the figure of them" (*NA*, p. 319). Amphialus is a less willing actor, as his name ("between two seas") implies. He "can be painted by nothing, but by the true shape of vertue" (*NA*, p. 68), but that shape is altered by erotic longing and familial pressure. As part of his mother's forces, he is a rhetorical Proteus and illusionist before his various audiences, "conforming himselfe after their humors. To his friends, friendlines; to the ambitious, great expectations; to the displeased, revenge; to the greedie, spoyle. . . . he knewe, how violently rumors doo blow the sailes of popular judgements, & how few there be, that can

discerne betweene trueth and truthlikenes, betweene showes
and substance" (*NA*, p. 371). Cecropia, however, reigns as laureate. She is her own Petrarchan lover, inventing hyperbolic
conceits to her own glory: "Their eyes admired my Majestie,
& happy was he or she, on whom I would suffer the beames
therof to fall. Did I goe to church? it seemed the very Gods
wayted for me, their devotions not being solemnized till I was
ready. Did I walke abroad to see any delight? Nay, my walking
was the delight it selfe" (*NA*, p. 364). Political machinations
are for her a struggle between creative wit and a brazen world.
The unleashing of the lion and bear failed because "blind Fortune" hates "sharpe-sighted inventions"; the Phagonian revolt
failed because "those louts were too gross instruments for del-
icate conceits" (*NA*, p. 365). Her final plot stretches her to the
fullest range of her powers, even as it brands those powers as
the ultimate vice: a determinedly atheistic world view.

   That view is established in Cecropia's debate with Pamela,
whom she tests as a substitute for the recalcitrant Philoclea.
Here, in the most famous of the Arcadian debates, the oppositions of Sidney's imagination crystallize into aesthetic and religious extremes. Noting that Pamela has been "woorking uppon a purse . . . so well proportioned" that "the cunningest
painter might have learned of her needle," and that her appearance shows she has not forgotten the "counsaile of a glasse,"
Cecropia tempts her with a praise of beauty as the touchstone
of consciousness and power. It is the mind's glory to be able to
"discerne Beautie," she reminds the princess, and a woman's
beauty is her army—her lips "may stande for ten thousand
shieldes," her eyes "tenne thousand . . . shot" (*NA*, pp. 403–
4). She then tunes her speech to a *carpe diem* theme, which in
turn modulates into a vision of time as *kairos*, fleeting opportunity that must be seized as it runs by: "Beauty goes away,
devoured by Time, but where remaines it ever flourishing, but
in the hart of a true lover?" Pamela, then, must not "lose the
hold of occasion, while it may not only be taken, but offers,

nay sues to be taken: which if it be not now taken, will never hereafter be overtaken" (*NA*, p. 405).[22]

Pamela's attitude remains of a piece with the design of her purse: scrupulously "proportioned." She understands her stitched detail work is but "an ornament of the principal work," and she responds to her aunt's praise of that work as a "treasure itself" by scorning the significance of "this outward glasse, intitled Beautie" (*NA*, p. 403). When Cecropia encourages her to seize the moment, she rises effortlessly from the fleshly to the spiritual, invoking her obedience to her father and her God. Pamela's majestic virtue, more pronounced in Sidney's revisions, now grows perhaps a little onerous as she snubs both sensuous beauty and the "weakenes" of earthly lovers (*NA*, p. 404). A sixteenth-century reader would no doubt have sympathized with her in the circumstances and applauded her courage, but would also, I suspect, have been quite capable of responding ironically to her prim uprightness.[23] And yet Sidney, the master ironist, now avoids irony; too much is at stake as he prepares to transform his heroine into a pre-Christian Scholastic who will proclaim the ultimate principles of order that the *New Arcadia* has sought since Strephon and Claius's opening lament for the lost Urania.

Cecropia sets the debate to that higher key when she determines to pry Pamela loose from her "heavenly conceits" with an atheist's full rhetorical arsenal. Religion, she instructs, is merely an expression of human need, a device by "politicke wittes" to "hold mans witte in well doing" and a shield to protect the foolish from such terrors as thunder. Religion is not only an instrument of power and a mark of ignorance, but the product of a fantastic, and ultimately self-defeating, imagination:

> All things follow but the course of their own nature, saving only Man, who while by the pregnanacie of his imagination he strives to things supernaturall, meane-while he looseth his owne naturall felicitie. Be wise, and that wisedome shalbe a God unto thee; be

contented, and that is thy heaven: for els to thinke that those powers (if there be any such) above, are moved either by the eloquence
of our prayers, or in a chafe by the folly of our actions; caries as-
much reason as if flies should thinke, that men take great care
which of them hums sweetest, and which of them flies nimblest.

(*NA*, pp. 406–7)

Cecropia's call to natural felicity is more than a reprise of Basilius's "let not certain imaginative rules" speech. It takes as its
assumption Plangus's nihilistic vision of "human kind" as
"balls to the stars" while "higher powers . . . idly sit above"
(*NA*, p. 227) and is only a short distance from Gloucester's
"flies to wanton boys" (*King Lear* 4.1.36). The stage is set for a
decisive response.

Pamela makes it by snaring Cecropia's aberrant wit within
a regulated cosmos. It is not the religious but the irreligious
who are fantastical: "most miserably foolish, since wit makes
you foolish" (*NA*, p. 407). Human knowledge itself could not
exist in a universe without wisdom, she insists, and to deny the
argument from design leads to a "bottomlesse pitt of absurdi-
ties" (*NA*, pp. 407–8). Chance could not have made "all things
of nothing," and even if there had been eternal substances,

> the heavie partes would have gone infinitely downewarde, the light
> infinitely upwarde, and so never have mett to have made up this
> goodly bodie. For before there was a heaven, or a earth, there was
> neyther a heaven to stay the height of the rising, nor an earth,
> which (in respect of the round walles of heaven) should become a
> centre.
>
> (*NA*, p. 408)

Both Cecropia's and Pamela's speeches are drawn from a repertoire of traditional arguments—skepticism, Lucretian ma-
terialism, and stoicism, as well as Renaissance defenses of the
Ancient Theology.[24] Sidney obviously relishes the opportunity
to display his erudition and to bring it to bear on creating the
Arcadia's most notable image of virtue, a saved pagan who by

the force of reason alone can recognize and celebrate the constancy of her Creator's infinite wisdom.

Scholars have traced the speculative sources of Pamela's argument, but the impact of one text has been overlooked; Pamela's theology is at several points a canny reflection of Sidney's own *Apology for Poetry*. The "All," the "inexpressable harmony," is fashioned by a creative act that goes beyond the raw stuff of nature, "a right heavenly Nature, indeed, as it were unnaturing them, doth so bridle them" (*NA*, p. 409). Her Creator, in other words, "with the force of a divine breath . . . bringeth things forth far surpassing [nature's] doings" (*Apology*, p. 101). Pamela's attack on Cecropia's secular reasoning similarly follows the *Apology*'s attack on historians. The historian, to recall the *Apology*'s argument, is caught in a foolish world, and so he can only follow the logic of "because it rained yesterday, therefore it should rain today"; his writing, then, "draweth no necessary consequence." Pamela likewise attacks Cecropia's appeal to physical beauty because this beauty is "without any further consequence" (*NA*, p. 403). According to her atheistical aunt, "yesterday was but as to day, and to morrow will tread the same footsteps of his foregoers." Pamela responds that this very succession proves "constancie"; even as Cecropia would "take away consequents," "all things" reveal to us the "necessitie of consequence" (*NA*, p. 408). And, for good measure, Pamela echoes Sidney's mockery of the tautologies of philosophers—"learned men have learnedly thought . . . in Nature we know it is well to do well" (*Apology*, p. 113): "But you will say it is so by nature, as much as if you said it is so, because it is so" (*NA*, p. 408).

Pamela's cosmology and theology may parallel the *Apology* because the two spring from common sources in Sidney's reading; but if Sidney is indeed revising his heroic fiction with the *Apology* in mind, there is a more deliberate reason: Pamela echoes Sidney's terms for poetry because that is precisely what she observes: she is looking at the poet's golden world *from the inside.* Sidney turns to philosophy not merely to reaffirm his speculative and spiritual allegiances but in order to invoke those allegiances on behalf of his poetic creation; his heroine's defense of her Creator's design allows Sidney to conjure his aesthetic goals, to proclaim the goodness of his creation against the demonic poet lurking within it. The flux of experience that the work comes increasingly to represent is made bearable by Pamela's lofty confidence: "This worke is steady and permanent" (*NA*, p. 408).

The intellectual and emotional advantages of speaking through a critical voice within the fiction are enormous. Pamela argues not for a world of conjectured consequence but for what is, to her, a world of real consequence. By casting his critical terms in a theological form, Sidney can at a crucial moment allow himself to imagine the world of his poem as assuming the ontological and aesthetic stability that an epic poet and critic such as Tasso would long for, a coherence that promises to hold together the variety of the poetic heterocosm within a larger unity of "discordant concord." If the poet has "no end either fixed in advance or determined by art," Tasso warns in the *Discorsi del poema eroico*, multiplicity and indeterminacy could force the "process . . . [to] go on *ad infinitum.*" Pamela's cosmos where "each thing [is] directed to an end" promises that "from an unitie many contraries should proceede still kept in an unitie: as that from the number of contrarieties an unitie should arise" (*NA*, p. 409). Sidney, moreover, demands that we recognize the power of Pamela's stance. The arguments she has devastated are not merely ad hoc rhetorical ploys; Cecropia has spoken "earnestly, because she spake as she thought" (*NA*, p. 406), and when she is exposed, so, too, is the nothingness at the heart of her self-assertion: "So fowly was the filthinesse of impietie discovered by the shining of her [Pamela's] unstayned goodnes" (*NA*, p. 411). Sidney appears at last to have realized the goal of the heroic: to make "magnanimity and justice shine throughout all misty fearfulness and foggy desires" (*Apology,*

p. 119); if Euarchus missed the mark in the original, Pamela now triumphs.

Pamela's triumph, however, is one that by its very nature can only be contingent. Few understand better than Sidney the paradox of a fictive creature appealing to ontological orders outside the fiction, a difficulty Milton would exploit mercilessly in his attack on Charles I's use of Pamela's earlier prayer from this same captivity episode (*NA*, pp. 382–83). Her prayer, Milton charged, merely proceeds "from the mouth of a Heathen fiction praying to a heathen God; & that in no serious Book, but the vain amatorious Poem of Sr *Philip Sidneys Arcadia*; a Book in that kind full of worth and witt, but among religious thoughts and duties not worthy to be nam'd; nor to be read at any time without good caution."[25] Though Pamela's rhetoric promises to open a channel to a higher dimension of reality, her vision is less a narrative *telos* than a counterweight that permits the release of yet further, opposite extremes. The narrative remains an imaginative roller coaster both prior to and following the debate, hurling us from moral commentary to battlefield slaughter, to beauty, and back; from "trayling guts," dismembered heads and limbs, and gouged-out eyes (*NA*, pp. 388–89), to the "delight" of "rich furniture, guilte swords, shining armours," to the tyranny of "often-changing fortune," a vision of "Terror": "now all universally defiled with dust, bloud, broken armours, mangled bodies, tooke away the maske, and sette foorth Horror in his owne horrible manner" (*NA*, p. 392). The succeeding debate, after explicitly setting aright the polarities of virtue and vice, is itself succeeded by a grinding of the Manichaean struggle to a standstill, leaving as the only outlet for either side a return to the compulsive aestheticizing of the earlier books. First to emerge from Basilius's ranks is Phalantus, long freed from his tournament of images in book 1, but still eager to please Artesia. His letter of challenge to Amphialus turns combat into theater:

Languishing in idlenesse, I desire to refresh my minde with some exercise of armes, which might make knowne the dooers, with delight of the beholders. . . . The place I thinke fittest, the Iland within the Lake, because it standes so well in the view of your Castell, as that the Ladies may have the pleasure of seeing the combate.

(*NA*, p. 413)

Sidney had previously used Phalantus to probe the artificiality of tournament imagery, but now revels in those artifices, elaborating in loving detail the trappings of both horses: Amphialus's, with its gold enamel and gems, together with branches and leaves made "so artificiallie" that "as the horse moved, it seemed indeed that the leaves wagged, as when the winde plaies with them"; Phalantus's white horse, tricked out as a dish of cream and fruit, with strawberry spots on his body, his mane and tail dyed crimson, and a bit counterfeiting vine branches that "brought foorth a cluster of grapes, by the workeman made so lively, that it seemed, as the horse champed on his bitte, he chopped for them, and that it did make his mouth water" (*NA*, p. 415).

Johan Huizinga notes that the "fiction that chivalry ruled the world," with its "bizarre accoutrements and pompous staging," represents both a serious longing for the sublime life and a "crying falsehood," and so elicits "an unstable equilibrium between sentimentality and mockery."[26] It is the instability that grows increasingly apparent at this point. Though the first combat is fought with the highest honor and sportsmanship, it is both gratuitous and futile. The defeated Phalantus simply deserts the siege "to seeke his adventures other-where," a wandering knight in search of a lost world of romance, while Amphialus reenacts his victories on the island stage over a succession of challengers, but failing in every instance to please the one spectator he longs to please, Philoclea, who is "ever sorriest, when he had best successe." Basilius, for his part, is humiliated by these tournament defeats and calls for a champion to end Amphialus's string of triumphs, a call that will prove to be disastrous. For here the *New Arcadia* once again reflects back on itself, only to annihilate its own images of perfection.

Argalus and Parthenia, as we have seen, overcome disfigurement and separation in book 1 to stand as a symbol of union and harmony. Book 3 presents us with an almost mystical image of their double riches, "each making one life double, because they made a double life" (*NA*, p. 420). Basilius's call, however, is irresistible to Argalus, because he has been "reading in a booke the stories of *Hercules*" (*NA*, p. 420). He is victimized by the affective power of heroic images, which "inflameth the mind with desire to be worthy," as the *Apology* so praises them, images to which the *New Arcadia* stands as a monument. Parthenia pleads with Argalus to relent, but he is "caried away by the tyrannie of Honour" (*NA*, p. 422). His assurance "I shal live, doubte not: for so great a blessing as you are, was not given unto me, so soone to be deprived of it" (*NA*, p. 421) displays in its passive constructions his faith in a higher power, the benevolent Providence Pamela so confidently invoked only a few pages earlier.

When he confronts Amphialus, benevolence has been withdrawn. The "notable example of the woonderfull effectes of Vertue" (*NA*, p. 426) that the combat supposedly demonstrates is smothered by images of butchery and gushing wounds (*NA*, pp. 423–26). Parthenia's agonized cry, "O God, what hath bene my desert to be thus punished" (*NA*, p. 426), is scarcely answered by Argalus's bland assurance that his death "pleaseth him, whose wisdome and goodnesse guideth all" (*NA*, p. 427). The guiding wisdom seems still more remote when Amphialus's next slaughtered victim, a mysterious "Knight of the Tomb" whose costume pictures "a gaping sepulchre" embroidered with "blacke wormes, which seemed to crawle up and downe, as ready alreadie to devoure him" (*NA*, p. 445), proves to be the grief-stricken Parthenia.

John Danby reads the deaths of Argalus and Parthenia as part of the larger theme of Christian patience. Their happiness was only "a temporary balance in the midst of tensions. The tensions constantly change, and constantly threaten the stability maintained by commanding them. . . . In good fortune or in bad, we need to centre our mind on that which is above the flux."[27] But by now any attempt to rise above the "midst of tensions" and "flux" is painfully ironic. The exquisite imagery with which Parthenia's wounds are pictured, an alabaster neck with dainty rivulets of the purest red (*NA*, p. 447) may distance the event but also sets our teeth on edge. So, too, does Basilius's attempt to "make Honour triumph over Death" by giving "order for the making of marble images, to represent them, & each way enriching the tombe," a gesture as vexing as the resolve of Capulet and Montague to erect golden statues to their dead children at the end of *Romeo and Juliet*.

Amphialus's murderous exhibitions on the island theater end only when he meets a more skilled performer. "Never game of death better plaid," the narrator approvingly tells us, as Amphialus receives from Musidorus "upon the bellie, so horrible a wound, that his guts came out withall" (*NA*, p. 461).

The closing of one theater, however, only marks the opening of another, this one under Cecropia's direction. Her productions aim for the grimmest possible images, advertising the imminent decapitation of both princesses and Pyrocles: "And to make [Basilius] the more feare a present performance, she caused his two daughters & *Zelmane* to be led unto the wals, where she had made a scaffold, easie to be seene by *Basilius*: and there caused them to be kept, as ready for the slaughter" (*NA*, p. 465). The public show is cancelled, but Cecropia sets to work in earnest by moving indoors, setting up her theatricals in her private hall. After scourging the princesses and terrorizing them with "noices of horror" and "sudden frightings in the night" (*NA*, pp. 470–73), she announces to Philoclea that

now she was come to the last parte of the play . . . she bad her
prepare her eies for a new play, which she should see within a fewe
houres in the hall of that castle . . . when the houre came that the
Tragedie should beginne, the curtaynes were withdrawen from before the windowes of *Zelmane,* and of *Philoclea.*

(*NA*, pp. 475–76)

Pyrocles and Philoclea witness what seems to be "The Beheading of Pamela," and its sequel follows a few days later for Pyrocles: "seven or eight persons in a cluster upon the scaffold:
who by & by retiring themselves, nothing was to be seene
thereupon, but a bason of golde, pitifully enameled with
bloud, and in the midst of it, the head of the most beautifull
Philoclea" (*NA*, p. 482). In a world filled with shocks—the disfiguring of Parthenia in book 1, the butchering of the rebels in
book 2, and the slaughter of Argalus and Parthenia in book 3—
this is the most terrible of all. Pyrocles' outburst goes beyond
his momentary doubt awaiting trial in the *Old Arcadia*; it denies
Pamela's cosmic harmonies with a cry that William Elton compares to Lear's raging on the heath:[28] "O tyraunt heaven, traytor
earth, blinde providence; no justice, how is this done? how is
this suffered? hath this world a governement? If it have, let it
poure out all his mischiefes upon me" (*NA*, p. 483). If Sidney
has trouble with his epic end, he still refuses to accept a tragic
one; tragedy is defused by a literalizing of the scene's basic metaphor. The play of death proves to have been *only* a play, a
sadistic theatrical illusion. Artesia, killed earlier, stood in for
Pamela, her severed head serving as a prop, and Philoclea's head
in the basin is another piece of stage trickery, one employing a
hollow scaffold and a bottomless basin through which to poke
her head as she "played the parte of death" (*NA*, p. 488).

As readers make their way through Cecropia's house of horrors, they must at some point wonder if there is any didactic
purpose in subjecting Pyrocles, or themselves, to this succession of monstrous images. We may, with some justification,
fall back on appeals to "negative exempla" that teach the ne-

cessity of patience in a cruel world, or even the importance of learning to guard against the abuses of the poetic imagination. But when Sidney fractions off the demonic poet, he uses her not to restrain his own fiction but to set free the darkest side of the "Zodiac of the wit," what Pyrocles properly calls "the worst, which mans wit could imagine" (*NA*, p. 490). We seem to be thrown back to the storm at sea in the second book, where "the terriblenesse of the continuall motion, the dissolution of the fare being from comfort, the eye and the eare having ougly images ever before it, doth still vex the minde, even when it is best armed against it" (*NA*, p. 193). "The feigned," Sidney claims, has the power to move because it "may be tuned to the highest key of passion"; the direction of movement, however, is no longer certain: "*Pyrocles*, who had felt (with no smal distance of time) in himself the overthrow both of hope and despaire, knew not to what key he should tune his mind, either of joy, or sorrow. But finding perfite reason in neither, suffred himselfe to be caried by the tide of his imagination" (*NA*, p. 490).

That Sidney still hoped to ride through the swelling tide of his own imagination seems clear when the "perplexed" Basilius sends for a second oracle and receives further directions from "celestiall providence," "not in darke wonted speeches, but plainely to be understood" that the battle will be won (*NA*, p. 510); certainly the disabling of Amphialus and the death of Cecropia (*NA*, p. 492) bode well for a military victory. But Sidney himself, I think, felt much of Pyrocles' agitation when he finally broke off his revision in the midst of yet another struggle, this time a deadly contest of swordsmanship. Here, the massive strength of Anaxius forces the still-disguised Pyrocles to fall back, once again, on his "divers faynings" (*NA*, p. 518).

Fulke Greville published the *New Arcadia* as a fragment but could not resist speculating about its completion. If the reader has found some profitable diversity in what he has read, Greville writes in his *Life of Sidney*, "let him conceive if this excellent Image maker had liv'd to finish, and bring to perfection, this extraordinary frame of his own Common-wealth . . . what a large field an active spirit should have had to walk in."[29] For Greville, this image maker's intention was clear enough, "to limn out such exact pictures, of every posture of the mind," but for most readers the embodiment of such an intention challenges any "large design."[30] For the critical problem is not what the *New Arcadia* would have looked like had Sidney finished it, but whether it was possible for him to have finished it. If Pamela's orderly cosmos had truly been his own, as Edwin Greenlaw argues, he would have composed a work as perfectly rounded as her walls of heaven, a work both various and harmonious because it could call on objectively established meanings.[31] He would have been able, in other words, to "discover the infinitely various modes of human action . . . imitate all the modes of human action in ordered and rhythmic relationship."[32] But when Sidney sets about to "limn out . . . every posture of the mind," he finds himself producing an endless proliferation of images. It is one of the ironies of his revision that the original romance, a genre so often associated by Renaissance critics with fantastic excess, is ultimately a more controlled piece of work. For all its play and paradox, it still follows the meticulous five-act structure of Terentian comedy. The *New Arcadia*, by contrast, grows beyond Sidney's most strenuous efforts to shape it. Once Cecropia has been eliminated and Amphialus carried off, Sidney confronts his protagonists with yet another embodiment of repression, the brutal Anaxius, leading even the patient Pamela to exclaim, "see how many acts our Tragedy hath" (*NA*, p. 503).

The great struggle of the *New Arcadia* is finally not between Basilius and Cecropia, but between Sidney's desire for an overarching form, for a symmetrical architectonic, and the centrifugal forces of the imagination that challenge all teleology. It is

this tension that makes the work so dynamic but also so difficult. As Kenneth Myrick notes, if Sidney had been content to
hang his images from a looser form, if "he had left all his episodes independent, they would be easy enough to follow. They
could be read once and forgotten, without greatly confusing
the unity of the fable."[33] The difficulty results from his "trying
to weave every episode into the central pattern," a pattern that
finally testifies not to a whole and coherent vision, but to the
enormous pressures that vision struggles to contain. Myrick
rightly notes that Sidney's art is "directed toward design and
not chaos," an ideal that is figured in Kalander's garden: "it
seemed that arte therein would needes be delightfull by counterfaiting his enemie error, and making order in confusion"
(*NA*, p. 17). But as we seek the work's design, we find ourselves pointing not to a stable architectonic but toward an expanding universe where fundamental relations become war-
ring oppositions. An elaborate system of family relationships,
for example, attempts to bind the characters together, but we
cannot recall it without also recalling that in episode after episode we have read of a father alienated from his son, a son from
his father, mother from son, mother from daughter, brother
from brother, husband from wife. The moral struggle upward
and the immoral sink downward in a narrative that pulls us
from pious and abstract didacticism one moment to sadism and
horror the next; if Sidney is compiling an encyclopedia of virtuous and vicious types, it has no final entry, and no index.

Sidney broke off his revisions when he found himself writing an infinite book. For the world his poetic fictions represent
is not Pamela's spherical and geocentric cosmos but an infinite
universe whose center is everywhere and whose circumference
nowhere.

WILLIAM SHAKESPEARE
AND
DRAMATIC FICTIONS

INTRODUCTION TO PART THREE

When Sidney tells us in the *Apology* that we do not accept a poet's fictions as literally true, one of his examples is the experience of attending a stage play: "What child is there that, coming to a play, and seeing *Thebes* written in great letters upon an old door, doth believe that it is Thebes?" (*Apology*, p. 124). This patent lack of credibility is the result, in part, of the sheer physicality of the medium: "No audience, finally, ever forgets it is at a play," a recent critic writes.[1] For Sidney, this physicality makes drama the least flexible of poetic kinds. Dramatists must remember that they are not working in a purely discursive medium, but that "many things may be told which cannot be showed, if they know the difference betwixt reporting and representing. As, for example, I may speak (though I am here) of Peru, and in speech digress from that to the description of Calicut; but in action I cannot represent it without Pacolet's horse" (*Apology*, p. 135).

Sidney nonetheless recognizes the disturbing imaginative potential of drama, and it is for this reason, I think, that his discussion of drama in the *Apology* engages his strictest Neoclassicism. He argues for the unities of time and place and against the mingling of kings and clowns in a "mongrel tragicomedy" not because he wants to maintain a fragile dramatic illusion but because he wants to restrict the playwright's wit, to defuse his potential for excess.[2] Indeed, to order the fancies of the *Old Arcadia*, Sidney resorts to the five-act Terentian structure. Correspondingly, when he needs an image for excess and misrule in the characters themselves, he summons theatrical metaphors. The disorientation of desire in the *Old Arcadia* becomes part of the "very stage-play of love" for the narrator; Plangus, in his melancholy nihilism, compares humanity and its futile dreams to "players plast to fill a filthy stage" (*OA*, p. 147); and at the end of the work (itself a piece of tragicomedy), Philanax can think of no harsher attack on Pyrocles than to charge him with being an actor, one who hides behind a succession of masks. Finally, and most disturbingly, the *New Arcadia*'s demonic Cecropia is represented as a playwright whose tragedy, "The Beheading of Philoclea," is imagined in terms of an actual Elizabethan stage device at which Sidney himself may have marveled in a performance of some play like *Appius and Virginia*, which features the sensational beheading of the heroine. Clearly, the sententious *Gorboduc* was not the only kind of drama Sidney might have enjoyed, and Sidney's fascination with the illusion is indicated by his accurate description of how the beheading was staged.[3]

What makes theatricality so powerful a metaphor for Sidney is the physicality he claimed limited it, a physicality that by its very nature suggests the tense interplay between human fictions and the world we call real. For even as drama exhilarates us by granting a physical presence to the projected, counterfactual worlds of poetic invention, that power also disturbs us in its ability to blur our assumed boundaries between the realms of play and earnestness. The earliest theatrical anecdote figures this ambiguity as an archetypal confrontation between the Athenian lawmaker Solon and the first great man of the theater, Thespis. It records the former's distress at the latter's "lying" to his audience, and his fear, despite assurances that all is done in play, that its subversive implications would infect the serious business of life.[4] Solon's discomfort touches the heart of drama's power, which has since antiquity been expressed by the trope of the *theatrum mundi*, comparing the stage and the world. No period is more fascinated with or repelled by this trope than the English Renaissance, when, despite mounting Puritan opposition to stage plays, dramatic metaphors point to the "essential quality of the age . . . the theatrical nature of life."[5] Dramatic metaphors symbolize extremes of optimism and pessimism in Renaissance culture throughout Europe—from Pico's man-the-miracle to Machiavelli's man-the-hypocrite, from a celebration of God's harmonious cosmos and its orderly reflection in the state to the exposure of the terrible futility of human institutions and the sovereign's manipulative illusions of power.

It is this very span of possibilities that makes drama a fitting completion to a study of Renaissance minds and their fictions. We have seen in Cusanus and Sidney an intensifying self-consciousness about the implications of human invention. Both writers present an idealized sense of limitless fecundity that remains critically qualified—implicitly in the structural instabilities and unresolvable paradoxes of Cusanus's thought, and explicitly in Sidney's thematic preoccupation with the volatile nature of poetic fictions. This critical awareness achieves a full and compelling articulation in the major dramas of the English Renaissance. That the public stage of the late sixteenth century—scarcely a place devoted to philosophical or critical speculation—should become such an arena may seem surprising. But by the last two decades of the century, Tudor drama had developed a broad and flexible repertoire, an extraordinary theatrical vocabulary vitally concerned with the pleasures and perils of human feigning. The frequent representation of characters, from player-kings to anarchic clowns, engaged in manipulating appearances and weaving plots makes central actions of the mind's versatility and inventiveness. Indeed, Bacon's sympathetic but sober analysis of the apparent divinity of poetry—"it doth raise and erect the mind, by submitting the shews of things to the desires of the mind"[6]—gains force in the context of stage plays. For they present not merely a world in the shape of human desire, but the spectacle of characters, be they motivated by joy, malice, or desperate necessity, in the very act of attempting to refashion the world in that shape. The exercise of power and the powers of artifice yield one of the theater's central analogies.

The analogy is most potent when Tudor drama takes as its primary imaginative focus the age's preoccupation with order and disorder. When the theater entertains questions of moral, political, or metaphysical importance, its structure may be surprisingly open-ended and relativistic; yet even when drama serves a rigorously normative view, the deployment of privileged truths within a theatrical context prepares the ground for the more problematic explorations that will follow in the 1580s and 1590s. In some ways, the complexity is inevitable. "It is not good to stay too long in the theatre," Bacon warned,[7] but the self-reflexiveness of drama, its tendency to exploit the suggestiveness of its own medium, makes us less certain about our ability to leave behind the realm of fictions. Drama may not transform us into everyday liars, as Solon seems to have feared, but the inescapability of the *theatrum mundi* trope forever threatens to complicate our understanding of the very ground upon which we imagine ourselves to stand.

The dramatic medium Shakespeare inherited was a highly charged field, one already sensitive to questions about human fictions and their relation to authoritative patterns of order. When Shakespeare exploits these energies, he increasingly directs his attention toward the potential embodied by such questions, rather than toward their answers. His historical and tragic worlds neither affirm nor deny Tudor visions of order and harmony; they concentrate, rather, on what is at stake in the mind's longing to behold, or to challenge, such visions. We see this concentration evolving in Shakespeare's earliest histories, where fixed coordinates of political and moral life are continually invoked, but prove no more absolute than Cusanus's conjectural points of reference, or Sidney's Arcadian perspectives. These plays lead us to the greater achievements of *Richard II* and *Hamlet*, where the ambiguities of metaphor and fiction making are represented with an epistemological subtlety and a range of implication comparable to the constructive work of any Renaissance philosopher or poetic theorist.[8]

9

PLAY AND EARNEST

THE MEANING OF OUR SUPPOSES

The power and pathos of human feigning are a central motif for the Renaissance stage, one whose origin may be traced back to the reemergence of Western drama from the church liturgy. Ironically, the institution that sought to abolish theatrical spectacle becomes the site of its rebirth, forcing that institution's privileged symbols to coexist with an art form marked, in Jonas Barish's phrase, by "ontological subversiveness."[1] Whatever the legacy of medieval religious drama for Tudor plays, no contribution is more important than its juxtaposition of fixed forms of orthodoxy with the volatility of theatrical representation. In medieval drama, such juxtaposition was not necessarily a source of tension. The hypothetical could prove quite apt for the presentation of the miraculous.[2] In St. Ethelwold's *Regularis concordia*, for instance, one of the brethren enters "as if [*acsi*] to take part in the service," and joins the three Marys at Jesus' sepulchre. "As if" is the path to truth when the actors hold up a cloth "as if [*ac*] making known the Lord has risen."[3] Even when drama moves out of the church and its projected world takes on a new inner density, it maintains its equilibrium. The gratuitous realm of game and play, the "created world" of nonearnest activity, V. A. Kolve remarks, still holds to a didactic function, "a lie designed to tell the truth about reality."[4]

Play and earnest, however, form an unstable compound. For even as these nonearnest, projected worlds determinedly

point beyond themselves to higher truth, they inevitably release the less manageable forces of the imagination. Evidence
of instability ranges from local abuses to more deeply seated
anxieties. Monstrously masked priests gesturing and singing
obscenely in the church, uneasiness about representations of
evil in religious plays, and more general discomfort about human feigning as an abomination to God's truth, all indicate a
potential for trouble.[5] No form of religious drama magnifies
that potential more than the morality plays of the fifteenth and
sixteenth centuries. Like its predecessors, the morality play
pictures man's relation to the eternal; *Everyman* is one extant
masterpiece that takes to heart its own advice to the audience:
"in the begynnynge / Loke well, and take good heed to the
endynge" (lines 10–11). But other moralities engage a theatrical self-enjoyment less willing to accept *Everyman*'s stringent
logic of self-denial, in which the time has passed for "sporte
and playe" (line 201). Because of the shift in focus from liturgy
and the pageant of sacred history to an allegorical analysis of
the individual mind, the morality openly represents—in its
mischievous Vices—the mercurial inventiveness of play making itself. Mental events that ought to be suppressed are dra-
matically exciting. *Mankind* (ca. 1470) notoriously exploits its
audience's desires by halting the action and extorting fees before allowing its chief devil to take the stage and its fullest
horseplay to unfold, including a visit to the Court of Mischief,
where the language of authority degenerates into parodic gib-
berish. Evil, theologians comfortingly tell us, is the absence of
being and is therefore merely ludicrous; evil figures on the stage
are to be ridiculed and rejected.[6] But morality Vices have an
undeniable stage *presence*. The personified Vices in a play such
as *Mankind*, writes Bernard Spivack, "because of their comic
and dramatic vitality, become theatrically fascinating. . . .
Proclaiming the moral superiority of virtue, they uniformly
demonstrated the dramatic superiority of vice." Pious intentions are challenged by the "profane excitement of the play."[7]

The key to that excitement lies not so much in slapstick or the scurrilous jest as in the free play mischief seems to promise. When the single Vice emerges from the group of Vices, his aggressiveness, which is also the aggression of performance, casts him as a restless deceiver with no motivation beyond an insatiable delight in his activity. He is a master of disguise who feigns laughter and tears with equal facility; his ingenious plotting and juggling with language not only demonstrate the Protean skills of the actor, but point to the playwright himself. For, like his creator, the Vice is a master of fictive invention, an artificer of "as if," and when his type is enriched by cross-fertilizations with the fool, the pattern of misrule, and the subtle schemers of intrigue plays, he becomes a virtual projection of power and delight, a comic release of human ingenuity. Serious historical and moral dramas will also regard him as the "projection of a fear," an inexplicable aggressor against official hierarchy, as we shall see, but first we should recognize the kind of poetic wit he represents.[8]

In early comedies such as *Gammer Gurton's Needle* (1553) and *Jack Juggler* (ca. 1555), the Vices' plots are motivated by little more than the sheer joy of making.[9] Whether their goals are domestic chaos, or, as in the latter play, the bizarre appropriation of another's identity through the powers of acting, they manifest a world open to the fiction maker, to his pleased discovery that "A man . . . might make a playe" (*GGN* 2.2.7–10). Fixed points and formal structures seem to lose their authority. Diccon, a lunatic from Bedlam, boasts that none can "defyne / Which way my iourney lyeth, . . . be it by nyght, or daye, / South, east, north or west, I am neuer out of my waye!" (*GGN* 2.1.7–10); Jack Juggler conquers his victim's appeals to personal memory or to the simple fact that "I am I." The more sophisticated techniques of intrigue comedy are not dependent on a single mischief maker; Gascoigne's *Supposes* (a translation of Ariosto's *I suppositi*) generalizes the forces that seek expression in the Vice, projecting a fluid play world filled with ingenious schemers.[10] Reality comes to seem like a game of cards, continually "in play . . . fauoring now this way, now y' way" (3.2.11–12), and while the play's characters may blame fortune, we understand that the world's volatility is largely generated by their own witty excesses, their having turned their world into a sophist's arena whose contours suggest the most far-fetched paradoxes (4.7.14–15, 4.4.43–47). These plays, moreover, seem to embody the most extreme forms of Nominalism. Stable knowledge gives way to a play of language. Language itself points to the merest *flatus vocis*: "Will you say a thing and not sticke to it to trie it?" complains one of Diccon's victims; "stick to it," the Bedlam replies, "mary sir I defy it!" (*GGN* 4.2.44–45). Gilson's famous complaint about Nominalism's inability to prove that "this world of ours is not a vast phantasmagoria behind which there is no reality to be found" momentarily finds a local habitation and a name in the worlds of Diccon, Jack, and Gascoigne's assorted pranksters.

The habitation is, of course, only momentary. The conventions of comedy itself dictate a return to a normative scheme in these plays' conclusions. Such formal resolutions may even suggest a higher coherence; Joel Altman notes that comedies of wit often snare their characters in epistemological binds that exhaust their resources, only to release them by a providential turn of events.[11] And yet these plays may often be less than fully committed to absolute closure. An exposed Diccon is asked to "bridle" his tongue, "cease a-while to fable" (*GGN* 5.2.219–20), but answers by boasting of the five hundred successes he has had since his release from Bedlam—a string of plots that stretches in the mind's eye to infinity. *Supposes* closes uniting families and lovers, and yet refuses to release them from the play's radical metaphor of the "suppose," the "mystaking or imagination of one thing for an other." The prologue tells us that in a "Comedie called Supposes" the very name may "driue into euery of your heades a sundry Suppose, to suppose the meaning of our supposes," and while the tangled plot is unraveled, the search for "the meaning of our supposes" does not entail their constraint. Rather, the play asks only for a pragmatic agreement that we have been sufficiently entertained: "if you suppose that our supposes haue giuen you sufficient cause of delighte, showe some token, whereby we may suppose you are content" (5.10.48–50). Even as the play satisfies us with the benevolent geometry of its well-plotted confusion, it reminds us how far the "as if" of stage action has moved from a ritualistic affirmation of the eternal to a symbolic enactment of human imagining.

Jack Juggler likewise places itself in the realm of human concerns. Its classical source, Plautus's *Amphitryon*, depends upon a god's supernatural powers of transformation, but Jack's plot relies on the skills of a mischievous actor. Its view of those skills eventually becomes a dark one, and suggests issues discussed in the final section of this study. While the prologue asks us to regard the action as a mere "fantasticall conceite" containing no "mattiers substancyall" (lines 79, 74), the play seems dedicated to upsetting all complacency, most forcefully in its bitter epilogue, which tells us that the preceding show has been an "example playne" of a world ruled by "power and might" (lines 1200, 1193).[12] All we "affirme, or denye" is subject to compulsion (lines 1177, 1206), whether it be that of the plain tyrant or the "cunning sophist" (lines 1199, 1184). If the world is open to contrivance, to the schemes of human ingenuity, it is for that very reason a world of risk, one in which human "making" may declare itself "by strenth, force, and vyolence" (line 1154). It is, in other words, the kind of world that haunted writers throughout the Renaissance—one that, as we have seen, repeatedly drives a writer such as Cusanus to retreat from the openness of conjectural play to the strictest authoritarianism, and that leads Sidney from the freedom of the poet's golden world to the horrors of Cecropia's castle. It is also the world of Tudor history plays, which presents problems of fiction making in an often disturbing political light.

MORAL HISTORIES

The vision of a fluid reality subject to continual revision and subtle schemers eager to oblige is deeply antithetical to Tudor ideology, whether Protestant or Catholic. "Ontological subversiveness" may be diffused into game playing by comedy, but the earnest subjects of history and political authority seek, in Irving Ribner's phrase, a "substantialist metaphysics."[13] If in *Respublica* (1553) we hear the lament that nothing seems "permanent or stable" and that things "as waving seas, doe flowe and ebbe" (lines 439, 443), we are also assured that God can restore true order at any moment, and He does so by the play's conclusion as His heavenly daughters crush, imprison, or convert the play's Vices. And if we consider the politics of drama as well as the politics in drama, we cannot help but be impressed by how Tudor authority increasingly attempts to control the potential unruliness of plays and interludes. Documents of the period voice concern not only about public disturbances, but also about a psychic wandering into "dyvers and sondrye kyndes of vyce and synne" that habitual playgoing can engender.[14]

Such anxieties about the gratuitous self-pleasuring of human invention are an intrinsic feature of Tudor orthodoxy. According to Richard Hooker, the "unquiet wit" is the archenemy, for he cannot be satisfied by the comely and hierarchical cosmos.[15] Though the mind of man may properly be "delighted with contemplation in itself" (1.8.5), some grow obsessed with their self-activity, until, like the fallen angels who were infatuated "by reflex of their understanding upon themselves," they lash out at the very order that produced them:

"Of certain turbulent wits it is said, 'Illis quieta movere magna merces videbatur': they thought the very disturbance of things established an hire sufficient to set them on work" (1.7.1). God becomes for them a mere projection of their own restless conceit: they believe it is the "will of God to have those things done which they fancy; their opinions are as thorns in their sides, never suffering them to take rest till they have brought their speculation into practice."[16] They may quote "five hundred sentences of holy Scripture" but all is founded upon subjective conjecture:

> What warrant have they, that any one of them [Scriptural passages] doth mean the thing for which it is alleged? Is not their surest ground most commonly, either some probable conjecture of their own, or the judgment of others taking those Scriptures as they do? . . . the most which can be inferred upon such plenty of divine testimonies is only this, That *some things* which they maintain, as far as *some men* can *probably conjecture*, do *seem* to have been out of Scripture *not absurdly* gathered.
>
> (2.7.9)

They are sophistic jugglers of probability, who will indulge their obsessions "as long as wit by whetting itself is able to find out any shift, be it never so sleight, whereby to escape out of the hands of present contradictions. . . . whether it be by misconstruction of the sense or by falsification of the words" (3.5.1).

Hooker's specific target is the Puritans, and the charge of a hyperkinetic imagination is, as we have seen, a common one in Renaissance controversies. But the closest analogue to Hooker's anarchist for whom "the very disturbance of things" is sufficient motivation is the stage Vice (a fine bit of irony if one considers Puritan attitudes toward the stage). When sixteenth-century writers transform the morality play into a vehicle for historical and political themes, they are quick to exploit the menace that lurks behind this type. Unregulated theatricalism becomes the dominant metaphor for any social, political, or religious force threatening the order of things, as if exposing the deceptiveness and illusoriness of all challenges to measured authority.

The metaphor's neatness is doomed to complication, however, for the playwright can affirm order only in a theatrical context, in the service of a regime notoriously committed to its own theatrical displays.[17] A closer look at some of the more prominent history plays reveals the first signs of this complication, the shifting strategies by which playwrights attempt to align the energies of drama with an official world picture celebrating stasis, order, and didactic control.

The first political morality play, John Skelton's *Magnificence*, is shrewdly aware of both the political and theatrical implications of display; even as it warns against courtly excesses, it keeps a steady eye on its own didactic enterprise. A summary of the play's action and quaint allegorical personages does not do justice to local subtleties, but will reveal the earnestness of its message. Sportive Liberty initially submits to Measure, but when princely Magnificence is seduced by the play's Vices, especially by Fancy, Magnificence squanders his wealth and becomes an egotistical monster, proclaiming his superiority to Alexander, Cyrus, Hercules, Charlemagne, Arthur, and Fortune itself. Inevitably, he falls, suffers the consequences of Adversity, Poverty, and Despair, and then repents, curbing his "wantonness" thanks to Perseverance.

Counterpointing this unambiguous moral curve is Skelton's self-consciousness about moral theater.[18] He was, of course, already an experienced hand at didactic discourse. His earliest extant poem cries out against the "frantyk frensy" of the commoners who killed their "naturall lord," the Earl of Northumberland: they were "stark Mad" and their "wilful foly" marks the limit of the poet's representations; he can only cry out against that folly, but "can not fayne" it. Skelton the playwright, however, must feign at least some version of it, must show those vagaries on stage by plotting their motions and writing their lines:

> Frantic Fancy Service I hight;
> My wits be weak, my brains are light;
> . . . .
> I blunder, I bluster, I blow and I blother;
> I make on the one day and I mar on the other;
> Busy, busy, and ever busy,
> I dance up and down till I am dizzy;
> I can find fantasies where none is;
> I will have it so, I will have it this.
>
> (1022–41)

A large measure of the play's dramatic life depends upon its Vices' ability to "find fantasies where none is"—their exploitation of the simple fact that, as Diccon would put it, a man might make a play. They may, it is true, explicitly warn us against their "Two faces" (line 710) or their histrionics; Courtly Abusion sports an outrageous hairdo and struts in the latest French fashions: "Beyond measure / My sleeve is wide, / . . . / All of pleasure / My hose straight tied, / My buskin wide, / Rich to behold, / Glittering in gold" (lines 848–54). But it would be too single-minded to ignore Skelton's self-investment in the play's forces of misrule. The prince's admiration for Courtly Abusion's rhetoric—"with pleasure I am surprised / Of your language, it is so well devised; / Polished and fresh is your ornacy" (lines 1530–32)—echoes Caxton's praise for Skelton's translations, their "polysshed and ornate terms."[19] Skelton's notorious sense of self-importance is reflected, too, in the seduced Magnificence, and his tumbling Skeltonics are sounded in the Vices' rhythms and verbal play: "Thy words hang together as feathers in the wind," exclaims the delighted prince over Folly's rhymes; "Thou art a fine merry knave" (lines 1819, 1827). Skelton's task is to harness play in an earnest cause, and he remains fully conscious of that task's delicacy. For, as Counterfeit Countenance reminds us when he lists the world's liars, his legions include counterfeit preachers, minstrels, lawyers, and those who "counterfeit earnest by way of plays" (line 427).

By a masterful stroke, Skelton sharpens his didactic focus by self-consciously turning his own dramatic technique into a metaphor for intrigue and deception. As David Bevington notes, Skelton outdoes his contemporaries in the use of doubling, the assignment of more than one role to each actor in a small company. The "constant reshuffling and alternation of the characters," writes Bevington,

> creates an atmosphere of intrigue during the phase of conspiracy and delusion. Conspirators appear and disappear, giving the impression that something mysterious is going on behind the scenes . . . the device not only solves a casting limitation but is structurally relevant to a dramatic presentation of duplicity. The hints of deviltry off stage are as effective as the visible machinations on stage.[20]

If theatrical trickery mirrors political trickery, Skelton is called upon to redeem his play as well as his morality hero. Both redemptions begin simultaneously with the entrance of Adversity before the now trembling Magnificence. The former turns to the audience and after warning of the fate of those who "follow their fancies in folly to fall" (line 1898) he excludes this play as an instance of folly. If we understand the fiction, we will find it is no lie; it does not merely "counterfeit earnest by way of plays," but rather, "though we show you this in game and play, / Yet it proveth earnest, ye may see, every day" (lines 1949–50). The final fifty lines insist repeatedly that this has been a particular kind of play, "devised to make you disport," a "disport and game" (lines 2534, 2567), but a game that, like Skelton's early prose *Speculum principis*, "a mirror encleared is . . . / This life inconstant for to behold and see" (lines 2520–

21). The play enacts its own thesis: the "free liberty / To sport" is redeemed when "measure is ruler," for "measure is treasure" (lines 79–80, 124, 125). The play's measure lies in its ultimate, didactic intention:

> This matter we have moved, you mirths to make
> Pressly purposed under pretence of play,
> Showeth wisdom to them that wisdom can take.
> (lines 2548–50)

Playing becomes earnest by a redoubling of play: the pretense has itself been a pretense. Through this paradox, Skelton would not only legitimize his poetic enterprise, but also coerce acceptance from any potential objector; those who balk at his claims to wisdom, he implies, pass judgment on themselves.

Skelton's conclusion may seem defensively oblique, but it adroitly manages the play's justification. In a work such as John Bale's *King Johan*, however, which bluntly demands a more immediate relation between fiction and reality, we find ourselves with a more deeply problematic, and eccentric, vision. For even as Bale cultivates the impression of rigorous historical accuracy in his play—including a (somewhat bogus) list of historical authorities (lines 2200–2206)—his vision leads him to what one critic calls a "fictional world of his own creating."[21] To that end, he merges and unmerges fact and abstraction, turning the historical King Johan into a timeless hero and translating the Vices into Johan's historical adversaries: Sedition, for example, becomes Stephen Langton, and Usurped Power becomes Pope Innocent III. Bale leaps, too, from the thirteenth to the sixteenth century, from England to Rome and back again, in order to show us an English martyr who falls before papal treachery only to rise from his historical ashes after three centuries as a triumphant Henry VIII and as an idealized version of that other sixteenth-century Johan, Johan Bale.

Even as Bale exploits every liberty the play world allows, he surpasses Skelton in turning theatricality into a metaphor of

evil. After Johan's opening warning against "sophysteres" who
would distort the abundance of God's "scriptur" and his vow
to "reforme the lawes and sett men in good order," the widow
England reports a dangerous invasion of hypocrites, with
"dysgysed heades in ther hoodes . . . in dyvers coloure and
shappe" (lines 36–38). They are followers of the "wyld bore of
Rome" who live wrapped up in "fantasyes, dreames and lyes,"
a traveling theatrical company, "wandring lyke most dysgysed
players" (lines 66ff.). Their English ally, Sedition, is a consummate liar and actor, entering with the oath "I will tell tales, by
Iesus" (line 43). He is a parody Pico's wonderful chameleon,
boasting of his ability to ascend the Catholic hierarchy:

> In euery estate of the clargye I playe a part:
> Sumtyme I can be a monk in a long syd cowle,
> Sumtyme I can be a none and loke lyke an owle,
> . . . .
> Sumtyme the bysshoppe with a myter and a cope,
> . . . .
> Yea, to go farder, sumtyme I am a cardynall;
> Yea, sumtyme a pope, and than am I lord ouer all,
> Bothe in hevyn and erthe and also in purgatory,
> And do weare iij crownes when I am in my glorye.
> (lines 194–210)

Catholicism becomes a rising tide of theatricality. The Vice
Dissimulation directs a fantastic Catholic service (lines 698ff.);
Treason has "played" priest "vnderneth *Benedicite*" (lines
1812–14); and the pope serves as a casting director as he plots
Johan's excommunication (lines 1056–60). The Catholics are
rich in stage properties; besides the excommunication props of
cross, bell, book, and candle, Sedition appears at one point
with a bag of bizarre relics, ranging from "a bone of the bles-
syd trynyte" to "a scabbe of saynt Iob," and items not on stage
are catalogued: "Your fyers, your waters, your oyles, your aul-
ters, your ashes, / Your candlestyckes, your cruettes, your
salte, with suche lyke trashes" (lines 1829–30).[22] Johan does

bear a few kingly symbols, such as a crown and scepter, but he gives them up to prevent a bloodbath, and we are reminded at the end by Verity that truth is essentially distinct from properties: "The crowne of it selfe without the man is nothynge" (line 2235).

King Johan stands fast against the theatrical horde, lamenting the clergy's having "left the scriptur for menns ymagynacyons" (line 335), but none believe his cry that the country is now swept by an unreal fiction. Nobility ignores his insistence that the significance of his excommunication is "but a fantasy in yowr ymagynacyon" (line 1495). True authority itself is mocked as if it were the fiction. Sedition tells Johan early that he will find his royal power a mere suppose: "Ye suppose and thynke that ye cowd me subdewe. / Ye shall neuer fynd yowr supposycyon trewe" (lines 231–32), and his chilling prophecy is realized when Johan attempts to prove his authority's foundation in Scripture. Nobility scoffs at his supposed sophistry: "Good lord, what a craft haue yow thes thynges to convaye!" (line 1519). Johan ends a solitary figure, overwhelmed by the forces of evil, the first such tragic hero in English drama.[23] The world fades from him as if an insubstantial dream, his support "vanyshed awaye, as it were a wynter myste. / All they are from me; I am now left alone" (line 1541–42).

Bale, of course, never doubts the true moral orientation of history; but it is only his license as a dramatic maker, his freedom to leap from the particular to the general, from the historical to the abstract and back again, that allows him to *represent* that truth. Johan is reborn in the sixteenth century as Imperial Majesty. The vowed order and reform of the play's opening can now be realized and old scores settled, as Sedition returns to the stage, leaping over three centuries and still plying his protean trade ("I am not he," he cries when recognized), only to be snared at last (lines 2484–86).

But if the resolution is to satisfy his audience, Bale must free both his protagonist and his play from any suspicion of will-

272 · William Shakespeare

fulness or wish-fulfillment. When Clergy slyly suggests that Imperial Majesty's final supremacy is enacted for the sake of his "pleasure," the kingly figure explodes: supremacy is not based on the "pleasure of my person," but on "God's truth":

> I wyll the auctoryte of Gods holy wurde to do it
> And it not to aryse of your vayne slypper wytt.
> That scripture doth not is but a lyght fantasye.
>
> (lines 2397–99)

The play itself is a typological mirror, as "the interpretour" tells us about midway through the action, truly representing the global struggle between good and evil: "Thys noble kynge Iohan, as a faythfull Moyses, / Withstode proude Pharao for hys poore Israel" (lines 1107–8). Near the play's end, Bale insists on the historical dimension of his typology, as Verity endorses the play's factuality over Polydore Vergil's unflattering historical portrait:

> I assure ye, fryndes, lete men wryte what they wyll,
> Kynge Iohan was a man both valeaunt and godlye.
> What though Polydorus reporteth hym very yll
> At the suggestyons of the malicyouse clergye?
> Thynke yow a Romane with the Romanes can not lye?
> Yes! Therfor, Leylonde, out of thy slumbre awake,
> And wytnesse a trewthe for thyne owne countrayes sake.
>
> (lines 2193–99)

There is a poignant irony in the call for "Leylonde" to awake and witness. The appeal, added sometime after 1547, is to Henry VIII's antiquary, John Leland, who shared Bale's passion for history. Insanity gripped Leland in 1547, from which he was never to recover, an insanity that, Bale suggests in his preface to *The Laboryouse Journey & Serche of Iohan Leylande*, may have been the consequence of a "poetical wit."[24] But once we have read *King Johan*, it is Bale's own poetic wit that is a matter of concern, the capacity he surely thought revealed universal truth shining through history, but that just as surely demonstrates the fantastic extremes to which theater can go in constructing doctrinal perspectives. *King Johan* threatens to transform historical interpretation into a war of fictions, the theatrical Catholics in the play against Bale's ostentatious distortions throughout the play. The play stands today less as a monument to "substantialist metaphysics" than as an instance of the disorienting forms of controversy that the Reformation fostered—even, for one critic, as "an exercise in psychopathic Protestantism."[25]

Thomas Sackville and Thomas Norton's *Gorboduc* (1562) for some marks a new stability in the history play, the sign of didacticism's renewed vitality and purposefulness inspired by *The Mirror for Magistrates*.[26] *Gorboduc*'s literary achievements are often cited—a logical plot structure, symbolic dumb shows, and the introduction of blank verse for drama. Its stability, however, is purchased at enormous dramatic cost. For even while the rhetoric of violence fills its Argument— "killed," "revenge," "cruelty," "rebellion," "terribly destroyed"—the play sets its scenes, as Wolfgang Clemen notes, at " 'points of rest' between actual incidents." Events may be ghastly, but they are also ghostly: "The 'dramatic present' plays a negligible part. We very often get the feeling that the 'real play' is being performed elsewhere, on another stage, and that the speakers are gazing across at this stage from the enclosed space in which they are sitting quietly together like a play-reading society."[27] The play's intellectual vigor has been impressively defended,[28] but it is a vigor that shuns theatricalization. Cruder in almost every way, the popular drama *Cambises* (ca. 1561) is nonetheless a more valuable indicator of the conflicting impulses embodied in Tudor histories.

Unlike *Gorboduc*, Thomas Preston's play is committed to the necessities of stage action: a body is flayed ("with a false skin" is the helpful stage direction), a heart cut out, and a hidden bladder of vinegar is punctured to display a stab wound. Add to such violence the slapstick of low comedy and a crew of mythological, allegorical, and historical personages, and we have a bizarre miscellany of stage effects that purports to bear the play's self-declared moral purpose. *Cambises* was, however, not only successful and memorable enough to be parodied by Shakespeare thirty years later; it also touches on subtler problems. Intermittently beneath the blood and thunder lie tantalizing moments of self-awareness that ask us whether "didactic drama" might not be an oxymoron.

The prologue announces the play's didactic intentions, enrolling it in the lists of mirrors for magistrates as a cautionary tale about the fall of Cambises, king of Persia. It is, however, also a mirror for didacticism; Cambises is, we are reminded, the son of Cyrus, one of Renaissance humanism's favorite *exempla*, thanks to Xenophon's idealizing *Cyropaedia*. Thomas Elyot, Thomas Hoby, and Sidney all praise that perfect pattern of a prince, as does the prologue here: "Cirus . . . did deserve, as I do read, the lasting blast of fame" (lines 15–16). The play then proceeds to turn the relations of fathers and sons into a nucleus for an initial gathering of models of moral instruction. Cambises seems at first to have profited from his father's example. He cites Cyrus's "worthy facts," and a relieved counselor rejoices that one "so yoong such profit should conceive" (lines 9, 23). Before invading Egypt, Cambises selects Sisamnes as his regent because of his "gift of wit" (line 62), and the latter declares that if he prove unvirtuous, he himself should be made the subject of an *exemplum*:

> Such execution then commence—and use it to this end—
> That all other, by that my deed, example so may take,
> To admonish them to flee the same by feare it may them make!
> (lines 90–92)

When Cambises returns to discover Sisamnes' corruption, he does, indeed, turn him into a speaking picture, particularly for the benefit of Sisamnes' son: "Call Otian, this iudges sonne, / And he shal heare and also see what his father hath doon" (lines

413–14). The spectacle instructs but hardly delights; not only is Sisamnes executed, but his body is flayed, while Otian cries out that such a sight is beyond "natures mould" (line 465). View it he does, however, and dutifully interprets it as a mirror: "O king, to me this is a glasse: with greefe in it I view / Example that unto your Grace I doo not prove untrue" (lines 469–70).

Yet we never witness the salubrious effects on Otian, who simply vanishes from the play. What remains instead is the sadistic impulse behind the performance. Having killed and mutilated a father before his son, Cambises mounts a complementary spectacle. When his one honest counselor cautions him against "certain vices," namely the "vice of drunkenness," Cambises proves his sobriety by shooting an arrow into the counselor's son's heart. As the heart is cut out for presentation to the father, Cambises applauds his work's besotted decorum: "After this wine to doo this deed I thought it very fit" (line 564).

The abruptness with which Cambises-virtuous becomes Cambises-vicious is explained by Willard Farnham, Irving Ribner, and others as Preston's awkward stitching together of the anecdotes of his source, Richard Taverner's *Garden of Wysdom*, which uses Cambises both as a positive example of stern moralism, the performer of "One Good Deed" as Preston's title has it, and a negative example of tyranny.[29] But Preston's use of his protagonist's contradictions is cagier than they allow; Cambises presents an image of human volatility that resists didactic "squaring," a creature for whom instruction can have only a temporary effect and whose own pose as moral tutor is subject to instantaneous self-parody. From the beginning, he has little real essence beyond an unstable and aggressive will. Even as the figure of Councell encourages him in the opening scene to persevere in his "vertuous life" and praises his military prowess as leading to a "supernal seat," his attitude toward Cambises' virtue is tense and defensive: "in that cup to drinke have no delight; / To martiall feats and kingly sport fix all your whole delight" (lines 33–34). Indeed, the figure of Shame proleptically bewails the king's "Lechery and drunkenness" even before his early "One Good Deed," and his vicious deeds bear an uncanny resemblance to his virtuous ones. When Cambises forces his cousin into an incestuous marriage, her cry, "It is a thing that Natures course doth utterly detest" (line 910) echoes Otian's response to the "good" punishment of Sisamnes.

Accentuating, instigating, and symbolizing human caprice is the figure of Ambidexter, one of the great Tudor Vices: "The king himselfe was godly up trained; / He professed vertue— but I think it was fained. / He plaies with both hands, good deeds and ill" (lines 607–9).[30] Running "this way and that way," he sows dissension throughout the social hierarchy, whether through obscenity and slapstick among country clowns and ruffian soldiers or by evoking the queasy anxiety of court suspicion in a scene where the king determines to kill his brother. Pretending to have overheard the latter pray for the king's death, Ambidexter refuses, like Diccon the Bedlam, either to affirm or deny the charge; ambiguity itself is enough to provoke paranoia and murder:

KING.   . . . doost thou presume to fill my princely eares with
        lyes?
        . . . .
        How saist thou? Speake the truth: was it so or no?
AMB.   I thinke so, if it please your Grace, but I cannot tell.
KING.   Thou plaist with both hands, now I perceive well!
        But, for to put al doubts aside, and to make him leese his
        hope,
        He shall dye

                                                    (lines 683–89)

A final attempt to instruct and reform the king occurs at his wedding celebration, a mirror of Tudor court spectacle. "Yonder is a royal court!" we are told, "There is triumphing, and sporte upon sporte, / . . . Masking and mumming, with eche kinde of thing" (lines 938–43). The king again indulges his sadistic sportiveness by forcing a young dog to fight a lion while the dog's brother watches, and cheerfully applauds the friendship that wins the day when both dogs join to chase the lion away. The new queen seizes the didactic moment: playing Nathan to David, she transforms what had been merely a "wonder great" to the amoral king into a moral commentary on the king's fratricide. There is, however, room for only one exegete in Persia, and the queen is killed for her interpretive presumption. The play seems to have lost its own moral bearings as well when the queen's elegiac farewell to the ladies of the court becomes an occasion for new comic routines by a wailing Ambidexter: "A, a, a, a! I cannot chuse but weepe for the queene! / . . . Oh, Oh! my hart, my hart! O, my bum will break!" (lines 1133–35).[31]

Cambises does not, of course, discard its didactic purpose. Though we may suspect some ironic hyperbolizing when the tyrant enters at the play's conclusion, a bloody sword thrust into his side as he insists "a iust reward for my misdeeds my death doth plaine declare" (line 1173) we cannot deny that the play has cautioned against abandoning the "moderate life" lived within its "square." And yet when the epilogue offers apologies in case the author has "squared amisse," we are reminded as well of the pressures of writing for the stage. To teach and delight may be a critical ideal, but the practice is fraught with ambiguities. If Preston's "Lamentable Tragedie mixed Full of Plesant Mirth" finally affirms the substantial order of things, it also suggests that playwrights must learn to play with both hands. *Cambises* may make this discovery seem a modest accomplishment, but its place in the development of Tudor drama shows that the medium can be exploited for more difficult and paradoxical representations.

"THE MAIESTIE OF THEIR PEN"

When the French moralist Matthew Coignet assaulted the poetic imagination, he included "comedies [that] are compounded of fixions, fables and lyes," and "playes" that turn "upside down all discipline and good manners." He made an exception, however, for "fables taken out of hystories, whereof, there maye growe some edifying";[32] there is a similar appeal to history as a substantial ground in the prologue to the *True Tragedy of Richard III* where a personified Truth promises Poetrie that he will "adde bodies" to poetic "shadowes" (lines 8–10). The staging of history, however, also raises the risks. The comic world may be turned upside down with no further consequences than a few bruised shins and confused gulls; in history plays, Tudor society's basic assumptions about authority become part of the theatrical display. Stephen Gosson warns of the implications: "If a true Historie be taken in hand, it is made like our shadows, longest at the rising and falling of the Sunne, shortest of all at hie noone. For the Poets driue it most commonly vnto such pointes as may best showe the maiestie of their pen in Tragicall speaches . . . or painte a fewe antickes to fitt their owne humors with scoffes & tauntes."[33] The playwright's narcissistic virtuosity turns the objective world he presumably reflects into a mere background against which to display his own unruly imaginings.

One need not endorse Gosson's attack to acknowledge the force of his remarks. Moral histories pit the agents of misrule—conceived in terms of fraud, randomness, or pointless versatility—against a stolid orthodoxy that inevitably overwhelms them. Yet the very staging of the conflict forces into prominence the energies of human contrivance upon which the theater itself depends. In the process, it threatens either to cast orthodoxy in a merely defensive role, an impersonal limit to the imagination, or to expose it as merely an authorized version of those very energies.[34] Seen from this point of view, Tudor drama reenacts the dilemma of symbolic forms in the Renaissance, which we have already noted in Cusanus's *ars coniecturalis* and Sidney's poetics: an art form that would point from human inventiveness to stable, objective truth also figures their problematic relationship.

This ambiguous potential motivated a good deal of Renaissance controversy. It underlies Wenck's attack on Cusanus as an obsessive meddler seeking to discard traditional fixed points of reason for the sake of his own dangerous fictions; it also lies behind the conservative responses to "errant" innovations of poetry and poetics in the Italian Renaissance. But the unsettling of assumptions inspires art as well as anxiety, becoming a central resource of the major historical and tragic dramas of the late sixteenth century. Examples spring readily to mind. For Hieronimo in Thomas Kyd's *The Spanish Tragedy*, the visions of Revelation become images of estrangement; his "tortur'd" and "restless" soul beats "at the windows the brightest heavens, / Soliciting for justice and revenge: But they are plac'd in those empyreal heights / Where, countermur'd with walls of diamond, / I find the place impregnable" (3.7.10–17). Having sought in vain for either divine or civic justice after his son's murder, Hieronimo finds satisfaction only in "sport" and "invention," a diabolic play-within-a-play that suddenly turns deadly earnest. Here is a play that challenges us to find the proper place of man's schemes and artifices. The entire action is itself cast as a play-within-a-play, observed by Revenge and a Ghost, a layering of fictions that has sent critics in different directions seeking a message. Does Hieronimo's revenge show human contrivance and violence in opposition to God's law? Or do they serve the ends of an inscrutable "heavenly justice"? Or is the play's very presentation of heavenly justice merely a projection of man's "lust for retribution"?[35] The most spectacular instances of such obstinate questions are, of course, in Christopher Marlowe's plays. At their center lies a conflict instigated by the restless human imagination seeking to fashion its own world, whether through military conquest, infinite riches in a little room, homosexual fantasy, or the magician's "lines, circles, letters, and characters." If we note that at the end of these plays the insatiable hero collapses into sterility, that his laboring brain, after violating traditional boundaries, can beget only "a world of idle fantasies," as Mephostophilis says of Faustus's, it is not because we have returned to the doctrinal origins of Marlowe's art, but because of the uncompromising purity, and so hopelessness, of Marlowe's tragic disjunctions.[36]

Less pure, and richer, are the historical and tragic predicaments in Shakespeare.

10

THE FIRST TETRALOGY

THE *HENRY VI* PLAYS

The Earl of Warwick's surprise attack in *3 Henry VI* seeks to restore the Lancastrian Henry VI to the throne. Pulling the crown from the head of the Yorkist King Edward, Warwick ridicules his fantasy of power:

> for his mind, be Edward England's king;
> But Henry now shall wear the English crown
> And be true King indeed; thou but the shadow.
>   (4.3.48–50)

The release of Henry from the Tower, however, signals only another displacement of authority. The weak king has enjoyed the safety of "incaged birds" and now resigns the government to his liberators, Warwick and Clarence, themselves only recent defectors from the Yorkist side. Suddenly possessed of the power for which so many have schemed throughout the three-play series, Warwick vows:

> We'll yoke together, like a double shadow
> To Henry's body, and supply his place
>   (4.6.49–50)

His simile betrays him. The Yorkist Edward may have been but the shadow of a king, but can any shadow, however multiplex, supply the place of body? The distinct boundary between fancy and reality has been blurred by political necessity. This hasty readjustment of terms recapitulates the *Henry VI* plays, a world where visions of stability are anchored only to the contingent, and where once-privileged coordinates lie open to human manipulation.

The treacherous flux of history is a preoccupation from the plays' first scene, the funeral of "Henry the Fifth, too famous to live long!" (*1 Henry VI*, 1.1.6), a ceremony itself disrupted by the wrangling of ambitious aristocrats. The first play also presents the genesis of the Wars of the Roses out of the shadowy motives of power politics. "What means this silence?" asks Richard Plantagenet. "Dare no man answer in a case of truth?" (2.4.1–2). Here, in a debate without stated topics, we hear the rhetoric of feuding parties proclaiming clear and distinct truths on their own behalves: the solution is "so naked," "so clear," "so shining," "so evident" that no rational mind could deny it, but Warwick confesses his confusion at these "nice sharp quillets of the law," and Somerset answers the challenge for a clear "argument" with a threatening gesture to "my scabbard" (2.4.17,60). The meaning of "this silence" shapes a language only in "dumb significants" (2.4.26) with the plucking of red and white roses as badges for the opposing factions. King Henry later expresses bafflement over this world of unexplained passion and arbitrary symbols. The dispute to him is "a toy, a thing of no regard," and he grandly puts on a red rose, declaring, "I see no reason, if I wear this rose, / That one should therefore be suspicious I more incline to Somerset than York" (4.1.152–54).

In a superb reading of the play, Sigurd Burckhardt casts Henry as a Platonist or medieval Realist whose belief in the priority of universals—the Rose and the Crown before any particular rose or crown—is lost in a world of accident:

> The wholeness and purity of conceptual forms is not sustainable in the world of choice and action; in action we become partial and partisan. . . . the universality and permanence of conceptual forms is a linguistic illusion. . . . What we have treated with contempt as "accidental" becomes in the highest degree "substantial"; in the world of action the redness or whiteness of a rose, the En-

glishness or Scottishness of a crown, is likely to be much more determinative than its conceptual "essence."[1]

Burckhardt's reading is of a piece with his larger interpretation of Shakespearean meanings: symbols, he argues, often begin as arbitrary counters, but in a manner both "binding and revelatory," they are seen "acquiring meaning." Dramatic action is not mimetic, but rather an analogue for the way meaning is generated in the world of accident; Shakespeare discovers "within the realities of his craft and circumstances the truth of world and stage alike."[2] Burckhardt's argument is wonderfully suggestive, but his vision of the accidental acquiring substance must be qualified by its inverse: the stage figures the world only by figuring the world as a stage. Exploiting the uncertainties of his predecessors, Shakespeare uncovers the expressive *un*realities of his craft. If, as Burckhardt implies, the play represents a Nominalist hunger for particular truth, its "dumb significants" also suggest a world where the substantial must be sought through verbal and historical "supposes." It is a world of existential loss as well as gain, one that shows us not only how meaning can become binding and revelatory but how it is bled out of an order that had once seemed objectively stable.[3]

The play dramatizes this loss in the fall of characters who see themselves as the guardians of their culture's values and symbols. They are not naive escapists like King Henry; rather, they are sophisticated, powerful, alert to the exigencies of action, but the creatures of a passing era. The most impressive figure is Lord Talbot, hero of the French wars. In *1 Henry VI*, he is invited by the Countess of Auvergne to what the Duke of Burgundy mistakes for "peaceful comic sport" (2.2.45), but which proves to be an ambush, a "plot" to rival the murder of Cyrus (2.3.4–6). Talbot's arrival sets the countess to gloating:

> Is this the Scourge of France?
> Is this the Talbot, so much fear'd abroad
> That with his name the mothers still their babes?

I see report is fabulous and false:
I thought I should have seen some Hercules,
A second Hector, for his grim aspect
And large proportion of his strong-knit limbs.
Alas, this is a child, a silly dwarf!
It cannot be this weak and writhled shrimp
Should strike such terror to his enemies.

(2.3.14–23)

Behind the plotter's humiliating taunts lies a note of disappointment. She had invited "warlike Talbot, for his acts / So much applauded" (2.2.35–36), but the flesh does not fill out his mythical dimensions; he is no Hercules or Hector, but an aging soldier. Nevertheless, she consoles herself that she has penetrated through the "fabulous and false": "Long time thy shadow hath been thrall to me, / For in my gallery thy picture hangs; / And now the substance shall endure the like" (2.3.35–37). The relations between shadows and substance are not as simple as she imagines. Talbot's response, "No, no, I am but shadow of myself: / You are deceived, my substance is not here," strikes her as an insoluble paradox—"He will be here, and yet he is not here: / How can these contrarieties agree?"— until the blowing of his martial horn, the sound of drums, and the entrance of his soldiers provide the answer: "Are you now persuaded / That Talbot is but shadow of himself? / These are his substance, sinews, arms, and strength" (2.3.49–50, 56–57, 60–62). If brave Talbot triumphs on the stage, as Nashe was to recall the play, he does so as a creature of the stage.[4] He is able to figure forth the objective old order only through his untroubled mastery of the actor's paradox; the power of performance, as Burckhardt suggests, is the analogue to the performance of power, the "strength / With which he yoketh your rebellious necks, / Razeth your cities, and subverts your towns, / And in a moment makes them desolate" (2.3.62–65).

Heroic performers such as Talbot rely, however, on a historical context whose symbols are perceived as pure and unequivocal. Hence he strips the knightly garter from the cowardly John Falstaff to preserve "this ornament of knighthood," "the sacred name of knight" (4.1.29, 40). But in the same scene, his king obtusely puts on the red rose, marking the emergence of a more oblique world of meaning. Talbot is trapped in this transition, whose sweep is international. His doom is foreshadowed in the opening act through the witchcraft of his arch foe, Joan of Arc, whose spells disorient him: "My thoughts are whirled like a potter's wheel; / I know not what I am, nor what I do" (1.5.19–20). She brings a cunning kind of theatricality to bear as she takes Rouen, dressing her soldiers as peasants and directing them to "Take heed, be wary how you place your words; / Talk like this vulgar sort of market men / That come to gather money for their corn" (3.2.3–5). The trick is respectable enough for Musidorus in the *New Arcadia*, but here aligns Joan with the kind of histrionic villainy one finds in the Catholic invasion in Bale's *King Johan*.⁵ Her witchcraft includes the juggling of appearances and rhetoric, and she produces some of the play's most ringing appeals to patriotism only to mock the constancy of her auditor's allegiances: "Turn and turn again!" (3.3.85). It is the sound of her mocking that closes Talbot's career as well. He dies with his son's corpse in his arms, defying "antic death" with a vision of "Two Talbots winged through the lither sky" (4.7.18, 21), but his transcendence is checked by Joan's sneer at William Lucy's lofty eulogy: "The Turk, that two and fifty kingdoms hath, / Writes not so tedious a style as this. / Him that thou magnifiest with all these titles, / Stinking and fly-blown lies here at our feet" (4.7.74–76).⁶

Humphrey, Duke of Gloucester, is another patriot who clutches for an order that seems to crumble in his grasp. He brings a written bill of accusations against the scheming Winchester only to have them torn from his hand and to be confronted: "Com'st thou with deep-premeditated lines, / With written pamphlets studiously devis'd"; make your charges, he

is insultingly commanded, "without invention" (3.1.1–2, 5).
"Extemporal speech" is not the sign of sincerity that Winchester pretends, Humphrey reminds the court, but only of the improvisational opportunist: "Think not, although in writing I preferr'd / The manner of thy vile outrageous crimes, / That therefore I have forg'd, or am not able / Verbatim to rehearse my method penn'd" (3.1.6, 10–13). Gloucester emerges in *2 Henry VI* as the final defender of England's symbolic sturdiness. Learning that England's conquests in France are to be relinquished for the sake of Henry's marriage to the French Margaret, he protests:

> Fatal this marriage, cancelling your fame,
> Blotting your names from books of memory,
> Razing the characters of your renown,
> Defacing monuments of conquer'd France,
> Undoing all, as all had never been!
> (1.1.98–102)

But symbols of permanence are quickly swept away.[7] Humphrey's effectiveness is limited to a few minor episodes, such as the exposure of a faked miracle of cured blindness (2.1), a victory quickly forgotten when the specter of witchcraft is raised one more time. He is framed through his wife's treasonous dealings with sorcerers and conjurers. It is the fate of the one honest man to be accused of playacting; the French Margaret brands him in terms Robert Greene may have recalled in making his notorious "upstart crow" remark about Shakespeare:

> Seems he a dove? His feathers are but borrow'd,
> For he's disposed as the hateful raven:
> Is he a lamb? His skin is surely lent him,
> For he's inclin'd as is the ravenous wolves.
> Who cannot steal a shape that means deceit?
> (3.1.75–79)

He is doomed in the end by being written into the theatrical contrivances of others: "Their complot is to have my life; / . . . mine is made the prologue to their play; / For thousands more, that yet suspect no peril, / Will not conclude their plotted tragedy" (3.1.147, 151–53).

In a disintegrating world, theatricality becomes the means for discrediting one's foes or for seizing power. The worst humiliation the French can inflict on Talbot in *1 Henry VI* is to reduce him to a "public spectacle," a motley to the view:

> In open market-place produc'd they me
> To be a public spectacle to all;
> Here, said they, is the Terror of the French,
> The scarecrow that affrights our children so.
>
> (1.4.39–42)

English society falls meanwhile to the manipulators and fiction makers, the "turbulent wits" who haunted Tudor moralists and dominated Tudor comedies and moral histories. The Bishop of Winchester grumbles, "Each hath his place and function to attend: / I am left out; for me nothing remains; / But long I will not be Jack out of office" (1.1.173–75); Suffolk admits only half-facetiously, "I have been a truant in the law / And never yet could frame my will to it; / And therefore frame the law unto my will" (2.4.7–9); and in *2 Henry VI* York secretly schemes: "Faster than spring-time showers comes thought on thought, / And not a thought but thinks on dignity. / My brain, more busy than the labouring spider, / Weaves tedious snares to trap mine enemies" (3.1.337–40).

Shakespeare takes the political morality play one step further, striking with canny accuracy at Tudor anxieties with his trilogy's self-conscious theatrics. York's staging of Jack Cade's serio-comic rebellion in *2 Henry VI* anatomizes not only the threat to order but the assumptions of order. Cade is the hero and Vice of a history-play-within-a-play, York's "substitute" who is fitted with a false name and claim to the throne to allow York to "perceive the commons' mind, / How they affect the house and claim of York" (3.1.374–75). The play's the thing; Cade's first public rally begins with a search for stage properties: "Get thee a sword, though made of a lath," jokes one follower (4.2.1). His comic introduction, complete with sniggering tradesmen, soon gives way to his sweeping assault on England's official culture; all gentility and learning are to be destroyed: "All scholars, lawyers, courtiers, gentlemen, / They call false caterpillars" (4.4.35–36); "pull down the Savoy," Cade cries, "others to the Inns of Court: down with them all" (4.7.1–2). Cade becomes the bogeyman of literacy: Lord Say's ability to speak Latin condemns him to death (4.7.55), as does Lord Stafford's ability to speak French (4.2.162ff.). A clerk's possession of a book with red letters proves him a conjurer, and his ability to sign his name, rather than making a cross, condemns him to hanging "with his pen and ink-horn about his neck" (4.2.81ff.). Cade is, however, more than a bullying anarchist. True, he makes the usual Vice-cries—"then are we in order when we are most out of order"—and in his attack on Lord Say he struts in the guise of a humanist's nightmare:

> Thou hast most traitorously corrupted the youth of the realm in erecting a grammar-school; and whereas, before, our forefathers had no other books but the score and the tally, thou hast caus'd printing to be us'd; and contrary to the King his crown, and dignity, thou hast built a paper-mill. It will be prov'd to thy face that thou hast men about thee that usually talk of a noun, and a verb, and such abominable words as no Christian ear can endure to hear.
>
> (4.7.30–39)

But his tone abruptly modulates, and we are allowed to glimpse his provocation—the mechanisms of power through which the literate have suppressed his class:

> Thou hast appointed justices of the peace to call poor men before them about matters they were not able to answer. Moreover, thou hast put them in prison; and because they could not read, thou hast hanged them.
>
> (4.7.39–44)

The glimpse is only momentary, and Cade is soon again the murderous buffoon. But our perspective has been complicated, and when Lord Say remarks to the Kentish rebels about their land, " 'tis 'bona terra, mala gens,' " which he slyly mistranslates as "Sweet is the country . . . / The people liberal, valiant, active, wealthy" (4.7.54, 59–60), we are caught between laughing at the rebels' ignorance and squirming at the evidence that proves Cade's point. It is the coercive force of literacy and eloquence that Cade attacks, and as he sentences the felicitously named Lord Say to death, he remarks, "I feel remorse in myself with his words; but I'll bridle it: he shall die, and it be but for pleading so well for his life" (4.7.100–102). Indeed, it is an aristocrat's eloquence that finally does Cade in, as Lord Clifford's speech turns the mob against him. "Was ever feather so lightly blown to and fro as this multitude? The name of Henry the Fifth hales them to an hundred mischiefs" (4.8.55–57) is Cade's bitter aside.

Cade's rebellion is ultimately sterile, a mere shadow of York's master plan. It does, however, serve to emphasize how problematic the locus of authority has become in the series. York's seizure of power at the end of *2 Henry VI* makes the issue explicit. York demands Clifford's obedience, and he in turn points to Henry:

> This is my king, York; I do not mistake;
> But thou mistakes me much to think I do.
> To Bedlam with him! Is the man grown mad!
> (5.1.129–31)

But who belongs inside Bedlam and who outside is not clear:

> CLIFFORD: Why, what a brood of traitors have we here!
> YORK: Look in a glass, and call thy image so.
> I am thy king, and thou a false-heart traitor.
> (5.1.141–43)

Were the action not murderous, we might think we were back in the world of Tudor comedy, with its mad pranksters and multiple supposes. How can we know the traitor from the hero? All opposing sides—French against English, York against Lancaster—claim to be fighting for God and the right. Even though Shakespeare invokes the true line of succession in each of the three plays (Part 1, act 2, scene 5; Part 2, act 2, scene 2; Part 3, act 1, scene 1), proving each time York's superior claim to the throne, with the final recitation convincing King Henry himself, he characterizes York as am ambitious schemer, less appealing than the pious, incompetent Henry.[8]

The plays further unsettle us by forcing us to reflect on the glory that has passed. Was the old order truly a golden age of substantial truths, or is that a nostalgic fantasy, a longing for a period that seemed simpler only because the illusions of power worked more smoothly? Warwick at the start of *3 Henry VI* enforces York's princely right by threatening to "fill the house with armed men, / . . . Write up his title with usurping blood," and by stamping his foot, the cue for soldiers to enter (1.1.170ff.), behavior less gracious than, but reminiscent of, Talbot's summoning his shadow's substance with a martial horn in Part 1. The only clear difference between the eras is the degree of volatility. Substance, once achieved, can become shadow again with terrifying suddenness. When he falls into Lancastrian hands in Part 3, York's longing to play the role of king is grimly mocked with a paper crown by the taunting, murderous Margaret, who likens him to a professional clown:

> Stamp, rave, and fret, that I may sing and dance.
> Thou woulds't be fee'd, I see, to make me sport;
> York cannot speak unless he wear a crown.
> A crown for York! and, lords, bow low to him!
> Hold you his hands whilst I do set it on.
> (*Putting a paper crown on his head.*)
> Ay, marry, sir, now looks he like a king!
> (1.4.91–96)

An oath seems scarcely more than a *flatus vocis* in Parts 2 and 3. York dismisses his to Henry, Henry his to York, and Clarence his to the Lancastrians. Such slippage becomes the basic fact of political and social life: as the gamekeepers blandly explain to King Henry as they arrest him, their oaths are to the king, whoever he may be at the moment (Part 3, 3.1.72ff.). A man may find himself at any time playing the fool, including the mighty kingmaker Warwick, who in Part 3 grandly woos the French king's sister for Edward after York's murder: "Myself have often heard him say, and swear, / That this his love was an eternal plant, / Whereof the root was fix'd in Virtue's ground" (3.3.123–25). The sworn fixity he invokes lasts less than fifty lines as letters arrive announcing Edward's sudden marriage to Lady Elizabeth Grey. And yet one who would act on the stage of history cannot afford to hesitate, to feel for a surer foundation. Edward would ride cautiously on fortune's wheel; his father's example tempts him to "forget / Our title to the crown, and only claim / Our dukedom till God please to send the rest," or, on a less pious note, "we'll debate / By what safe means the crown may be recover'd" (4.7.46–47, 51–52). But his supporters demand he play the role of king or not play at all. "I came to serve a king and not a duke," Montgomery protests:

> What talk you of debating? In few words:
> If you'll not here proclaim yourself our King,
> I'll leave you to your fortune and be gone
> To keep them back that come to succour you.
> Why shall we fight, if you pretend no title?
> (4.7.49, 53–57)

The pun on "pretend" says more than Montgomery would admit; he demands a fiction worth fighting for.

In a world of shifting allegiances and problematic meanings, the heroic spirit can only rush into action, as does brave Warwick in Part 3, hoping that his full-throated hyperboles will drown out the agonizing sense of unreality in his heart:

> Then let the earth be drunken with our blood;
> I'll kill my horse because I will not fly.

> Why stand we like soft-hearted women here,
> Wailing our losses, whiles the foe doth rage;
> And look upon, as if the tragedy
> Were play'd in jest by counterfeiting actors?
> Here on my knee I vow to God above
> I'll never pause again, never stand still,
> Till either death hath clos'd these eyes of mine,
> Or fortune given me measure of revenge.
>
> (2.3.23–32)

He directs his curses against the manipulative Lancastrians, who have, as he earlier puts it, "wrought the easy-melting King like wax" (2.1.171). But it is to their cause that he will soon defect, and for whose cause he will die. And while he dies like Talbot, looking toward heaven for release, he also echoes Joan's mockery over Talbot's corpse: "Lo now my glory smear'd in dust and blood! / . . . nothing left me but my body's length. / Why, what is pomp, rule, reign, but earth and dust?" (5.2.23–27).

The *Henry VI* trilogy once seemed to E. M. W. Tillyard's followers the "simple and obvious" work of a young didact in "no need of ambiguities."[9] Though Shakespeare's later histories are subtler, there is no simple ideological point of origin in these early efforts. If there is an allusion to the "Homily against Disobedience and Willful Rebellion" in *2 Henry VI*, it is, as J. P. Brockbank notes, spoken by a murderous pirate intent on justifying his "lynch law":

> All the acts of retribution in this play and the next are invested in an atmosphere of evil—images sickening and grotesque. . . . Suffolk's death is an act of lynch law, and one of several similar happenings which is at once a satisfying act of retribution, and therefore a recognition of the chronicle "Providence"; and "a barbarous and bloody spectacle" (IV.i.174) and therefore a moral and aesthetic challenge to the validity of that Providence.[10]

What had been a peculiar juxtaposition of didacticism and amoral spectacle in a play such as *Cambises* has become a subtler means of complicating moral response. Shakespeare's aim is not subversion but a dramatic exploration of Tudor ideals as expressions of human desire, a part of historical process rather than its authorized explanation.

If that exploration seems brutal, it can also be poignant. In Part 3, King Henry is driven from battle by his ferocious queen and seeks the consolation of literary fiction. Sitting on a molehill, he imagines himself a shepherd, "blowing of his nails" and the battle—"like to the morning's war" between day and night—is transformed through further simile into an image of the sea as a battleground between tide and wind. Henry appears to be inventing epic similes, regarding violent action through pastoral (cf. *Aeneid* 2.304ff.), but only for the sake of wishing himself into a nostalgic vehicle:

> Oh God! methinks it were a happy life
> To be no better than a homely swain;
> To sit upon a hill, as I do now,
> To carve out dials quaintly, point by point,
> Thereby to see the minutes how they run—
> . . . .
> So minutes, hours, days, weeks, months, and years,
> Pass'd over to the end they were created
> Would bring white hairs unto a quiet grave.
> Ah, what a life were this!
>
> (2.5.21–41)

Henry longs to escape historical flux, to inform time with meaningful shape toward a peaceful end. He will soon discover that there is no exit when the dead York's deformed son, now ironically invested with loyal Gloucester's title, visits him in the Tower of London with his dagger drawn.

Nor is Henry the only victim of futile supposing. The new

King Edward IV imagines his future reign as the advent of brighter genres:

> And now what rests but that we spend the time
> With stately triumphs, mirthful comic shows,
> Such as befits the pleasure of the court?
>
> (5.7.42–44)

The mirth of this world will prove more demonic than courtly and belongs to the new king's brother, the future Richard III.

RICHARD III

Thomas Nashe may have felt inspired by the sight of brave Talbot triumphing on the stage, but for characters in the plays, such as the Duchess of York, Shakespeare's version of the Wars of the Roses fashions very few lasting images of virtue and valor. She laments in *Richard III*:

> I have bewept a worthy husband's death,
> And liv'd with looking on his images:
> But now two mirrors of his princely semblance
> Are crack'd in pieces by malignant death;
> And I, for comfort, have but one false glass,
> That grieves me when I see my shame in him.
>
> (2.2.49–54)

The deaths of her husband and two of her three sons mark a progressive degeneration from exemplar to icastic image, then from icastic to the fantastic. All that remains is the distorted shape in a "false glass."

That shape is Richard of Gloucester's, who emerges in *3 Henry VI* as the most obsessive of a savage world of schemers:

> like one lost in a thorny wood,
> That rents the thorns and is rent with the thorns,
> Seeking a way, and straying from the way;

Not knowing how to find the open air,
But toiling desperately to find it out—
Torment myself to catch the English crown:
And from that torment I will free myself,
Or hew my way out with a bloody ax.
(3.2.174–81)

For most of *Richard III*, Richard's obsession is more joyful than it is tormenting. His search for advantage fully indulges a mental agility that would wrest the fragments of a degenerating world to its own purposes. Attempts to explain his cruel exhilaration have led literary historians, quite rightly, to his theatrical antecedents and cousins, the Vice and the "villain as hero."[11] But these types do not so much identify him as point to energies that have always sought expression in such types and that now attempt to shape a world-view of their own. Richard's animosity is strangely philosophical, directed not merely against political rivals, but toward a suffocating and sinister cosmos. Love, he charges in his first great soliloquy in *3 Henry VI*, "did corrupt frail Nature with some bribe" to "disproportion me in every part, / Like a chaos" (3.2.155, 160–61). The start of *Richard III* finds him charging Nature itself with instigating the malice:

I, that am curtail'd of this fair proportion,
Cheated of feature by dissembling Nature,
Deform'd, unfinish'd, sent before my time
Into this breathing world, scarce half made up
(1.1.18–21)

Richard's deformity allows those threatened by him to contain him in their imaginations, safely locating him far down the scale of being: he is a "dog," a "poisonous toad," a "bottled spider," a "foul swine." We are continually offered such images as an index to Richard's depravity, and Richard's unremitting villainy adds force to the censure. But Richard for much of the action outpaces the play's moral categories. Critics since Lamb have noted how Richard turns his deformities into a sign of his uniqueness, as if transforming deprivation into power.[12] Robbed of an external form, he finds an informing principle within: "I can . . . frame my face to all occasions," he says in *3 Henry VI*:

> I can add colours to the chameleon,
> Change shapes with Proteus for advantages,
> And set the murderous Machiavel to school
> (3.2.182ff.)

Richard is at once stereotypical and uncategorizable. A. P. Rossiter sees in him the "volcanic Renaissance energies" that crack the stratified medieval world order.[13] "Who would not admire this our chameleon?" Pico says of man; his "self-transforming nature . . . symbolized by Proteus" makes him the miracle of creation. Yet Richard is just as surely a demonic parody of Renaissance man's most optimistic self-image. He is the paragon of a world where malevolent desire replaces the *amor platonicus*, and where the bestiality of "this breathing world" replaces the *anima mundi*. His self-fashioning compulsively overreaches its models: he *adds* colors to the chameleon, is *more* versatile than Proteus, and casts the Machiavel—who had already exposed to the age the darker side of transforming natures—as a mere schoolboy (3.2.191–93). Richard is Shakespeare's first great focal point for a psychic hunger that defies the corporate world of sameness at any cost:

> I have no brother, I am like no brother;
> And this word "love," which greybeards call divine,
> Be resident in men like one another,
> And not in me: I am myself alone
> (5.6.80–83)

We hear this voice again in *Richard III*'s first soliloquy, pitting "Our," "Our," "Our" against the demands of "I," "I," "I." What that "I" represents can never be made explicit, for it is generated from a coincidence of opposites: the union of deprivation and vigor. Its appetites betray both an absence of being and the most intensely dramatic form of existence possible; his will to power captures the imagination because it, more than any other motive in the play, projects the shapes of human desire.[14] Richard seems virtually to carve out a world of his own as he makes a bid for poetic omnipotence. Though he cannot caper nimbly in a lady's chamber, no love poet ever spoke with greater forcibleness than he when courting Lady Anne over the coffin of his victim, her father-in-law, Henry VI:

> Was ever woman in this humor woo'd?
> Was ever woman in this humor won?
> . . . .
> Having God, her conscience, and these bars against me,
> And I no friends to back my suit
> But the plain devil and dissembling looks?
> And yet to win her! All the world to nothing!
> (1.2.227–37)

He rivals evidence, conscience, even God Himself, armed only with dissembling looks at a few Petrarchan conceits. A gambler facing impossible odds—"All the world to nothing"—he also stands before us as a poetic genius, a creator *ex nihilo* who leaves behind the brazen nature that has cheated him from birth to deliver his own masterful intrigues.

His creations are, of course, not entirely out of "nothing." As I have already suggested, he depends upon a world coming undone—"a giddy world" (2.3.5), "a reeling world" (3.2.37). Here he finds matter for his conceit, juggling fragments of meaning: "Plots have I laid, inductions dangerous, / By drunken prophecies, libels, and dreams"; "I clothe my naked villainy / With odd old ends stol'n forth of Holy Writ" (1.1.32–33, 1.3.336–37). Nothing makes this world's disintegration more evident than the attempts of others to shore up its ruins in resistance to Richard's will. Clarence invokes God's law against murder to hold off Richard's hired assassins, but only manages to set into motion a debate where, in Wilbur Sanders's excellent analysis, "the issues of allegiance and justice are tossed and jostled back and forth, every rationalisation being undercut by the next. . . . It is an infinite regression of crime and punishment."[15] The old Queen Margaret likewise demands for herself a privileged status, with similar results. Presuming to expose this Yorkist world of fantasy, she invokes the old crimes and contentions of the *Henry VI* plays:

> I call'd thee then vain flourish of my fortune;
> I call'd thee, then, poor shadow, painted queen,
> The presentation of but what I was,
> The flattering index of a direful pageant;
> . . . .
> A dream of what thou wast; a garish flag
> To be the aim of every dangerous shot;
> A sign of dignity; a breath, a bubble;
> A queen in jest, only to fill the scene.
> (4.4.82ff.)

But the remembrance of things past is disastrous for her choric pretensions, for then she was the "she-wolf of France" sadistically taunting York with a paper crown. The crimes she recalls evoke contradictory constructions; might they not be the fulfillment of York's curse and God's punishment on her? "God, not we, hath plagued thy bloody deed" is Richard's opportunistic reading, and he is not alone: "No man but prophesied revenge for it," Dorset recalls (1.3.169ff.). Each side is locked in a battle of conjectural histories stretching backward into the abysm of time. Even Moulton, who places Margaret in a nemesis pattern that "shuts in the play like a veil," sees the veil here lifting to open up "a vista of nemeses receding further and further back into history."[16]

For all her formal laments and retributive schemes, the highest role Margaret achieves is that of Richard's rival poet, a competing voice toward which Queen Elizabeth would turn for lessons in rhetoric: "O thou, well skill'd in curses, stay awhile / And teach me how to curse mine enemies" (4.4.116–17). Here Margaret proves herself experienced in fantasy and *energeia*: "Think thy babes were sweeter than they were, / And he that slew them fouler than he is: / Bettring thy loss makes the bad-causer worse: / Revolving this will teach thee how to curse" (4.4.120–23). But in a world up for grabs, Richard grabs best. He neatly counterpunches against Margaret's telegraphed imprecations, striking home with her name before she can complete their predictable course. "O, let me make the period to my curse!" she protests, but too late; "Tis done by me, and ends in 'Margaret' " (1.3.238–39).

He also outplays the others through his extraordinary agility, his ability to invent a contrivance for every situation. At one moment he is a Petrarchan lover; at another, a wise old uncle. He seems to have ingested the world of the *Henry VI* plays into his repertoire, mimicking the plain-speaking Duke Humphrey in his outcry against upstarts at court (1.3.47, 78–82), and the pious, retiring King Henry in his "holy and devout" show of "zealous contemplation" as he reluctantly accepts the crown from his co-conspirator Buckingham. Richard, some critics have noted, seems uncannily to be writing the plot of *Richard III* itself; the effect is in large measure achieved by Richard's mastery of "if," his success in bending events to his own hypothetical constructions. Only a fool like Hastings can laugh at Richard's victims who "think themselves . . . safe" while gloating "that I know our state secure" (3.2.65, 79). Hastings's security founders on a conditional. Balking at Richard's further forgeries against his enemies—"If they have done this deed"—he finds his life lost for an "if": "If? . . . / Talk'st thou to me of ifs! Thou art a traitor: / Off with his head!" (3.4.73–76). Richard has established a monopoly on "if," and only his co-conspirator is allowed the luxury of playing so: "Canst thou," Richard sounds his protégé, "quake and change thy colour, / . . . / As if thou were distraught and mad with terror?" (3.5.1–4). When Hastings's severed head is returned to the stage, Buckingham poses a question that turns into a challenge: "Would you imagine, or almost believe, / . . . that the subtle traitor / This day had plotted, in the council-house, / To

murder me and my good Lord of Gloucester?" (3.5.34–38).
The point is not that others *do* believe, but that, like an audience
at a play, they are compelled to assent. The Scrivener makes
this explicit when he arrives on stage with the official charges
against Hastings:

> Here is the indictment of the good Lord Hastings,
> Which in a set hand fairly is engross'd,
> That it may be today read o'er in Paul's
> . . . .
> Here's a good world the while!
> Who is so gross
> That cannot see this palpable device?
> Yet who's so bold but says he sees it not?
> (3.6.1–3,10–12)

The charges are no less contrived by Richard's mind than by
the Scrivener's hand, the sheer overtness of their fictionality
testifying to the furthest point of Richard's mastery.[17]

Richard's exploitation of a disintegrating world continues until
he finds himself unraveling as well. He has sustained his vision
of a continuously expanding circle of power through Machia-
vellian contrivances, but his drives are incompatible with Machiavelli's chilling lucidity. Despite the histrionic powers assigned to the Prince and the quasi-aesthetic nature of his *virtù*,
Machiavelli's focus yields a remorseless literalness of vision: "I
thought it fitter to follow the effectual truth of the matter, than
the imagination thereof: And many Principalities and Repub-
liques have been in imagination, which neither have been seen
nor knowne to be indeed: for there is such a distance between
how men doe live and how men ought to live; that hee who
leaves that which is done, for that which ought to bee done,
learnes sooner his ruine, than his preservation."[18] Richard is
driven, rather, by an idealizing, poeticizing impulse, however
perverse. As early as *3 Henry VI*, he longs for kingship as if it
were the poet's golden world made actual: "Do but think /

How sweet a thing it is to wear a crown, / Within whose circuit is Elysium / And all that poets feign of bliss and joy" (1.2.28–31). "I'll make it my heaven to dream upon a crown," he later soliloquizes, and though he reproaches himself for dreaming—"I do but dream on sovereignty; / Like one that stands upon a promontory / And spies a far-off shore where he would tread" (3.2.134–36)—it is the vision, not the crown itself, that is his heaven. The very distance "between my soul's desire and me . . . between me and home" is the impetus that sustains his joyous feigning.

Distance, as we have seen, figures prominently in Renaissance visions of creative action. Whereas some traditions regard beauty as a congruence between subject and object, for Cusanus it is also the gulf between finite and infinite that drives the mind to realize its boundless fecundity as it seeks "all beauty the mind can picture." Richard, too, is inspired by his own hunger, but finally he can only parody such ideal possibilities. His goal is all too attainable, and once his supposed terminus is achieved, he degenerates from a creature of infinite variety into a creature of indeterminacy, his limitless power descending into formless desire. He grows forgetful of his own orders, is easily confused; the master of equivocation misunderstands his own messenger and must bribe him after striking him. "My mind is changed," he tells us, but now his transformation binds him. Richard is no longer Proteus, but the king, and as John Palmer shrewdly observes, "anything he may have to do next must necessarily be something of an anti-climax. The first, fine careless rapture is exhausted. All he can do henceforth is to maintain his position."[19] "He's sudden if a thing comes into his head," his brother Edward says of him in *3 Henry VI*, and his continual translation of thought into action keeps him in flight. He cannot think standing still.

Richard's dilemma, and the play's, is that the dynamics of human invention have been conceived purely in terms of a war between the subject and its objects; in his drive for poetic omnipotence, Richard has consumed rather than transformed his world. His translation of idea into practice recoils into solipsism, for anything perceived to be external to the "I" must be destroyed, whether it be on the Lancastrian side, the Yorkist side, or within his own intimate circle. Buckingham flourishes as if in ideal friendship; "my other self, my counsel's consistory," Richard names him. But he must also remain one of "many simple gulls" (1.3.328), and a moment's hesitation in acting out Richard's wish to have the two princes murdered is enough to highlight the "otherness" of this alter ego. Richard suspects Buckingham of looking "into me with considerate eyes" and of growing "circumspect," and resolves that "The deep-revolving, witty Buckingham / No more shall be the neighbour to my counsels" (4.2.42–43). The mere plea for "some little breath, some pause" is enough to make the rupture decisive and irremediable; Richard cannot bear the thought of an independent mind outside his own, of a deep-revolving wit that does not turn exactly on his axis.

"All the world to nothing" was his boast, and now that boast mocks him. His imagined Elysium disintegrates as soon as it is built—"My kingdom stands on brittle glass" (4.2.61)—and there is less and less material with which to shore it up; "Swear . . . by something that thou hast not wrong'd," Elizabeth challenges (4.4.373). The man of dreams, we learn, is now haunted by nightmares (4.1.82–84). Where he had once seemed as inexorable as history itself, pressing ever into the future, Richard is finally cursed by the past. On the eve of his destruction on Bosworth Field, the world he has suppressed returns to the stage as shadows in the night, ghostly supporters of his conqueror, Henry Tudor, Earl of Richmond.

CONCLUDING ORDER

Robert Ornstein's contention that "Richard is the only antagonist worthy of Richard," and that *Richard III* dramatizes "Richard's failure rather than Richmond's success" seems entirely just.[20] For even though intimations of the supernatural echo through the play in the form of prophecies, dreams, and ghosts, promising an overarching design,[21] the play's very life depends on Richard's comic villainy and the corrosive effects it has on all such system building. A. P. Rossiter, still one of the play's best commentators, finds in the very providentialism of Shakespeare's histories evidence of a mind outrunning static patterns. Schemes of Order and Degree "falsified his fuller experience of men. Consequently while employing it as a FRAME, he had to undermine it, to qualify it with equivocations: to vex its applications with sly or subtle ambiguities: to cast doubts on its ultimate human validity, even in situations where its principles seemed most completely applicable."[22] The collision of Richard's "seductive appeal" with the play's rigid providentialism leaves us with a vision not of absolutes but of "relatives, ambiguities, irony, a process thoroughly dialectical."[23] Wilbur Sanders put the matter more bluntly. Richard's parodies of the moral order "envelop the moral and the Christian in a cloud of ambiguity. . . . Richard releases a sense of incipient absurdity about the very postures he hypocritically adopts."[24]

And yet, it is the parodied, the absurd, that "wins" in the end, and that seems, in retrospect, to have been winning all along. King Edward's deathbed warning, "Take heed you dally not before your King, / Lest He that is the supreme King of kings / Confound your hidden falsehood" (2.1.12–14), seems ludicrous when first uttered, particularly in light of the gulling to which he is immediately subject. But Rivers, Grey, Vaughan, and Hastings all come to see themselves as victims of Margaret's supernatural curses (act 3, scenes 3 and 4), and Buckingham recalls Edward's terms when his end accords with his false vow: "That high All-Seer which I dallied with, / Hath turn'd my feigned prayer on my head, / And given in earnest what I begg'd in jest" (5.1.20–22). God becomes a morality playwright, turning jest into earnest to round off the play, seizing the detachable oaths of human schemers to weave them into a closed system of significances that traps Richard as well.[25]

A juggler of "odd old ends," the heroic villain who reveled in his freedom from prophetic formulae—"How chance the prophet could not, at that time, / Have told me—I being by—that I should kill him?" (4.2.98–99)—is frozen into the text of providential history. It is an irony that has darkened his declarations of autonomy from his first soliloquy of the play—"I am determined to prove a villain" (1.1.30)—and that returns with crushing finality in his last:

> What do I fear? Myself? There's none else by;
> Richard loves Richard, that is, I am I.
> Is there a murderer here? No. Yes, I am!
> Then fly. What, from myself? . . .
> . . . .
> My conscience hath a thousand several tongues,
> And every tongue brings in a several tale,
> And every tale condemns me for a villain
> (5.3.183ff.)

"I," "me," "my," "myself" sound thirty-seven times in the thirty-line soliloquy, but can mount no resistance to the determined end. The quasi-divine "I am I" fragments into agitated self-division, only to rejoin in grim monotony; the teller of tales finds every tale "condemns me for a villain." Determination dies in its fulfillment.

We are in part relieved by the cessation of Richard's murderous tyranny, but what consolation are we offered for the loss of his vitality? An enormous one, if we are to judge by Henry Tudor's reaffirmation of a sacramental cosmos, political unity, and peace: "We have ta'en the sacrament, / We will unite the white rose and the red" (5.5.18–19). Yet the victorious Richmond is dreary and wooden compared even to a defeated Richard crying for a horse, and Max Reese's contention that Richmond's "lifelessness . . . shows how seriously Shakespeare took him" is perhaps the most depressing note possible with which to usher in the golden age of the Tudors.[26] Order is restored with promises of "smooth-fac'd peace" and "smiling plenty" but also with a draining of energy that carries its own hint of menace. Richard has practiced his bloody coercion on the stage, but from us has asked only for laughter and applause. Henry Tudor frees his fellow characters from the nightmare of Richard's reign, but when upon his own coronation he extends his gaze from the stage to us, it is to demand: "What traitor hears me and says not amen?" It is perhaps this prospect that has led critics with very different views of the play to share a final sense of tragic loss.

Its tragedy is, however, determinedly self-limiting. Shakespeare's achievement in *Richard III* parallels that of its titular hero; its great stage success simultaneously marks Shakespeare's "mastery of the known world of drama"[27] and his confrontation with that world's limits. By the play's end, he has used up its possibilities, even as Richard has used up his. For the play turns on the great Marlovian conflict of the individual and the cosmos, but achieves release only by reduction, resolving its antinomies by collapsing them into each other. Even as Richard is finally shrunken to a puppet of Providence, there is an unsettling familiarity in the workings of that Providence. Its shedding of innocent blood for the sake of a larger scheme, its ironic tripping up of its enemies, its pulling the strings of puppetlike characters mark not so much an end of Richard's Vice-trickery as an upward displacement of its practices. The end of *Richard III* suggests not the triumph of a moral universe, but a playwright's effort to circumscribe his creation, to close off and make manageable the energies of which he is not yet in full possession by casting their image on a cosmic scale and calcifying them into the authorized truths of an inscrutable God.

Richard's ultimate dismantling, at once political and imaginative, does not indicate Shakespeare's "fixed dislike of individualism" in the face of Tudor orthodoxy, as Reese would have it,[28] but rather the discovery of how much more complex a drama he would need to present fiction-making man and the world of his experience.

II

THE SUBSTANCE OF *RICHARD II*

ANAMORPHOSIS

In act 2, scene 2 of *Richard II*, Bushy finds the queen "too much sad" after the king's departure for Ireland. She admits that she knows no cause for her grief, but thinks it a vague premonition:

> Some unborn sorrow ripe in Fortune's womb
> Is coming towards me, and my inward soul
> With nothing trembles; at some thing it grieves
> More than with parting from my lord the king.

Bushy seizes on her paradoxical relation of nothing and something to propose a new perspective on her melancholy:

> Each substance of a grief hath twenty shadows,
> Which shows like grief itself, but is not so.
> For sorrow's eye, glazed with blinding tears,
> Divides one thing entire to many objects,
> Like perspectives, which, rightly gaz'd upon,
> Show nothing but confusion; ey'd awry,
> Distinguish form. So your sweet Majesty,
> Looking awry upon your lord's departure,
> Find shapes of grief more than himself to wail,
> Which, look'd on as it is, is nought but shadows
> Of what it is not; then, thrice-gracious queen,
> More than your lord's departure weep not—more's not seen,
> Or if it be, 'tis with false sorrow's eye,
> Which, for things true, weeps things imaginary.
>
> (2.2.14–27)

The general sense of Bushy's conceit seems clear enough: the queen's grief is like an optical illusion, which, when seen for what "it is," proves to be made up only of "shadows," "things imaginary." Yet the terms of Bushy's analogy are themselves unstable, shifting and realigning as we read them. Part of the problem lies in the perspective metaphor itself, which conflates two possibilities: a prismatic breaking up of images (as when Venus multiplies Adonis's wounds, gazing through the refractions of her tears in *Venus and Adonis*), and an anamorphic composition, a painting of grossly, but cunningly, distorted images that must be regarded from an oblique point of view in order to "distinguish form."¹ If we are willing to overlook the discrepancy, it is because we understand both as serving the same consoling function.

There are, however, other disturbances. The curious quibbling on the terms "rightly" and "awry" makes the relation between the two parts of Bushy's analogy a skewed one, comparing the viewer's proper relation to a painting ("like perspectives . . . ey'd awry") to the queen's misinterpretation of events ("looking awry"). As Dover Wilson succinctly notes, "the perspective is 'rightly gazed upon' when 'eyed awry' "; that is, when looked at from the angle indicated in the distortions of the work itself.² Looking awry at the king's departure, however, is the wrong thing to do; Bushy insists she regard it for what it is, no more. The difficulty may again be overcome, but only by an intellectually strenuous realignment: the reversal of right and awry cooperates with the world of warped images; the return to semantic normality, when "awry" can once again mean incorrect, underscores the recommended shift to political reality. But such a rationale still elides the "confusion" and "shadow" of lines 19 and 23. If facing the world aright dissolves the "shapes of grief," their amorphous shadows haunt the canvas. Indeed, they make their pressure felt throughout the analogy in touchy grammatical moments. Lines 14 and 22 contrast the singular "substance" of reality to the plural "shadows" of illusion, yet in each case the succeeding lines use the singular for the illusory ("shows," "is not so," "is naught but shadows / Of what is not"). Elizabethan grammar allows the relative to take a singular verb,[3] but the very nature of Bushy's distinction forces us to pause, to sort out substance and shadow in a way that keeps the lines of division uncertain. The paradox, in fact, only escalates after he has finished his speech, and the quibbling ends only when events prove the queen's conceit, though created out of nothing, to have been the proper perspective all along.

The difficulties of Bushy's conceit may mark the strain of its own ingenuity, revealing the decadence of courtly rhetoric. But its tortuousness also discloses the problem at the heart of *Richard II*, a play whose characters insist on coherent and substantial patterns behind the turbulence of events, only to find their most confident gestures and perspectives drawn into the uncertainties they decry.

THE DREAM OF ORDER

The opening scene swells with the promise of substance, a stage rich with majesty and pomp as the king addresses his noble uncle:

> Old John of Gaunt, time-honoured Lancaster,
> Hast thou according to thy oath and band
> Brought hither Henry Herford thy bold son,
> Here to make good the boist'rous late appeal
> (I.I.I–4)

The ceremonial scene, like the name of Lancaster, invokes time-honored harmony to resolve all conflict: the "old" sponsors the "bold," supervising "boist'rous" energy to good effects.

Even Bolingbroke's dual accusation of treason and murder against Mowbray is cast in terms that appeal to traditional design: "By that, and all the rites of knighthood else, / Will I make good against thee," he vows, and Mowbray answers just as decorously, "I'll answer thee in any fair degree / Or chivalrous design of knightly trial" (1.1.75–76, 80–81). But their rhetoric, as Derek Traversi notes, is already strained by hyperbole,[4] and despite claims for honest grounds beneath their terms, decorum falls to a "bitter clamour of two eager tongues": Mowbray engages Bolingbroke in a contest of overstatement, declaring his willingness to "run afoot / Even to the frozen ridges of the Alps" to fight Bolingbroke, and the latter, not to be outpaced in geographical fantasy, announces his willingness to fight at "the furthest verge / That ever was survey'd by English eye."

The expansiveness of these world-encompassing terms threatens the decorous design less than does the silence behind the hyperbole. When Richard remarks, "How high a pitch his resolution soars!" he takes note not only of Bolingbroke's grand manner, but of a tacit threat to the crown. For Bolingbroke's exposure of Mowbray's part in the murder of Thomas of Woodstock borders on an exposure of the king as well: both Holinshed and the *Mirror for Magistrates* indict Richard as the instigator of his uncle Woodstock's death. The very obliqueness of the opening scene, far from being a defect in the play as it is sometimes regarded, registers the pressure of what cannot publicly be said. Bolingbroke's overstatement, Richard's double sense, and Mowbray's tortuous evasions ("I slew him not, but to my own disgrace / Neglected my sworn duty in that case") all radiate from the unnameable center of this public performance: the king's guilt.

Here is a more complex game than the hypocritical posturings of *Richard III*. There the violations of order were clearly that, and though we may admire the theatrical energy of the villainous Richard, we are reminded that he is a deformed egotist, one who is determined to prove a villain. In *Richard II*, violation lurks behind the opening scene like some mythic first crime, one that Bolingbroke compares to the murder of Abel. Nor are the fictionalizers mere Machiavels; even John of

Gaunt, the embodiment of the patriotic old order, upholds the illusions of Richard's court, despite the knowledge of Richard's guilt he reveals in the second, private, scene of act 1. "Each of them is lying," John Palmer astutely notes of act 1, scene 1, "and everyone knows they are lying, but each, according to the rules of the game, must be believed."[5] The stark confrontation of order and disorder in *Richard III* gives way to a world where the very fabric of a culture depends on a communal maintenance of fiction, a culture even Tillyard characterizes as "an elaborate game" where "means matter more than ends."[6]

The preponderance of means over ends, one corollary of a world ruled by the "philosophy of as if," must not be confused with the cynical manipulation of commonplaces in the first tetralogy. For all their self-conscious playacting, the characters of *Richard II* are genuinely motivated by ideal longings, seeking to shore up their dream of a world order. Though Mowbray understands the ways of the world, he cherishes a more sublime principle as well:

> The purest treasure mortal times afford
> Is spotless reputation—that away,
> Men are but gilded loam, or painted clay.
> · · · · · · · · · · · · · · · ·
> Mine honour is my life, both grow in one,
> Take honour from me, and my life is done.
> (1.1.177ff.)

When both Mowbray and Bolingbroke refuse to be reconciled, Richard, too, supplements his weakness with an appeal to a larger harmony: "Since we cannot atone you, we shall see / Justice design the victor's chivalry" (1.1.202–3).

The following scenes, however, darken the context within which any meaningful action can be staged. Gaunt is crippled by the ambiguity of owing loyalty to a king who has murdered his brother. What had once stood as a balanced edifice of duties has become a tangle of mutually exclusive obligations, and

Gaunt looks to the highest possible order for resolution: "Since correction lieth in those hands / Which made the fault that we cannot correct, / Put we our quarrel to the will of heaven" (1.2.4–6). But Woodstock's widow will not let Gaunt retreat so quickly to the eternal. In a formal, emblematic speech that reveals a mind as traditional and ceremonial as his own, she insists that Gaunt's inaction is less pious than suicidal, and the scene ends without resolution, in impotence and melancholy exhaustion: "I may never lift / An angry arm against His minister," Gaunt answers the duchess, who departs for Plashy's "empty lodgings and unfurnish'd walls." The only hopeful note in scene 2 is the duchess's anticipation of the redeeming violence of the impending chivalric combat, but scene 3 denies this final recourse. Expectations of dramatic release and resolution build through the prolonged formality of ritualistic introductions, only to collapse when the anxious king banishes both contestants, closing down the court world's final self-righting mechanism.

The promise of significant action yields to action threatening all significance. Mowbray, who had boasted that he would run to the frozen Alps, is numbed by the prospect of silent years awaiting him in distant lands where English is unknown: "My native English, now I must forgo, / . . . dull unfeeling barren ignorance / Is made my gaoler to attend on me. / . . . What is thy sentence then but speechless death, / Which robs my tongue from breathing native breath?" (1.3.160ff.) Mowbray becomes an actor without a context, a purposeless wanderer without coordinates who strangely echoes such drifters of Tudor comedy as Diccon the Bedlam, but stripped of the Vice's joyous theatrical energy: "Now no way can I stray— / Save back to England all the world's my way" (1.3.206–7).

Gaunt is similarly oppressed by the courtly game, which has degenerated into a mirthless comedy where rule and misrule are indistinguishable. Again tormented by loyalties wrenched out of alignment, Gaunt must consent to Bolingbroke's banishment and can advise his son only to retreat into a fantasy world of imagined revels and supposes:

> Think not the king did banish thee,
> But thou the king. Woe doth the heavier sit
> Where it perceives it is but faintly borne.
> Go, say I sent thee forth to purchase honour,
> And not the king exil'd thee; or suppose
> Devouring pestilence hangs in our air,
> And thou art flying to a fresher clime.
> Look what thy soul holds dear, imagine it
> To lie that way thou goest, not whence thou com'st.
> Suppose the singing birds musicians,
> The grass whereon thou tread'st the presence strew'd,
> The flowers fair ladies, and thy steps no more
> Than a delightful measure or a dance;
> For gnarling sorrow hath less power to bite
> The man that mocks at it and sets it light.
>
> (1.3.279–93)

Self-delusion and tricks of perspectivism ("Look what thy soul holds dear, imagine it / To lie that way thou goest, not whence thou com'st") are inadequate. None knows better than Gaunt that his son's exile shows his "own life destroyed," and Bolingbroke's critique shatters his half-hearted fictions:

> O, who can hold a fire in his hand
> By thinking on the frosty Caucasus?
> Or cloy the hungry edge of appetite
> By bare imagination of a feast?
> Or wallow naked in December snow
> By thinking on fantastic summer's heat?
>
> (1.3.294–99)

The longing to restore the fragile network of beliefs and ceremony becomes an obsession for the remainder of *Richard II*. Gaunt on his deathbed idealizes the passing world in the play's most famous speech:

> This royal throne of kings, this scept'red isle,
> This earth of majesty, this seat of Mars,

This other Eden, demi-paradise,
This fortress built by Nature for herself
Against infection and the hand of war,
This happy breed of men, this little world
                    (2.1.40–45)

The speech rolls up a series of magnificent but discordant mythic terms. "We do not expect to find Mars in Eden," M. M. Mahood remarks,[7] but he must be there, even as Gabriel and his guard must scout Milton's Eden, for Gaunt's is a defensive paradise, a fortress against an infected world. The "little world" is built as much by Gaunt's imagination as by Nature, and after nineteen lines of opulent metaphor—"precious stone," "blessed plot," "teeming womb"—the vision collapses in a bitter predicate: "is now leas'd out—I die pronouncing it— like to a tenement or pelting farm."[8] The dream of autonomy sinks back into the images of isolation and self-annihilation from which it arose: England "is now bound in with shame, / With inky blots and rotten parchment bonds; / That England, that was wont to conquer others, / Hath made a shameful conquest of itself" (2.1.61–66; cf. 38–39). Gaunt would "enforce attention" with the "deep harmony" traditionally granted the "tongues of dying men" (2.1.5–7), but when Richard enters, fresh from his cruellest scene (1.4), Gaunt's rhetoric succeeds not in reforming the king but in making a final conquest of itself. After a self-pitying play on his name, Gaunt chastises the king in terms that are dismissed as the ravings of a "lunatic lean-witted fool, / Presuming on an ague's privilege" (2.1.115–16).

Gaunt is hardly to blame. Futile rhetoric is the final outlet in a world where the king wastes his state's financial and psychic resources. But Gaunt's high-mindedness should not obscure the fact that the play never shows us an age of deep harmonies. Cosmic order is always qualified, as in Bolingbroke's tight-lipped homage to the kingly logos that reduces his exile from ten years to six: "How long a time lies in one little word! / Four lagging winters and four wanton springs / End in a word: such is the breath of kings" (1.3.213–15). Order is more a matter of efficacy than ideals, its ability not only to satisfy the longing for a sublime life, but also to coerce even the disillusioned into endorsing its terms. Richard's error, however, has been to press his manipulation of reality too far; he revises the rules of the game as he goes along and so exposes his divine right as mere subjective willfulness. When Richard, to finance his Irish wars, seizes the inheritance due the banished Bolingbroke, even the politic York warns him that the structure of custom cannot be violated without also annulling the king's power, his very identity, which that structure makes possible.

> Take Herford's rights away, and take from time
> His charters, and his customary rights;
> Let not to-morrow then ensue to-day:
> Be not thyself. For how art thou a king
> But by fair sequence and succession?
> (2.1.195–99)

"THERE LIES THE SUBSTANCE"

The world of *Richard II* presents a culture of lost equilibrium struggling to reanimate its exhausted myths even as it reveals to us the vulnerability of those myths. It also presents us with a paradox. For as Richard's political fortunes wane, his frantic responses to the turmoil seize center stage. A shallow figure in the first two acts, a posturing magnifico who abuses his power, Richard is imaginatively reconstituted by the rupture of the very order upon which he has always depended.[9]

York's conventional moral critique of Richard is sufficient for acts 1 and 2: "Will doth mutiny with wit's regard" (2.1.28). Bolingbroke's rebellious and triumphant return, however, inaugurates a more fundamental exploration of the wit itself, be-

ginning with Richard's grandiose address to his land as he prepares to meet Bolingbroke's forces:

> Feed not thy sovereign's foe, my gentle earth,
> Nor with thy sweets comfort his ravenous sense,
> But let thy spiders that suck up thy venom
> And heavy-gaited toads lie in their way,
> . . . .
> Mock not my senseless conjuration, lords:
> This earth shall have a feeling, and these stones
> Prove armed soldiers ere her native king
> Shall falter under foul rebellion's arms.
>
> (3.2.12ff.)

The Orphic allusion is clear; less clear is the intention behind
it. Richard would step beyond the symbolic Orphism of Sidney's *Apology*, or Lorenzo's fictions in *The Merchant of Venice*
("the poet / Did feign that Orpheus drew trees, stones and
flood," 5.1.79–80). Richard's allusion is not a tale of, or about,
poetic feigning, but a claim he makes for himself as king, the
literal extent of which is unnervingly vague. "Mock not my
senseless conjuration" is not only a plea for rhetorical license,
but a command to supporters who grow nervous at the prospect of a king who does not merely utter hyperboles, but who
is careless about the limitations of his tropes. He would picture
himself as both military leader and World Soul, animating and
ordering the lifeless and subrational, calling forth nature in his
holy war; even the bishop of Carlisle, who later defends Richard as the "figure of God's majesty," delicately reminds him
that the stage of history demands practical action to make all
claims substantial: "The means that heaven yields must be im-
brac'd / And not neglected; else, heaven would, / And we will
not; heavens offer, we refuse / The proffered means of succour
and redress" (3.2.29–32). The duke of Aumerle speaks more
bluntly: Richard's delay has allowed Bolingbroke to grow

"strong and great in substance and power"; Richard must enter the field to establish his own substance.

Richard, however, appears to be stalled at the point of transition between metaphor and its embodiment; he attempts to substantiate his conceit not through action but by adding to it another traditional analogy comparing royal power to the sun. Just as thieves range freely when the "searching eye of heaven is hid" but flee the light of day, so, too, when Bolingbroke, who "hath revell'd in the night,"

> Shall see us rising in our throne the east,
> His treasons will sit blushing in his face,
> Not able to endure the sight of day,
> But self-affrighted tremble at his sin.
> Not all the water in the rough rude sea
> Can wash the balm off from an anointed king;
> The breath of worldly men cannot depose
> The deputy elected by the Lord;
> For every man that Bolingbroke hath press'd
> To lift shrewd steel against our golden crown,
> God for his Richard hath in heavenly pay
> A glorious angel: then, if angels fight,
> Weak men must fall, for heaven still guards the right.
> (3.2.50–62)

Richard's insistence on his own terms lays out the fundamental assumptions of his "world picture," a vision of an orderly universe where such correspondences and analogies as the "*roi soleil*" have an ontological depth. No longer careless of tradition, Richard becomes the spokesman of the most conservative orthodoxy. Yet by *not* standing outside of his culture's ideals, by insisting that its official world order is literally and objectively real, the orthodox Richard of the play's second half forces a profounder crisis than could any villain of the histories.[10] He begins with the unqualified premise that he is God's anointed, and resolves the entire issue into a simple proposition: "If angels fight, / Weak men must fall." The metaphysical, he maintains, is prior to the practical, but his terms already betray him;

he opposes Bolingbroke's forces with "angels" in "heavenly pay" as supplements to his "golden crown," a pun on the spirit-made-cash whose flippancy exposes the instability of Richard's confidence. He merely sidesteps the challenge, and as the circle of his power shrinks, he finds himself dodging within an increasingly constricted area. In the eighty lines that follow, Richard is forced to recognize the ineluctable: his Welsh forces have deserted and his favorites have been beheaded; there is no escape from history. Salisbury's lament reminds Richard of the irony of his metaphysical presumptions: "O, call back yesterday, bid time return, / And thou shalt have twelve thousand fighting men!" (3.2.69–70).

Trapped in the rush of events, Richard fluctuates wildly between unreasonable hope and unseemly despair. Aumerle's plea "remember who you are" evokes a new fantasy of the kingly logos: "Is not the king's name twenty thousand names? / Arm, arm my name! a puny subject strikes / At thy great glory" (3.2.85–87), but the report that the king's favorites have been put to death turns the glory into dust:

> Our lands, our lives, and all, are Bolingbroke's,
> And nothing can we call our own but death;
> And that small model of the barren earth
> Which serves as paste and cover to our bones.
> For God's sake let us sit upon the ground
> And tell sad stories of the death of kings:
> How some have been depos'd, some slain in war,
> Some haunted by the ghosts they have deposed,
> Some poisoned by their wives, some sleeping kill'd,
> All murthered—for within the hollow crown
> That rounds the mortal temples of a king
> Keeps Death his court, and there the antic sits,
> Scoffing his state and grinning at his pomp,
> Allowing him a breath, a little scene,
> To monarchize, be fear'd, and kill with looks;
> Infusing him with self and vain conceit,
> As if this flesh which walls about our life
> Were brass impregnable; and, humour'd thus,

Comes at the last, and with a little pin
Bores thorough his castle wall, and farewell king!
Cover your heads, and mock not flesh and blood
With solemn reverence; throw away respect,
Tradition, form, and ceremonious duty;
For you have but mistook me all this while.
I live with bread like you, feel want,
Taste grief, need friends—subjected thus,
How can you say to me, I am a king?

(3.2.151–77)

Richard no longer imagines himself as a director of the *anima mundi*, but as the microcosm of a dead, physical world, shrunken to "that small model of the barren earth." In his Orphic speech, he warned his audience to "mock not my senseless conjuration"; now he parodies his own grandeur: "Mock not flesh and blood / With solemn reverence." The forms of power— "respect, / Tradition, form, and ceremonious duty"—become flickering illusions, the empty gestures of a theatrical performance. Only a few lines earlier, Scroop used the metaphor of child actors to discredit the rebels' pretensions: "Boys, with women's voices, / Strive to speak big, and clap their female joints / In stiff unwieldy arms against thy crown" (3.2.113– 15). Richard now sees his own kingship as pretense, a "little scene" within his mind, staged for the amusement of Death in a dreamlike court where "the antic" is the true locus of power, a jester who toys with the king, fooling him with vain conceit until he punctures his fantasy with a little pin.

Ernst Kantorowicz has called *Richard II* a tragedy of the king's two bodies, a play about the rupture between the mortal who plays the king and his role as God's Anointed. It is in this scene, Kantorowicz argues, that Richard sees his "fiction of royal prerogatives" vanish, and as the "fiction of the oneness of the double body breaks apart" Richard must confront the fact of his "feeble manhood":

A curious change in Richard's attitude—as it were, a metamorphosis from "Realism" to "Nominalism"—now takes place. The Universal called "Kingship" begins to disintegrate; its transcendental "Reality," its objective truth and god-like existence, so brilliant shortly before, pales into a nothing, a *nomen.*[11]

For Kantorowicz, Richard confronts his own physical reality— "a *physis* now void of any metaphysis whatever." But Richard is never truly disillusioned. The scene he hastily constructs is a new fantasy, inspired by despair rather than complacency. As Edward Dowden remarks with irritation, Richard takes "aesthetic satisfaction" in "that sweet way I was in to despair" (3.2.205).[12] His mind in this scene plays over Astrophil's paradox: "I am not I; pity the tale of me." The king is not himself; we must pity the tale of him, one of the "sad stories of the death of kings."

If his metaphysical universal evaporates, Richard immediately replaces it with a literary universal, a timeless pattern governed by the wheel of fortune and memorialized by poets and chroniclers. His gesture bears a resemblance to, but also marks an important advance over, Richard III's boasted superiority to the murderous Machiavel and his self-comparison to the Vice Iniquity. There a character places his performance within a literary context, but in terms that stiffly and ostentatiously display Shakespeare's own self-consciousness as a dramatic maker. The character is necessarily flattened even as he raises our anticipation; he becomes a superb, but obvious, product of a dramatist's workshop, a puppet that points to the very materials out of which it has been constructed. When the invention thus outstrips its sources, our attention is directed past the character to the creator himself.

Richard II turns Shakespeare's literary self-consciousness to a subtler effect. Richard II's sad stories are almost certainly those Shakespeare was reading in Hall, Holinshed, and the *Mirror for Magistrates*, but as Tillyard rightly suggests, they also refer to Chaucer's *Monk's Tale* and its succession of *de casibus* tragedies.[13] The second allusion is important, not because it evokes an idealized medieval atmosphere, as Tillyard has it, but because Chaucer was a poet at the court of the historical Richard II. Shakespeare shows us Richard at a moment of crisis, reaching out for poetic tales he might have heard in his fourteenth-century world and writing himself into them even as he calls our attention to the sixteenth-century historical narratives of which Richard inevitably was to become a part. Shakespeare's gesture toward his sources fuses with Richard's gesture toward his; the fashioning of *Richard II* becomes an analogue for the self-fashioning of Richard II.

It is this rendering of Richard's inner life, engaged in acts of poetic invention, that gives Shakespeare's fallen king an irresistible fascination. As Bolingbroke comes to dominate the world in the play, Richard dominates the world of the play. Deposition may lurk in the former's mysterious mind, but it is the latter who introduces the term and gives it dramatic shape; having located his story among the death of kings, he casts himself with perverse pleasure as its suffering hero:

> What must the king do now? Must he submit?
> The king shall do it. Must he be depos'd?
> The king shall be contented. Must he lose
> The name of king? a God's name, let it go.
> I'll give my jewels for a set of beads;
> My gorgeous palace for a hermitage;
> My gay apparel for an almsman's gown;
> My figur'd goblets for a dish of wood;
> My sceptre for a palmer's walking staff;
> My subjects for a pair of carved saints,
> And my large kingdom for a little grave,
> A little little grave, an obscure grave
>
> (3.3.143–54)

Having assumed for so long the political mythology joining his mind, the state, and the cosmos, Richard is obsessed by gaps, picturing an unreal fall in an unreal world, as if history were a shift of scene and a player's backstage doubling, an exchange of one role's symbolic costume and properties for those of another.[14] The only resistance he can offer is that of paradox: "Cousin, I am too young to be your father, / Though you are old enough to be my heir" (3.3.204–5). Finally, he undoes himself in terms as formal and ceremonious as any spectacle of state: "Now, mark me how I will undo myself . . . / With mine own tears I wash away my balm, / With mine own hands I give away my crown, / With mine own tongue deny my sacred state, / With mine own breath release all duteous oaths; / All pomp and majesty I do forswear" (4.1.203–11). Comforted by the frame of artifice, he gives voice to his outrage by projecting himself into the role of typological interpreter, computing how many more times he has been betrayed than was Christ ("He, in twelve, / Found truth in all but one; I, in twelve thousand, none"). Inspired by his fantasy of martyrdom, he almost succeeds in humiliating Bolingbroke by forcing him to enact symbolically his rebellion ("Here, cousin, seize the crown").

But his fictions inevitably return him to his favorite subject, himself, and he turns the necessary property, the crown, into the conceit of a deep well into which he sinks, a bucket filled with tears. When he attempts to reclaim the voice of moral interpreter, threatening Northumberland with the sinfulness of treason "mark'd with a blot, damn'd in the book of heaven," that metaphor, too, becomes a figure for his self-reflexiveness. Asked to read a list of accusations, Richard retorts: "I'll read enough / When I do see the very book indeed / Where all my sins are writ, and that's myself."

The book is, in fact, a mirror, a property that appears on stage as Richard pronounces "myself":

> RICH.   Give me that glass, and therein will I read.
> No deeper wrinkles yet? hath sorrow struck
> So many blows upon this face of mine
> And made no deeper wounds? . . .
> . . . .
> A brittle glory shineth in this face;
> As brittle as the glory is the face,
> (*Dashes the glass against the ground*)
> For there it is, crack'd in a hundred shivers.
> Mark, silent king, the moral of this sport—
> How soon my sorrow hath destroyed my face.

BOL.   The shadow of your sorrow hath destroy'd
The shadow of your face.

RICH.   Say that again.
The shadow of my sorrow? ha! let's see—
'Tis very true, my grief lies all within,
And these external manners of lament
Are merely shadows to the unseen grief
That swells with silence in the tortur'd soul.
There lies the substance.

                             (4.1.276ff.)

Richard again pretends to invent a public, moral emblem, and not finding his reflected image sufficiently wrinkled, he shatters the mirror as part of a new dramatic event, a "sport" whose "moral" is the fragility of glory. When Bolingbroke rejects its histrionic self-indulgence with a quibble on "shadows," Richard seizes his terms even as he seized his father's estate, annexing their riches and turning them into his own plaything. But he plays with a new purpose. He is now a master at his craft, turning over the words and scrutinizing them with a "let's see" before fashioning them into a new metaphor. What he constructs is a way of seeing, a perspective on the ambiguous shadows of his performance, but one that, unlike Bushy's consoling perspective on the shadowy griefs of the queen, affirms sorrow as a vanishing point for his composition: "the tortur'd soul."

The course of act 4, scene 1, reveals the method in Richard's madness, a proto-Cartesian exercise in radical doubt, an "inverted rite," as Walter Pater calls it, where Richard divests himself of all prior assumptions, stripping himself down to the point where he feels he must himself vanish: "I must nothing be," "I have no name, no title; / No, not that name was given me at the font, / But 'tis usurped" (4.1.201, 255–57). Though this may appear to be the bleakest of imaginative sequels to Cusanus's *idiota* and his vision of man—the conflation of regal power and amnesia evolving wholly into the latter—there is a regeneration of sorts. For once Richard has pared away the universals of crown, majesty, and statutes, there remains the seemingly irreducible speaking voice, conspicuously and hyperbolically discoursing on the fact of its nothingness. Here Richard finds his *cogito*, the quiddity of self in the midst of negation: "There lies the substance."

In his final scene, Richard attempts to move out from this internal fixed point to construct a comprehensible model of the external world and his experience of it.

> *(Enter Richard alone)*
> RICH. I have been studying how I may compare
> This prison where I live unto the world;
> And, for because the world is populous
> And here is not a creature but myself,
> I cannot do it. Yet I'll hammer it out.
> My brain I'll prove a female to my soul,
> My soul the father, and these two beget
> A generation of still-breeding thoughts,
> And these same thoughts people this little world,
> In humours like the people of this world;
> For no thought is contented.
>
> (5.5.1–11)

His "let's see" of act 4 has become an explicit study for comparisons; he enters as a self-conscious maker of metaphor. Finding no objective correspondence between tenor and vehicle, he complains, "I cannot do it," only to complete the line with "Yet I'll hammer it out." In his first scene, Richard's "we cannot do" was resolved by an appeal to the ideal of "Justice"; in his last, the royal "we" becomes the particular "I," and "cannot" is overcome through an appeal to the mind's own powers of invention. The act of the mind is Richard's final mode of action.

Richard the betrayed Christ now plays Richard the creating God of Genesis, ironically fulfilling an ideal of Renaissance philosophers and literary critics. Adam and Eve were instructed to be fruitful and multiply, and Richard, too, peoples his world with his soul and brain, male and female principles that "beget a generation of still-breeding thoughts." But any suggestion of the human maker as analogue to the divine Maker is ironic; there is no *afflatus* for Richard, only anxiety. He is again obsessed by loss, and the proliferation of thought recoils on the supposedly secure center. Richard assumes the role of a critical Abélard, setting his thoughts and scriptural passages against each other in his own *Sic et Non*:

> The better sort,
> As thoughts of things divine, are intermix'd
> With scruples, and do set the word itself
> Against the word,
> As thus: "Come, little ones"; and then again,
> "It is as hard to come as for a camel
> To thread the postern of a small needle's eye."
> (5.5.11–17)

Both quotations are from Matthew 19, and if read in context they are not contradictory. The first is addressed to innocent children; the second to the wealthy who find their treasure in earthly things. Yet they become opposites for one who can no longer tell whether he is an innocent child or one of the damned. At one moment Richard imagines his close relation to the Absolute; the next, the unpassable barrier that separates him from it. The paradox of immanence and transcendence turns fully tragic.

The peopling of the microcosm, then, becomes at once a sign of the mind's fecundity and its fragmentation, a poetic power impelled by the discovery of its vulnerability.

> Thoughts tending to ambition, they do plot
> Unlikely wonders: how these vain weak nails
> May tear a passage thorough the flinty ribs
> Of this hard world, my ragged prison walls;
> And for they cannot, die in their own pride.
> Thoughts tending to content flatter themselves
> That they are not the first of fortune's slaves,
> Nor shall not be the last—like silly beggars
> Who, sitting in the stocks, refuge their shame,
> That many have and others must sit there;

And in this thought they find a kind of ease,
Bearing their own misfortunes on the back
Of such as have before indur'd the like.
Thus play I in one person many people,
And none contented.

(5.5.18–32)

Richard's conceit becomes a retrospective on the action of the play, now refracted through a series of fantastic distortions. He perversely describes his thoughts of escape as little Bolingbrokes, tending to ambition and plots, their attack on the "flinty ribs" conflating Bolingbroke's threats against the "rude ribs" of his earlier refuge in act 3, scene 3 with the name of that refuge, Flint Castle. They also become versions of Richard himself, dreamers who "plot / Unlikely wonders" only to find themselves isolated and dying in their pride. This sense of enclosure produces one of the play's most involuted conceits, of thoughts easing themselves by thinking of previous thoughts, becoming failed Stoics who can endure their fate only by thinking of all the other slaves of fortune. The abstract play of thoughts thinking of thoughts crystallizes in the image of beggars sitting in stocks, each consoled by the humiliation of his predecessors, but each doomed to serve in the identical capacity for his successors. The final image, then, winds itself into a metaphor of a metaphor, yet the psychological weight is felt immediately by Richard, a king who has made himself a beggar, and whose fantasies can only reenact his sorrows: "Thus play I in one person many people, / And none contented." Here is Shakespeare's first interior view of the protean mind, one far subtler than the exciting, but relatively simple, externality of the histrionic Vice. We see it from within and are dazzled by the changing shapes of its thought, and experience at the same time its suffocating anxiety:

Sometimes am I king,
Then treasons make me wish myself a beggar,
And so I am. Then crushing penury
Persuades me I was better when a king;

Then am I king'd again, and by and by
Think that I am unking'd by Bolingbroke,
And straight am nothing. But whate'er I be,
Nor I, nor any man that but man is,
With nothing shall be pleas'd, till he be eas'd
With being nothing.

(5.5.32–41)

Richard may be a poetic maker at his craft, representing his
world in miniature, but he can no more rebuild his world
through language than he could marshal rocks and angels to
defend his kingdom. He draws the world of the play into his
mind until there is nothing left for him except that mind and
its longing for self-annihilation.

Because Richard is given to moral commentary, we may feel
encouraged to make our own. Certainly the play provides us
with suitable terms: Richard's microcosm cries out for contrast
to Gaunt's vision of England as "this little world" populated,
not with sorrowful thoughts, but by a "happy breed of men."
Richard's longing for self-annihilation also carries us back to
Gaunt's warning that "light vanity, insatiate cormorant, /
Consuming means, soon preys on itself." Richard himself,
upon hearing music outside his cell, echoes York's warning not
to subvert time's order:

I wasted time, and now doth time waste me;
For now hath time made me his numb'ring clock;
My thoughts are minutes, and with sighs they jar
Their watches on unto mine eyes, the outward watch,
Whereto my finger, like a dial's point,
Is pointing still, in cleansing them from tears.
Now sir, the sound that tells what hour it is
Are clamorous groans which strike upon my heart,
Which is the bell—so sighs, and tears, and groans
Show minutes, times, and hours. But my time
Runs posting on in Bolingbroke's proud joy,
While I stand fooling here, his Jack of the clock.

(5.5.49–60)

Our fascination with Richard's eccentric performance, however, carries us beyond the sententiae of the old order. The conceit builds, as do so many of Richard's speeches, to the point
of ludicrousness, but at the same time opens up psychic dimensions undreamt of in Gaunt's or York's philosophy, possibilities untouched, too, by Richard III's frantic self-divisions
on Bosworth field, Henry VI's pastoral fantasy on the molehill
(also about managing time), or even by Marlowe's great heroes. Richard neither flees from nor succumbs to his ruin. His
working mind, rather, traces the unbreakable circularity of human awareness and in the process touches the productive as
well as the destructive impulses running through its circuits.
The inner voice that calls him to acknowledge his painful failure also reenacts the creative ground of that failure. He has always ordered the world through subjective conceit and now
forces upon himself the realization that this is the only way he
can order it, even as he reviles himself for doing so: "I stand
fooling here, his Jack of the clock."[15]

It is only at the moment of death—the only end to the mind's
inventions—that the "I" finds its way out of the labyrinth.
After lashing out at his assassins in a fine, but futile, burst of
action, Richard finally settles his beating brain while directing
a final religious drama, dissolving the "I" in the silent space
between body and soul:

> Mount, mount my soul! thy seat is up on high,
> Whilst my gross flesh sinks downward, here to die.
>   (5.5.111–12)

TRANSITION AND TRAGEDY

Once Richard's world decomposes into a swirl of fictions and
conceits, the play returns us to the political and historical reality
that continues to exist outside his mind. What new forms of
coherence does this world offer those who are finally spared the
caprices of their unstable king?

If the old order was from the first an elaborate game, one sustained by the force of tradition, but which trembled from the start at the brink of collapse, the new order finds itself from its very inception struggling with centrifugal forces that threaten to break it up. Bolingbroke's first appearance as king, mediating the Aumerle-Bagot dispute in act 4, scene 1, recalls Richard's first appearance in act 1, scene 1 attempting to mediate between Bolingbroke and Mowbray. The new king handles his crisis more efficiently, but the second dispute also reveals how much more badly the world has come undone. Character after character joins the fray, first one side then the other gaining support, each giving the lie to the other until the word *lie* itself scatters its meanings in a series of puns as overdone as any of Richard's verbal plays. "Dishonourable boy," Surrey sneers at Fitzwater, who has just charged "thou liest," "That lie shall lie so heavy on my sword / That it shall render vengeance and revenge / Till thou, the lie-giver, and that lie do lie / In earth" (4.1.65–69).

If Richard faces a transition from Realism to Nominalism as Kantorowicz suggests, his universal kingship paling into a mere *nomen*, his experience is reenacted throughout this scene. So overworked are the terms of honor and daring (act 4, scene 1.21, 41, 44, 48, 55, 65, 70, 71, 73, 74, 85, 91), that they cease to signify that which breathes life into gilded loam and painted clay, as Mowbray believed in the opening scene, each repetition taking us closer to the level of the *flatus vocis*. Aumerle dramatizes this exhaustion of signs when he finds that he has run out of gloves with which to challenge his accusers, and must plead, "Some honest Christian, trust me with a gage."[16] The banished Mowbray is invoked finally as one who holds the key to the controversy, but when Bolingbroke calls for his former foe to return, the bishop of Carlisle laments, "That honourable day shall ne'er be seen." Mowbray has died after fighting in the Crusades. If honor and glory have clear significance anywhere, it is on fields far removed from England, the consequences of which Carlisle himself experiences when the dispute is suspended and Richard's impending deposition becomes the issue. "What subject can give sentence on his king? / And who sits here that is not Richard's subject?" Carlisle's challenge evokes what skeptics call the "problem of the criterion": if we call into question not merely our judgments, but the very standard by which we judge, what will protect us from logical and political anarchy?[17] "Kin with kin, and kind with kind, confound. / Disorder, horror, fear, and mutiny, / Shall here inhabit" (4.1.141–43). Northumberland's blunt response makes Carlisle aware that his fixed point of judgment has *already* been eroded: "Well have you argued, sir, and, for your pains, / Of capital treason we arrest you here" (4.1.150–51). His arguments have become detachable set-pieces, to be applauded for their artifice ("Well have you argued") but now implicated in the very swirl of chaos they decry; Carlisle has entered, as it were, a new gravitational system, which charts his eloquent arguments by a new set of coordinates, locating in the realm of "treason" what were once grand warnings against treason.

The play will not allow us to witness this scene as the substitution of one closed system for another. Their tensed proximity continually pulls them open, and much of the play's attention is directed toward the spectacle of characters struggling to locate themselves in the flux. York superbly embodies this struggle, vacillating from act 2 on from one side to the other until, in a desperate act of self-deception, he convinces himself that Richard has willingly adopted Bolingbroke as his heir. Like Warwick in *3 Henry VI*, he is momentarily chilled by the unreality of events:

> As in a theatre the eyes of men,
> After a well-grac'd actor leaves the stage,
> Are idly bent on him that enters next,
> Thinking his prattle to be tedious;
> Even so, or with much more contempt, men's eyes
> Did scowl on Richard.
>
> (5.2.23–28)

A. P. Rossiter complains of Shakespeare's apparent failure to represent more clearly the reasons why the populace York observes would shift its support, but that omission is, I think, Shakespeare's point. As York's simile suggests, the king falls not because he is corrupt or frivolous, but because he has met a better actor: "at last out-fac'd by Bolingbroke" (4.1.286).[18] But York evades the implications of his own terms, and insists instead upon binding all into a consoling, if inscrutable, harmony: "But heaven hath a hand in these events, / To whose high will we bound our calm contents." Like Gaunt before the melancholy duchess, York refers all questions to the All-Seer, and so desperate is his need to imagine a divine director ordering the *theatrum mundi* that he pleads with Bolingbroke in the following scene to execute his only son for treason against the new regime.

If York is at all sympathetic, it is because he crystallizes the audience's own discomfort. The deposition of a ruler was a theme of such importance in the waning years of Elizabeth that it cried out for resolution. But none is possible in a play whose structure is built over so many gaps and omissions. The plot is set in motion by the murder of Woodstock, a crime whose details are never made clear, and ends with the murder of Richard, a crime that springs either from deception or misinterpretation—Bolingbroke's melancholy lament within Exton's hearing. The intervening struggle is really a non-struggle between Richard's fantastic overstatement and the mysterious understatement of the new "silent king." Where language does not avoid the matter, there is a deflection of matter from language; the play is conspicuous in its use of privative terms ("unhappied," "uncurse," "unkiss," "unking'd"), all of which point to a negative dramatic center, the inverted rite of deposition.[19]

Critics sometimes fill the gap by taking Richard at his own word, pronouncing his death a "martyrdom," the "keystone to an affirmed moral order."[20] S. K. Heninger comments perceptively on the hypothetical or problematic nature of the play's moral claims, but still attempts to locate its moral coordinates through an imagistic pattern: "The sun-king concept is an ideal, an absolute, a fixed-point, the hub of fortune's wheel about which Richard and Bolingbroke turn."[21] But it is the nature of the play to make us doubt all fixed points, whether they be allusions to sun kings, royal martyrs, fallen Edens, or Tudor theories of obedience. All is implicated, finally, in the problematic motions of rhetoric and history.

If there is any hope for reintegration, it lies in the future, and the future in this play lies with Bolingbroke. He is the "bold son" of the play's first lines, who naively believes that self-affirmation can find an outlet in traditional combat: "My lance's point [will] . . . furbish new the name of John a Gaunt, / Even in the lusty haviour of his son" (1.3.74–77). He becomes the play's most successful role player when he is forced to recognize the disorder of things, a world where human identity cannot merely be refurbished but must be continually recreated.[22] From the moment of his banishment, his aggressively critical mind rejects his father's "bare imagination," and when he learns that the physical vestiges of his name have been effaced—

> you have fed upon my signories,
> Dispark'd my parks and fell'd my forest woods,
> From out my own windows torn my household coat,
> Rac'd out my imprese, leaving me no sign,
> Save men's opinions and my living blood,
> To show the world I am a gentleman
> (3.1.22–27)

—he turns to his own *virtù*, his capacity for autonomous action.

Bolingbroke's victory, it is often argued, charts a transition from the late Middle Ages to the early modern world, from Richard's decadent and fevered fantasy to cooler political calculation, but it does so without a sense of liberation, Burckhardtian or otherwise. Not only does York's vision of a passing of actors continue to haunt us, but our first glimpse of the newly crowned Henry IV is of a man suddenly aged by a generation; the bold son has become a fretful father: "Can no man tell me of my unthrifty son?" (5.3.1). There is no "new spring of time," no passage "From Richard's night to Bolingbroke's fair day." Bolingbroke's demonstrations of autonomy and self-movement degenerate into cruelly manipulative exhibitions of his own misery, his own isolation and dread: "Have I no friend will rid me of this living fear?" he laments within Exton's hearing, luring his supporter into a regicide that will prove to be anything but a binding up of uncertainties.

There is a cunningly contrived room in Urbino that creates what one commentator has called "an exalted, humanistic illusion."[23] The walls are decorated with wood inlays that, when viewed from the center of the room, create the illusion of statuettes, shelves stacked with books, and tables displaying musical instruments. Should the observer leave the center, however, all turn into flat, distorted shapes, those strange, misshapen forms characteristic of anamorphic art. *Richard II* creates a similar environment, a world where once clearly drawn shapes have degenerated into ambiguous shadows. All its inhabitants must struggle to find the deposed vantage, a proper perspective through which to re-form their reality, whether they are locked behind the bare walls of Pomfret Castle or ride triumphantly into London bathed in the light of political success. Carlisle suggests that Mowbray found that point outside England, fighting in the Crusades, and it is appropriate that Bolingbroke end the play with a resolve to do the same: "I'll make a voyage to the Holy Land / To wash this blood from off my guilty hand." Heaven's self-proclaimed scourge and minister, who alludes in the opening and closing scenes of the play to Cain and Abel (1.1.104; 5.6.43), fears at the end that he may be playing Pilate.

Twice he reminds us in the succeeding *Henry IV* plays of his longing to go to the Holy Land (Part 1, act 1, scene 1; Part 2, act 3, scene 1). Eventually, a fatal illness forces him to reveal a prophecy made many years before: "I should not die but 'in Jerusalem'" (*2 Henry IV*, 4.5.237). It is with some discomfort that we recognize a long-held death wish behind his cherished quest, but a more unsettling irony is revealed when he learns that his deathbed is to lie only in what "vainly I supposed the Holy Land." Final justification becomes the vainest suppose of all: the Holy Land is replaced by a mere *nomen*; his deathbed lies in a room that bears only the name of "Jerusalem."

"KING OF INFINITE SPACE": HAMLET AND HIS FICTIONS

As drama's most frequently interpreted hero lies dying in the final act of *Hamlet*, he is obsessed with those who will misinterpret him. He commands Horatio to "report me and my cause aright / To the unsatisfied . . . in this harsh world draw thy breath in pain, / To tell my story" (5.2.331–32, 340–41). It relieves Hamlet to think of his story put "aright" by a speaker such as Horatio; but can the latter, whose philosophy excludes so much in heaven and earth, "truly deliver" the substance of what has happened? The "cause" he must report is driven by a violation of assumptions so fundamental that no character or spectator can ever convince another that he has truly gotten it right.

Like the histories, *Hamlet* presents nostalgic glimpses of stabler times and of stabler interpretations. Horatio's historical narrative of Old Hamlet's combat with Old Fortinbras in the first scene recalls a world controlled by a "seal'd compact / Well ratified by law and heraldry" (1.1.86–87). Acts of violence were governed by chivalric codes, the mark of a stable social order that encouraged an optimistic ideal of the human personality: "The courtier's, soldier's, scholar's, eye, tongue, sword; / Th' expectancy and rose of the fair state, / The glass of fashion and the mould of form" (3.1.151–53). Ophelia's recollection of Hamlet the humanist prince, whose inheritance should have included both the throne of Denmark and a comprehensible universe, seems remote from the melancholy figure whose orations on the dignity of man are indissolubly linked to their bitter negation:

> What a piece of work is a man! How noble in reason! how infinite in faculties! in form and moving, how express and admirable! in action, how like an angel! in apprehension, how like a god! the beauty of the world! the paragon of animals! And yet, to me, what is this quintessence of dust?
>
> (2.2.302)

If the history plays represent the advent of a broad cultural anxiety, *Hamlet* anatomizes that anxiety. By act 4, Richard II longs to "melt myself away in water drops" (4.1.262) when he witnesses Bolingbroke's efficient manipulation of power, and Hamlet, faced with a similar spectacle in the first act of his play, also longs to "melt, / Thaw, and resolve . . . into a dew" (1.2.129–30). Richard ends his play deposed from his throne and, his queen suggests, from his senses. This is Hamlet's circumstance in the first act of a play that goes on to dramatize a vaster and more terrifying kind of deposition, a wrenched displacement from the expectancy of the state to the "boundary situation" of tragedy.[1] Nor is that situation settled by the play's close—however insistently we and the play's characters may long for a resolution—when Hamlet yields his story to silence, or to the problematic and partial version Horatio will tell the unknowing world.

HAMLET *VIATOR*

Hamlet, the prince and the poem, both demand and frustrate explanation, a situation the play's own would-be interpreters discover too well: "Hath there been such a time—I would fain know that—/ That I have positively said ''Tis so,' / When it prov'd otherwise?" (2.2.152–54). Polonius's conjecture about the "very cause of Hamlet's lunacy" (2.2.49) is plausible, as Gertrude concedes—"It may be, very like"—but Polonius must be certain. The pains of love produce melancholy in a predictable sequence: frustration, sadness, weakness, madness; they follow as the night the day. Any mystery, rightly gazed upon, becomes for Polonius transparent allegory, the kernel of truth awaiting his interpretive eye: "I will find / Where truth is hid, though it were hid indeed / Within the centre" (2.2.156–58). If he seems in his ramblings a little overfond of indirections to find directions out, it is a self-indulgence born of his confident knowledge of the ways of the world. One may construct circular windlasses (2.1.65), but the true direction is, in the end, always known.

Polonius disastrously misses the mark, hunting the trail of policy until he finds himself in the line of fire, but his tragedy is less a sign of senility than of a competence that has lost its context. By act 2, scene 2 we have heard the Ghost's story and know more than Polonius; more, too, than Rosencrantz and Guildenstern, who would also pluck out the heart of Hamlet's mystery. And yet, like them, we find interpretive clarity an *ignis fatuus*. *Hamlet* begins in darkness and anxiety, fearful questions and sickness at heart that skew our responses to even the brightest public scenes. We enter the play at the very edge of Elsinore, where Horatio has been brought to bear witness to some "thing" of mystery. "*Oratio* next to *ratio*," Sidney writes, is "the greatest gift bestowed upon mortality," but Horatio the scholar, whose name encloses both, cannot draw into the light of discursive understanding a Ghost that is "something more than fantasy." He can only address it as "illusion," clutching at a series of fragmented hypotheses and conjectures: "If," "If," "If," "Or if," "they say," "I have heard," "So have I heard, and do in part believe it." Horatio's strength marks his limitations; he is a creature of consummate rationality who can, even as he is harrowed "with fear and wonder" (1.1.44), note the Ghost's expression, his complexion, the color of his beard, and report the details to Hamlet. In the midst of amazement he can even count the moments like the measured ticking of a clock. So he answers Hamlet's "Stay'd it long?" "While one with moderate haste might tell a hundred" (1.2.236–37). But for all his acuteness, he confronts a world as removed from his capacities as it is from Polonius's. He brings Hamlet to the ramparts only to beg him to hold back, picturing the solitary confrontation as a scene of vertigo, "the dreadful summit of the cliff" whose dizzying prospect "puts toys of desperation" into the mind. Hamlet's refusal to "be ruled" proves to Horatio that "he waxes desperate with imagination"; but it establishes for us Hamlet's fitness for this world: "Be thou a spirit of health or goblin damn'd, / Bring with thee airs from heaven or blasts from hell, / Be thy intents wicked or charitable, / Thou com'st in such a questionable shape / That I will speak to thee. I'll call thee Hamlet, / King, father, royal Dane" (1.4.40–45). Facing a mystery that spans the extremes of human wonder and belief, Hamlet calls out his own name, invoking not only the relationship of son to father but the mind's longing for "thoughts beyond the reaches of our souls" (1.4.56).

His range, paradoxically, exceeds even that of the Ghost itself. For despite its awesomeness and mystery, the Ghost presents a stable picture of human nature:

> But virtue, as it never will be moved,
> Though lewdness court it in a shape of heaven,
> So lust, though to a radiant angel link'd,
> Will sate itself in a celestial bed
> And prey on garbage.
>
> (1.5.53–57)

Whereas the Ghost adheres to a sure sense of moral interiority, of a core possessor whose virtue or lust dominates external appearance, the younger Hamlet has already presented a more unsettling moral vision:

> So, oft it chances in particular men
> That, for some vicious mole of nature in them,
> As in their birth, wherein they are not guilty,
> Since nature cannot choose his origin;

By the o'ergrowth of some complexion,
Oft breaking down the pales and forts of reason;
Or by some habit that too much o'erleavens
The form of plausive manners—that these men,
Carrying, I say, the stamp of one defect,
Being nature's livery or fortune's star,
His virtues else, be they as pure as grace,
As infinite as man may undergo,
Shall in the general censure take corruption
From that particular fault. The dram of eale
Doth all the noble substance of a doubt
To his own scandal.

(1.4.23–38)

Human "origin" is prior to moral control and choice, and its relation to Providence is uncertain. "It chances," rather, to be under the sway of "fortune's star," leading man's "noble substance" to the brink of annihilation. Whether its "pales and forts of reason" are undermined from within or corrupted by external pressures of "general censure," human substance is characterized less by guilt than by an inexplicable vulnerability. The tensed juxtaposition of "virtues . . . infinite" and nothingness conflates the two extremes between which human nature is traditionally located at the midpoint of creation. For it is a sense of dislocation that has become Hamlet's ruling obsession. He, too, has lost his accustomed field of action, but unlike Polonius and Horatio he cannot call on an unreflecting confidence or a cautious rationality for protection.

We first see him as a singular figure in black disgusted by the unctuous competence of Claudius at court. Once the embodiment of humanity's best self-image, Hamlet clings to the vestiges of his substantiality, "that within which passes show" (1.2.85), against a corrosive theatricality; he would "know not seems" or the "actions that a man might play." What, then, is left for him to know? His loyalty to an idealized past threatens those protected vestiges from within; his moralizing against the weary, stale, flat, and unprofitable uses of this world entails self-cancellation. The degree to which he reviles Claudius is inversely proportional to his own capacity for heroic action: "My father's brother, but no more like my father / Than I to Hercules" (1.2.152–53). Against this damning comparison, the Ghost's injunction offers Hamlet a clear focus, an utter simplicity of motive. But even as Hamlet craves that invigorating purpose—"My fate cries out, / And makes each petty arture in this body / As hardy as the Nemean lion's nerve" (1.4.81–83)—his self-comparison to the lion killed by Hercules disqualifies him from the blunt extroversion of his father, for whom angry words led swiftly to violent deeds: "In an angry parle, / He smote the sledded Polacks on the ice" (1.1.62–63). The very assumptions upon which Old Hamlet's conduct had rested, that composite of piety and violence so familiar to Renaissance politics, elude Hamlet's grasp. The Ghost, with its call for vengeance, invokes not only a lost equilibrium, but the schizophrenia of a dying culture. Its return to Denmark is, in C. S. Lewis's phrase, "permanently ambiguous";[2] no world view, no theory of divine scourging or demonic impersonation, is adequate to it because it draws its primary dramatic force not from any single frame of reference, but from the way we see it take hold of Hamlet's mind. It is for him a spectral reflection of a world that can no longer reconcile its contradictions: the Ghost binds Hamlet to revenge, but calls murder "most foul"; it evokes Christian ritual and value—lamenting its death without the sacrament, referring Gertrude's judgment "to heaven," commanding Hamlet to taint not his mind—and yet commands one of the "foul crimes" for which it suffers, and taints the prince's mind with an obsessive and graphic tale of political outrage and sexual degradation.

Hamlet never questions the morality of revenge because he would suppress contradiction by negation: "Yea, from the table of my memory / I'll wipe away all trivial fond records, / All saws of books, all forms, all pressures past" (1.5.98–100). But the complexities of consciousness and culture, of pressures past, cannot be effaced so easily. Hamlet immediately associates his task with the weight of history, the need to set time back into joint, even as he longs to separate himself from the social forms that have betrayed him. When the strain of his ambivalence forces him "to put an antic disposition on" it is to allow him to reconnoiter a world that seems itself to have gone mad. As the prince, "his choice" is "circumscrib'd" (1.3.22); as the wronged and disinherited prince he is even more narrowly "bound." But as the antic prince he is temporarily released both from the demands of a court he finds so nightmarish and from the revenge to which he had promised to sweep "with wings as swift / As meditation" (1.5.29–30). Madness bends meditation to test indirections, giving the *viator* time to feel his way through a world grown alien.

Because it is a world where theater passes for reality, Hamlet summons the primitive power of theatricality itself. The antic disposition taps an already volatile sense of self and makes of Hamlet a parodist of what were once fixed points of reference: love, marriage, kingship, respect for the dead, are either mocked or hysterically affirmed. Linguistic norms are fair game as well; if the Ghost has sent Hamlet's speech into "wild and whirling words," Hamlet plays relentlessly with "words, words, words"—he is Shakespeare's most prolific quibbler— and seems irresistibly drawn to parody the voices he hears around him.[3] At once Vice and Fool, he creates havoc with his sneaking mischief, his "miching mallecho"; Jack Juggler, Diccon the Bedlam, Ambidexter, together with Shakespeare's own Jack Cade and Richard III, lurk behind his cruel jokes and pointed nonsense.

But the same constraints that distance Hamlet from the simplicity of the blunt Revenger distance him from the amoral and anarchic joys of the Vice. He cannot jettison conscience: no character is as morbidly obsessed by moral values as he, and no character is more burdened by the sheer awareness of consciousness. The Vice in Hamlet is fed by a profound melancholy, one that forever turns back on the depths of its own agitation. He is speaking tropically about himself when he advises Polonius to watch his daughter because the sun can "breed": "Let her not walk i' th' sun. Conception is a blessing. But as your daughter may conceive—friend, look to 't" (2.2.183). It is Hamlet who is "too much in the sun" (1.2.67); his vision of diseased sexuality, the nunnery scene suggests, mirrors the dangerous fecundity of his own frantic conceptions in a world of depraved opportunities, "with more offenses at my beck than I have thoughts to put them in, imagination to give them shape, or time to act them in" (3.1.125). The mind races to keep up with its own monstrous possibilities.

Both the world and the mind have become distracted globes, fields of action upon which only fitful bursts of activity or tortuous soliloquy can be performed. But between them lies an *orbis tertius*, a globe of self-conscious fictions. It is this field that Hamlet would make his own. The displaced *uomo universale*, deprived of the courtier's, soldier's, and scholar's outlets, longs to explore this new virtuosity. It is more than warm memory, then, that provokes his enthusiastic greeting to the players from Wittenberg.

HAMLET AND AENEAS

Like many a Renaissance fiction-maker, Hamlet turns to classical models, even those of indirect transmission, and his first conscious choice is the avenging Pyrrhus. It is difficult to read or hear the Player's speech Hamlet requests without noting its uncanny, if ambiguous, reflection of Hamlet's own situation. A blackened avenger delays momentarily, then drives toward fulfillment; yet he is a "hellish" figure who slaughters a "reverend . . . father" and evokes the anguish of a matronly Hecuba. Whether we find in its curious alignments evidence of Oedipal patterns, moral commentary on blood revenge, or the intractability of received material, the speech seems calculated to intrigue us with its cross-references.[4]

One of the speech's most important cross-references is its framing circumstance: this is "Aeneas' tale to Dido." Hamlet longs to hear Aeneas's autobiographical tale because its narrator bears so profound a resemblance to him. Like Hamlet, Aeneas bears witness to the death of his culture. He is the *Aeneid*'s reluctant hero, a melancholy personality forced into public, heroic action by the supernatural promptings of ghosts, omens, and prophecies. "My fate cries out," Hamlet exclaims; isolated from the world he once knew, he is driven to reform the time, which is out of joint. Aeneas, too, is an exile: "His fate / had made him fugitive" (1.1–2; 2–3),[5] and he might well lament, "O cursed spite." "Aeneas," writes Wendell Clausen, "enters the poem wishing he were dead, the only epic hero to do so":[6] "O, three and four times blessed were those who died before their fathers' eyes beneath the walls of Troy" (1.133–35; 94–96). Hamlet's first soliloquy ("O, that this too too solid flesh") quickly establishes a temperamental similarity. Hamlet mourns for what is past, sees his father in his mind's eye, and suffers that within that passes show; the weight of Aeneas's past is literally enacted by the carrying of his father on his shoulders, and is psychologically borne in a deep interior: "his pain / is held within, hidden" (1.291–92; 209). Aeneas may unburden his heart in his tale to Dido, but he will inevitably abandon her, driving her to madness and suicide, even as Hamlet will abandon, madden, and destroy Ophelia.

"Hamlet's world is pre-eminently in the interrogative mood," writes Maynard Mack, and its questionable shape is powerfully prefigured in the *Aeneid*.[7] Aeneas's world is one of obscure omens and phantoms of loved ones at which he clutches in vain. The promise of a coherent vision often seems as elusive as the words and symbols of the Sibyl's leaves, all "in place and order" until her door is opened; then the verses "flutter through the hollow grotto," never to be rejoined. Though Aeneas fulfills his role as the "pious" hero, founder of a new culture in the West, the darkness of his experience is never fully exorcised. The epic's turning point, the visit to the underworld (6), proceeds from a giant elm of empty dreams to a gate of ivory, passageway of false dreams. The glory of military conquest is similarly vexing; the gleam of Aeneas's crest is compared to a sinister comet and the "blazing Dog Star, bringer of diseases . . . saddening the skies" (10.382–84; 273–75), and his final triumphs over Mezentius and Turnus are tainted by their strange melancholy and cruel violence.

Nonetheless, Brooks Otis's reading of a "resurrection" into objective and public action in the epic's second half points up an important contrast to *Hamlet*.[8] Aeneas, through all his sorrow and uncertainty, is sustained by promises of the authenticity of his quest and of a final, creative outlet. Others may produce finer sculptors, orators, and astronomers, his father's ghost tells him, but the Romans will master the greatest of human arts: "the rulership of nations" (6.1129–37; 847–53). Aeneas joins himself to the future, bearing Vulcan's illustrated shield, "glad / for all these images, though he does not know what they mean," for he has been assured by a prophetic vision, and by a voice on the Tiber, that his commitment is not to "empty / fictions sleep has feigned" (8.51–52; 42). Hamlet, like Aeneas, is a bringer of disease and death, but the justification for his grim heroism is less certain.[9] There is for him no underworld to visit, where a paternal spirit points toward the future. The underworld, rather, forces itself on him, confronting him with an inescapable past; beyond that, it is a graveyard heaped with bones, or an undiscovered country, puzzling the will. Nor is there a great sea voyage from the old East to the new West; Hamlet's sea voyage returns him to the land from which he set out, naked and alone. A Renaissance man seeking direction in *imitatio*, Hamlet only accentuates his distance from his classical model, reproducing Aeneas's dilemmas, not his resolution. The tale to Dido takes him only to the grieving Hecuba and the paradox of a player's tears:

> O, what a rogue and peasant slave am I!
> Is it not monstrous that this player here,
> But in a fiction, in a dream of passion,
> Could force his soul so to his own conceit
> That from her working all his visage wann'd;
> Tears in his eyes, distraction in's aspect,
> A broken voice, and his whole function suiting
> With forms to his conceit? And all for nothing!
> For Hecuba!
> What's Hecuba to him or he to Hecuba,
> That he should weep for her?
>
> (2.2.542–52)

The player's passion is generated out of nothing, "in a fiction"; like Sidney's poet, his matter springs from "his own conceit." Richard III's extroverted boast "All the world to nothing" turns inward with a tone of disbelief: "All for nothing!" Hamlet would dearly love to be Denmark's Aeneas, rising from enigma to authenticity, beyond "actions that a man might play"; but locked in a prison called Denmark, one may negotiate illusion only by complete immersion in it. The disorienting nature of such a passage is made clear throughout the soliloquy that closes act 2, scene 2. Hamlet contrasts his own "motive" and "cue" to the player's, not to set off his reality, but to picture a greater performance ("He would drown the stage with tears"). Hamlet then oscillates between self-reproach and fantasy, calling himself "John-a-dreams" (cousin perhaps to Richard II's "Jack of the clock"), then dreaming up an imaginary antagonist ("Who calls me villain") for a round of rhetorical shadowboxing, then reproaching himself for his self-indulgent histrionics ("Why, what an ass am I!").

But out of such vagaries comes a surer sense of purpose, something missing from the wilder theatrics of the antic disposition. He accuses himself of saying "nothing," but it is the poet's nothing he has uttered, and the final voice we hear is that of the deliberating artist, a voice we have heard in Richard II's "let's see" and "I'll hammer it out" (4.1.294; 5.5.5): "About, my brains. Hum—I have heard / That guilty creatures, sitting at a play, / Have by the very cunning of the scene / Been struck so to the soul that presently / They have proclaim'd their malefactions" (2.2.584–88). Confidence swells together with renewed echoes of Sidney's *Apology*. Dramatic fictions can draw tears from even the most "abominable tyrant," according to Sidney, tenting to the quick the hidden "ulcers" of corruption (*Apology*, pp. 117–18).[10] If Hamlet cannot complete the part of Aeneas, passing from ambiguous images to historical reality, he will draw reality into his images, not only composing a spectacle for the court, but making a spectacle of the court: "I'll observe his looks . . . The play's the thing / Wherein I'll catch the conscience of the king."

THE PURPOSE OF PLAYING

The succeeding scene proves the efficacy of playing, but, as is so often the case in *Hamlet*, in a way we do not expect. Polonius arranges his own little play to catch Hamlet's conscience and unknowingly catches Claudius's: "How smart a lash that speech doth give my conscience!" the king winces in an aside as he watches Polonius direct Ophelia with her devotional book, revealing to us, for the first time, the truth of the Ghost's accusations (3.1.50). The anticipated effect follows an unexpected cause, and our longing to see the proper cause and effect joined primes us for Hamlet's revision of *The Murder of Gonzago*.

It is a hunger for propriety that informs Hamlet's aesthetic tastes as well. He has already praised the restraint of an "honest method" before the Player's Speech (a judgment that proved to be less than accurate), and now, before *The Murder of Gonzago*,

Hamlet devotes his closest attention to his medium. His advice to the players can scarcely be called Shakespeare's own essay— Hamlet would not have been pleased by *Hamlet*. It reveals, rather, Hamlet's urge to rewrite the part he has been playing, to stabilize the imagination through critical self-consciousness.

> Do not saw the air too much with your hand, thus, but use all gently; for in the very torrent, tempest, and, as I may say, whirl-wind of your passion, you must acquire and beget a temperance that may give it smoothness.
>
> (3.2.4)

His longing to temper the "wild and whirling words" of his antic disposition leads him to a peculiar hybrid of Polonian pontificating and Sidneyan Neoclassicism and didacticism:

> Be not too tame neither, but let your own discretion be your tutor. Suit the action to the word, the word to the action; with this special observance, that you o'erstep not the modesty of nature; for any-thing so o'erdone is from the purpose of playing, whose end, both at the first and now, was and is to hold, as 'twere, the mirror up to nature; to show virtue her own feature, scorn her own image, and the very age and body of the time his form and pressure.
>
> (3.2.16)

If the mirror Hamlet holds up is a revenge tragedy, it is just as surely a history play. Players are "the abstract and brief chron-icles of the time," he insists (2.2.518), and his play embodies his perspective on recent Danish history.

Although Hamlet may not employ a proscenium-arched stage, there is something radically perspectival about his little court drama. He presents a scene upon which he has brooded in his mind's eye, now projected into a conspicuously artificial construction for all to see. Like perspective art, the play is de-signed to draw the viewer into its own illusory space. Alberti's understanding of the power of perspective to place "both the beholder and the painted things he sees . . . on the same plane," finds its analogue in Hamlet's scheme to subdue the court to his aesthetic control.[11] For though Hamlet's aim is to strip away Claudius's deception, the play he calls *The Mousetrap* must first catch the observer's response within its own design and use the very cunning of the scene to turn that response into the culminating theatrical moment. Claudius's fiction played as reality will succumb to Hamlet's reality played as fiction, a conquest to end all fictions when poisoning in jest becomes vengeance in earnest.

So plotted, it is no wonder that Hamlet's play, unlike *Hamlet* itself, begins by charting a world of scrupulous measurements. The Player King and Queen, in stiff couplets, compute the length of their love ("thirty dozen moons with borrowed sheen / About the world have twelve thirties been") and the balancing of love and fear ("women's fear and love hold quantity, / . . . as my love is siz'd, my fear is so") (3.2.162–65). We anticipate a neatness of design, and according to Dover Wilson, we are not disappointed. The play is a "complete success," he argues, a "central point," "the point at which all the threads of the plot may be expected to meet."[12] But the reduction of Hamlet's obsessions to symbolic form is far more problematic. Granville-Barker and others have shown how the lines of Hamlet's composition lead our mind's eye in unexpected directions.[13] The play seems concerned more with catching the conscience of the queen than that of the king, its scandalous taunts far from the supposed purpose of playing: "A second time I kill my husband dead / When second husband kisses me in bed" (3.2.179–80). Often noted as well is the return of the disturbing conflations of the Player's speech: the original murderer and the revenger are collapsed into one dramatic figure, "Lucianus, nephew to the King." "Come," Hamlet exhorts him. "The croaking raven doth bellow for revenge." But who is revenging whom? If the revenger simply reproduces the original crime, the act of revenge, as the Greek tragedians knew, becomes an endless repetition of murder and revenge.[14]

The confused reflections of Hamlet's mirror stem in part

from the shifting lines that refer two players, the Player King and Lucianus, to three potential referents: Old Hamlet, Claudius, and Hamlet. They are intensified by the convergence of the entire play into the personality of its author. As in a dream where several figures may stand as versions of the dreamer, so in the play Hamlet's characters all carry elements of himself. The affinity between Lucianus and Hamlet is clear. But so too is that between the Player King and Hamlet. For this is not the sanguine militarist who "smote the sledded Polacks on the ice," but someone who is "sick of late," "far from cheer and [his] former state," terms that echo Hamlet's about himself: "I have of late—but wherefore I know not—lost all my mirth" (2.2.292). Has the revenge impulse become so self-directed that Hamlet stages a psychomachia, where his inhibiting melancholy is destroyed by an archaic, vengeful side of his personality? There remains yet further self-reference: the Player King's warning to his Queen of the frailty of memory and purpose both recalls the Ghost's injunction, "Remember me," and anticipates his whetting of "thy almost blunted purpose." *The Mousetrap* may have been set to catch the conscience of both king and queen, but in effect it catches the conscience of its author in the play of equivocations. Hamlet conceived of the play as a triple test of Claudius's guilt, of the Ghost's word, and of his own mind: "If his occulted guilt / Do not itself unkennel in one speech, / It is a damned ghost that we have seen, / And my imaginations are as foul / As Vulcan's stithy" (3.2.78–82). But if Hamlet's imagination is suspect, so, too, are its creations, which display the stamp of his obsessive imaginings.

If he would join with Horatio in censure of the king's seeming as he had planned, he might still, in Granville-Barker's terms, "bridge fiction to fact." But he is too exultant over the triumph his fiction brings him—"Would not this . . . get me a fellowship in a cry of players, sir?" (3.2.269)—to notice Horatio's odd reticence: "Half a share," the same sort of caution Horatio sounded when hearing the credulous soldiers' ghost lore: "So have I heard, and do in part believe it" (1.1.165). Horatio did "very well note" Claudius, but Hamlet, so ready to "take the Ghost's word" does not note Horatio's evasive answer to his query: "Didst perceive?" Nor does Horatio appear eager to clarify. For he may have perceived something more disturbing at the play than evidence of hidden regicide. He is silent for the rest of the scene, and does not speak again until the prince has been sent to England and Ophelia has gone mad, herself "speak[ing] things in doubt." "Her speech is nothing," a gentleman reports,

> Yet the unshaped use of it doth move
> The hearers to collection; they yawn at it,
> And botch the words up to fit their own thoughts.
> (4.5.7–10)

Only then does Horatio speak, warning that Ophelia "may strew / Dangerous conjectures in ill-breeding minds" (4.5.14–15). Horatio's seeming lack of concern for Ophelia is less surprising than his solicitousness for a regime he must by now know is corrupt. Hamlet may admire Horatio's stoicism, his ability to take "Fortune's buffets and rewards . . . with equal thanks," and call him "that man / That is not passion's slave" (3.2.65–66, 69–70); but Horatio's reaction to what he calls "dangerous conjectures" here, and his earlier fear that Hamlet has grown "desperate with imagination," shows us the cost of that determined equilibrium, and explains why, after agreeing to Hamlet's plan (3.2.85–87), he retreats behind equivocation and silence. The bitterly intense and paradoxical *Murder of Gonzago* has shown Horatio a mind deeply threatening to his own, and to the running of the state, a mind whose complexity outruns its ability to compose itself, forever poised at "the dreadful summit of the cliff."[15] Hamlet's success leaves him utterly isolated.

Yet he takes no notice of Horatio's reticence, for he feels himself to have reached the summit of his power. Denmark may still be a prison, a Cecropian castle of theatrical horrors, but he imagines that he has seized control of the mechanisms of illusion and gained an aesthetic, if not a political, sovereignty. He plays the master of conjecture, bullying the diplomatic Polonius by shaping and unshaping the ambiguous forms of a cloud—now like a camel, now like a weasel, now like a whale—because that archetype of questionable shapes, the Ghost "like the king," has been verified, his word worth "a thousand pound" (3.1.279). Here, Hamlet believes, is the fixed vantage point for which he has so long sought.

HAMLET'S SEQUELS

Hamlet's supposed vantage, and advantage, has been won only through the ambiguous shapes of his own play, and he is reluctant to leave the stage he controls. Left alone at the scene's end, he continues his play as a private fantasy, in a soliloquy that assumes Lucianus's voice: " 'Tis now the very witching time of night, / When churchyards yawn, and hell itself breathes out / Contagion to this world. Now could I drink hot blood" (3.2.378–80).[16] But between *The Mousetrap*'s abrupt termination and his forced exile from Denmark, Hamlet's mastery continually breaks down, and we find him repeatedly struggling to recompose himself and his world into poetic and dramatic order.

Planning a confrontation with his mother, he revises his revenger's stance by confessing to role playing: "I will speak daggers to her, but use none. / My tongue and soul in this be hypocrites" (3.2.386–87). Yet before he can reach her, he stumbles onto the scene for which he should have been priming himself: Claudius is apparently kneeling in prayer, at Hamlet's mercy. Having shuttled between fantasies of acting and action, he finds himself equivocating:

> Now might I do it pat, now 'a is a-praying;
> And now I'll do't—and so 'a goes to heaven,

And so am I reveng'd. That would be scann'd:
A villain kills my father; and for that,
I, his sole son, do this same villain send
To heaven.
Why, this is hire and salary, not revenge.

(3.3.73–79)

Hamlet sticks at the hypothetical "might." He turns opportunity into a quickly sketched plot, but one whose consequences undo the opportunity. The critical mind scans only to defer the play it might enact.

Up, sword, and know thou a more horrid hent.
When he is drunk asleep, or in his rage;
Or in th' incestuous pleasure of his bed;
At game, a-swearing, or about some act
That has no relish of salvation in 't—
Then trip him, that his heels may kick at heaven,
And that his soul may be as damn'd and black
As hell, whereto it goes.

(3.3.88–95)

Hazlitt's reading of Hamlet rationalizing his delay is no longer in critical favor, but it provides an important insight. Hamlet is, in Hazlitt's terms, "the prince of philosophical speculators"; because he "cannot have his revenge perfect, according to the most refined idea his wish can form, he declines it altogether."[17] I would only propose that Hamlet's "idea" is as poetical as it is speculative. Hamlet demands the prerogatives of both playwright and actor. He seeks omnipotence over his world and will wait until he can send Claudius to hell, even as Marlowe sends Faustus. But Hamlet's world is not so tractable, and neither is his intelligence privileged with the playwright's control. His surmise is riddled with irony, the most obvious instance being Claudius's failure at prayer. Hamlet, the perfect opportunity before him, unknowingly replicates his intended victim: "Like a man to double business bound / I stand in pause where I shall first begin, / And both neglect" (3.3.41–43). The juxtaposition of two soliloquies, a unique moment in Shakespeare, creates the eerie sense of minds passing in the night, oblivious to their parallel torments. The interior depths of another mind lie beyond the grasp of Hamlet's fictions.[18] The following scene, however, shows Hamlet still reaching for those depths, only to set in motion a chain of consequences he had not "scann'd." He comes to Gertrude as the teacher whose mirror will illuminate what Sidney calls "the secretest cabinet of our souls" (*Apology*, p. 106): "You go not till I set you up a glass / Where you may see the inmost part of you," a program immediately compromised when the queen mistakes the poet's trope for the Nero he would not be, her cries for help, in turn, betraying Polonius, who is killed by a thrust through the arras. Hamlet, who fancied himself the master of conjecture, who mocked Polonius by having him guess at the shapes of clouds, lunges at a muffled cry and an amorphous shape behind a curtain, one which, for a fleeting moment, looked to him very like the king.

With the death of Polonius, Hamlet's roles as moral teacher and antic become indistinguishable. His pretensions untouched by Polonius's corpse at his feet ("I took thee for thy better"), Hamlet presents notable images of virtue and vice— the portraits of his father and uncle—and almost succeeds, as Nathan does with David in Sidney's anecdote, in showing his audience its own filthiness: "Thou turn'st my eyes into my very soul / And there I see such black and ingrained spots / As will not leave their tinct." But the unrelenting, almost pathological, intensity of Hamlet's images ("the rank sweat of an enseamed bed") provokes cries of "no more . . . no more . . . No more" until the Ghost's entry halts the performance in midflight, even as Claudius's call for light had halted *The Murder of Gonzago*.

Gertrude's inability to see the Ghost presents us with more than an enigma about the spirit world's selective visibility. In a court more joyous than that of Elsinore, Theseus could be amused by "seething brains" and "shaping fantasies, that apprehend / More than cool reason ever comprehends."

> The lunatic, the lover and the poet
> Are of imagination all compact
> . . . .
> The poet's eye, in a fine frenzy rolling,
> Doth glance from heaven to earth, from earth to heaven;
> And as imagination bodies forth
> The forms of things unknown, the poet's pen
> Turns them to shapes, and gives to airy nothing
> A local habitation and a name.
> (*A Midsummer Night's Dream* 5.1.3–17)

We have long known that Hamlet apprehends more than cool reason ever comprehends, that his frenzied eye glances even further than from heaven to earth: "airs from heaven or blasts from hell." We also know of his fascination with fiction making, with a Player's ability to cry "for nothing." But when Gertrude calls his one fixed point "vacancy," "incorporal air," "the very coinage of your brain / The bodiless creation ecstasy / Is very cunning in," Hamlet protests and for the moment so do we; we *see* the Ghost, and so have others. And yet in a play that so often asks us to think about the nature of theater, and has so worried the boundaries of what it means to be or not to be, we cannot be sure where to locate our ontological markers. It is a dizzying moment and immediately refers us to an ethical dilemma: what kind of poetic world is Hamlet constructing about his assumed fixed point? He demands acknowledgment of his sanity: "My pulse as yours doth temperately keep time" (a speech we should recall when Hamlet offers his insanity defense to Laertes in the play's final scene), and then launches into a didactic program complete with philosophical underpinnings: role playing merges with Scholastic *habitus*: "Assume a virtue, if you have it not. / That monster custom, who all sense doth eat, / Of habits devil, is angel yet in this, / That to the use of actions fair and good / He likewise gives a frock or livery / That aptly is put on" (3.4.160–65). Repeated performance reforms the performer; this is perhaps Hamlet's most optimistic defense of drama's efficacy, fairly reversing the terrible vulnerability he earlier felt before the vicious mole of Nature. The "stamp of one defect . . . nature's livery" gives place to a new "frock or livery. . . . For use almost can change the stamp of nature" (3.4.164–68). Yet he ends the scene with a reminder of what else the theater puts into play, reverting to the cruel gloating and amoral hilarity of the Vice as he anticipates new mischief, " 'tis the sport to have the engineer / Hoist with his own petar," and drags Polonius's corpse offstage: "I'll lug the guts into the neighbour room" (3.4.206–7, 211).

The four scenes that present the Player's speech, *The Murder of Gonzago,* and Hamlet's private encounters with Claudius and Gertrude show us a Hamlet longing for the coherent force of fictions and seeking to take on drama's power of concentration. But in none of these scenes does Hamlet set his world aright. His constructions net him only fragile oases of power, which quickly dissolve into nihilism: "We fat ourselves for maggots." Nor does the play itself ever settle our discomfort about the mind's hunger for its own inventions; it only widens its focus to show us the universality of that ambiguous, but inescapable, human craving.

The widest, and most disturbing, of such visions occurs with Hamlet's crossing of Fortinbras's path and his meditation on the latter's purposefulness. Here Hamlet conceives a poetics of heroism that takes as its sure sign of divine afflatus ("with divine ambition puffed") an eagerness for mass slaughter. As the captain tells Hamlet: "Truly to speak, and with no addition, / We go to gain a little patch of ground / That hath in it no profit but the name" (4.4.17–19). To speak without illusion is to note that men die for an illusion, even if their goal is but a name, a *flatus vocis.* The gnawing sense of unreality in the first tetralogy and the probing questions of *Henry V* about a ruler's responsibility for the butchering of his men (act 4, scene 1) are topics Hamlet ignores in his fascination with the very gratuitousness of combat. The fecundity of "godlike reason" is its capacity to invent motivation *ex nihilo*: "Rightly to be great / Is not to stir without great argument, / But greatly to find quarrel in a straw, / When honour's at the stake" (4.4.53–56). Fortinbras is the poet of relentless will and aggression who never lacks an end because he fills every void with "a fantasy and trick of fame." If he lacks "great argument," he will fight "for an egg-shell"; if he cannot assault Denmark, a barren spot in Poland will do as well. As in his soliloquy on Hecuba, Hamlet insists his course is more than mere fiction: "How stand I, then, / That have a father kill'd, a mother stain'd." But the examples he draws to spur his dull revenge come from a world where men die for "the question of this straw" (4.4.26), and where their leaders find "quarrel in a straw" (4.4.55), a world, for all its purposefulness, with little to dignify it above the madness of Ophelia in the following scene, as she "spurns enviously at straws" (4.4.6).

THE FINAL MAKER

Hamlet's sea voyage, like much of his thinking, returns him to his point of departure. Yet he returns as if transformed, for the tale we hear in his letter to Horatio speaks of a Hamlet who seizes occasion. The adventure, it is true, is elaborately distanced from us, its offstage heroics reported by Horatio reading a letter; it recounts, too, an opaquely romantic narrative of a prince at sea who seems closer to Sidney's Pyrocles waving his sword on the broken mast than to the Hamlet we know. Indeed, as Hamlet later describes it, the adventure begins as a war of theaters—"Ere I could make a prologue to my brains, / They had begun the play—I sat me down; / Devis'd a new commission; wrote it fair" (5.2.30–32). But Hamlet seems reformed by his new genre. His revision of Claudius's orders for his death is quite unlike the revision of *The Murder of Gonzago* in its brutal efficacy. Equally important, there are no fantasies of poetic omnipotence; Hamlet takes pains to minimize, even cancel, his powers of calculation and will, crediting a "rashness" that submits him to a higher maker:

> Our indiscretion sometime serves us well,
> When our deep plots do pall; and that should learn us
> There's a divinity that shapes our ends,
> Rough-hew them how we will.
>
> (5.2.8–11)

Hamlet's "divinity that shapes our ends" redeems the haunting entropy of *The Murder of Gonzago*: "Our thoughts are ours, their ends none of our own."

Religious terminology is scarcely new to the play, but it makes increasing claims for itself, and demands on us, as the play winds toward its conclusion. Does Hamlet's seeming acceptance solve his and the play's dilemmas? What are the dimensions of his apparently transformed perspective? The key, many have felt, lies somewhere in Hamlet's inner life: "To trace the steps by which Hamlet arrived at this state of mind," writes Hardin Craig, "is to master the meaning of the play."[19] Shakespeare seems willfully to have blocked that mastery; once Hamlet returns to Denmark, there is an abrupt cessation of soliloquy. But that cessation is itself a most tantalizing clue. Hamlet has accused his "brains still beating" (Claudius's phrase) with turning awry his great enterprise, and has pictured himself trapped in an intellectual dance of regression, one step forward, three backward: "A thought which, quarter'd, hath but one part wisdom, / And ever three parts coward" (4.4.42–43). Returned to a starting point, Hamlet begins a final drive toward chastening, even cancelling, those intricate turnings, a longing for self-displacement that culminates in his final affirmation of Providence.

Hamlet, writes Harry Levin, "takes place in an open universe; its signs and omens, though evident, are equivocal," and it is never more open than in its determined efforts at closure, efforts that begin in the graveyard.[20] The grave makers' banter about guilt and willful action sets the scene, introducing the terms "Christian" or "Christen" four times, but taking their black humor no further than to complaints about the aristocracy's unfair privileges of suicide. Nor does Hamlet's succeeding meditation on death steady our view of a Christian universe, despite the fact that his language echoes that of spiritual meditation; his is a peculiarly spiritless imagining of the body turned to dust, with no interest in tracing the soul's progress to the everlasting.[21] His progress is marked by the skulls that are tossed up, and he reflects on familiar obsessions: fratricide (Cain's jawbone) and ruthless politicians. The meditation expands outward, not upward, by recalling the recurrent nightmare of the history plays, from Jack Cade's assault on law courts and the literate to Richard II's despairing "throw away respect / Tradition, form, and ceremonious duty." Hamlet entertains the collapse of all social forms and social personalities: the politician, the courtier, the lady, and the lawyer are only bones "to play at loggets." Where are the lawyer's "quiddities now, his quillets, his cases, his tenures, and his tricks," where the land buyer's "statutes, his recognizances, his fines, his double vouchers, his recoveries" (5.1.96)? All lie in the wasteland of dead selves and symbols. The final human "maker," as the scene's first riddle has already told us, is the grave maker.

The grave maker began his profession the day young Hamlet was born, as if waiting thirty years to bury him, and this is fitting. The meditator implicates himself in death with a completeness unparalleled in the play. The skull of Yorick sets him up a glass:

> Alas, poor Yorick! I knew him, Horatio: a fellow of infinite jest, of most excellent fancy; he hath borne me on his back a thousand times. And now how abhorred in my imagination it is! My gorge rises at it. Here hung those lips that I have kiss'd I know not how oft. Where be your gibes now . . . ?
>
> (5.1.179)

The antic of Claudius's court meets his predecessor in office, his father's fool. A fellow of infinite jest now chapfallen; the irony returns us to Hamlet's thwarted humanism, his repeated juxtaposition of infinite possibility and nothingness: virtues may be "as infinite as man may undergo" but will be undone by a "dram of eale" (1.4.34–36); a piece of work "noble in reason" and "infinite in faculties" is the "quintessence of dust" (2.2.302); Hamlet could count himself "king of infinite space" were it not that he has bad dreams (2.2.254). But now the meditation wings swiftly from "man's death" to "*my* death," not a prayer that this "flesh *would* melt" but the insistence that it inevitably *will* melt. The rhetorical balance of "My gorge rises at it. Here hung those lips" equates the lips that no longer hang to the gorge that will no longer rise. The thought is "abhorred in my imagination" in part because the picture implies its own effacement, the end of imagining altogether. Rather than step back to compose a perspective, Hamlet would collapse his own point of view into general annihilation.

The attempt of consciousness to cancel itself in thought cannot of course be completed. Writers from Epicurus to Freud have explained that "my death" is strictly unimaginable; no thought experiment transforming oneself into one dead can annul the thinker, the "spectator" having the thought.[22] The effort of self-cancellation is nonetheless crucial; Hamlet transforms his brooding over mortality into a purposeful "negative way," a stripping down of the self until thought must reconstitute itself. That it must is implied by the conspicuously dramatic nature of Hamlet's examination of Yorick's skull, perhaps the most famous interview in theatrical history. The scrutiny that begins "Let me see" inevitably leads to further vision:

HAMLET. To what base uses we may return, Horatio! Why may not imagination trace the noble dust of Alexander till 'a find it stopping a bung-hole?
HORATIO. 'Twere to consider too curiously to consider so.

HAMLET. No, faith, not a jot; but to follow him thither with
modesty enough, and likelihood to lead it, as thus:
Alexander died, Alexander was buried, Alexander re-
turneth to dust; the dust is earth; of earth we make
loam; and why of that loam whereto he was converted might they not stop a beer-barrel?
Imperious Caesar, dead and turn'd to clay,
Might stop a hole to keep the wind away.
(5.1.197)

Horatio is as wary as ever of his friend's desperate imagination,
and Hamlet meets his objections by again playing critic. He
does not overstep the "modesty of nature" (3.2.18); there is
"modesty enough and likelihood to lead it": death to burial to
dust to earth to loam is a plot both necessary and probable.
Hamlet's Neoclassicism, however, has by now caught up to his
practices, far beyond Sidney's with its mingling of kings and
clowns in a heap of dust, Caesar and inanimate clay.

But have those practices changed as well? Surely this is the
same mind that pictured "outstretched heroes" as "beggars'
shadows" (2.2.263) and a king going a "progress through the
guts of a beggar" (4.3.31). The turning of dark obsessions into
jest and sport—bones into loggets and dead heroes into jin-
gles—and the cruel contest of hyperbole with Laertes over
Ophelia's grave, mark very little by way of "regeneration."
The tone of "detached, bemused irony" that Eleanor Prosser
professes to hear in her denial of the scene's nihilism is at best
intermittent and shot through with sardonic laughter and
muted hysteria.[23] And yet Hamlet *has* achieved a new kind of
self-measuring, which paradoxically reaches its clearest expression in the midst of ranting: "This is I, Hamlet the Dane."
Hamlet would be reborn in the graveyard, but reborn as a social creature, a public performer—"*This*," one character
among others—no longer the subjective, isolated consciousness aloof from the play.

Hamlet emerges from the graveyard picturing a world
where he is no longer at the center of things, nor pushed to the

dizzying edge, for Providence is now assumed as its center and circumference. The two paradoxes that have haunted him, the mind's generation of fictions out of nothing and the juxtaposition of man's infinity and his nothingness, seem resolved in each other. Man is less the maker than the thing made, truly a "piece of work" because God's fiction created *ex nihilo* and protected by that Maker from slipping back into nothing. Once the higher Artificer is assumed, the need to master rival plots and set time back into joint vanishes. All is already in place, and Hamlet need only submit to the king's next contrivance, "to play" with Laertes (5.2.192, 199, 245), confident that one Theater subsumes all fragmentary theaters. The mind that has struggled with the mightiest of opposites—"to be or not to be"—finally conflates affirmation and denial. In the time between Hamlet's "Let be" and "Let it be" (5.2.216, 330), the play that has strained for release explodes in a torrent of murderous action, leaving the king, the queen, and Laertes dead, and Hamlet at the brink of the "undiscovered country."

"IF YOU DESIRE TO KNOW THE CERTAINTY" (4.5.137)

"If only men's minds could be seized and held still! They would see how eternity, in which there is neither past nor future, determines both past and future time."[24] Augustine's stability of vision is what Hamlet seeks in his echo of Matthew 10:29–31: "There is a special providence in the fall of a sparrow. If it be now, 'tis not to come; if it be not to come, it will be now; if it be not now, yet it will come" (5.2.211). Horatio, whose scenario from the start has been "Heaven will direct it" (1.4.91), can at last find comfort in Hamlet's shaping divinity: "That is most certain" (5.2.11).

We have throughout the play been drawn by, and made suspicious of, the "desire to know the certainty"—Claudius's line as he snares Laertes in his contrivance (4.5.137)—and at the end we again feel the siege of contraries. For if Hamlet has struggled with a historical and psychological world of paradox, we have attended to a theatrical world that repeatedly violates our expectations on almost every level of response, frustrating our longing for clarity with blocked action, contradictory frames of reference, and incongruous systems of value. Now that Hamlet, the prince and the poem, are released from their torments, their "frustrated energy" fulfilled in "significant action," we long to partake fully of the experience.[25] But Shakespeare has calculated a swerve into the dramatic effect, to produce a doubling back of the play's final movement in our minds the moment the thrust of the action has slowed. We find ourselves questioning what, and how, the action has signified, an effect that relies, in part, on memory. As in the histories, conjectures about the divine have been tossed about with ease, from Claudius's hypocritical moralizing about Hamlet's "will most incorrect to heaven" and his invocation of the "divinity that hedges round a king" to Hamlet's self-appointment as Heaven's "scourge and minister" after stabbing Polonius and his providentialism after the gratuitous murders of Rosencrantz and Guildenstern. His "I'll lug the guts" and "They are not near my conscience" lack even the momentary remorse we hear in Claudius's efforts at prayer.

Problems of action lead us to problems of character. Hamlet's final "maturity" is a topic often discussed by critics, but the form he assumes presents us, I think, with the work's most "questionable shape." We cannot without discomfort endorse Horatio's hopeful vision of flights of angels singing Hamlet to his rest. "Thy commandment all alone shall live / Within the book and volume of my brain," Hamlet promises the Ghost (1.5.102–3); that one commandment has never been love and the book and volume have proven, despite frantic efforts at self-editing, to be endlessly complex. Self-revision returns with "A man's life's no more than to say 'one'" (5.2.74), but can we accept this as a perception of final unity when it entails the un-

savory casuistry with which Hamlet absolves himself of blame
for the deaths of Laertes' father and sister, disposing of "Hamlet's madness" as a thing of darkness no longer acknowledged
his? Does Hamlet recover moral and psychic order or place
himself in a situation that cuts off possibility, denying the king
of infinite space time to dream by allowing himself only the
"interim," "to say 'one' "—and nearly losing that opportunity
until learning "in thee there is not *half* an hour's life" (5.2.307;
my emphasis)? Has Hamlet, in other words, found a lucidity
beyond human fictions, a fullness transcending consciousness,
or has he merely reified his own desire for a limit to thought?

The play will not let us pluck out the heart of its mystery.
Appeals to Providence subside as quickly as they well up as
Hamlet, in his dying moments, worries not about his eternal
lot but about his earthly reputation and endorses Fortinbras's
claim to the Danish throne. When he deputizes Horatio to "tell
my story," to "report me and my cause aright," he asks not for
the play we have seen but for a rectified account, the tale of a
prince as it *ought* to be told.

Horatio, in his account to Fortinbras, momentarily surprises us. His own "most certain" providentialism fades before
a vision of "woe or wonder" and murderous irony: "So shall
you hear / Of carnal, bloody, and unnatural acts; / Of accidental judgments, casual slaughters; / . . . purposes mistook /
Fall'n on th' inventors' heads" (5.2.372–78). His tale, however,
has its own "cause"; for like the late prince, Horatio knows
how to mount a play within a play: "Give order that these bodies / High on a stage be placed to the view" (369–70). It is one
that Fortinbras is eager to have performed:

> Let us haste to hear it,
> And call the noblest to the audience.
> For me, with sorrow I embrace my fortune;
> I have some rights of memory in this kingdom,
> Which now to claim my vantage doth invite me.
> (5.2.378–95)

Fortinbras and Horatio become collaborators, staging a court drama for the noblest. If we hear in the "sorrow" of Fortinbras's embrace a repetition of Claudius's "weighing delight and dole" (1.2.13), it is because he is a creature who sees in drama an unambiguous technique of perspective and power, vantage and advantage. Horatio has his own motives: "Let this same be presently perform'd, / Even while men's minds are wild, lest more mischance / On plots and errors happen" (5.2.385–87). His *Tragedy of Hamlet, Prince of Denmark* will be a lesser thing than ours because its author could never bear the problematic distance between event and interpretation, the space *Hamlet* inhabits. He must close off all "plots and errors," those "dangerous conjectures in ill-breeding minds" (4.5.15).

Hamlet ends with Fortinbras setting the new play in motion, directing the action and fixing roles: "Let four captains / Bear Hamlet like a soldier to the stage" (one of whom has recently explained to Hamlet the absurdity of the assault on Poland). Fortinbras justifies the probability of his fiction—"he was likely, had he been put on, / To have prov'd most royal"—and even orders the accompaniment, "the soldier's music." He is the militarist as Neoclassicist, demanding decorum and revising the unseemly: "Such a sight as this / Becomes the field, but here shows much amiss." Together with Horatio and his flights of angels, he will rewrite Hamlet into the role of Lord Talbot, the aristocratic hero of *1 Henry VI* who finds substance in martial valor and dies defying "antic death" with a vision of his soul "winged through the lither sky" (4.7.18, 21). Rival constructions will be drowned out by the soldier's music and the rites of war that thunder loudly at the play's last line, Fortinbras's stage direction: "Go, bid the soldiers shoot."

Shakespeare's *Hamlet* is both more fundamental and more sophisticated than the play Horatio and Fortinbras imagine. For it is a "history" play in an ultimate sense, one that reactivates in its audience the mingled awe and anxiety that drove Renaissance minds to pour out the age's fantastic array of competing religious, philosophical, superstitious, scientific, and aesthetic explanations of the world. It draws to a powerful, dramatic resolution but one that, once experienced, opens out again in our minds. The play concludes by making us Hamlet's heirs, ambivalent kings of infinite space.

AFTERWORD

Hamlet disturbs some critics, Francis Fergusson argues in *The Idea of the Theater*, because it seems to lack the "finality of conceptual truth wherein the reason could find its satisfaction and its rest." Fergusson responds to this complaint by advancing a "oneness of analogy," a principle of coherence he traces to the Middle Ages. The play's bewildering complexities, he argues, converge in "analogical relationships" pointing to the "supreme analogue," its "underlying substance."[1] This kind of argument, I think, will always be attractive to literary historians who caution readers not to praise or blame Renaissance texts in terms of modern values. As they properly note, Renaissance metaphysics and aesthetics tended to refer the relativism and strife of worldly activity to a deeper network of correspondences; signaling an originating unity. The implications of this unity are both formal and thematic—even ideological. If we read Renaissance texts correctly, these historians urge, "we end by seeing into the general, the principle, the quiddity. . . . we see it in essence . . . grounded even in *ultimate* reality."[2] Yet Fergusson also admits that much of the power of *Hamlet* derives from the pressure of opposing impulses. By the end of his discussion he wonders if the play does not also represent another aspect of Renaissance culture, one more modern than medieval: "By what process was the clue to the vast system of medieval analogies lost, the thread broken, and the way cleared for the centerless proliferation of modern culture? . . . *Hamlet* can be regarded as a dramatization of the process which led, in the Renaissance, to the modern world and its fragmentary theaters."[3]

Fergusson's ambivalence about *Hamlet* reenacts a continuing, and I think irresolvable, controversy about the Renaissance itself. If one tradition of scholarship finds the "broad and central road" of the period to be one of "orthodox conservatism," another sees the Renaissance as a period of radical transformation—even, perhaps, as the "most psychically disturbed era in European history."[4] One of the goals of this study has been to explore the grounds of such disagreement. Notions of quiddity (or the Quiddity of quiddity), underlying coherence, and architectonic form are indeed crucial for many Renaissance writers, but forms of order, I have been arguing, are often most in evidence when they are most under stress. Though Cusanus and Sidney invoke cosmic harmony and ethical patterning, they also remain preoccupied with the mind's effort to invent—both to find and to create—the forms of order it craves. Such effort inspires a full range of responses. One may revel in claims that the mind is the measure of all things, the coiner of value and the rival of nature, or that poetic eloquence is the starting point for all learning, yet the humanism that sponsors such optimism also offers its dark parody. Is our sense of self-worth, our civilization itself, Erasmus's Folly asks, anything more than a web of human fictions spun from, and sustained by, self-love?[5]

An emblem of such ambiguity is offered by the painting reproduced as the frontispiece of this book, Parmigianino's *Self-Portrait in a Convex Mirror*, perhaps the best-known example of Renaissance fascination with illusionism and curved mirrors. The narcissism is striking: the beautiful, youthful face—"more of angel than of man," thought Vasari—appears in an image that is the first to acknowledge openly the function of mirrors in self-portraiture, Sydney Freedberg notes.[6] The face is set back far enough to avoid being disfigured by the curved surface, yet the image is memorable precisely because of its peripheral distortions: the warped window, the monstrously elongated hand. If, as Freedberg argues, the painting retains its harmony despite its violations of Renaissance ideals, it is partly because of the perfection of its circular shape. Here we see the portrait as microcosm, a globe unto itself, for the painting not only imitates the circular form of the mirror, but is executed upon a wooden hemisphere. And yet the image has always astonished its viewers, from Parmigianino's day to our own, for its eccentricity as well as for its centric shape. Vasari praises its realism, but also calls attention to the artist's "caprice," his indulgence in "*bizarrie.*" The work is at once a powerful illusion and a reveling in illusion—a masterful, ingenious artifact. As John Ashbery writes, "The whole is stable within / Instability, a globe like ours, resting / On a pedestal of vacuum, a ping-pong ball / Secure on its jet of water . . . pure / Affirmation that doesn't affirm anything."[7]

Sidney tells us that the poet "nothing affirms," but he also holds out the promise of something more comprehensive and substantial than the bizarre and the astonishing. Even so, the notable images that he and the later Elizabethans create repeatedly ask us to pause and wonder, as does Parmigianino's, about what it is that we comprehend. Passages that appeal to us as exemplars of the Renaissance world-view prove, upon closer inspection, to be ironically framed, even radically compromised. A homily against disobedience is spoken by a murderous pirate (the lieutenant in *2 Henry VI*); the divine right of kings by a usurper and murderer (Claudius in *Hamlet*); the universal significance of degree, priority, and place by a wily and politic manipulator (Ulysses in *Troilus and Cressida*); a vision of cosmic harmony by a would-be seducer of another man's wife, one who in the classical original finally receives an arrow through his throat for his troubles (Antinous in Sir John Davies's *Orchestra*). My point is not that Renaissance men and women despaired of achieving some kind of truth. "Your If is the only peacemaker. Much virtue in If," Touchstone advises in *As You Like It*. If so, there is a very human truth to be learned from it. Nor did they feel that life on earth was inevitably a tissue of illusion. An aggressive separating of the illusory from the true is one frequent and powerful response. But Shakespeare, for one, understood that such activity could unfold further ironies. I have focused on the early histories; the later histories also make the point, and fairly bluntly at times. Hotspur is impatient with Glendower's self-mythologizing: the earth may have shaken at the Welshman's birth, but it would have done so "if your mother's cat had but kittened." Yet Hotspur himself is one whose "imagination" and absorption in a "world of figures" drive him "beyond the bounds of patience" (*1 Henry IV*). His allies understand his error: one must not depend upon "conjecture, expectation, and surmise," the "great imagination / Proper to madmen." But they, too, will be fooled by the expectation of an old-fashioned honor, which evaporates in no more time than it takes for a pious Machiavel to invoke God and "Christian care" (*2 Henry IV*). The second tetralogy would seem to resolve the cycle with the triumphant Henry V, "the mirror of all Christian kings," but no play reminds its audience more explicitly how much of its own imagination is involved in creating the picture of its desires "within this wooden O" where we "make imaginary puissance" and "entertain conjecture": "Play with your fancies"; "Work, work your thoughts"; "eke out our performance with your mind." Nor is that picture without its disquieting ambiguities,[8] the greatest of which is perhaps the Epilogue's reminder of how quick bright things come to confusion, an anticipation of the violent and paradoxical world of the *Henry VI* plays, with which Shakespeare launched his historical series. If Shakespeare ends his active career with *The Tempest*, it is with the understanding that a play of exquisite analogies must also acknowledge things of darkness. A storm becomes a means to harmony, but a "most majestic vision . . . Harmonious charmingly" may also imply the self-absorbing vanity of art (4.1.41–

139). Indeed, a banquet of "harmony" can make men mad (3.3.18, 88–90); healing and transformation also entail the "rough magic" of manipulation. In the end, the world that has been reconciled is a various place: for the young, it is a brave new world; for the old, a place to meditate the grave. If all are substantially united, it is not only in triumphant homecoming, but also by being "such stuff as dreams are made on."

Our indulgence sets Prospero free, but the longing to distinguish the idols of the mind from authentic truth remains perhaps the sixteenth century's most important legacy to the seventeenth. From Bacon and Hobbes to Herbert and Milton, philosophers, poets, and theologians affirm their allegiances to a genuine order of truth beyond the merely fictive. Yet the enduring preoccupation in the late Renaissance and the Baroque with illusionism itself suggests that affirmation will continue to be energized by an urgent and inescapable awareness of the need both to question and to affirm.

NOTES

INTRODUCTION

1. William J. Bouwsma, "The Renaissance and the Drama of Western History," *American Historical Review* 84 (1979): 1–15, especially pp. 10–14.

2. *The Mind's Road to God*, trans. George Boas (Indianapolis: Bobbs-Merrill, 1953), p. 4. For the intimate relation of vision to meaning, see the discussions of image and metaphor in Bonaventure by Anthony Nemetz, "The *Itinerarium Mentis in Deum*: The Human Condition," and Marigwen Schumacher, "Mysticism in Metaphor," both in *S. Bonaventure, 1274–1974* (Rome: Collegio S. Bonaventura, 1973), 2: 345–59 and 361–86 respectively.

3. The problematic nature of Petrarch's account is stressed in Robert M. Durling, "The Ascent of Mt. Ventoux and the Crisis of Allegory," *Italian Quarterly* 18 (1974): 7–28.

4. Angus Fletcher, *The Transcendental Masque: An Essay on Milton's Comus* (Ithaca: Cornell University Press, 1971), p. 106.

5. Dominick LaCapra, *Rethinking Intellectual History: Texts, Contexts, Language* (Ithaca, N.Y.: Cornell University Press, 1983), pp. 28–29.

6. Johan Huizinga, *Homo Ludens: A Study of the Play Element in Culture* (1950; reprint, Boston: Beacon Press, 1962), p. 180.

7. Ernst Cassirer, *The Individual and the Cosmos in Renaissance Philosophy*, trans. Mario Domandi (New York: Barnes and Noble, 1963); Alexandre Koyré, *From the Closed World to the Infinite Universe* (Baltimore: Johns Hopkins University Press, 1957); Dorothy Koenigsberger, *Renaissance Man and Creative Thinking: A History of Concepts of Harmony, 1400–1700* (Hassocks, England: Harvester Press, 1979).

8. On perspective as a species of fiction making, see Claudio Guillén, "On the Concept and Metaphor of Perspective," in *Comparatists at Work*, ed. S. G. Nichols, Jr., and R. B. Vowles (Waltham, Mass.: Blaisdell, 1968), pp. 29–90; Ernest B. Gilman, *The Curious*

Perspective: Literary and Pictorial Wit in the Seventeenth Century (New Haven: Yale University Press, 1978); and Harry Berger, Jr., "The Renaissance Imagination," *Centennial Review* 9 (1965): 36–78, especially pp. 52–60.

9. John Calvin, *Institutes of the Christian Religion,* ed. J. T. McNeill, trans. F. L. Battles (Philadelphia: Westminster Press, 1960), 1: 64–65 (1.5.12).

INTRODUCTION TO PART ONE

1. "Das Vermächtnis des Nikolaus von Kues: Der Brief an Nikolaus Albergati nebst der Predigt in Montoliveto," ed. Gerda von Bredow, Sitzungsberichte der Heidelberger Akademie der Wissenschaften (Heidelberg: Carl Winter, 1955), p. 46.

2. I have used the Heidelberg edition, *Nicolai de Cusa opera omnia iussu et auctoritate Academiae Litterarum Heidelbergensis ad codicum fidem edita* (Leipzig-Hamburg: Felix Meiner, 1932–), specifically: vol. 1, *De docta ignorantia,* ed. Ernst Hoffman and Raymond Klibansky (Leipzig, 1932); vol. 2, *Apologia doctae ignorantiae,* ed. Raymond Klibansky (Leipzig, 1932); vol. 3, *De coniecturis,* ed. Josef Koch and Karl Bormann (Hamburg, 1972); vol. 4, *Opuscula I (De Deo abscondito, De quaerendo Deum* et al.), ed. Paul Wilpert (Hamburg, 1959); vol. 5, *Idiota de sapientia, De mente, De staticis experimentis,* ed. Ludwig Baur (Leipzig, 1937); vol. 7, *De pace fidei,* ed. Raymond Klibansky and Hildebrand Bascour (Hamburg, 1959); vol. 11, fasc. 1, *De beryllo,* ed. Ludwig Baur (Leipzig, 1940), fasc. 2, *De Possest,* ed. Renata Steiger (Hamburg, 1973), fasc. 3, *Compendium,* ed. Bruno Decker and Karl Bormann (Hamburg, 1964); vol. 12, *De venatione sapientiae* and *De apice theoriae,* ed. Raymond Klibansky and Hans Senger (Hamburg, 1982); vol. 13, *Directio speculantis seu de Non Aliud,* ed. Ludwig Baur and Paul Wilpert (Hamburg, 1950). Where the Heidelberg series was not available, I have used Nikolaus von Kues, *Werke,* ed. Paul Wilpert (Berlin: Walter de Gruyter, 1967). International bibliographies of editions and studies appear in *Mitteilungen und Forschungsbeiträge der Cusanus-Gesellschaft* (Mainz: Matthias-Grünewald-Verlag, 1961–), 1 (1961): 95–126; 3 (1963): 223–37; 6 (1967): 178–202; 10 (1973): 207–34; 15 (1982): 121–47. Translations quoted or consulted are cited in the notes below.

1. LEARNED IGNORANCE

1. Tertullian, *On Prescription against Heretics,* in *The Ante-Nicene Fathers,* ed. Alexander Roberts and James Donaldson (New York:

Charles Scribner's Sons, 1899), 3:246 (*PL* 2, cols. 22–23). For an influential survey of some of the topics covered here, see Etienne Gilson, *Reason and Revelation in the Middle Ages* (New York: Charles Scribner's Sons, 1938).

2. *Ante-Nicene Fathers*, 3: 248.

3. Peter Damian, "The Book of the 'Lord Be With You,' " in *Selected Writings on the Spiritual Life*, trans. Patricia McNulty (London: Faber and Faber, 1959), p. 54.

4. "On the Perfection of Monks," in ibid., p. 85.

5. *Theologia Germanica*, trans. Susanna Winkworth, rev. ed. (New York: Pantheon Books, 1949), pp. 116–17.

6. Ibid., p. 138.

7. *The Cloud of Unknowing and Other Works*, trans. Clifton Wolters (New York: Penguin Books, 1978), pp. 73, 111.

8. Boethius, *The Consolation of Philosophy*, trans. Richard Green (New York: Bobbs-Merrill, 1962), p. 5.

9. Quoted in R. W. Southern, *Medieval Humanism and Other Studies* (Oxford: Basil Blackwell [1970]), pp. 39, 40. See also M.-D. Chenu, *Man, Nature, and Society in the Twelfth Century*, ed. and trans. Jerome Taylor and Lester K. Little (Chicago: University of Chicago Press, 1968), passim.

10. All quotations from Plotinus are from *The Enneads*, trans. Stephen Mackenna, 2nd ed., revised by B. S. Page (London: Faber and Faber, 1962).

11. This tension in Plotinus's thought has been noted in A. H. Armstrong, *An Introduction to Ancient Philosophy* (1947; reprint, Boston: Beacon Press, 1963), p. 192. But see E. R. Dodds, *Pagan and Christian in an Age of Anxiety* (Cambridge: Cambridge University Press, 1965), pp. 24–26, which argues for a chronological development in Plotinus's views.

12. For Augustine on the mind's deforming restlessness, see *De Trinitate* 12.11.16; on the act of doubting, *De civitate Dei* 11.26; on the principle of knowledge, *De Trinitate* 9.6.9.

13. Etienne Gilson, *History of Christian Philosophy in the Middle Ages* (New York: Random House, 1955), p. 77.

14. Epistle 55, in *A Select Library of the Nicene and Post-Nicene Fathers*, 1st ser., ed. Philip Schaff (Buffalo: Christian Literature Co., 1886), 1: 310. See also *De doctrina Christiana* 2.6.7–8 and 3.5.9.

15. See A. H. Armstrong, "St. Augustine and Christian Platonism," in *Augustine: A Collection of Critical Essays*, ed. R. A. Markus (New York: Doubleday, 1972).

16. Saint Augustine, *Confessions*, trans. R. S. Pine-Coffin (1961; reprint, Baltimore: Penguin, 1971), p. 241 (10.35).

17. See Joseph Anthony Mazzeo, "St. Augustine's Rhetoric of Silence," in *Renaissance and Seventeenth-Century Studies* (New York: Columbia University Press, 1964), and Stanley E. Fish, *Self-Consuming Artifacts* (Berkeley and Los Angeles: University of California Press, 1972), pp. 21–43. Cf. Fish's strict reading and Mazzeo's allowance for self-enjoyment, pp. 17–18.

18. *Epistola* 130.15, *PL* 33, col. 505, quoted in F. Edward Cranz, "Saint Augustine and Nicholas of Cusa in the Tradition of Western Christian Thought," *Speculum* 28 (April 1953): 310.

19. I am indebted here to the interpretations of Plato's *Parmenides* by A. E. Taylor, *Plato: The Man and His Work* (1926; reprint, New York: World, 1956), pp. 349–70, and by Francis Cornford, *Plato and Parmenides* (New York: Bobbs-Merrill, n.d.), pp. v–x, and 131–34.

20. For "material figures" and "poetic representations," see *On the Heavenly* [or *Celestial*] *Hierachy* 1.3 and 2.1 respectively, in *The Works of Dionysius the Areopagite*, trans. John Parker (1897–99; reprint, Merrick, N.Y.: Richwood, 1976), 2: 3, 5. On the objective nature of Dionysian symbol, see Chenu, *Man, Nature, and Society*, p. 126. For the career of poetic myths and allegorical fictions in later medieval thought, see Winthrop Wetherbee, *Platonism and Poetry in the Twelfth Century: The Literary Influence of the School of Chartres* (Princeton: Princeton University Press, 1972), chapter 1, and Brian Stock, *Myth and Science in the Twelfth Century: A Study of Bernard Silvester* (Princeton: Princeton University Press, 1972), chapter 1.

21. *Dionysius the Areopagite on the Divine Names and the Mystical Theology*, trans. C. E. Rolt (1920; reprint, New York: Macmillan, 1951), pp. 194, 198.

22. For "superlative" terms, see John the Scot, *Periphyseon: On the Division of Nature*, ed. and trans. Myra L. Uhlfelder (Indianapolis: Bobbs-Merrill, 1976), 1.14, pp. 23–27. For the hydra metaphor, see ibid., 4.7, p. 242. Surveys of Dionysian thought and influence, together with generous references to essential studies, appear in "Denys L'Areopagite," in *Dictionnaire de spiritualité ascétique et mystique* (Paris: Beauesne, 1957), 3: 245–430, and Bernard McGinn, "Pseudo-Dionysius and the Early Cistercians," in *One yet Two: Monastic Tradition East and West*, ed. M. Basil Pennington (Kalamazoo: Cistercian Publications, 1976), pp. 200–241.

23. Bernard's emphasis on self-love is stressed by Southern, *Medieval Humanism*, p. 34. Southern notes the bitterness of the dialectical controversies in "Lanfranc of Bec and Berengar of Tours," in *Studies in Medieval History Presented to Frederick Maurice Powicke*, ed. R. W. Hunt et al. (Oxford: Clarendon Press, 1948), pp. 27–48, and *The Mak-*

ing of the Middle Ages (New Haven: Yale University Press, 1953), p. 195. Bernard's complaint about boundary stones is from *Contra quaedam capitula errorum Abaelardi* (epistola 190), quoted in Josef Pieper, *Scholasticism: Personalities and Problems of Medieval Philosophy*, trans. Richard and Clara Winston (New York: Pantheon Books, 1960), pp. 82–83.

24. Anselm's concern about Nominalism appears in *De incarnatione verbi* 1, and his acceptance of patristic authority in the preface to the *Monologion*. (R. W. Southern notes the importance of obedience for Anselm in *St. Anselm and His Biographer* [Cambridge: Cambridge University Press, 1963], pp. 102ff., but also notes Anselm's very flexible sense of speculative "limits" on pp. 53, 88, and 94.) *Fides quaerens intellectum* was the original title of the *Proslogion*, Anselm writes in the preface to that work (Schmitt, 1: 94); *credo ut intelligam* appears in chapter 1 of the *Proslogion* (Schmitt, 1: 100). Modern disagreement over the precise meaning of these claims is discussed in John McIntyre, *St. Anselm and His Critics* (London: Oliver and Boyd, 1954), pp. 15–38.

25. Citations of *Cur Deus homo* are from *A Scholastic Miscellany: Anselm to Ockham*, ed. and trans. Eugene Fairweather (Philadelphia: Westminster Press, 1956), and page numbers refer to that edition. Whether Anselm genuinely intended his arguments to be effective against unbelievers is a much-debated point. Two views may be mentioned. R. W. Southern suggests that the appeal to an unbeliever, though the unbeliever is "probably imaginary" in the earlier *Proslogion*, is informed in *Cur Deus homo* by a need to answer Jewish criticisms of the doctrine of the Incarnation (*St. Anselm and His Biographer*, pp. 88–91). Paul Vignaux argues, however, that in Anselm's works, and in medieval speculation in general, the unbeliever functions more or less as a dialectical sparring partner (*Philosophy in the Middle Ages*, trans. E. C. Hall [New York: Meridian, 1959], pp. 43–50). The testing of the mind's argumentative agility is a recurrent motif in Anselm's work; the *Monologion*, Anselm tells us, answers the desires of his brethren "that nothing at all in the meditation would be argued on Scriptural authority" (*Anselm of Canterbury*, ed. and trans. Jasper Hopkins and Herbert Richardson [Toronto and New York: Edwin Mellen Press, 1974]), 1: 3.

26. Here Anselm may have in mind Augustine's warning that "when you hear a symbolic exposition given of a passage of Scripture which records events, you should first of all get it clear in your mind that the event recorded took place as it is recorded; otherwise, if you take away the basis of fact, you may find yourselves attempting to

376 · Notes to Pages 14–17

on air" (*sermo* 2.6; quoted by R. L. P. Milburn, *Early Christian Interpretations of History* [London: Adam and Charles Black, 1954], p. 155). Augustine, however, is concerned with the factuality of biblical history underlying symbolic interpretation, Anselm, with the reality, or unreality, of thought itself.

27. Eadmer, *The Life of St. Anselm, Archbishop of Canterbury*, ed. and trans. R. W. Southern (New York: Thomas Nelson and Sons, 1962), pp. 60–61. See also R. W. Southern, *Saint Anselm and His Biographer*, p. 83.

28. Translations of the *Proslogion* are from *Scholastic Miscellany*, ed. and trans. Fairweather.

29. Eadmer, *Life of St. Anselm*, pp. 60–61.

30. Called the "ontological" proof by Kant in his criticism of it, it continues to be defended and attacked by philosophers. For substantial bibliographies, see John H. Hick and Arthur C. McGill, eds., *The Many-Faced Argument: Recent Studies on the Ontological Argument for the Existence of God* (New York: Macmillan, 1967), pp. 357–70, and Jasper Hopkins, *A Companion to the Study of St. Anselm* (Minneapolis: University of Minnesota Press, 1972), pp. 261–65.

31. For the suggestion that this shift exposes a problem in Anselm, see F. Edward Cranz, "Cusanus, Luther, and the Mystical Tradition," in *The Pursuit of Holiness in Late Medieval and Renaissance Religion*, ed. Charles Trinkaus and Heiko A. Oberman (Leiden: E. J. Brill, 1974), p. 95.

32. M. J. Charlesworth, *St. Anselm's "Proslogion" with "A Reply on Behalf of the Fool" by Gaunilo and "The Author's Reply to Gaunilo"* (Oxford: Clarendon Press, 1965), pp. 163, 165.

33. See Southern, *St. Anselm and His Biographer*, p. 65. "Historical studies," Arthur McGill notes, continue to seek "Anselm's unspoken assumption which allows him to see his argument not just as moving within a closed circle of subjective reasoning, but as providing a compelling demonstration of God's real existence" (*The Many-Faced Argument*, pp. 70–71).

34. Albert's attack on anti-intellectualism is quoted in David Knowles, *The Evolution of Medieval Thought* (New York: Random House, 1962), p. 249. His cautious attitude toward "the mental universe of Greco-Arabian learning" as "specifically other than the patristic world of Christian faith," is discussed in Gilson, *History of Christian Philosophy*, pp. 277–79, 668 n. 3.

35. *Summa contra gentiles* 2.38. See Gilson, *Reason and Revelation*, p. 77.

36. A helpful survey of shifting trends in historiography is Wil-

liam J. Courtenay, "Nominalism and Late Medieval Religion," in *The Pursuit of Holiness*, ed. Trinkaus and Oberman, pp. 26–59.

37. Heiko A. Oberman, *The Harvest of Medieval Theology: Gabriel Biel and Late Medieval Nominalism* (Cambridge, Mass.: Harvard University Press, 1963), p. 68.

38. For mysticism as a response to the challenges of late-medieval thought, see Steven Ozment, "Mysticism, Nominalism, and Dissent," in *The Pursuit of Holiness*, ed. Trinkaus and Oberman, especially pp. 80–83, and Cranz, "Cusanus, Luther, and the Mystical Tradition," in ibid., p. 96.

39. Raymond Bernard Blackney, *Meister Eckhart: A Modern Translation* (New York: Harper and Brothers, 1941), p. 169. For emphasis on intellect and knowing in Eckhart, see C. F. Kelley, *Meister Eckhart: On Divine Knowledge* (New Haven: Yale University Press, 1977), Gilson, *History*, pp. 438–42, and Vignaux, *Philosophy in the Middle Ages*, pp. 180–87. Anti-intellectualist implications are discussed by Ozment, "Mysticism, Nominalism, and Dissent," pp. 83–85.

40. Reiner Schürmann, *Meister Eckhart, Mystic and Philosopher: Studies in Phenomenology and Existential Philosophy* (Bloomington: Indiana University Press, 1978), pp. 3–47, 70–74, 166–68.

41. Southern, *Medieval Humanism*, pp. 24–25.

42. Unless otherwise noted, translations of *De docta ignorantia* are from Jasper Hopkins, *Nicholas of Cusa on Learned Ignorance: A Translation and an Appraisal of "De docta ignorantia"* (Minneapolis: Arthur J. Banning Press, 1981), which is more accurate than Germain Heron's translation, *Of Learned Ignorance* (London: Routledge and Kegan Paul, 1954).

43. *Metaphysics* 2.1.

44. Cassirer claims that Cusanus is "the first modern thinker" because "his first step consists in asking not about God, but about the possibility of knowing God" (*The Individual and the Cosmos in Renaissance Philosophy*, trans. Mario Domandi [New York: Barnes and Noble, 1963], p. 10). Jasper Hopkins complains about the vagueness of Cassirer's statement: "The same observation could be aptly made about the first step taken by Moses Maimonides and by Thomas Aquinas" (*A Concise Introduction to the Philosophy of Nicholas of Cusa* [Minneapolis: University of Minnesota Press, 1978], p. 15). From a somewhat different perspective, I argue that Cassirer does indeed establish Cusanus's modernity. Hopkins seems, in part, to agree; see *Nicholas of Cusa on Learned Ignorance*, p. 43.

45. For the interpretive controversy over Cusanus's difficult no-

tion of *contractio*, see Jasper Hopkins's polemical study, *Nicholas of Cusa's Metaphysic of Contraction* (Minneapolis: Arthur J. Banning Press, 1983).

46. See chapter 2.

47. *De ludo globi* 2, discussed in Cassirer, *Individual and Cosmos*, p. 44.

48. Cassirer, *Individual and Cosmos*, p. 41.

49. Nicholas's account of his mission appears in his letter to Cardinal Caesarini, appended to *De docta ignorantia*. This important quest for *coincidentia* was not without historical irony. Not only did the unification prove ultimately to be illusory, but Nicholas's part in the mission had its roots in yet further dissention at home. He went to Greece as part of the minority, pro-papal party, after splitting with the raucous majority at the Council of Basel. See also Aeneas Sylvius's portrait of a shrewd and overzealous Cusanus authorizing his mission with a "false decree," cited in note 59, below.

50. At the end of book 1, Cusanus echoes Dionysius by suggesting a negative approximation: "The negations which remove the more imperfect things from the most Perfect are truer than the others. For example, it is truer that God is not stone than that He is not life or intelligence; and [it is truer that He] is not drunkenness than that He is not virtue" (1.26). Commentators sometimes rely on the notion of an asymptote to picture Cusanus's progress toward an unreachable goal. See, e.g., Maurice de Gandillac, *La Philosophie de Nicolas de Cues* (Paris: Editions Montaigne, 1941), p. 166 n., and Donald F. Duclow, "Pseudo-Dionysius, John Scotus Eriugena, Nicholas of Cusa: An Approach to the Hermeneutic of Divine Names," *International Philosophical Quarterly* 12 (1972): 269–72. But given the premise of an infinite gulf between finite and infinite, such appeals have, at best, a provisional status. The inconsistency inherent in Cusanus's appeals to approximation is also noted by Hopkins, *Concise Introduction*, p. 20; for stronger terms, see D. J. B. Hawkins's introduction to Heron's translation: "Nicholas is now on the edge of an abyss. If the sense in which positive attributes can be assigned to God is exclusively causal and relative to creatures, then we know nothing at all of what God is in himself and even the paradoxical doctrine of the reconciliation of contraries is left without a foundation. This would be genuine agnosticism, but Nicholas stops just in time" (p. xx). Hawkins then cites Cusanus's affirmative theology, but finds it inadequate.

51. In a stimulating essay, Karsten Harries draws analogies to Eckhart to argue that Cusanus allows man to "transcend all perspectival limitations" through a "god-like power" ("The Infinite Sphere:

Comments on the History of a Metaphor," *Journal of the History of Philosophy* 13 [1975]: 7, 11, 15). I am arguing, however, that despite Cusanus's strong attraction to notions of self-transcendence, he continually returns to the perspectival. Cusanus does argue that the merging exercise aids the *intellectus*, which is beyond reason, but the problem remains, as I will argue in the next chapter.

52. For the belief, derived from Pythagoreanism, that mathematics reveals the true structure of Being, see Vincent Foster Hopper, *Medieval Number Symbolism: Its Sources, Meaning and Influence on Thought and Expression* (New York: Columbia University Press, 1938). S. K. Heninger, Jr., *Touches of Sweet Harmony: Pythagorean Cosmology and Renaissance Poetics* (San Marino, Calif.: Huntington Library, 1974), is also an attractive study of the subject. I am here, however, tracing a poetics that is in many ways antithetical to what Heninger calls "Pythagorean poetics." For more specific commentary on Cusanus's attitude, see chapter 2, note 22, below.

53. Hopkins defends Cusanus's "way of doing philosophy," but notes with some displeasure his "implausible" arguments, which compare so unfavorably to the detailed debates and distinctions of his Scholastic predecessors: "He is all too content merely to sketch and to hint. Yet, we his contemporary readers are left with no idea of what he might have been hinting at when at the end of I, 6 he alludes with no small measure of hyperbole, to 'an infinity of similar considerations' which shows clearly that the unqualifiedly Maximum is Absolute Necessity" (*Nicholas of Cusa on Learned Ignorance*, p. 8).

54. I have preferred Heron's less literal translation here. The Latin reads: "Neminem mortalium comprehendere iudicium illud ac eius iudicis sententiam manifestum est, quoniam, cum sit supra omne tempus et motum, non discussione comparativa vel praesumptiva ac prolatione vocali et signis talibus expediur, quae moram et protractionem capiunt" (*Opera omnia*, 1: 149).

55. Johannes Wenck, Cusanus's Scholastic contemporary, attacked *De docta ignorantia* on this point. Cusanus, he charges, "exceedingly dishonors Jesus by universalizing him," because he "destroys the individuality of Christ's humanity" and so "destroys the doctrine of the true humanity of Christ." "How can the humanity of Christ be fully absolute? . . . His humanity was not free from time. Nor was it above time and incorruptible absolutely; for in that case Christ would not have been truly dead. . . . This universalization was fallaciously suggested to him [Cusanus] by his own abstract understanding." Wenck's attack is translated in Jasper Hopkins, *Nicholas of Cusa's Debate with John Wenck: A Translation and an Appraisal of "De ignota*

litteratura" and "Apologia doctae ignorantiae" (Minneapolis: Arthur J. Banning Press, 1981). (For a discussion of Wenck's attack on Cusanus's epistemology, see chapter 2, below.) The problem of Cusanus's Christology was raised in modern times by, among others, T. Whittaker in "Nicholas of Cusa," *Mind* 34 (1925): 436–54, who saw it as a mere appendix with no real relation to the rest of his thought. Cassirer vigorously defended the importance of Christology for Cusanus in *Individual and Cosmos,* pp. 38–40, and a detailed study of Christology appears in Rudolf Haubst, *Die Christologie des Nikolaus von Kues* (Freiburg: Verlag Herder, 1956). One cannot doubt that Cusanus saw himself as an orthodox Christian, but whether or not his Christology integrates his epistemological themes is another matter. H. Lawrence Bond argues that it functions in precisely that way in "Nicholas of Cusa and the Reconstruction of Theology: The Centrality of Christology in the Coincidence of Opposites," in *Contemporary Reflections on the Medieval Christian Tradition: Essays in Honor of Ray C. Petry,* ed. George H. Shriver (Durham: Duke University Press, 1974), pp. 81–94, but there are still demurrers on this point. See, for example, Jasper Hopkins, *Concise Introduction,* pp. 27–28; Lewis White Beck, *Early German Philosophy* (Cambridge, Mass.: Harvard University Press, 1969), p. 70 n. 31, and James E. Beichler, *The Religious Language of Nicholas of Cusa* (Missoula, Mont.: American Academy of Religion and Scholars Press, 1975), pp. 115–28.

56. See Beichler, *Religious Language,* chapter 4, for a lively argument that Cusanus's preoccupation with the language of knowledge and wisdom led to a radical transformation of his religious discussion.

57. Examples are given in Ernst Robert Curtius, *European Literature in the Latin Middle Ages,* trans. Willard R. Trask (New York: Harper and Row, 1963), p. 321. Citation to *De apice theoriae* should be to theorem 5.

58. See Paul E. Sigmund, *Nicholas of Cusa and Medieval Political Thought* (Cambridge, Mass.: Harvard University Press, 1963), and Morimichi Watanabe, *The Political Ideas of Nicholas of Cusa* (Geneva: Librairie Droz, 1963).

59. The "Hercules" remark appears in *De gestis concilii Basiliensis commentariorium libri II,* ed. and trans. D. Hay and W. K. Smith (Oxford: Clarendon Press, 1961), pp. 14–15. Aeneas had been a conciliarist at Basel and his characterization of a "versatile and shrewd" Nicholas sounds more Odyssean than Herculean. Cusanus's late frustration, which Aeneas blames on the former's "pride" and desire to guide "St. Peter's skiff" himself, is in *The Commentaries of Pius II,* trans. F. A. Gragg, Smith College Studies in History, vol. 22 (North-

ampton, Mass.: Dept. of History of Smith College, 1937), pp. 499–502. The anecdote ends with Cusanus making his way home in bitter tears, only to return later, with a "meeker spirit."

60. Cassirer, *Individual and Cosmos*, pp. 60, 1. For a contrast to Cassirer's view of Cusanus as a Renaissance optimist, see Rudolf Stadelmann's dark interpretation of him as the herald of later Renaissance skepticism and pessimism in *Vom Geist des ausgehenden Mittelalters: Studien zur Geschichte der Weltanschauung von Nicolaus Cusanus bis Sebastian Franck* (Halle: Niemeyer, 1929), pp. 39–65. Robert Hoopes attacks *De docta ignorantia* as an instance of "non-rational despair," but does not elaborate (*Right Reason in the English Renaissance* [Cambridge, Mass.: Harvard University Press, 1962], p. 93).

61. For the importance of freedom from intellectual authority, see *Idiota de sapientia*, book 1. The late *Compendium*, chapter 8, portrays man as drawing an intellectual map of the world in a *homo cosmographicus* conceit. Southern's romance claim appears in *The Making of the Middle Ages*, chapter 5. He is, however, less than enthusiastic about the Renaissance quest for variety. Contrasting its "new humanism" to that of the Middle Ages, he writes: "The nobility of man was expressed in his struggle with an unintelligible world rather than in his capacity to know all things" (*Medieval Humanism*, p. 60).

62. For Cassirer on participation, see *Individual and Cosmos*, pp. 22–24. The *universum* quotation is from Thomas P. McTighe, "Nicholas of Cusa's Theory of Science and Its Metaphysical Background," in *Nicolò Cusano agli inizi del mondo moderno*. (Florence: Sansoni, 1970), p. 333.

63. See Harries, "Infinite Sphere," pp. 5–6, and Hopkins, *Concise Introduction*, p. 13. A standard study of the philosophical history of the figure is Dietrich Mahnke, *Unendliche Sphäre und Allmittelpunkt* (Halle: Max Niemeyer Verlag, 1937). Compare also the daring use of the figure by the English Metaphysical poet Thomas Traherne, for whom it becomes a symbol of the endlessly expanding human mind, especially in "My Spirit" (*Centuries, Poems and Thanksgivings*, ed. H. M. Margoliouth [Oxford: Oxford University Press, 1958], 2: 50–56).

2. CONTROVERSY AND THE ART OF CONJECTURE

1. Ernst Cassirer, *The Individual and the Cosmos in Renaissance Philosophy*, trans. Mario Domandi (New York: Barnes and Noble, 1963), p. 19.

2. Paul E. Sigmund, *Nicholas of Cusa and Medieval Political Thought* (Cambridge, Mass.: Harvard University Press, 1963).

3. Vincent Martin, "The Dialectical Process in the Philosophy of Nicholas of Cusa," *Laval théologique et philosophique* 5 (1949): 213–68.

4. D. J. B. Hawkins, *A Sketch of Medieval Philosophy* (London: Sheed and Ward, 1946), p. 148.

5. Wenck's attack has recently been reedited, with a translation, in Jasper Hopkins, *Nicholas of Cusa's Debate with John Wenck: A Translation and an Appraisal of "De ignota litteratura" and "Apologia doctae ignorantiae"* (Minneapolis: Arthur J. Banning Press, 1981). Translations of Wenck and of Cusanus's *Apologia* are from this volume, as are page numbers for Wenck. Still valuable for its introduction is the older edition of E. Vansteenberghe, *Le "De ignota litteratura" de Jean Wenck de Herrenberg contre Nicolas de Cues*, Beiträge zur Geschichte der Philosophie des Mittelalters, vol. 8, no. 6 (Münster: Aschendorff, 1910).

6. See Charles Trinkaus, "Protagoras in the Renaissance: An Exploration," in *Philosophy and Humanism: Renaissance Essays in Honor of Paul Oskar Kristeller*, ed. Edward P. Mahoney (New York: Columbia University Press, 1976), pp. 199–205.

7. *The Basic Works of Aristotle*, ed. Richard McKeon (New York: Random House, 1941), p. 750 n. 54. All quotations from Aristotle are from this edition.

8. St. Thomas Aquinas, *The Disputed Questions on Truth*, trans. Robert W. Mulligan, S.J. (Chicago: Henry Regnery Company, 1952), 1: 50 (q. 1, a. 12).

9. Etienne Gilson, *The Christian Philosophy of St. Thomas Aquinas* (New York: Random House, 1956), p. 30.

10. See, especially, Thomas McTighe, "Nicholas of Cusa's Theory of Science and Its Metaphysical Background," in *Nicolò Cusano agli inizi del mondo moderno* (Florence: Sansoni, 1970), 317–38. F. Edward Cranz, "The Transmutation of Platonism in the Development of Nicolaus Cusanus and of Martin Luther," in ibid., pp. 92–93, notes that Cusanus moves only gradually to a denial of multiple quiddities, but that he does so explicitly in his last work. Jasper Hopkins, by contrast, emphasizes Cusanus's claims that he establishes different quiddities (*Apologia*, p. 33), in, for example, *Nicholas of Cusa On Learned Ignorance: A Translation and An Appraisal of "De docta ignorantia"* (Minneapolis: Arthur J. Banning Press, 1981), pp. 11, 21–24, and study cited in chapter 1, note 45, above. The juxtaposition of the fullness and nothingness of creation may be from Eckhart. See Bernard J. Muller-Thym, *The Establishment of the University of Being in the Doctrine of Meister Eckhart of Hochheim* (New York: Sheed and Ward, 1939), pp. 7–14 and chapter 3.

11. Adolfo P. Carpio, "The Anarchy of Systems and the Theory of Truth," in *Proceedings of the XIth International Congress of Philosophy* (Amsterdam: North-Holland Publishing Co., 1953), 1: 16. For the crucial role of *adaequatio*, see E. Gilson, *The Christian Philosophy of St. Thomas Aquinas*, pp. 230–31.

12. Documents relevant to this controversy are edited by E. Vansteenberghe, in *Autour de la docte ignorance: Une Controverse sur la théologie mystique au XVe siècle*, Beiträge zur Geschichte der Philosophie des Mittelalters, vol. 14, nos. 2–4 (Münster: Aschendorff, 1915). For the attack on "fictiones, ymmaginaciones, putaciones et estimaciones," see p. 213.

13. Letter of 14 September 1453, in ibid., p. 114. The warning about a *visionem fantasticam* appears in a letter of 22 September 1452, ibid., p. 112.

14. Ibid., p. 115. On loving the good *sub ratione boni*, see pp. 111–12.

15. For Cusanus on the copulation of negation and affirmation, see ibid., pp. 114–15. C. E. Rolt argues that the marble statue metaphor is Dionysius's own qualification of radical negation (*Dionysius the Areopagite on the Divine Names and the Mystical Theology* [London: Macmillan, 1951], p. 195 n.1). I cannot agree; the discussion there firmly distinguishes negative and affirmative ways. The metaphor may represent one of Dionysius's "dissimilar similitudes," which call attention to their own inadequacy.

16. See Maurice de Gandillac, *La Philosophie de Nicolas de Cues* (Paris: Editions Montaigne, 1942), p. 207. A similar point about Cusanus's later descriptions of quasi-empirical experiments is made by E. J. Dijksterhuis, *The Mechanization of the World Picture*, trans. C. Dikshoorn (1961; reprint, New York: Oxford University Press, 1969), p. 231.

17. These early thought experiments may be considered "self-consuming artifacts," to borrow Stanley Fish's term. See *Self-Consuming Artifacts: The Experience of Seventeenth-Century Literature* (Berkeley and Los Angeles: University of California Press, 1972). Self-consumption, however, is only one half of Cusanus's dialectical play.

18. Cassirer, *Individual and Cosmos*, p. 177.

19. Hans Vaihinger, *The Philosophy of "As If,"* trans. C. K. Ogden (1924; reprint London: Routledge & Kegan Paul, 1949). For Cusanus's fondness for "as if" constructions, see Hopkins, *Nicholas of Cusa on Learned Ignorance*, p. 179, nn. 44, 47.

20. For the "lambda formula," see *Plato's Cosmology: The Timaeus of Plato*, trans. with a running commentary by Francis Cornford (London, 1937), pp. 66–68. Nicolas LeFevre de la Boderie published

the *figura universi* together with translations of Pico's *Heptaplus* and Francesco Giorgio's *De harmonia mundi* in 1579, and Athanasius Kircher used Cusanus's *figura paradigmatica* superimposed over the *figura universi* in 1650. For reproductions, see S. K. Heninger, Jr., *The Cosmographical Glass: Renaissance Diagrams of the Universe* (San Marino, Calif.: Huntington Library, 1977), pp. 92–97. Cusanus's mathematical experiments were not universally admired in his age, however. Regiomontanus in 1471 calls him "a ridiculous geometer, whose vanity has led him to fill the world with humbug" (quoted in Eugenio Garin, *Portraits from the Quattrocento*, trans. Victor A. and Elizabeth Velen [New York: Harper and Row, 1972], p. 130). De Gandillac criticizes the apparent arbitrariness of the *figura universi* and suggests that Cusanus later lost interest in it (*La Philosophie de Nicolas de Cues*, pp. 322–23).

21. E. R. Dodds notes that in Proclus we find "the assumption that the structure of the cosmos exactly reproduces the structure of Greek logic . . . ontology becomes so manifestly the projected shadow of logic as to present what is almost a *reductio ad absurdam* of rationalism" (Proclus, *The Elements of Theology*, trans. E. R. Dodds, 2nd ed. [Oxford: Clarendon Press, 1963], p. xxv). A. H. Armstrong makes a similar point about Plotinus: "The great levels of being which he recognizes are projections on to the cosmic plane of the stages of human consciousness" (*An Introduction to Ancient Philosophy* [1947; reprint, Boston: Beacon Press, 1968], p. 190).

22. Cusanus's views about number and universal order may be discerned in his comments about the Pythagoreans. In *Idiota de mente*, chapter 6, he compliments their intelligence, but cannot believe they held number to be the principle of things, because it proceeds from our mind (*ex nostra mente procedit*). We enjoy dealing in number as in our own works (*delectabiler multum versamur in numero quasi in nostro proprio opere*). Perhaps they meant by number the image of ineffable divine number, he ventures. In *De beryllo*, he returns to the issue. The *Pythagorici* should realize that mathematicals and numbers are not "substances or principles" of things, but "rational entities of which we are the creators" (*non esse substantias aut principia rerum sensibilium, sed tantum entium rationis, quarum nos sumus conditores*). Some studies that have emphasized this aspect of Cusanus's mathematics include Karl Jaspers, *Anselm and Nicholas of Cusa* (New York: Harcourt Brace Jovanovich, 1974), pp. 63–70; McTighe, "Nicholas of Cusa's Theory of Science," cited in note 10 above; and two articles by Karsten Harries, "Cusanus and the Platonic Idea," *New Scholasticism* 37 (April 1963), especially p. 192, and "The Infinite Sphere: Comments on the

History of a Metaphor," *Journal of the History of Philosophy* 13 (1975), especially p. 15, where Harries observes that mathematical certainty "has its foundation in that man is dealing here only with his own creations."

23. Aquinas discusses the ability to go beyond metaphor in *ST* 1.13.3. George Klubertanz points out that Aquinas also grounds his metaphors in "the same kind of ontological similarities which are directly expressed in analogous predication" (*St. Thomas Aquinas on Analogy* [Chicago: Loyola University Press, 1960], p. 81).

24. Quotations are from Henry Bett, *Nicholas of Cusa* (London: Methuen, 1932), p. 180, and de Gandillac, *La Philosophie de Nicolas de Cues*, p. 169.

25. Nancy S. Struever, "Metaphoric Morals: Ethical Implications of Cusa's Use of Figure," in *Archéologie du signe*, ed. Lucie Brind'Amour and Eugene Vance, Papers in Mediaeval Studies, no. 3 (Toronto: Pontifical Institute of Mediaeval Studies, 1982), pp. 305–34. Quotations are from pp. 310, 309, 313, 314. Wittgenstein is cited on p. 315 n.26. A different kind of study, but one that makes a similar argument about the nonreferentiality of the mind's conjectural world, is Pauline Moffitt Watts, *Nicolaus Cusanus: A Fifteenth-Century Vision of Man*, Studies in the History of Christian Thought, vol. 30 (Leiden: E. J. Brill, 1982), especially chapter 3.

26. N. Struever, "Metaphoric Morals," pp. 317, 311.

27. K. Harries, "The Infinite Sphere," pp. 12–13.

28. For Cusanus's tinkering with the *intellectus*, see de Gandillac, *La Philosophie de Nicolas de Cues*, pp. 198–204, and Jasper Hopkins, *A Concise Introduction to the Philosophy of Nicholas of Cusa* (Minneapolis: University of Minnesota Press, 1978), p. 172, n. 175. For a related suggestion concerning Cusanus's preference for horizontal over vertical conceptions of mental effort, see Phillip Damon, "History and Idea in Renaissance Criticism," in *Literary History and Historical Understanding*, ed. Phillip Damon, Selected Papers from the English Institute (New York: Columbia University Press, 1968), especially pp. 36–37.

29. Eusebio Colomer, *Nikolaus von Kues und Raimund Llull* (Berlin: Walter de Gruyter, 1961).

30. Marshall Clagett, *Nicole Oresme and the Medieval Geometry of Qualities and Motions* (Madison: University of Wisconsin Press, 1968), pp. 12–13, 164–69, 438–39.

31. "The Commentaries on the *Isagoge* of Porphyry," in *Selections from Medieval Philosophers*, ed. and trans. Richard McKeon (New York: Charles Scribner's Sons, 1: 92.

32. "Glosses of Peter Abailard on Porphyry," in ibid., 1:237–38. For much of what follows, see Martin N. Tweedale, "Abailard and Non-Things," *Journal of the History of Philosophy* 5 (October 1967): 329–42, which discusses the different kinds of "non-things" in Abélard's thought and suggests "a dimly felt anxiety as to what we should say exists or does not exist." See also John Boler, "Abailard and the Problem of Universals," in *Journal of the History of Philosophy* 1 (October 1963): 37–51. I am also indebted to the unpublished study of F. Edward Cranz, "New Dimensions of Thought in Anselm and Abélard as against Augustine and Boethius," which the author generously lent me.

33. McKeon, *Selections*, 1: 238. See also Tweedale, pp. 334–35, and Boler, p. 47.

34. Heiko A. Oberman, "Some Notes on the Theology of Nominalism with Attention to Its Relation to the Renaissance," *Harvard Theological Review* 53 (1960): 62.

35. *The Unity of Philosophical Experience* (New York: Charles Scribner's Sons, 1937), pp. 80–81. The specific doctrine that sets off Gilson's attack is God's ability to conserve in us the intuition of a nonexistent. For citations of some articles sparked by Gilson's provocative charges, see Gilson, *History of Christian Philosophy in the Middle Ages* (New York: Random House, 1955), p. 784, n. 7.

36. See Philotheus Boehner, *Collected Articles on Ockham* (New York: St. Bonaventure, 1956), especially "The Realistic Conceptualism of William of Ockham," pp. 156–74. See also Heiko A. Oberman, "The Shape of Late Medieval Thought: The Birthpangs of the Modern Era," and William J. Courtenay, "Nominalism and Late Medieval Religion," in *The Pursuit of Holiness in Late Medieval and Renaissance Religion*, ed. Charles Trinkaus and Heiko A. Oberman (Leiden: E. J. Brill, 1974), pp. 3–25 and 26–59 respectively. Oberman notes that though Nominalism replaces "eternal structures of being" with a deep sense of contingency, "contingency should not be understood to mean unreliable" (p. 13).

37. E. A. Moody, *The Logic of William of Ockham* (London: Sheed and Ward, 1935), p. 303.

38. Gordon Leff, *William of Ockham: The Metamorphosis of Scholastic Discourse* (Manchester: Manchester University Press, 1975), p. 243. This detailed study is in part a "retraction" by Leff, an attempt to clear Ockham of the charges of skepticism and of the excesses of later "Ockhamism": Ockham, Leff writes, sought to safeguard "concepts from the status of merely mental constructs." Nevertheless, Leff makes it clear that the central theme of Ockham's works is "the dis-

crepancy between the conceptual and the ontological," which led Ockham to discard the "assumption of a pre-existing harmony between concepts and reality" (pp. xx–xxi).

39. *Selections*, ed. McKeon, 1:239; *Die Logica "Ingredientibus,"* ed. Bernhard Geyer, Beiträge zur Geschichte der Philosophie des Mittelalters, vol. 21, no. 1 (Münster: Aschendorff, 1919), 20:31–36.

40. *Die Logica "Ingredientibus,"* ed. Geyer, 20:1.

41. William of Ockham, *Philosophical Writings*, ed. and trans. Philotheus Boehner (New York: Bobbs-Merrill, 1964), p. 44.

42. Boehner, *Collected Articles*, p. 146, takes Maurice De Wulf to task for failing to observe Ockham's distinction between *fictum* (a "mental picture" or "thought object") and *figmentum* (an "unreal" "fiction"). Nevertheless, the reality of the *fictum* is problematic for Ockham; see discussion below, and also Boehner, p. 162, n. 10. Compare, too, Abélard's analogous uses of *fictum* and *figmentum* in *Die Logica "Ingredientibus,"* ed. Geyer, pp. 20–21, 315, and Anselm's in *Cur Deus homo*, *PL* 158, cols. 365, 406; Schmitt, 2: 52, 104. For a general discussion, see Leff, *Ockham*, pp. 89–104, 172–74.

43. *Selections*, ed. McKeon, 1:239; Ockham, *Philosophical Writings*, pp. 44–45.

44. *Selections*, ed. McKeon, 1:250. The need to look through figments appears in the context of a similar discussion by Abélard of the mind's ability to fashion imaginary forms, in *Die Logica "Ingredientibus,"* ed. Geyer, pp. 313:35–37 and 315:28–34. I am indebted here to Cranz, "Cusanus, Luther, and the Mystical Tradition," in *The Pursuit of Holiness*, ed. Trinkaus and Oberman, p. 95, and "New Dimensions," cited above in note 32.

45. Ockham, "The Seven *Quodlibeta*," in *Selections*, ed. McKeon, 2:389; see Leff's discussion, *Ockham*, pp. 99–101.

46. This argument is well represented by Hopkins, *Concise Introduction*, pp. 32–36, and *Nicholas of Cusa on Learned Ignorance*, pp. 21–26. Cusanus's Nominalist leanings, however, are suggested by Cranz, "Cusanus, Luther, and the Mystical Tradition," in *The Pursuit of Holiness*, ed. Trinkaus and Oberman, p. 99; by Giovanni Santinello, *Introduzione a Nicolò Cusano* (Bari: Editori Laterza, 1971), p. 80; and by Rudolf Haubst, *Studien zu Nikolaus von Kues und Johannes Wenck*, Beiträge zur Geschichte der Philosophie und Theologie des Mittelalters, vol. 38, no. 1 (Münster: Aschendorff, 1955), p. 134. Cusanus is not often interpreted as a Realist, but see J. N. Hillgarth, *Ramon Lull and Lullism in Fourteenth-Century France* (Oxford: Clarendon Press, 1971), pp. 270–75.

47. Hans-Georg Gadamer admits there is difficulty in determin-

ing "what this natural word is supposed to be," but endorses its "methodological sense" because its promise of harmony in diversity frees us from the "relativistic consequences" of modern thought (*Truth and Method*, trans. William Glen-Doepel [London: Sheed and Ward, 1975], pp. 395–97). I agree with Gadamer's assessment of the term's function, but I would stress that the *vocabulum naturale* reveals a felt need as much as it does an achieved stability.

48. For my translations of *De idiota*, I have consulted *The Idiot in Four Books* (London: William Leake, 1650; reprint, San Francisco: California State Library, 1940); *Unity and Reform: Selected Writings of Nicholas de Cusa*, ed. and trans. John Patrick Dolan (Indiana: University of Notre Dame Press, 1962), pp. 101–27, 241–60 (books 1, 2, and 4); and Nicholas de Cusa, *Idiota de Mente*, trans. Clyde Lee Miller (New York: Abaras Books, 1979) (book 3). I retain the Latin name *idiota* because "layman" may not quite express the paradox of his learned ignorance and "idiot" is perhaps too Dostoevskian. Walter Kaiser, *Praisers of Folly* (Cambridge, Mass.: Harvard University Press, 1963), places him in the tradition of Renaissance wise fools.

49. Nancy S. Struever, *The Language of History in the Renaissance* (Princeton: Princeton University Press, 1970), pp. 45–46.

50. Anton C. Pegis, "Concerning William of Ockham," *Traditio* 2 (1944): 465.

51. Ozment, "Mysticism, Nominalism, and Dissent," in *The Pursuit of Holiness*, ed. Trinkaus and Oberman, pp. 78, 80.

52. Oberman, "Theology of Nominalism," especially pp. 63–69.

3. PROTEUS AND THE VISION OF GOD

1. For relations between the divine *vis entificativa* and the human *vis assimilativa*, see Ernst Cassirer, *The Individual and the Cosmos in Renaissance Philosophy*, trans. Mario Domandi (New York: Barnes and Noble, 1963), pp. 43 and 68, and Clyde Lee Miller's introduction to Nicholas de Cusa, *Idiota de mente* (New York: Abaris Books, 1979), especially pp. 22–23 on the ambiguity of *assimilatio* and a "creative or 'poetic'" view of cognition (p. 22). Robert Durling uses Cusanus's terms in a discussion of Renaissance poetics in *The Figure of the Poet in Renaissance Epic* (Cambridge, Mass.: Harvard University Press, 1965), pp. 131–32. See also chapter 4, notes 11 and 12, and chapter 5, note 7, below. More generally, Pauline Moffitt Watts, *Nicolaus Cusa-*

nus: A Fifteenth-Century Vision of Man (Leiden: E. J. Brill, 1982), argues that there is a progression in Cusanus's thought from estrangement to a positive assertion of the mind's ability to create its "own conjectural universe" (p. 110) and freely to invent a cultural world (p. 206). Erwin Panofsky has written in several places about sixteenth-century attitudes toward artistic creativity; see, e.g., *The Life and Art of Albrecht Durer* (Princeton: Princeton University Press, 1955), pp. 279–82, and "Artist, Scientist, Genius: Notes on the 'Renaissance-Dämmerung,'" in *The Renaissance: Six Essays* (New York: Harper and Row, 1962), especially pp. 167ff.

2. E. J. Dijksterhuis, *The Mechanization of the World Picture*, trans. C. Dikshoorn (1961; reprint, New York: Oxford University Press, 1969), p. 231.

3. This feature of *De idiota* is also discussed in Donald F. Duclow, "Pseudo-Dionysius, John Scotus Eriugena, Nicholas of Cusa: An Approach to the Hermeneutic of the Divine Names," *International Philosophical Quarterly* 12 (June 1972): 260–78.

4. Verbal abundance evokes different responses in Cusanus's later works, according to context. In *De venatione sapientiae* (33), linguistic diversity is the consequence of the imprecision of post-Adamic language, and the quest for highest wisdom requires silence; in *Compendium* (6–8), the fashioning of letters, syllables, and words distinguishes human intelligence from that of animals, and the variety of words manifests the variety of the mind.

5. *Rhetoricorum libri V*, quoted in Nancy Struever, *The Language of History in the Renaissance* (Princeton: Princeton University Press, 1970), p. 58.

6. See Terence Cave, *The Cornucopian Text* (Oxford: Clarendon Press, 1979), pp. 11–12.

7. For Cusanus's reliance upon, and divergence from, Augustine, see F. Edward Cranz's important essay, "Saint Augustine and Nicholas of Cusa in the Tradition of Western Christian Thought," *Speculum* 28 (April 1953): 297–316. Much has been written on Cusanus as a kindred spirit of the humanists. See, especially, Cassirer, *Individual and Cosmos*, passim (though Cassirer's argument for the former's direct influence on the latter is generally rejected). Charles Trinkaus's *In Our Image and Likeness* (Chicago: University of Chicago Press, 1970), concentrates on Italian figures and so mentions Cusanus only in passing, but does note that his "affinity" to Italian humanism is "striking" (1: xvi).

8. See Cassirer, *Individual and Cosmos*, pp. 43–44.

9. Valuable discussions of this issue appear in Thomas Greene,

"The Flexibility of the Self in Renaissance Literature," and A. Bartlett Giamatti, "Proteus Unbound: Some Versions of the Sea God in the Renaissance," in *The Disciplines of Criticism: Essays in Literary Theory, Interpretation, and History*, ed. Peter Demetz et al. (New Haven: Yale University Press, 1968), pp. 241–64 and 437–75, respectively, and in Stephen J. Greenblatt, *Sir Walter Ralegh: The Renaissance Man and His Roles* (New Haven: Yale University Press, 1973).

10. See Erwin Panofsky, *Studies in Iconology: Humanistic Themes in the Art of the Renaissance* (New York: Harper and Row, 1962), pp. 50–51 and note 53. Cassirer gives an optimistic reading of Cusanus's Prometheanism in *Individual and Cosmos*, pp. 94–97. An essential essay on anxiety in the Renaissance, with extensive notes, is William J. Bouwsma, "Anxiety and the Formation of Early Modern Culture," in *After the Reformation: Essays in Honor of J. H. Hexter*, ed. Barbara C. Malament (Philadelphia: University of Pennsylvania Press, 1980), pp. 215–46.

11. Michael Seidlmayer, "Nikolaus von Kues und der Humanismus," in *Humanismus, Mystik und Kunst in der Welt des Mittelalters*, ed. Josef Koch (Leiden: E. J. Brill, 1953), pp. 1–38. Cusanus does, in fact, discuss the endless torment of "knowledge that is ignorance," but insists that this is the fate of those who turn away from infinite wisdom, i.e., the opposite of true *docta ignorantia*. See Watts, *Nicolaus Cusanus*, pp. 82, 128.

12. A similar conclusion is reached by Miller, introduction, *Idiota de mente*, p. 28.

13. Quotations from Nicholas of Cusa, *The Vision of God*, trans. Emma Gurney Salter (London: J. M. Dent and Sons, 1928). For the theatrical nature of *De visione Dei*, I am indebted to Jackson Cope's discussion in *The Theater and the Dream: From Metaphor to Form in Renaissance Drama* (Baltimore: Johns Hopkins University Press, 1973), pp. 15–22. As will be apparent, I interpret Cusanus's drama differently. To anticipate: Cope sees the work moving toward a validation of mental picturing by beginning with man as the painter of an icon of God and ending with God as the painter of man. Cusanus, I argue here, does not resolve the dilemma of human conceptualizing through pictorialism, but rather invents pictorial representations of that dilemma. The description of God as mixing colors is clearly a *humanly* imagined metaphor for God, a conjecture based on the icon itself. A parallel is found in *De docta ignorantia* when Cusanus, alluding to The Wisdom of Solomon 11:21, justifies man as measurer through God's use, in creation, of "arithmetic, geometry, music, and likewise as-

tronomy" (2.13). As Karl Jaspers shrewdly notes: "Cusanus is speaking allegorically, momentarily putting the imitative human mind in the place of the original. . . . Hence mathematical thinking is human thinking. Man, not God, is the mathematician" (*Anselm and Nicholas of Cusa*, trans. Ralph Manheim [New York: Harcourt Brace Jovanovich, 1974], p. 72).

14. This conflation is also noted by Edgar Wind, *Pagan Mysteries in the Renaissance*, rev. ed. (New York: W. W. Norton, 1968), p. 220, n. 11.

15. Jaspers, *Anselm and Nicholas of Cusa*, p. 50.

16. Dorothy Koenigsberger, *Renaissance Man and Creative Thinking: A History of Concepts of Harmony, 1400–1700* (Hassocks, England: Harvester Press, 1979), chapter 3. For further analogies with Alberti, and for Cusanus's aesthetics in general, see Giovanni Santinello, *Il pensiero de Nicolò Cusano nella sua prospettiva estetica* (Padua: Liviana, 1968), and "Nicolò Cusano e Leon Battista Alberti: Pensieri sul bello e sull' arte," in *Nicolò da Cusa: Relazioni tenute al convengo interuniversitario di Bressanone nel 1960* (Florence: Sansoni, 1962); Joan Gadol, *Leon Battista Alberti: Universal Man of the Early Renaissance* (Chicago: University of Chicago Press, 1969); and Kathi Meyer-Baer, "Nicholas of Cusa on the Meaning of Music," *Journal of Aesthetics and Art Criticism* 5 (June 1947): 301–30.

17. Erwin Panofsky, *Renaissance and Renascences in Western Art* (New York: Harper and Row, 1972), p. 123.

18. Cusanus's anticipation of Vico has been noted by Jaspers (*Anselm and Nicholas of Cusa*, p. 108), among others.

19. M. de Gandillac bases the distinction between Cusan *verisimile* and poetic verisimilitude on the former's promise of progressive movement toward truth (*La Philosophie de Nicolas de Cues* [Paris: Editions Montaigne, 1942], p. 168). I have been arguing throughout this section, however, that Cusanus's progression argument is insufficient to prevent the distinction from blurring. See chapter 1, note 50.

20. Eugenio Garin, *Science and the Civic Life in the Italian Renaissance*, trans. Peter Munz (Garden City, N.Y.: Doubleday, Anchor Books, 1969), p. 9.

21. The three Hopkins quotations are from *Nicholas of Cusa on God as Not-Other: A Translation and an Appraisal of De Li Non Aliud* (Minneapolis: University of Minnesota Press, 1979), p. 7; *Nicholas of Cusa on Learned Ignorance: A Translation and an Appraisal of De docta ignorantia* (Minneapolis: Arthur J. Banning Press, 1981), pp. 15–16; and *Not-Other*, p. 21, respectively.

22. John Colet, *Two Treatises on the Hierarchies of Dionysius*, trans. J. H. Lupton (London: Bell and Daldy, 1869), p. 7 (in Latin, p. 169). See chapter 1, n. 20, above.

23. The game leads the dialogue to serious issues: the creativity of the arts, the mind as register of value, etc. The originating context, however, is typically oblique; the game, as Bachelard informed M. de Gandillac, is a mechanical impossibility (*Oeuvres choisies de Nicolas de Cues* [Aubier: Editions Montaigne, n.d.], pp. 515–16, n. 4). Compare the impossible probabilities of *De docta ignorantia*'s thought experiments and the impossible empiricism of *De staticis experimentis*.

24. Hopkins, *A Concise Introduction to the Philosophy of Nicholas of Cusa* (Minneapolis: University of Minnesota Press, 1978), pp. 72–73. The pseudo-Dionysian "dissimilar similitude" contributes to this impression of Metaphysical wit. *Discordia concors* is, of course, Dr. Johnson's phrase for wit in general, and Metaphysical wit in particular, in "Cowley" (*The Lives of the Poets*, ed. G. B. Hill, 3 vols. [Oxford: Clarendon Press, 1905], 1:20). For a discussion of the "gap" between tenor and vehicles, see Earl Miner, *The Metaphysical Mode from Donne to Cowley* (Princeton: Princeton University Press, 1969), chapter 3.

25. Wind, *Pagan Mysteries*, p. 200; Hopkins, *Concise Introduction*, pp. 18, 173, n. 9.

26. Hopkins, *Concise Introduction*, pp. 126–31.

27. De Gandillac, *La Philosophie de Nicolas de Cues*, p. 294, n. 6.

28. Hopkins, *Not-Other*, p. 12. But see also Nancy Struever's defense of what she calls Cusanus's "grammatical fantasies" in "Metaphoric Morals: Ethical Implications of Cusa's Use of Figure," in *Archéologie du signe*, ed. Lucie Brind'Amour and Eugene Vance, Papers in Mediaeval Studies, no. 3 (Toronto: Pontifical Institute of Mediaeval Studies, 1982), pp. 305–34.

29. James Beichler's comment is to the point: "While it is true that the construction *ac si* with pluperfect subjunctive does not denote a situation contrary to fact, as an expression of traditional Christian belief concerning the divine inspiration of the scriptures the statement is not without ambiguity" (*The Religious Language of Nicholas of Cusa* [Missoula, Mont.: American Academy of Religion and Scholars Press, 1975], p. 121.) The art of conjecture often brings pressure to bear on difficult points in orthodoxy; for further questions about Cusan orthodoxy, see Beichler, pp. 196–98, n. 44.

30. Compare Wenck's attack on Cusanus: God demands, he writes, that "we may behold with quietude—to be still." Cusanus's restlessness makes him a "false prophet" who forgets the words of John 10: "Scripture cannot be broken," and Galatians 1, which gives

"scriptural teaching precedence" (Jasper Hopkins, *Nicholas of Cusa's Debate with John Wenck* [Minneapolis: Arthur J. Banning Press, 1981], p. 22).

31. "Epistola Nicolai de Cusa ad Rodericum Trevino," printed with *De auctoritate presendendi in concilio generali,* ed. Gerhard Kellen, Sitzungsberichte der Heidelberger Akademie der Wissenschaften, 1935–1936, no. 3 (Heidelberg: Carl Winter, 1935), pp. 107–10.

32. *Sermo* 180, quoted in Beichler, *Religious Language,* p. 153.

33. Nicholas of Cusa, "Where Is He Who Is Born King of the Jews?" in *Late Medieval Mysticism,* ed. Ray C. Petry, Library of Christian Classics, vol. 8 (Philadelphia: Westminster Press, 1957), p. 390.

34. Quotations from Jaspers, *Anselm and Nicholas of Cusa,* pp. 112, 57, and "Sermon on the Eucharist," in *Late Medieval Mysticism,* p. 385.

35. Beichler, *Religious Language,* p. 152.

36. See Claude J. Peifer, *Monastic Spirituality* (New York: Sheed and Ward, 1966), pp. 293–302, and R. W. Southern, *The Making of the Middle Ages* (New Haven: Yale University Press, 1953), pp. 223–25. Cusanus expresses his wish to live at Tegernsee in his letter to Gaspar Aindorffer of 16 August 1454, in *Autour de la docte ignorance: Une Controverse sur la théologie mystique au XVᵉ siècle,* ed. E. Vansteenberghe, Beiträge zur Geschichte der Philosophie des Mittelalters, vol. 14, nos. 2–4 (Münster: Aschendorff, 1915), p. 139.

37. Edmond Vansteenberghe, *Le Cardinal Nicolas de Cues (1401–1464)* (Paris: Edouard Champion, 1920), p. 275.

38. Cassirer, *Individual and Cosmos,* p. 60; see also p. 38.

39. Nancy Struever, *The Language of History in the Renaissance* (Princeton: Princeton University Press, 1970), p. 90.

INTRODUCTION TO PART TWO

1. Eugenio Garin, *Science and the Civic Life in the Italian Renaissance,* trans. Peter Munz (Garden City, N.Y.: Doubleday, Anchor Books, 1969), p. 9.

2. I have in mind such studies as F. J. Levy, "Sir Philip Sidney Reconsidered," *English Literary Renaissance* 2 (1972): 5–18; Louis Adrian Montrose, "Celebration and Insinuation: Sir Philip Sidney and the Motives of Elizabethan Courtship," *Renaissance Drama,* n.s., 8 (1977): 3–35; Richard McCoy, *Rebellion in Arcadia* (New Brunswick: Rutgers University Press, 1979); and Arthur F. Marotti, " 'Love Is Not Love': Elizabethan Sonnet Sequences and the Social Order," *English Literary History* 49 (1982): 396–428. The Greville quotation is

from *The Life of the Renowned Sir Philip Sidney*, ed. Nowell Smith (Oxford: Clarendon Press, 1907), p. 38, and Sidney's remarks about his vocation are from *An Apology for Poetry*, ed. Geoffrey Shepherd (1965; reprint, London: Thomas Nelson and Sons, 1973), p. 95.

3. Thomas Moffett, *Nobilis; or, A View of the Life and Death of a Sidney*, trans. Virgil B. Heltzel and Hoyt H. Hudson (San Marino, Calif.: Huntington Library, 1940), pp. 6, 70–71; Greville, *Life*, p. 6.

4. *The Prose Works of Sir Philip Sidney*, ed. Albert Feuillerat (Cambridge: Cambridge University Press, 1962), 3:252–53. Bruno's influence on Sidney has been argued by Frances Yates in essays now reprinted in *Lull & Bruno: Collected Essays*, vol. 1 (London: Routledge and Kegan Paul, 1982). Though I do not agree with her readings of Sidney, I think Bruno does have important things to tell us about later English poetry and poetics, especially about the "Metaphysicals." His interpretation of Cusanus develops the Metaphysical potential of the earlier thinker, as I plan to argue elsewhere. See above, chapter 1, n. 63, and chapter 3, n. 24. See also Joseph Anthony Mazzeo, "A Critique of Some Modern Theories of Metaphysical Poetry," *Modern Philology* 50 (1952): 88–96.

5. Joel Spingarn, *Literary Criticism in the Renaissance* (1899; reprint, New York: Harcourt, Brace and World, 1963), p. 164; see also pp. 170–71; Kenneth Myrick, *Sir Philip Sidney as a Literary Craftsman* (1935; reprint, Lincoln: University of Nebraska Press, 1965), p. 216. For a response to Spingarn and Myrick on this point, see Cornell March Dowlin, "Sir Philip Sidney and 'Other Men's Thought,'" *Review of English Studies* 20 (October 1944): 257–71.

6. Quotations in part 2 will be drawn from the following editions: *An Apology for Poetry*, ed. Geoffrey Shepherd (1956; reprint, London: Thomas Nelson and Sons, 1973); *The Poems of Sir Philip Sidney*, ed. William A. Ringler, Jr. (Oxford: Clarendon Press, 1962); *The Countess of Pembroke's Arcadia (The Old Arcadia)*, ed. Jean Robertson (Oxford: Clarendon Press, 1973); *The Prose Works of Sir Philip Sidney*, ed. Albert Feuillerat, vol. 1 (for the *New Arcadia*) (1912; reprint, Cambridge: Cambridge University Press, 1969). In debatable questions of spelling or titles, e.g., Astrophil or Astrophel, *Apology* or *Defence*, I adopt forms used in these editions, but retain variants used in critical studies in quotation.

4. ITALIAN RENAISSANCE CRITICISM

1. Joel Spingarn, *Literary Criticism in the Renaissance* (1899; reprint, New York: Harcourt, Brace and World, 1963), p. 3.

2. Tertullian, *Apology, De spectaculis*, trans. T. R. Glover, Loeb ed. (1931; reprint, London: Heinemann, 1953), pp. 286–87. Tertullian's attack is part of the broader charge of idolatry he leveled against public exhibitions. See Jonas A. Barish, "The Antitheatrical Prejudice," *Critical Quarterly* 8 (Winter 1966): 329–48). For Abélard on allegory, see Winthrop Wetherbee, *Platonism and Poetry in the Twelfth Century* (Princeton: Princeton University Press, 1972), pp. 38–43, and Brian Stock, *Myth and Science in the Twelfth Century* (Princeton: Princeton University Press, 1972), pp. 52–55. Abélard on "pernicious elation" is quoted in Richard McKeon, "Renaissance and Method in Philosophy," in *Studies in the History of Ideas*, vol. 3 (New York: Columbia University Press, 1935), p. 62; Aquinas is quoted in Ernst Robert Curtius, *European Literature in the Latin Middle Ages*, trans. Willard Trask (New York: Harper and Row, 1963), p. 217.

3. For a fuller discussion, and much related material, see Murray Wright Bundy, *The Theory of Imagination in Classical and Medieval Thought*, University of Illinois Studies in Language and Literature, vol. 12, no. 2 (Urbana: University of Illinois Press, 1927).

4. See Baxter Hathaway, *The Age of Criticism: The Late Renaissance in Italy* (1962; reprint, Westport, Conn.: Greenwood Press, 1972), chapter 8. Bundy argues that Plato himself turns in his later dialogues to a more exalted sense of the imagination (*Theory of Imagination*, pp. 19–59).

5. Rosemond Tuve, *Elizabethan and Metaphysical Imagery* (Chicago: University of Chicago Press, 1947), pp. 41–42.

6. Ibid., pp. 224, 213.

7. Paul Oskar Kristeller, *The Philosophy of Marsilio Ficino*, trans. Virginia Conant (1943; reprint, Gloucester, Mass.: Peter Smith, 1964), pp. 44, 57.

8. See Ernst Cassirer, *The Individual and the Cosmos in Renaissance Philosophy*, trans. Mario Domandi (Philadelphia: University of Pennsylvania Press, 1972), pp. 69–72 and 113–14, and Charles Trinkaus, *In Our Image and Likeness: Humanity and Divinity in Italian Humanist Thought* (Chicago: University of Chicago Press, 1970), 2: 477–79.

9. *Platonic Theology* 13.3, trans. Josephine L. Burroughs, *Journal of the History of Ideas* 5 (1944): 233. For general discussion, see André Chastel, *Marsile Ficin et l'art* (Geneva: Librairie Droz, 1954), and Trinkaus, *In Our Image and Likeness*, 2: 482–86.

10. For the poetic heterocosm and its possible origin in Neoplatonism, see M. H. Abrams, *The Mirror and the Lamp: Romantic Theory and the Critical Tradition* (1953; reprint, New York: Norton, 1958), pp. 272–74, and note 12 below. For stimulating discussions concerning heterocosms in Renaissance thought, see Harry Berger, Jr., "The

Ecology of the Mind: The Concept of Period Imagination—An Out-line Sketch," *Centennial Review* 8 (Fall 1964): 409–34, and "The Re-naissance Imagination: Second World and Green World," *Centennial Review* 9 (Winter 1965): 36–78.

11. The Ficino quotation is from *Platonic Theology* 13.3, trans. Burroughs, p. 235; the "great analogy" is the subject of Milton Nahm's *The Artist as Creator* (Baltimore: Johns Hopkins University Press, 1956).

12. Quoted in Nesca A. Robb, *Neoplatonism of the Italian Renais-sance* (London: George Allen and Unwin, 1935), p. 238. E. N. Tiger-stedt credits Landino with originating the notion of the poet as a god-like creator, and argues that Landino was under the influence of Ficino's more general praise of man ("The Poet as Creator: Origins of a Metaphor," *Comparative Literature Studies* 5 (1968): 455–88).

13. Quoted in Kristeller, *Ficino*, p. 58.

14. "Concerning the Sun," in *Renaissance Philosophy*, trans. Ar-thur B. Fallico and Herman Shapiro (New York: Random House, 1967), 1: 122, 125. See also Kristeller, p. 83. Jackson Cope notes that Ficino transfers Cusanus's metaphor for God as an infinite circle to the sun, "in a passage that moves agilely from hypothetical to positive constructions" (*The Theater and the Dream: From Metaphor to Form in Renaissance Drama* [Baltimore: Johns Hopkins University Press, 1973], p. 26).

15. Kristeller, *Ficino*, p. 50. See also pp. 50–52 for qualification.

16. Ibid., pp. 93–94.

17. Quoted in Kristeller, *Ficino*, p. 98. See also the contrast drawn between Cusanus and Ficino by Harry Berger: "Ficino and Pico did not understand the implications of *serio ludere* as well as Cusanus or Plato did. . . . What they failed to appreciate was the potential use-fulness of the poetic as fictional, counterfactual, hypothetical, hetero-cosmic. Properly understood, *serio ludere* protects the mind from slip-ping into magic by keeping it alive to the fact that its symbols are only symbols, its fictions only fictions" ("Pico and Neoplatonist Idealism: Philosophy as Escape," *Centennial Review* 13 [Winter 1969]: 73).

18. Pico della Mirandola, *Heptaplus*, trans. Douglas Carmichael, in *On the Dignity of Man and Other Works* (1940; reprint, New York: Bobbs-Merrill, 1965), pp. 76–77. For a discussion of the metaphysical underpinnings of allegory, see Thomas P. Roche, Jr., *The Kindly Flame* (Princeton: Princeton University Press, 1964), chapter 1. For the further implications of the notion that "poetry should reproduce the order of the universe," see Maren-Sofie Røstvig, "Structure as Prophecy," in *Silent Poetry: Essays in Numerological Analysis*, ed. Ala-

stair Fowler (New York: Barnes and Noble, 1970). I am also indebted to F. Edward Cranz's unpublished paper, "Some Historical Structures of Reading and Allegory," which argues that Renaissance confidence in such schemes are far from stable; Cranz suggests that the dismantling of the hierarchical cosmos by thinkers like Cusanus signals a radical reappraisal of the possibilities of allegory.

19. Kristeller, *Ficino*, p. 308.

20. *The Renaissance Philosophy of Man*, ed. Ernst Cassirer et al. (Chicago: University of Chicago Press, 1948), pp. 207–8.

21. *Platonic Theology* 14.7, quoted in Trinkaus, *In Our Image and Likeness*, 2: 493–94, and Kristeller, *Ficino*, pp. 208–9. Eugenio Garin makes some highly rhetorical, but characteristically penetrating, comments on Ficino's anxiety:

> He donned the garments of a priest and turned toward Plato and Plotinus in order to find someone who might transform into hope the restlessness that troubled him, and to assure him that the meaning we are unable to discover here on earth, the positive certainty of things, is in reality up on high, where it will be revealed to us in the end. Both his Christianity and his Platonism helped him to keep alive at least one comforting doubt: "perhaps things as they appear to us are not true; perhaps, at present, we are asleep." Hence emerged the Ficino who was more sincere and more lively than the one who arranged everything in well-ordered and systematic concepts and substances which he could then place as a screen between himself and his bewilderment. His systematic universe was as fictitious as it was comforting.
>
> (*Science and the Civic Life in the Italian Renaissance*, trans. Peter Munz [Garden City, N.Y.: Doubleday, 1969], p. 4)

22. Erwin Panofsky, *Albrecht Dürer*, 3rd ed. (Princeton: Princeton University Press, 1948), 1: 165. See also Raymond Klibansky, Erwin Panofsky, and Fritz Saxl, *Saturn and Melancholy: Studies in the History of Natural Philosophy, Religion, and Art* (New York: Basic Books, 1964), and Chastel, *Marsile Ficin*, pp. 163–67.

23. Kristeller, *Ficino*, pp. 360–61.

24. There are numerous discussions of the struggle of poetic transcendence against historical and psychological chaos in the Italian Renaissance; see, e.g., Eugenio Donato, "Death and History in Poliziano's *Stanze*," *Modern Language Notes* 80 (January 1965): 27–40;

Robert Durling, *The Figure of the Poet in Renaissance Epic* (Cambridge, Mass.: Harvard University Press, 1965), chapter 6; and David Quint, trans., *The Stanze of Angelo Poliziano* (Amherst: University of Massachusetts Press, 1979), introduction.

25. Quotations are from *Boccaccio on Poetry*, trans. Charles G. Osgood (1930; reprint, New York: Bobbs-Merrill, 1956). Page numbers are cited in the text.

26. Boccaccio is grappling with a sense of cultural distance and difference often associated with Renaissance thought. See, especially, Erwin Panofsky, *Studies in Iconology* (1939; reprint, New York: Harper and Row, 1967), chapter 1. Boccaccio makes surreptitious use of medieval authorities, as Jean Seznec points out (*The Survival of the Pagan Gods* [Princeton: Princeton University Press, 1953], pp. 220–22), but this fact enriches rather than refutes Panofsky's thesis; Boccaccio's fudging exposes his acute consciousness of the problem. For a brilliant discussion of the consequences of early historical perspectivism, see Thomas M. Greene, "Petrarch and the Humanist Hermeneutic," in *Italian Literature: Roots and Branches*, ed. Giose Rimanelli and Kenneth John Atchity (New Haven: Yale University Press, 1976).

27. See Curtius, *European Literature in the Latin Middle Ages*, chapter 12.

28. *De oratore* 2.35. For the popularity of these and other Ciceronian tags, see Hanna H. Gray, "Renaissance Humanism: The Pursuit of Eloquence," *Journal of the History of Ideas* 24 (October–December 1963): 504, n. 19.

29. "Praeterea si exquirat inuentio: reges armare in bella: deducere naualibus: classes emittere: caelum terras & aequora describere: uirgines sertis & floribus insignire: actus hominum p qualitatibus designare: irritare torpentes: desides animare: temerarios retrahere. sontes uincire: & egregios meritis extollere laudibus & huiusmodi plura" (*Genealogiae* [Venice, 1494], reprinted in *The Renaissance and the Gods*, ed. Stephen Orgel [New York: Garland Publishing, 1976], 2: 104ʳ.

30. On the ambiguities of "invention," see Murray Wright Bundy, " 'Invention' and 'Imagination' in the Renaissance," *Journal of English and Germanic Philology* 29 (1930): 535–45, and Baxter Hathaway, *Marvels and Commonplaces: Renaissance Literary Criticism* (New York: Random House, 1968), pp. 56, 121. More generally, see Tuve, *Elizabethan and Metaphysical Imagery*, pp. 309ff.

31. Giuseppe Mazzotta argues that the *Genealogy* in part represents Boccaccio's reaction against the instability of his own fictional world in the *Decameron* ("The *Decameron*: The Marginality of Litera-

ture," *University of Toronto Studies* 42 [Fall 1972]: 64–81). See also Mazzotta, "The *Decameron*: The Literal and the Allegorical," *Italian Quarterly* 18 (Spring 1975): 53–73.

32. Boccaccio tells us in the preface that where the Ancients "fail me" or are "inexplicit," he will set down his own opinions "with perfect freedom of mind" (p. 12), and critics have often noted the broad range of that freedom. Osgood, for example, points to "lucubrations . . . that seem to us irresponsible, yet they gave large room and free play to Boccaccio's poetic imagination" (*Boccaccio on Poetry*, p. xxv).

33. The problem of poetic autonomy is sometimes located as a late Renaissance development, but see John Freccero, "The Fig Tree and the Laurel: Petrarch's Poetics," *Diacritics* 5 (Spring 1975): 34–40. It should be noted here, as well, that allegorical practice in the Renaissance could be far more flexible and open-ended than defensive appeals to ultimate clarity and doctrinal truths might suggest. For valuable discussions, see Rosemond Tuve, *Allegorical Imagery* (Princeton: Princeton University Press, 1966); Paul J. Alpers, *The Poetry of "The Faerie Queene"* (Princeton: Princeton University Press, 1967); Roche, *Kindly Flame*, chapter 1; and Michael Murrin, *The Veil of Allegory* (Chicago: University of Chicago Press, 1969). See also A. C. Hamilton's brief but cogent remarks on the subject in *The Structure of Allegory in "The Fairie Queene"* (Oxford: Clarendon Press, 1961), pp. 15–17.

34. Bernard Weinberg, "Robortello on the *Poetics*," in *Critics and Criticism: Ancient and Modern*, ed. R. S. Crane (Chicago: University of Chicago Press, 1952), pp. 346–47. For the relations between poetics and rhetoric, see Charles Sears Baldwin, *Medieval Rhetoric and Poetic (to 1400)* (New York: Macmillan, 1928); Donald L. Clark, *Rhetoric and Poetry in the Renaissance* (1922; reprint, New York: Russell and Russell, 1963); Bernard Weinberg, *A History of Literary Criticism in the Italian Renaissance* (Chicago: University of Chicago Press, 1961); and Marvin T. Herrick, *The Fusion of Horatian and Aristotelian Criticism, 1531–1555*, Illinois Studies in Language and Literature, vol. 32, no. 1 (Urbana: University of Illinois Press, 1946), especially chapter 4. See also two speculative and suggestive studies by Wesley Trimpi: "The Ancient Hypothesis of Fiction: An Essay on the Origins of Literary Theory," *Traditio* 27 (1971): 1–78, and "The Quality of Fiction: The Rhetorical Transmission of Literary Theory," *Traditio* 30 (1974): 1–118.

35. See Trinkaus, *In Our Image and Likeness*, 2: 712–21, and Murrin, *The Allegorical Epic* (Chicago: University of Chicago Press, 1980), pp. 27–50 and 197–202.

36. The union of eloquence and wisdom remains, of course, an

400 · Notes to Pages 117–19

ideal for the Renaissance, and rhetorical writers sometimes invoke metaphysics and theology to ennoble their art. "The order of God's creatures in themselves is not only admirable and glorious, but eloquent; then he that could apprehend the consequence of things, in their truth, and utter his apprehension as truly were a right orator," John Hoskins says (dedicatory address, *Directions for Speech and Style*, ed. Hoyt H. Hudson [Princeton: Princeton University Press, 1935], p. 2). The ideal, however, was often a distant one. See the following studies of this dilemma: Hanna H. Gray, "Renaissance Humanism: The Pursuit of Eloquence," *Journal of the History of Ideas* 24, no. 4 (1963): 497–514; William J. Bouwsma, *Venice and the Defense of Republican Liberty* (Berkeley and Los Angeles: University of California Press, 1968), chapter 1; Jerrold E. Seigel, *Rhetoric and Philosophy in Renaissance Humanism* (Princeton: Princeton University Press, 1968); and Nancy Struever, *The Language of History in the Renaissance* (Princeton: Princeton University Press, 1970).

37. Quoted in Seigel, *Rhetoric and Philosophy*, pp. 81–82. In addition to the studies cited in note 36, see Donald Kelley, *Foundations of Modern Historical Scholarship* (New York: Columbia University Press, 1970), pp. 31–32. More recently, Lawrence Manley has studied the place of the verbal arts in the "normative crisis of Renaissance thought" and has argued that the English Renaissance "witnessed the gradual displacement of the criterion of natural fitness by the idea that rectitude arises from the often arbitrary and unpredictable character of experience" (*Convention 1500–1750* [Cambridge, Mass.: Harvard University Press, 1980], p. 139).

38. *Institutes* 6.2, quoted in Bundy, *Theory of Imagination*, p. 106.

39. Quoted in Hathaway, *Age of Criticism*, p. 332; see ibid., pp. 331–35, and Robert L. Montgomery, *The Reader's Eye: Studies in Didactic Literary Theory from Dante to Tasso* (Berkeley and Los Angeles: University of California Press, 1979), pp. 107–16.

40. *Ragionamento sopra le cose pertinenti alla poetica*, quoted in Hathaway, *Age of Criticism*, p. 139.

41. See Hathaway, *Age of Criticism*, chapter 9.

42. Quoted in Weinberg, *History of Literary Criticism*, 1: 259. A classical source is Plutarch, "How the Young Man Should Study Poetry," *Moralia*, trans. Frank Cole Babbit (Loeb Classical Library) (New York: G. B. Putnam's Sons, 1927), pp. 71–197. Plutarch begins by discussing the monitoring of youths, and later self-monitoring, when reading poetic fictions; drug metaphors appear on pp. 78–81. For a recent discussion, see Margaret W. Ferguson, *Trials of Desire: Renaissance Defenses of Poetry* (New Haven: Yale University Press,

1983), pp. 148–49. See also Weinberg's discussion of Giacopo Grifoli in *History of Literary Criticism*, 1: 276.

43. See Hathaway, *Age of Criticism*, pp. 404–6 and, more generally, 316, 328, 436. See also Montgomery, *Reader's Eye*, pp. 94–107, especially pp. 100 and 106, and Bundy's introduction to Girolamo Fracastoro, *Naugerius sive de poetica dialogus*, trans. Ruth Kelso (Urbana: University of Illinois Press, 1924), especially pp. 14–15. Tuve minimizes Fracastoro's peculiarities by claiming that his Aristotelianism, "however different its metaphysical implications" from Platonism, still produces universals analogous to the Platonic Ideas (*Elizabethan and Metaphysical Imagery*, pp. 41–42, 56–57).

44. Quoted in Hathaway, *Age of Criticism*, p. 165. On this point, see also ibid., chapter 10, and *Marvels and Commonplaces*, pp. 50, 86.

45. Lionardo Bruni D'Arezzo, "Concerning the Study of Literature," in W. H. Woodward, *Vittorino da Feltre and Other Humanist Educators* (1897; reprint, New York: Bureau of Publications, 1963), p. 132. Weinberg notes a similar view in Robortello: "The impossible or the false . . . because it is incredible, has no place in poetry, no persuasive power, no possible moral effect" ("Robortello," p. 327).

46. See Weinberg, *History of Literary Criticism*, 1: 77, 93, 99–100, 153, 158; 2: 801; and Herrick, *Fusion*, pp. 28ff. For later developments of this controlling of the imagination through *res/verba* distinctions, see A. C. Howell, "*Res et Verba*: Words and Things," *English Literary History* 13 (1946): 131–42, and for parallels in historiography, see Kelley, *Foundations*.

47. Robortello is quoted in Weinberg, "Robortello," p. 325; Beni in Hathaway, *Age of Criticism*, p. 185; Tuve's comment from *Elizabethan and Metaphysical Imagery*, p. 213. For effective lying through paralogisms, see Hathaway, *Marvels and Commonplaces*, pp. 51, 58, 63, 111–12, 135. Tasso reacts strongly against such formulations; for him, the verisimilar can be either true or false, but leans toward the true, and he protests that poetry is "not a deceptive use of appearances, an art like the conjurer's" (*Discourses on the Heroic Poem*, trans. Mariella Cavalchini and Irene Samuel [Oxford: Clarendon Press, 1973], pp. 28–32).

48. For the poet as a second god, see F. M. Padelford, *Select Translations from Scaliger's Poetics* (New York: Holt, 1905), p. 6, and notes 11 and 12 above; for the Virgilian Idea, see H. B. Charlton, *Castelvetro's Theory of Poetry* (Manchester: University of Manchester Press, 1913), p. 153, and Weinberg, *History of Literary Criticism*, 2: 746–48.

49. See Hathaway, *Marvels and Commonplaces*, pp. 109–10.

50.   Selected translations from Cinthio's writings appear in Allan H. Gilbert, *Literary Criticism: Plato to Dryden* (1940; reprint, Detroit: Wayne State University Press, 1962), pp. 242–73; quotation on poetic liberty is from p. 269. For the controversy over Ariosto, and the problem of romance fictionality in general, see: Weinberg, *History of Literary Criticism*, 2: 954–1073; Hathaway, *Marvels and Commonplaces*, passim; Durling, *Figure of the Poet*, chapters 5 and 6; Alban K. Forcione, *Cervantes, Aristotle, and the "Persiles"* (Princeton: Princeton University Press, 1970), pp. 11–87; James Nohrnberg, *The Analogy of "The Faerie Queene"* (Princeton: Princeton University Press, 1976), pp. 5–22; and Patricia Parker, *Inescapable Romance* (Princeton: Princeton University Press, 1979), chapter 1.

51.   Gilbert, *Literary Criticism*, pp. 276, 278, 285.

52.   Unless otherwise indicated, translations of Castelvetro and Mazzoni are drawn from Gilbert, *Literary Criticism*, and translations of Tasso drawn from the Cavalchini and Samuel edition cited above in note 47. Page numbers are cited in the text.

53.   Hathaway, *Age of Criticism*, p. 178.

54.   Quoted in Charlton, *Castelvetro's Theory*, p. 35.

55.   Ibid., pp. 42–43; and Hathaway, *Marvels and Commonplaces*, p. 63.

56.   Quoted in Charlton, *Castelvetro's Theory*, pp. 113–14; see also Gilbert, *Literary Criticism*, pp. 319–20.

57.   Charlton, *Castelvetro's Theory*, p. 115. Buonamici's defense of Aristotle is an important sixteenth-century reaction to Castelvetro's literalness; for discussion see Weinberg, *History of Literary Criticism*, 2:689–99; Hathaway, *Marvels and Commonplaces*, pp. 84–86, and *Age of Criticism*, pp. 55–58. For a brief, but splendid, contrast between Castelvetro's restrictions and the intellectual autonomy of Cusanus and Ficino, see Phillip Damon, "History and Idea in Renaissance Criticism," in *Literary History and Historical Understanding*, Selected Papers from the English Institute (New York, 1967), pp. 33–37.

58.   *Age of Criticism*, p. 118. I am indebted to Hathaway's discussions of Mazzoni throughout.

59.   See my discussion of Abélard and Nominalist *ficta* in chapter 2.

60.   The remark on Mazzoni's cosmos is in *Age of Criticism*, p. 379. Bulgarini on metaphor is quoted in ibid., p. 358; see chapters 27 and 28 for a general discussion of the argument. One might note here that Tuve's view of Renaissance metaphor as "discovered, not conjectured," is asserted by Bulgarini, but is part of a controversy that also represents the opposite view.

61. Hathaway, *Age of Criticism*, pp. 379–81, and *Marvels and Commonplaces*, pp. 70–71.

62. Quoted in *Age of Criticism*, p. 77, and *Marvels and Commonplaces*, p. 94, where Hathaway compares Mazzoni's view to Sidney's *Apology*.

63. Tasso page numbers refer to edition cited in note 47, above.

64. There are many discussions of Tasso's critical and poetic trials. See Eugenio Donadoni, *Torquato Tasso, saggio critico*, 2nd ed. (Florence: La Nuova Italia, 1936), chapter 6; Durling, *Figure of the Poet*, chapter 6; Hathaway, *Age of Criticism*, pp. 153–54, 171–72, 390–96, and Forcione, *Cervantes, Aristotle, and the "Persiles,"* pp. 35–48.

65. For opposing readings of this passage, see Thomas M. Greene, *The Descent from Heaven: A Study in Epic Continuity* (New Haven: Yale University Press, 1963), pp. 214–15, and Annabel M. Patterson, "Tasso and Neoplatonism: The Growth of His Epic Theory," *Studies in the Renaissance* 18 (1971): 131–33. Tasso, according to Greene, lived in a world still seeking the "monolithic unity" of medieval thought, but could only achieve unity by "the papering over of divisions" (p. 202).

66. Letter to Maurizio Cataneo in Torquato Tasso, *Prose*, ed. Ettore Mazzali (Milan: R. Ricciardi, 1959), p. 888, quoted in John Charles Nelson's introduction to Fairfax translation, *Jerusalem Delivered*, trans. Edward Fairfax (New York: G. P. Putnam's Sons, n.d.), p. xviii. Further details of Tasso's madness appear in A. Solerti, *Vita di Torquato Tasso* (Rome: Loescher, 1895); and C. P. Brand, *Torquato Tasso: A Study of the Poet and of His Contribution to English Literature* (Cambridge: Cambridge University Press, 1965), chapters 1 and 8. Relations between Tasso's psychic and poetic instabilities are depicted by Durling, *Figure of the Poet*, pp. 205–10.

67. Damon, "History and Idea," p. 50.

68. Erwin Panofsky, *Idea: A Concept in Art Theory*, trans. Joseph Peake (New York: Harper and Row, 1968), p. 81.

5. SIDNEY'S FEIGNED *APOLOGY*

1. All quotations are from *An Apology for Poetry*, ed. and introd. Geoffrey Shepherd (1956; reprint, London: Thomas Nelson and Sons, 1973). Page numbers are cited in text.

2. Walter Davis, *Idea and Act in Elizabethan Fiction* (Princeton: Princeton University Press, 1969), p. 37. For Sidney as a Renaissance Neoplatonist, see in addition to Davis (chapter 2): F. Michael Krouse, "Plato and Sidney's *Defense of Poesie*," *Comparative Literature* 6 (1954):

138–47; John P. McIntyre, S. J., "Sidney's 'Golden World,' " *Comparative Literature* 14 (1962): 356–65; and William Wimsatt and Cleanth Brooks, *Literary Criticism: A Short History* (New York: Knopf, 1957), p. 174. For a view of Sidney in dialogue with the original Plato, see Irene Samuel, "The Influence of Plato on Sidney's *Defense of Poesie*," *Modern Language Quarterly* 1 (1940): 383–91. Besides the obvious metaphorical difference, Augustinian illumination is different from Platonic inspiration; the former deals with the general nature of cognition, the latter with a special poetic gift. But both fulfill similar functions in Renaissance poetics. The argument for Sidney's Augustinianism usually relies on the evidence of Mornay and Hoskins's hierarchy of inner "words," leading to the divine Logos. See *Apology*, ed. Shepherd, pp. 59, 157–58 n.; *An Apology for Poetry*, ed. and introd. Forrest G. Robinson (Indianapolis: Bobbs-Merrill, 1970), p. 17, n. 63; and Forrest G. Robinson, *The Shape of Things Known: Sidney's Apology in Its Philosophical Tradition* (Cambridge, Mass.: Harvard University Press, 1972), chapter 3.

3. Erwin Panofsky, *Idea: A Concept in Art Theory*, trans. Joseph Peake (New York: Harper and Row, 1968), pp. 91–92.

4. The disenchantment with, or distancing from, arguments for poetic inspiration in the later Renaissance has often been noted. See, for example, Baxter Hathaway on Fracastoro, *The Age of Criticism: The Late Renaissance in Italy* (1962; reprint, Westport, Conn.: Greenwood Press, 1972), pp. 405–6; Robert Durling, *The Figure of the Poet in Renaissance Epic* (Cambridge, Mass.: Harvard University Press, 1965), pp. 199–200, where Tasso's yearning for inspiration and his view of poetry as "rationalistic, autonomous *techné*" are found to be in conflict; and Richard Willis's effort to rationalize inspiration: poets behave "as if . . . roused by the divine breath, they seem to be transported," cited and discussed in J. V. H. Atkins, *English Literary Criticism: The Renascence* (1947; reprint, New York: Barnes and Noble, 1968), pp. 109–10.

5. See A. C. Hamilton, "Sidney's Idea of the 'Right Poet,' " *Comparative Literature* 9 (Winter 1957): 51–59.

6. This silence is part of Sidney's rhetorical strategy. He wants us to be able to say, as does John Buxton, that "Sidney describes the poet as a combination of vates, divinely inspired seer, and poet, or maker" (*Sir Philip Sidney and the English Renaissance* [London: Macmillan, 1954], p. 4). But Sidney is careful to leave us enough evidence to deduce a more precise set of theoretical distinctions.

7. A useful survey of attitudes toward the poet as "maker" appears in S. K. Heninger, *Touches of Sweet Harmony* (San Marino,

Calif.: Huntington Library, 1974), pp. 287–324. Sidney echoes the further analogy of human creativity to the divine, but he is oblique about the matter, compared not only to Cusanus, Ficino, and Scaliger, but also to other English apologists of the verbal arts, who, despite their caution, still invoke the analogy more directly. Thomas Wilson calls the eloquent man "halfe a GOD," in the preface to *The Arte of Rhetorique* (1553), ed. G. H. Mair from the 1560 edition (Oxford: Clarendon Press, 1909); Thomas Lodge alludes with favor to the ancient praise of Homer as *Humanus deus* in his *Defence of Poetry* (1579), in *Elizabethan Critical Essays*, ed. G. Gregory Smith (Oxford: Clarendon Press, 1904), 1:64. Sidney's indirectness cannot be accounted for in terms of religious scruples without also explaining why the pious Wilson did not share the same reluctance when he went halfway to asserting an equivalence. I suspect that Sidney is intrigued by the trope's claims for creativity, but views its ontological complacency with suspicion. Compare also George Puttenham's opening chapter, where after comparing God to a poet, he turns the analogy around, but only with a metaphorical dodge and a lower-case plural: "Poets thus to be conceived . . . be (by maner of speech) as creating gods" (*The Arte of English Poesie*, ed. Gladys Doidge Willcock and Alice Walker [1936; reprint, Cambridge: Cambridge University Press, 1970], p. 4).

8. William G. Crane, *Wit and Rhetoric in the Renaissance* (New York: Columbia University Press, 1937), p. 14. There are, to be sure, religious themes sounded in the passage, from the exhortation to give "right honour to the heavenly Maker" to the mention of "that first accursed fall of Adam." But these references are keyed to rhetorical ends; the emphasis in the *Apology* is on man as the maker of images, not man as the image made. Acknowledgment of the Fall and the infected will does not draw the discussion into the orbit of theology— although diverging claims have been made for it as an indication of Sidney's Calvinism, Thomism, or semi-Pelagianism—so much as it advertises the way poetry can grant an argumentative edge over the "incredulous." If poetic fictions now seem, oddly enough, to assume the function of Anselm's "necessary reasons" in disputing with hypothetical unbelievers, that impression is only momentary. For we soon discover that the passage on the hierarchy of makers, despite multiple echoes of Genesis, is not an explication of faith; still less is it an objective account of the vertical structure of being.

9. A. E. Malloch, "'Architectonic' Knowledge and Sidney's *Apologie*," *English Literary History* 20 (1953): 181–85.

10. See discussion in chapter 4.

11. Ficino, "Five Questions Concerning the Mind," in *Renaissance Philosophy of Man*, ed. Ernst Cassirer et al. (Chicago: University of Chicago Press, 1948), pp. 201–2. For an argument that Sidney's notion of poetic feigning may have been influenced by Ficino, see Cornell March Dowlin, "Sidney's Two Definitions of Poetry," *Modern Language Quarterly* 3 (1942): 579.

12. Sidney appears nonetheless to have been intrigued by geometry as a form of intellectual mastery and self-mastery. Languet admits its usefulness, but is concerned that it will exhaust Sidney's intellect and health. Sidney answers by including geometry as one of the "high and difficult objects" that free him from melancholy (*The Correspondence of Sir Philip Sidney and Hubert Languet*, ed. and trans. Steuart Pears [London: William Pickering, 1845], pp. 28–29). Alastair Fowler's numerological analyses of Sidney's poems are of some interest in this regard, although I do not share his sense of Sidney's Neoplatonic grounding; see Fowler's *Triumphal Forms* (Cambridge: Cambridge University Press, 1970), pp. 174–80, and *Conceitful Thought* (Edinburgh: Edinburgh University Press, 1975), pp. 38–58.

13. Hathaway, *Age of Criticism*, p. 332.

14. Robinson, *The Shape of Things Known*, p. 118.

15. See Murray Wright Bundy, "'Invention' and 'Imagination' in the Renaissance," *Journal of English and Germanic Philology* 29 (1930): 535–45, and Baxter Hathaway, *Marvels and Commonplaces: Renaissance Literary Criticism* (New York: Random House, 1968), pp. 56, 121.

16. William Rossky, "Imagination in the English Renaissance: Psychology and Poetic," *Studies in the Renaissance* 5 (1958): 49–73.

17. *Arte of English Poesie*, p. 19. Compare Puttenham's discussion of figurative speech as abuse and trespass: the "iudges *Areopagites*" forbade figurative speeches as "meere illusions to the minde" (p. 154). But see also the excellent discussion of Puttenham's pluralistic attitude toward rhetoric and illusionism in Lawrence Manley, *Convention: 1500–1750* (Cambridge, Mass.: Harvard University Press, 1980), pp. 176–88.

18. Quoted by Rossky, "Imagination in the English Renaissance," p. 56.

19. Wimsatt and Brooks, *Literary Criticism*, p. 171.

20. For arguments that his radical insistence on the poet's free feigning sets Sidney apart from such Italian sources as Scaliger and Minturno, see Cornell March Dowlin, "Sidney and Other Men's Thought," *Review of English Studies* 20, no. 80 (1944): 257–71, and Hamilton, "Sidney's Idea of the 'Right Poet.'"

21. Bernard Weinberg, *A History of Literary Criticism in the Italian Renaissance* (Chicago: University of Chicago Press, 1961), 1:31. By contrast, Jacob Bronowski has noted that in the *Apology* poetry appears to be straining in two directions at once, toward liberated ideality and a forced application to the concrete (*The Poet's Defence* [Cambridge: Cambridge University Press, 1939], pp. 39–56).

22. A. C. Hamilton, "Sidney and Agrippa," *Review of English Studies* 7, no. 26 (1956): 151–57. Similar claims are made in Hamilton's book on Spenser, cited in note 2.

23. Montaigne, *Essays*, trans. John Florio (London: J. M. Dent and Sons, 1938), 2: 244–45.

24. Kenneth Myrick, *Sir Philip Sidney as a Literary Craftsman* (1935; reprint, Lincoln: University of Nebraska Press, 1965), pp. 53–55.

25. There are several recent discussions of the disjunctions in Sidney's argument, sometimes refining the older question of the relative importance of Aristotelianism and Platonism for the *Apology*. See Michael Murrin, *The Veil of Allegory* (Chicago: University of Chicago Press, 1969), pp. 184–89 for Sidney's witty and unclassifiable conflation of metaphysical and Neoclassical views, and O. B. Hardison, Jr., "The Two Voices of Sidney's *Apology for Poetry*," *English Literary Renaissance* 2 (Winter 1972): 83–99 for a possible shift in attitude by Sidney. "The *Apology* . . . was written in two phases. . . . Before a thorough revision was possible Sidney died (leaving the *Apology*) incompletely harmonized," Hardison writes (p. 98). For Sidney's eclecticism as a conscious rhetorical design, see Virginia Riley Hyman, "Sidney's Definition of Poetry," *Studies in English Literature* 10 (Winter 1970): 49–62, on Sidney as strategically selecting from his tradition; Catherine Barnes, "The Hidden Persuader: The Complex Speaking Voice of Sidney's *Defence of Poetry*," *PMLA* 96 (May 1971): 422–27, for the work's "'poetic' intricacy" (p. 426); and Margaret W. Ferguson, *Trials of Desire: Renaissance Defenses of Poetry* (New Haven: Yale University Press, 1983), chapter 4.

26. See chapter 4, note 46, above. See also Philip's advice to his brother to avoid "Ciceronianisme the cheife abuse of Oxford, *Qui dum verba sectantur, res ipsas negligunt*" (*The Prose Works of Sir Philip Sidney*, ed. Albert Feuillerat [1912; reprint, Cambridge: Cambridge University Press, 1962], 3: 132).

27. Compare Cusanus's liberties in *De coniecturis*, where he sketches out a schematic World Soul and hierarchical cosmos after questioning them in *De docta ignorantia*, discussed in chapter 2.

28. Myrick, *Sidney as Literary Craftsman*, p. 298.
29. *Correspondence of Sidney and Languet*, ed. and trans. Pears, p. 29.
30. Ibid., p. 20.
31. Ibid., p. 23.
32. Some of the discussion concerning this argument's first published version suggests the need for more specific clarification. I am not arguing that Sidney regards morality as ultimately divorced from ontology, or that he denies the final goodness of God's creation, but rather that he regards reliance upon such absolutes to justify human activities such as fiction making to be epistemologically untenable.

6. ASTROPHIL'S POETICS

1. Theodore Spencer, "The Poetry of Sir Philip Sidney," *English Literary History* 12 (1945): 251–78. Quotation on p. 278.
2. C. S. Lewis, *English Literature in the Sixteenth Century* (Oxford: Clarendon Press, 1954), p. 327.
3. David Kalstone, *Sidney's Poetry: Contexts and Interpretations* (Cambridge, Mass.: Harvard University Press, 1965), pp. 106–7. Stella's place in these highly self-conscious sonnets has often been a point of critical concern. Hallett Smith's notion of a "double audience" seems to define *Astrophil and Stella* as a metasequence reflecting on a series of phantom sonnets; the poems Astrophil sends to Stella "are something in the background, a stage property in the drama, as if they existed before the series of *Astrophel and Stella* did" (*Elizabethan Poetry: A Study in Convention, Meaning, and Expression* [Cambridge, Mass.: Harvard University Press, 1952], pp. 148, 145). See also William Ringler, *The Poems of Sir Philip Sidney* (Oxford: Clarendon Press, 1962), p. xliv: "Stella herself is not directly addressed until sonnet 30, and she is only occasionally addressed thereafter. Astrophil is the central figure, everything is presented from his point of view."
4. Neil Rudenstine, *Sidney's Poetic Development* (Cambridge, Mass.: Harvard University Press, 1967), p. 200. For an extreme and disapproving view of the sequence's rhetorical seductions, see Richard Lanham, "*Astrophil and Stella*: Pure and Impure Persuasion," *English Literary Renaissance* 2 (1972): 100–115.
5. The self-critical nature of sonnets is discussed by Rosalie L. Colie in *Shakespeare's Living Art* (Princeton: Princeton University Press, 1974), chapters 1 and 2, especially pp. 50–67. See also John Freccero, "The Fig Tree and the Laurel: Petrarch's Poetics," *Diacritics* 5 (Spring 1975): 34–40.

6. For somewhat varied listings of these "critical sonnets," see Hallett Smith, *Elizabethan Poetry*, p. 143, n. 25, and Ringler, *Poems of Sidney*, p. 458. See also Kalstone, *Sidney's Poetry*, pp. 129–30.

7. For a discussion of this pun in Shakespeare, see William Empson, *Some Versions of Pastoral* (1935; New York: New Directions, 1968), pp. 136–38.

8. For "heart" as referring to "the mind in general," see Ringler, *Poems of Sidney*, p. 459. Critics sometimes feel it is necessary to disabuse modern readers of sentimentality, and so follow Rosemond Tuve's lead in *Elizabethan and Metaphysical Imagery* (Chicago: University of Chicago Press, 1947), p. 39, in emphasizing poetic invention over Spencer's claims in "Poetry of Sidney" for "sincerity" and "honest feeling" (p. 269). The point of the first sonnet's conclusion, I think, is that the Muse refers to *both* loving in truth and feigning in verse; to reject either slackens the poem's generative tension. Invention is, of course, the ultimate issue, for both Astrophil's sincerity and his invention are elements of Sidney's invention.

9. Ringler, *Poems of Sidney*, p. 458.

10. Rosalie Colie comments: "From the *logos* of Stella's name . . . all necessary words can be unfolded. . . . Stella's name, which, since it names her who is infinitely rich, opens out into an infinity of words to express that richness" (*Paradoxia Epidemica: The Renaissance Tradition of Paradox* [Princeton: Princeton University Press, 1966], pp. 192–93).

11. Lewis, *English Literature in the Sixteenth Century*, p. 329.

12. For a discussion of Astrophil in the context of Renaissance individualism, see Jerome Mazzaro, *Transformations in the Renaissance English Lyric* (Ithaca, N.Y.: Cornell University Press, 1970), chapter 3. Mazzaro offers Cusanus as an analogy on pp. 99–100.

13. Kalstone, *Sidney's Poetry*, pp. 130–31, 150; Robert Montgomery, *Symmetry and Sense: The Poetry of Sir Philip Sidney* (Austin: University of Texas Press, 1961), p. 76. See also Montgomery, p. 86: "It is clear enough that *Astrophel and Stella* is a tissue of shifting moods and states of mind, a kaleidoscope of the lover's sensations. What is less clear is the persistence of Astrophel's need to look into himself, to assess the ground he stands on, to question and establish the geography of his emotions." Anne Ferry closely analyzes Astrophil's self-exploration in *The "Inward" Language: Sonnets of Wyatt, Sidney, Shakespeare, Donne* (Chicago: University of Chicago Press, 1983), chapters 3 and 4.

14. Kalstone, *Sidney's Poetry*, pp. 137, 119. G. K. Hunter suggests that "*Astrophil and Stella* . . . is dominated by the brilliance of the

personality it reveals. The opposition . . . is set up between the self-justifying ego and the traditional formulas" ("Drab and Golden Lyrics of the Renaissance," in *Forms of Lyric*, ed. Reuben A. Brower [New York: Columbia University Press, 1970], p. 17). Some critics see less vitality and brilliance in Astrophil; Alan Sinfield, for example, regards the speaker as merely "tricksy" and "evasive" and his resistance to orthodoxy a sign of his moral turpitude ("Astrophil's Self-Deception," *Essays in Criticism* 28 [1978]: 1–18). For further discussion of moral criticisms of Astrophil, see end of chapter 6 and note 27 below.

15. For Astrophil's progressive isolation, see Richard B. Young, "English Petrarke: A Study of Sidney's 'Astrophel and Stella,'" in *Three Studies in the Renaissance: Sidney, Jonson, Milton* (New Haven: Yale University Press, 1958), pp. 46, 50.

16. Contrasting Sidney's approach to the "religious sublimation" of other sonneteers, Ringler justly notes that "Astrophil remains a realist and accepts the power of emotion as an empirical fact that cannot be denied" (*Poems of Sidney*, p. xlvii). The empirical is almost immediately transfigured in Astrophil's imagination, however.

17. Petrarchan lovers are notorious for transforming the world into an image of their love, but Astrophil does so with a particularly ostentatious wit. His comparisons, as J. W. Lever notes, have no "symbolic dimension"; there is little pretense of participation in another reality: "The objects he contemplates must be suffused with his own personality before they can arouse his poetic sympathy" (*The Elizabethan Love Sonnet* [London: Methuen, 1956], p. 85).

18. Thomas Stroup discusses this sonnet as embodying the *Apology*'s primary tenets in "The 'Speaking Picture' Realized: Sidney's 45th Sonnet," *Philological Quarterly* 29 (1950): 440–42.

19. Rosalie Colie discusses Sidney's development of this paradox out of Petrarch, in *Paradoxia Epidemica*, chapter 2.

20. "To the Curteous Reader," in *The Harmonie of the Church* (1591). All Drayton quotations are from *The Works of Michael Drayton*, 5 vols., ed. J. William Hebel, corrected edition (Oxford: Basil Blackwell, 1961). Quotation here, 1: 3.

21. For the Herculean ideal, see O. B. Hardison, Jr., "The Orator and the Poet: The Dilemma of Humanist Literature," *Journal of Medieval and Renaissance Studies* 1 (1971): 33–44.

22. Young, "English Petrarke," p. 77.

23. Ibid., p. 88. This claim has provoked rebuttals from Kalstone, *Sidney's Poetry*, p. 177, and Montgomery, *Symmetry and Sense*, pp. 102–3, 117.

24. For important studies, see Lawrence Babb, *The Elizabethan*

Malady (East Lansing: Michigan State College Press, 1951), and Bridget Gellert Lyons, *Voices of Melancholy* (1971; reprint, New York: W. W. Norton, 1975). For Astrophil as melancholic, see Montgomery, *Symmetry and Sense*, p. 105, n. 10; p. 116, n. 20.

25. The two strains of melancholy are discussed in Raymond Klibansky, Erwin Panofsky, and Fritz Saxl, *Saturn and Melancholy: Studies in the History of Natural Philosophy, Religion, and Art* (New York: Basic Books, 1964).

26. All Greville quotations are from *Poems and Dramas of Fulke Greville, First Lord Brooke*, 2 vols., ed. Geoffrey Bullough (Edinburgh: Oliver and Boyd, 1939).

27. See Montgomery, *Symmetry and Sense*, p. 117: "The resolution of the sequence lies in the irresolution of Astrophel."

28. Karl Murphy, "The 109th and 110th Sonnets of *Astrophel and Stella*," *Philological Quarterly* 34 (1955): 349–52, summarizes the arguments in favor of the addition and concludes against it. The addition is also rejected by Smith, *Elizabethan Poetry*, p. 155, Ringler, *Poetry of Sidney*, p. 423, and Montgomery, *Symmetry and Sense*, p. 188.

29. There are several versions of this argument with varying degrees of moral severity. For some examples, in addition to Sinfield, "Astrophil's Self-Deception," cited in note 14 above, see James J. Scanlon, "Sidney's *Astrophil and Stella*: 'See what it is to Love' Sensually!" *Studies in English Literature* 16 (1976): 65–74; and Andrew D. Weiner, "Structure and Fore Conceit in *Astrophil and Stella*," *Texas Studies in Language and Literature* 16 (Spring 1974): 1–25. More persuasive is Montgomery's discussion in chapter 7 of *Symmetry and Sense*, where the moral psychology of Astrophil's "wilful error" is placed in relation to other poetic concerns. For further contrast, see David Kalstone's eloquent defense of Astrophil's voice: "Sir Philip Sidney," in *English Poetry and Prose, 1540–1674*, ed. Christopher Ricks (London: Barrie and Jenkins, 1970), p. 56, and A. C. Hamilton's suggestion of "contradictory responses" in *Sir Philip Sidney: A Study of His Life and Works* (Cambridge: Cambridge University Press, 1977), pp. 104–6.

INTRODUCTION TO CHAPTERS 7 AND 8: SIDNEY'S TWO *ARCADIAS*

1. William Hazlitt, "Lectures on the Dramatic Literature of the Age of Elizabeth," in *The Complete Works of William Hazlitt*, ed. P. P. Howe (London: J. M. Dent and Sons, 1931), 6: 320–25. The Greville quotation is from *The Life of the Renowned Sir Philip Sidney*, ed. Nowell Smith (Oxford: Clarendon Press, 1907), pp. 15–16.

412 · Notes to Pages 184–87

2. *The Countess of Pembroke's Arcadia* (*The Old Arcadia*), ed. Jean Robertson (Oxford: Clarendon Press, 1973), p. 3.

3. Greville, *Life*, pp. 153–54. For the social motivation of a courtier's *sprezzatura*, see Kenneth Myrick, *Sir Philip Sidney as a Literary Craftsman* (1935; reprint, Lincoln: University of Nebraska Press, 1965), chapter 1. Myrick's general comments in this chapter on the conflict between "abounding energy" and the "distrust of the imagination" in English humanism are valuable.

4. Comparisons of the two versions and their respective merits are numerous. R. W. Zandvoort's *Sidney's Arcadia: A Comparison Between the Two Versions* (Amsterdam: Swets and Zeitlinger, 1929) is still useful for details. For more recent discussion, see Richard A. Lanham, "The Old Arcadia," in *Sidney's Arcadia*, Yale Studies in English, vol. 158 (New Haven: Yale University Press, 1965), chapter 1. Most agree the *New Arcadia* is a heroic poem, for which see Myrick, *Literary Craftsman*, chapters 4 and 5, but the *Old Arcadia* has been called both a romance and a heroic poem. See, e.g., Alan D. Isler, "Heroic Poetry and Sidney's Two *Arcadias*," *PMLA* 83 (1968): 368–79 (but see Myrick, pp. 134ff.). Most suggestive are claims for the work's elusiveness: Lanham, "The Old Arcadia," p. 358, and Stephen J. Greenblatt, "Sidney's Arcadia and the Mixed Mode," *Studies in Philology* 70 (1973): 269–78. Sidney was in Italy in 1574 and Myrick suggests that he may have been aware of the controversy over Ariosto (*Literary Craftsman*, pp. 91–92). Though neither *Arcadia* is an Ariostan romance, both are concerned with the pleasures and perils identified with that genre in Renaissance criticism.

7. THE *OLD ARCADIA*

1. If, as is sometimes suggested, the opening of the *Old Arcadia* represents some kind of "fall," it is not to inaugurate a religious allegory but to remind us that for Sidney only a fallen world is fully accessible to narrative.

2. See E. H. Gombrich, "Icones Symbolicae: The Visual Image in Neo-Platonic Thought," *Journal of the Warburg and Courtauld Institutes* 11 (1943): 163–92. Elizabeth Dipple notes an "ironic subsurface" in the work but argues that the image is "read as a neoplatonic embodiment of beauty for Pyrocles" ("Harmony and Pastoral in the *Old Arcadia*," *English Literary History* 35 [1968]: 317).

3. See Michael Murrin, *The Veil of Allegory* (Chicago: University of Chicago Press, 1969), pp. 184–89, and O. B. Hardison, Jr., "The

Two Voices of Sidney's *Apology for Poetry*," *English Literary Renaissance* 2 (Winter 1972): 83–99.

4. Sidney's curious provoking and evading of moral judgment has often been noted and discussed in terms of his ambivalences, his participation in the rhetorical tradition, and his psychological complexion. See, respectively, Neil Rudenstine, *Sidney's Poetic Development* (Cambridge, Mass.: Harvard University Press, 1967), chapters 1–3; Joel B. Altman, *The Tudor Play of Mind* (Berkeley and Los Angeles: University of California Press, 1978), pp. 97–106; and Richard C. McCoy, *Sir Philip Sidney: Rebellion in Arcadia* (New Brunswick: Rutgers University Press, 1979), passim. It is sometimes pointed out that Philanax's warning to Basilius echoes Sidney's *A Letter to Queen Elizabeth* (text in *Miscellaneous Prose of Sir Philip Sidney*, ed. Katherine Duncan-Jones and Jan Van Dorsten [Oxford: Clarendon Press, 1973], pp. 46–57). See the useful recent comparison in Dorothy Connell, *Sir Philip Sidney: The Maker's Mind* (Oxford: Clarendon Press, 1977), chapter 4. I take this not as the sign of political self-justification, but of Sidney's ability to transmute complex experience into a play of voices. Sidney's handling of Philanax in the final trial scene makes him a very curious defender of the Leicester point of view.

5. David Kalstone, *Sidney's Poetry: Contexts and Interpretations* (Cambridge, Mass.: Harvard University Press, 1965), pp. 88, 85.

6. Philoclea's longing for plainer speech is also evident when Pyrocles first reveals his true identity to her: "Shall I seek far-fetched inventions? Shall I seek to lay colours over my decayed thoughts? Or rather . . . let me keep the true simplicity of my word" (*OA*, p. 121). Sidney will complicate this sentiment when he gives it to Astrophil in *AS*, sonnet 1.

7. Franco Marenco argues that all external eruptions of disorder in the work are reflections of the anarchic desires lurking in the "illusory refuge" of these "highly refined . . . pleasure-seeking aristocrats" in "Double Plot in Sidney's Old *Arcadia*," *Modern Language Review* 64 (1969): 248–63. Marenco's extreme Calvinist reading seems antithetical to Richard A. Lanham's sense of "fun" as expressed in "The Old Arcadia," in *Sidney's Arcadia*, Yale Studies in English, vol. 158 (New Haven: Yale University Press, 1965), but like Lanham, Marenco has a keen eye for the ways in which the protagonists are compromised in the work.

8. See especially Altman, *Tudor Play of Mind*, pp. 93–94 and Lanham, "The Old Arcadia," chapters 3 and 4.

9. Lanham, "The Old Arcadia," emphasizes the element of game playing in many of the debates. Pyrocles' Neoplatonism is a "house

of cards," the debates, a "stylized 'Can-you-top-this?' "; if we take the debates too seriously, "we shall miss all the fun" (pp. 255, 256, 275). Musidorus's rhetoric is analyzed by P. Albert Duhamel, "Sidney's *Arcadia* and Elizabethan Rhetoric," *Studies in Philology* 45 (1948): 134–50. Duhamel demonstrates how Arcadian rhetoric is more closely reasoned than Euphuism. Though one may read this as a mark of intellectual seriousness, I regard it as an indication of the depths the *Old Arcadia* opens up to verbal and intellectual play.

10. For the animal symbolism here, see Marenco, "Double Plot," and Arthur F. Marotti, "Animal Symbolism in *The Faerie Queene*," *Studies in English Literature* 5 (1965): 78–79.

11. Lanham argues that we cannot feel sure we understand the moral orientation of the romance because the narrator will not "stay put" ("Old Arcadia," p. 325). See also Rudenstine, *Sidney's Poetic Development*, pp. 28–34, and A. C. Hamilton, *Sir Philip Sidney: A Study of His Life and Works* (Cambridge: Cambridge University Press, 1977), pp. 37–40.

12. The political meaning—the struggle between aristocracy and tyranny—is nicely laid out by William Ringler in *The Poems of Sir Philip Sidney* (Oxford: Clarendon Press, 1962), pp. 412–15. See also William D. Briggs, "Political Ideas in Sidney's *Arcadia*," *Studies in Philology* 28 (1931): 137–61, and Irving Ribner, "Sir Philip Sidney on Civil Insurrection," *Journal of the History of Ideas* 13 (1952): 152–72, for differing views of Sidney's political sympathies. Equally important, however, is the tale's surface: a beast fable about man's creation as king of animals, first from a spark of heavenly fire and then from a quality drawn from each animal, both virtuous and sinister: "heart," "active might," "secret cruelty," "easy to change." It is a mythic tale of the mind's emergence and estrangement from nature. The theme is further developed in the fourth eclogues with Agelastus's picture of human alienation, drawn from Job 7:14ff.: time and nature are cyclically regenerated, but "mankind is for ay to naught resolved . . . let us all against foul nature cry; / We nature's works to help, she us defaces" (*OA*, p. 347). None of the pastoral elegies sung in this final group of eclogues allows for the consolation of a higher perspective so conspicuous in, for example, Spenser's "November" eclogue or Milton's *Lycidas*.

13. The eclogues' challenges are emphasized in Kalstone, *Sidney's Poetry*, pp. 60–84; Rudenstine, *Sidney's Poetic Development*, pp. 35–41; and McCoy, *Rebellion*, pp. 45–52. For "Ye goat-herd gods," see, especially, William Empson, *Seven Types of Ambiguity* (1930; rev. ed., Norfolk, Conn.: New Directions, 1947), pp. 34–38, and Kalstone,

Sidney's Poetry, pp. 71–84. Elizabeth Dipple, by contrast, sees a "tight moral lesson" evolving in the eclogues that leads us to a Neoplatonic Idea. The Idea, however, proves to be concerned with the loss of the golden age, the "moral end of illustrating . . . chaos and disharmony" ("The Fore Conceit of Sidney's Eclogues," *Literary Monographs* 1 [1967]: 1–47).

14. See, respectively, Elizabeth Dipple, "Harmony and Pastoral in the *Old Arcadia*," *English Literary History* 35 (1968): 309–28, and Walter R. Davis, "A Map of Arcadia: Sidney's Romance in Its Tradition," in *Sidney's Arcadia*, Yale Studies in English, vol. 158 (New Haven: Yale University Press, 1965). Davis's study takes the composite *Arcadia* of 1593 as its text. For brief, but cogent, dismissals of otherworldly emphases, see Nancy Rothwax Lindheim, "Vision, Revision, and the 1593 Text of the *Arcadia*," *English Literary Renaissance* 2 (1972): 136–47, which sees Sidney's sphere of interest as the active life, and Kalstone, *Sidney's Poetry*, which makes a this-worldly argument for the Arcadian poems: Sidney "lingers over, indeed fiercely celebrates, the consequences of this fallen state" (p. 82).

15. For the fictional reconstructions in the trial scene, see Altman, *Tudor Play of Mind*, p. 101.

16. Philanax's abuses of rhetoric are discussed by Lorna Challis, "The Use of Oratory in Sidney's *Arcadia*," *Studies in Philology* 62 (1965): 561–76. The responses of Pyrocles and Musidorus after him are criticized by Lanham, "Old Arcadia," pp. 301–10, and McCoy, *Rebellion*, pp. 125–27.

17. For the importance of "public space" in civic humanism, see Nancy S. Struever, *The Language of History in the Renaissance* (Princeton: Princeton University Press, 1970), pp. 118ff.

18. See Erwin Panofsky's eloquent introduction to *Meaning in the Visual Arts* (Garden City, N.Y.: Doubleday, 1955).

19. A. Bartlett Giamatti discusses Renaissance ambivalence toward the figure of Proteus, which comes to symbolize both man's civilizing genius and his subversive drives ("Proteus Unbound: Some Versions of the Sea God in the Renaissance," in *The Disciplines of Criticism*, ed. Peter Demetz et al. [New Haven: Yale University Press, 1968], pp. 437–75).

20. Davis, "Map of Arcadia," p. 166; Lanham, "Old Arcadia," pp. 315, 234–35.

21. For criticisms of Euarchus's judgment, see D. M. Anderson, "The Trial of the Princes in the *Arcadia*, Book V," *Review of English Studies*, n.s., 8 (1957): 409–12; Clifford Davidson, "Nature and Judgment in the *Old Arcadia*," *Papers on Language and Literature* 6 (1970):

348–65; Jon S. Lawry, *Sidney's Two Arcadias: Pattern and Proceeding* (Ithaca, N.Y.: Cornell University Press, 1972), p. 149; and Stephen J. Greenblatt, "Sidney's *Arcadia* and the Mixed Mode," *Studies in Philology* 70 (1973): 269–78.

22. See, in addition to the studies cited in note 21 above, Kenneth Rowe, *Love and Parental Authority in Sidney's Arcadia*, University of Michigan Contributions in Modern Philology, no. 4 (Ann Arbor, Mich., 1947), which argues that "the *Arcadia* ends with an effect of ethical confusion," and Elizabeth Dipple, "Unjust Justice in the *Old Arcadia*," *Studies in English Literature* 10 (1970): 83–102.

23. Hamilton, *Sir Philip Sidney*, p. 41.

24. A. Bartlett Giamatti, *Play of Double Senses: Spenser's Faerie Queene* (Englewood Cliffs, N.J.: Prentice-Hall, 1975), p. 109.

25. Kalstone, *Sidney's Poetry*, p. 100. See also David Kalstone, "Sir Philip Sidney," in *English Prose and Poetry, 1540–1674*, ed. Christopher Ricks (London: Barrie and Jenkins, 1970), p. 52. There have been numerous claims for the role of Providence in the *Old Arcadia*; two of the more illuminating are Margaret E. Dana, "The Providential Plot of the *Old Arcadia*," *Studies in English Literature* 17 (1977): 39–57, and Myron Turner, "Distance and Astonishment in the *Old Arcadia*: A Study of Sidney's Psychology," *Texas Studies in Language and Literature* 20 (1978): 303–29. According to the latter, the *Old Arcadia* "offers no mediating term between the exuberant potency of the imagination and its fundamental powerlessness to lead the self out of its labyrinth. For the thread of invention which Arcadian consciousness grasps is merely human thought, the thread of its own being, and leads the self back into itself. . . . Salvation must come from without" (pp. 324–25).

26. Elizabeth Dipple, "Metamorphosis in Sidney's *Arcadias*," *Philological Quarterly* 50 (1971): 55.

27. Lawry, *Sidney's Two Arcadias*, pp. 30, 34, 35, 17; Marenco, "Double Plot," pp. 250, 263.

28. Lawry, *Sidney's Two Arcadias*, p. 35.

29. See Ringler, *Poems of Sir Philip Sidney*, pp. xxxvii–xxxviii.

30. I borrow the phrase from Davis, "Map of Arcadia," p. 166.

8. THE *NEW ARCADIA*

1. An ironic view of the princes in this scene is urged by Richard Lanham in "The Old Arcadia," in *Sidney's Arcadia*, Yale Studies in English, vol. 158 (New Haven: Yale University Press, 1965), p. 288;

see also Richard McCoy, *Sir Philip Sidney: Rebellion in Arcadia* (New Brunswick: Rutgers University Press, 1979), pp. 121–24. Nancy Rothwax Lindheim is more sympathetic and argues that the scene's philosophical concerns are with the active life, in "Vision, Revision, and the 1593 Text of the *Arcadia*," *English Literary Renaissance* 2 (1972): 136–47. It is nonetheless significant that the princes try to ground their (compromised) active lives in the fixed and eternal.

2. See Lily B. Campbell, "The Christian Muse," *Huntington Library Bulletin* 8 (1935): 29–70, and Katherine D. Duncan-Jones, "Sidney's Urania," *Review of English Studies* 17 (1966): 123–32. For the overloading of significance, see note 4 below.

3. E. M. W. Tillyard, *The English Epic and Its Background* (1954; reprint, New York: Oxford University Press, 1966), p. 303. Tillyard notes the clash of styles in this scene, which, A. C. Hamilton shows, is reinforced by a juxtaposition of sources, an abrupt shift from Montemayor's pastoralism to the violence of Heliodorus's romance (*Sir Philip Sidney: A Study of His Life and Works* [Cambridge: Cambridge University Press, 1977], pp. 129–31).

4. Duncan-Jones notes: "They praise her with hyperbolical conceits more exaggerated than any even in the most conceitedly erotic passages . . . in the main plot"; "the discrepancies between different levels of presentation appear to be imperfectly reconciled. Venus Urania, whom Ficino describes as begotten of the Angelic Mind, seems altogether too large a conception to be fused with the simple shepherdess" ("Sidney's Urania," pp. 123, 132).

5. Kenneth Myrick, *Sir Philip Sidney as a Literary Craftsman* (1935; reprint, Lincoln: University of Nebraska Press, 1965), p. 188.

6. The general critical emphasis on the didactic seriousness of the *New Arcadia*'s "speaking pictures" may be held in tension with what I take to be an opposite extreme, the irritation of Yvor Winters at Sidney's "joy of purely rhetorical invention." Winters's 1939 essay is on the lyric, but its terms are applicable to Sidney's prose: Sidney's "inventiveness," he complains, "is far in excess" of his "moral intelligence." Together with other late sixteenth-century poets, he is one of the "decadents, in the sense that their ingenuity exceeds their intelligence; they are concerned in some measure with the meaningless fabrication of procedure and only imperfectly with moral perception" ("The 16th Century Lyric in England: A Critical and Historical Reinterpretation," reprinted in *Elizabethan Poetry: Modern Essays in Criticism*, ed. Paul J. Alpers [New York: Oxford University Press, 1967], pp. 105–6).

7. David Kalstone, "Sir Philip Sidney," in *English Poetry and Prose, 1540–1674*, ed. Christopher Ricks (London: Barrie and Jenkins, 1970), p. 49.

8. Jon S. Lawry, *Sidney's Two Arcadias* (Ithaca, N.Y.: Cornell University Press, 1972), p. 187.

9. Tillyard, *English Epic*, p. 309. Tillyard follows John Danby's argument here: "Without Sidney's gravely beautiful handling of Pyrocles' dual nature at this point, the ensuing tangle would be either impossibly ridiculous or obscene" (*Poets on Fortune's Hill: Studies in Sidney, Shakespeare, Beaumont & Fletcher* [1952; reprint, Port Washington, N.Y.: Kennikat Press, 1966], p. 57).

10. For a contrast to Tillyard and Danby, see Mark Rose's claim that Sidney "intended his readers to find Pyrocles' disguise offensive" ("Sidney's Womanish Man," *Review of English Studies*, n.s., 15 [1964]: 354).

11. The tale of Pan and Syrinx appears in *Metamorphoses* 1.2.689ff.

12. The location of the Ladon episode, during a pause in the complicated retrospective narrative of book 2, emphasizes its self-conscious imaging of the narrative flow. Moralized mythology is, of course, a conspicuous feature of Renaissance texts, but Sidney's playfulness is not an isolated or eccentric instance. "The Middle Ages . . . assume a reality in the old myths, an essential truth variously reflected, but truth and reality nevertheless. The Renaissance, with its advance in classical scholarship, knew more and more about mythology, but took it less seriously. With increase of knowledge the conviction of reality declines, at least in artistic use, and the old myths tend to become mere playthings," says Charles Osgood (introduction to *Boccaccio on Poetry* [1930; reprint, New York: Bobbs-Merrill, 1956], p. xxiii). Osgood overstates the case, but he points to a significant tendency in writers such as Sidney.

13. I am citing Golding's 1567 translation, book 8, lines 211–24, from *Shakespeare's Ovid: Being Arthur Golding's Translation of the Metamorphoses*, ed. W. H. D. Rouse (1961; reprint, New York: W. W. Norton, 1966), p. 164.

14. For the serious as well as "decadent" nature of Tudor chivalry, see Arthur B. Ferguson, *The Indian Summer of English Chivalry: Studies in the Decline and Transformation of Chivalric Idealism* (Durham, N.C.: Duke University Press, 1960); see also Frances Yates, "Elizabethan Chivalry: The Romance of the Accession Day Tilts," *Journal of the Warburg and Courtauld Institutes* 20 (1957): 4–25; William Ringler, *The Poems of Sir Philip Sidney* (Oxford: Clarendon Press, 1962), p. 474.

15. The essential study of Sidney's additions, particularly on matters of form, is Myrick's *Sir Philip Sidney as a Literary Craftsman.* For a subtle argument about Sidney's analysis of heroism in the princesses as well as the princes, see Myron Turner, "The Heroic Ideal in Sidney's Revised *Arcadia*," *Studies in English Literature* 10 (1970): 63–82.

16. Walter Davis, "Thematic Unity in the *New Arcadia*," *Studies in Philology* 57 (1960): 129; Hamilton, *Sidney*, p. 152. Hamilton's chapter 5 contains a broad and useful survey of Sidney's didacticism, but he regards it as far more fundamental and efficacious than I do: "No one may enter truly into the work without leaving it a better person" (p. 168).

17. Nancy Rothwax Lindheim, "Sidney's *Arcadia*, Book II: Retrospective Narrative," *Studies in Philology* 65 (1967): 163–64, 166, 168, 170.

18. The passage has been attacked by Samuel Lee Wolff, *The Greek Romances in Elizabethan Prose Fiction* (New York: Columbia University Press, 1912); R. W. Zandvoort, *Sidney's Arcadia: A Comparison Between the Two Versions* (Amsterdam: Swets and Zeitlinger, 1929); and Mario Praz (quoted in Myrick, *Sir Philip Sidney as a Literary Craftsman*, p. 263); it has been defended by Alan D. Isler, "Sidney, Shakespeare, and the 'Slain-Notslain,'" *University of Toronto Quarterly* 37 (1968): 175–85, and Lawry, *Sidney's Two Arcadias*, pp. 241–42. Myrick confesses to initial shock at the passage, but decides (I think against his better instincts) that "Sidney is aristocratic in the best sense" in such scenes (*Sir Philip Sidney as a Literary Craftsman*, pp. 259, 263–64).

19. See Baxter Hathaway, *The Age of Criticism: The Late Renaissance in Italy* (1962; reprint, Westport, Conn.: Greenwood Press, 1972), chapter 9. Lindheim notes that Sidney's "dynamic conception of virtue" is "built upon a static conception of character" ("Retrospective," p. 185).

20. Lawry calls the painter an "anti-Cyrus" who seems to merit his injuries (*Sidney's Two Arcadias*, p. 242), and Kalstone suggests this is a critical defense of "stylized narrative" over the crude "copyist" ("Sir Philip Sidney," p. 46). Sidney distances himself from the painter, but he does not wholly divorce himself from him. He is, I think, consciously figuring forth his frustration by invoking those disturbing moments in classical epics when some version of the poet within the poem gets too close to the savage violence the poem describes. Compare Phemios the singer, spared in the *Odyssey*, book 22; Cretheus, the Muse's comrade, killed by Turnus in the *Aeneid*, book 9; and

Lampetides the singer, killed in Ovid's *Metamorphoses*, book 5. The Virgilian analogue presents the most unsettling instance, for the victim is clearly the poet's self-image:

> amicum Crethea Musis,
> Crethea Musarum comitem, cui carmina semper
> et citharae cordi numerosque intendere nervis;
> semper equos atque *arma virum* pugnasque *canebat*
> (9.774–77; emphasis added)

21. Lawry, *Sidney's Two Arcadias*, p. 250.

22. The vision of time as opportunity is alien to neither *Arcadia*, peopled as they are with scheming lovers as well as villains. Sidney's attribution of it to an atheistic world-view, however, marks his effort to suppress its imaginative appeal. For epic teleology in conflict with the protean multiplicity of *kairos*, see David Quint, "The Figure of Atlante: Ariosto and Boiardo's Poem," *Modern Language Notes* 94 (1979): 77–91.

23. Roger Ascham reports the complaint of Lady Jane Grey: "When I am in presence either of father or mother; whether I speak, keep silence, sit, stand, or go, eat, drink, be merry, or sad, be sewing, playing, dancing, or doing any thing else; I must do it, as it were, in such weight, measure, and number, even so perfectly, as God made the world"; her experience leads her not to the vision of goodness, but rather "I think myself in hell" (*The Scholemaster*, ed. R. J. Schoeck [Ontario: J. M. Dent and Sons, 1966], pp. 38–39).

24. For the debate's philosophical backgrounds, see Lois Whitney, "Concerning the Nature of the *Countess of Pembroke's Arcadia*," *Studies in Philology* 24 (1927): 207–22; Ronald Levinson, "The 'Godlesse Minde' in Sidney's *Arcadia*," *Modern Philology* 29 (1931): 21–26; and D. P. Walker, "Ways of Dealing with Atheists: A Background to Pamela's Refutation of Cecropia," *Bibliothèque d'humanisme et renaissance* 17 (1955): 252–77. Whitney also notes some inaccuracies in Pamela's argument.

25. *Eikonoklastes*, in *Complete Prose Works of John Milton* (New Haven: Yale University Press, 1962), vol. 3, ed. Merritt Hughes, p. 362. Hughes refers to the passage as a "famous literary misjudgment" (p. 362, n. 38) and suggests that Milton's irritation stems from Charles's placing of an invocation of Christ where Pamela had prayed for her earthly lover. Elsewhere Hughes attributes Milton's irritation to Charles's hypocrisy and points to Milton's example of Richard III

mouthing pieties ("New Evidence on the Charge that Milton Forged the Pamela Prayer in the *Eikon Basilike*," *Review of English Studies*, n.s., 3 (1952): 138–40. I suspect that Milton's disapproval also stems from the prayer's unreality; he allows himself to cite Shakespeare's play because "the Poet us'd not much licence in departing from the truth of History" (*Complete Prose Works*, 3: 362); Pamela, however, is overtly fictive, and fictions, however "full of worth and witt," require "good caution."

26. J. Huizinga, *The Waning of the Middle Ages*, trans. F. Hopman (1924; reprint, New York: Doubleday, 1954), p. 80.

27. Danby, *Poets on Fortune's Hill*, pp. 52–53.

28. William R. Elton, *King Lear and the Gods* (San Marino, Calif.: Huntington Library, 1966), p. 59.

29. Fulke Greville, *The Life of the Renowned Sir Philip Sidney*, ed. Nowell Smith (Oxford: Clarendon Press, 1907), pp. 14–15.

30. The major problem facing such speculation is how Sidney could have created a climactic trial scene after having subjected the protagonists to the Captivity Episode. That Sidney has reached an impasse is suggested by Elizabeth Dipple, "The Captivity Episode and the *New Arcadia*," *Journal of English and Germanic Philology* 70 (1971): 424; and Lindheim, "Vision," p. 147.

31. This general assumption is stated most explicitly by Edwin Greenlaw, "The Captivity Episode in Sidney's *Arcadia*," in *The Manly Anniversary Studies in Language and Literature* (Chicago: University of Chicago Press, 1923), pp. 62–63, and by Zandvoort, who argues that Pamela's speech "quivers with a religious fervour which must have come straight from the author's heart" (*Sidney's Arcadia*, p. 162).

32. I am quoting Francis Fergusson's characterization of the *Divine Comedy* in *The Idea of a Theater* (Princeton: Princeton University Press, 1949), p. 4.

33. Myrick, *Sir Philip Sidney as a Literary Craftsman*, p. 169.

INTRODUCTION TO PART THREE

1. Michael Goldman, *Shakespeare and the Energies of Drama* (Princeton: Princeton University Press, 1972), p. 9.

2. An argument for dramatic illusion is made by S. L. Bethell, *Shakespeare and the Popular Dramatic Tradition* (1944; reprint, New York: Staples Press, 1948), p. 20.

3. A similar device is illustrated in C. Walter Hodges, *The Globe Restored* (1953; reprint, New York: Norton, 1968), p. 73. Sidney may

also have learned about the trick from Reginald Scot's *Discoveries of Witchcraft*. See *The Poems of Sir Philip Sidney*, ed. William A. Ringler, Jr. (Oxford: Clarendon Press, 1962), p. 366.

4. Quoted in A. M. Nagler, *A Source Book in Theatrical History* (1952; reprint, New York: Dover, 1959), p. 3.

5. Anne Righter, *Shakespeare and the Idea of the Play* (London: Chatto and Windus, 1962), pp. 83–84. The studies on this topic are numerous; see especially Herbert Weisinger, "*Theatrum Mundi*: Illusion as Reality," in *The Agony and the Triumph* (East Lansing: Michigan State University Press, 1964), and Stephen J. Greenblatt, *Sir Walter Ralegh: The Renaissance Man and His Roles* (New Haven: Yale University Press, 1973), chapter 2.

6. *The Proficience and Advancement of Learning* in *The Works of Francis Bacon*, ed. James Spedding, Robert Ellis, and Douglas Heath (London: Longman et al., 1857–74), 3: 343–44.

7. Ibid., 3: 346.

8. Quotations from plays in part 3 are from the following editions: *Everyman*, in *Chief Pre-Shakespearian Dramas*, ed. J. Q. Adams (Boston: Houghton Mifflin, 1924); *Gammer Gurton's Needle*, in ibid.; *Jack Juggler*, ed. Eunice Lilian Smart and W. W. Greg, Malone Society Reprints (London: Oxford University Press, 1933); *Supposes*, in *Early Plays from the Italian*, ed. R. Warwick Bond (Oxford: Clarendon Press, 1911); *Respublica*, re-edited by W. W. Greg, Early English Text Society (London: Oxford University Press, 1952); *Magnificence*, ed. Paula Neuss, Revels Plays (Baltimore: Johns Hopkins University Press, 1980); *King Johan*, ed. Barry B. Adams (San Marino, Calif.: Huntington Library, 1969); *Gorboduc*, ed. Irby B. Cauthen, Jr., Regents Renaissance Drama (Lincoln: University of Nebraska Press, 1970); *Cambises*, in *Chief Pre-Shakespearian Dramas*, ed. J. Q. Adams; *The True Tragedy of Richard the Third*, ed. W. W. Greg, Malone Society Reprints (London: Oxford University Press, 1929); *The Spanish Tragedy*, ed. Philip Edwards, Revels Plays (London: Methuen, 1959); *Doctor Faustus*, ed. John D. Jump, Revels Plays (Cambridge, Mass.: Harvard University Press, 1962); *The First Part of King Henry VI*, ed. A. S. Cairncross (London: Methuen, 1962); *The Second Part of King Henry VI*, ed. A. S. Cairncross (London: Methuen, 1962); *The Third Part of King Henry VI*, ed. A. S. Cairncross (London: Methuen, 1964); *King Richard III*, ed. Antony Hammond (London: Methuen, 1981); *King Richard II*, ed. Peter Ure (London: Methuen, 1956); *Hamlet*, in *Shakespeare: The Complete Works*, ed. Peter Alexander (1951; reprint, London: Collins, 1970).

9. PLAY AND EARNEST

1. Jonas Barish, "The Antitheatrical Prejudice," *Critical Quarterly* 8 (1966): 331. For a fuller development of Barish's argument, see his *The Antitheatrical Prejudice* (Berkeley and Los Angeles: University of California Press, 1981).

2. On conflict between the Church and a "mimetic instinct," see E. K. Chambers, *The Mediaeval Stage* (1903; reprint, London: Oxford University Press, 1967). O. B. Hardison, *Christian Rite and Christian Drama in the Middle Ages* (Baltimore: Johns Hopkins University Press, 1965), argues on the contrary that what we think of as impersonation and mimesis are an outgrowth of the liturgy's own dramatic nature. Chambers notes the connection (2: 3ff.), but Hardison objects to his terms of opposition (pp. 15ff.).

3. Text in Karl Young, *The Drama of the Mediaeval Church* (Oxford: Clarendon Press, 1933), 1: 249–50.

4. V. A. Kolve, *The Play Called Corpus Christi* (Stanford: Stanford University Press, 1966), p. 32; see also chapter 1 passim.

5. See Glynne Wickham, *Early English Stages, 1300–1600* (New York: Columbia University Press, 1959–81), 3: 32–34, 175–76, 182–85; Jonas Barish, *The Antitheatrical Prejudice*, chapter 3; and the pages in E. K. Chambers, Karl Young, G. R. Owst, and Rosemary Woolf cited in ibid., p. 66, n. 1.

6. The tradition of "privative evil" is traced by Charlotte Spivack in *The Comedy of Evil on Shakespeare's Stage* (London: Associated University Presses, 1978).

7. Bernard Spivack, *Shakespeare and the Allegory of Evil* (New York: Columbia University Press, 1958), p. 123. See, however, the cautionary words of Spivack, ibid., p. 193, and Kolve, *Corpus Christi*, pp. 134ff., and the appraisal of Robert Potter, *The English Morality Play* (London: Routledge and Kegan Paul, 1975), pp. 34–36.

8. My characterization of the Vice is indebted to Spivack, *Shakespeare and the Allegory of Evil*. For the Vice as playwright, see ibid., pp. 150, 192; Northrop Frye, *Anatomy of Criticism* (Princeton: Princeton University Press, 1957), pp. 173–74, 216; and Michael Goldman, *The Actor's Freedom* (New York: Viking Press, 1975), pp. 44–45. See also Anne Righter, *Shakespeare and the Idea of the Play* (London: Chatto and Windus, 1962), pp. 68ff.; L. W. Cushman, *The Devil and the Vice in the English Dramatic Literature before Shakespeare* (Halle: N. Niemeyer, 1910); and Francis Hugh Mares, "The Origin of the Figure Called 'the Vice' in Tudor Drama," *Huntington Library Quarterly* 22 (1959): 11–29.

I borrow the expression "projection of a fear" from A. P. Rossiter's preface to *Woodstock: A Moral History* (London: Chatto and Windus, 1946), p. 15.

9. C. F. Tucker Brooke, *The Tudor Drama* (Boston: Houghton Mifflin, 1911), p. 163. On Diccon, see also Spivack, *Shakespeare and the Allegory of Evil*, pp. 323–27, and Joel B. Altman, *The Tudor Play of Mind* (Berkeley and Los Angeles: University of California Press, 1978), pp. 155–57.

10. See G. E. Duckworth, *The Nature of Roman Comedy* (Princeton: Princeton University Press, 1952), pp. 140–41, 315–16, and Harry Levin, "Two Comedies of Errors," in *Refractions* (New York: Oxford University Press, 1966), pp. 128–50.

11. Altman, *Tudor Play of Mind*, pp. 119, 146, 160–61, 164. For discussion of limited human games subsumed within a larger divine game in medieval drama, see also Kolve, *Corpus Christi*, chapter 8.

12. The victim's master dismisses the bizarre tale of his servant, but Plautus's original makes it clear that he is next in line for the same trick. For "dark" readings of *Jack Juggler*, see K. Marienstras, "*Jack Juggler*: Aspects de la conscience individuelle dans une farce du 16e siècle," *Etudes anglaises* 16 (1963): 321–30, and Jackson Cope, *The Theater and the Dream: From Metaphor to Form in Renaissance Drama* (Baltimore: Johns Hopkins University Press, 1973), which sees Jenkin as the victim of an "existential theft" and the play as a "metaphoric vehicle for a tenor which may be defined as theological, epistemological, or ontological" (pp. 108–11). David Bevington argues, however, that the epilogue was a late addition, transforming "modest courtly hedonism" into a Protestant polemic against "Catholic thought control" (*Tudor Drama and Politics* [Cambridge, Mass.: Harvard University Press, 1968], pp. 125–26).

13. Irving Ribner, *The English History Play in the Age of Shakespeare* (1957; rev. ed. London: Methuen, 1965), p. 22.

14. Wickham, *Early English Stages*, vol. 2, pt. 1, p. 327. More generally, see chapters 3 and 4. For further documents see E. K. Chambers, *The Elizabethan Stage* (Oxford: Clarendon Press, 1923), vol. 4, appendix D. The final mastery of courtly control over unruly theatrics itself becomes part of court symbolism. See Stephen Orgel's discussions of the antimasque and rational order in *The Jonsonian Masque* (Cambridge, Mass.: Harvard University Press, 1965), pp. 35, 118–19, 131–39, 158–69; *Ben Jonson: The Complete Masques* (New Haven: Yale University Press, 1969), pp. 13–15, 26–35; and *The Illusion of Power* (Berkeley and Los Angeles: University of California Press,

1975), chapter 2. The social significance of Tudor control is explored in Louis Adrian Montrose, "The Purpose of Playing: Reflections on a Shakespearean Anthropology," *Helios*, n.s., 7 (1980): 51–74.

15. Quotations from Richard Hooker, *Of the Laws of Ecclesiastical Polity* (1907; reprint, London: J. M. Dent, 1969).

16. Quoted in Peter Munz, *The Place of Hooker in the History of Thought* (London: Routledge and Kegan Paul, 1952), p. 30. I am indebted here to Munz's discussion.

17. For the development of court display up to Elizabeth, see Sydney Anglo, *Spectacle, Pageantry, and Early Tudor Policy* (Oxford: Clarendon Press, 1969), and for later developments, see Roy Strong, *The Cult of Elizabeth: Elizabethan Portraiture and Pageantry* (London: Thames and Hudson, 1977). The theatrical dimension is powerfully discussed in Stephen Greenblatt, *Renaissance Self-Fashioning: From More to Shakespeare* (Chicago: University of Chicago Press, 1980), pp. 28ff., 161ff.

18. Though the curve is unambiguous, the specific ground it traces is not. For two different views about the play's political and didactic interests, see Bevington, *Tudor Drama and Politics*, chapter 4, and William O. Harris, *Skelton's Magnyfycence and the Cardinal Virtue Tradition* (Chapel Hill: University of North Carolina Press, 1965).

19. Quoted in William Nelson, *John Skelton, Laureate* (New York: Columbia University Press, 1939), p. 4. Stanley Fish sees a complex Skelton, but speculates that by the time Skelton wrote *Magnificence*, he had come to realize that language was "man- rather than God-made" and that a devotion to eloquence was "a foolish and even sinful preoccupation with the products of the human mind" (*John Skelton's Poetry* [New Haven: Yale University Press, 1965], p. 130). Nelson, by contrast, may be overly impressed by tales of Skelton's wildness, but shrewdly assesses the paradox of Skelton's moral voice: "His own description of excess, embodied in the morality *Magnificence*, reads like a criticism of his works" (p. 236).

20. David Bevington, *From Mankind to Marlowe: Growth of Structure in the Popular Drama of Tudor England* (Cambridge, Mass.: Harvard University Press, 1962), pp. 135–36.

21. Bevington, *Tudor Drama and Politics*, p. 99. For Bale's historians see Barry B. Adams's introduction to *John Bale's King Johan* (San Marino, Calif.: Huntington Library, 1969), pp. 25–38.

22. Adams, *King Johan*, pp. 40–43. See also Edwin S. Miller, "The Roman Rite in Bale's *King John*," *PMLA* 64 (1949): 802–22.

23. S. P. Johnson, "The Tragic Hero in Early Elizabethan

Drama," in *Studies in the English Renaissance Drama in Memory of Karl Julius Holzknecht*, ed. J. W. Bennet et al. (New York: New York University Press, 1959), p. 159.

24. Quoted in introduction to *The Itinerary of John Leland*, ed. Lucy Toulmin Smith (London: G. Bell and Sons, 1906–10), p. xii. For Bale's association with Leland, see Lily Campbell, *Shakespeare's Histories: Mirrors of Elizabethan Policy* (San Marino, Calif.: Huntington Library, 1947), pp. 62–64, and Honor McCusker, *John Bale, Dramatist and Antiquary* (Bryn Mawr, Pa.: n.p., 1942), pp. 51–58.

25. M. M. Reese, *The Cease of Majesty* (London: Edward Arnold, 1961), p. 70. For a more sympathetic view of Bale's techniques, see John N. King, *English Reformation Literature* (Princeton: Princeton University Press, 1982), pp. 56–75. The sometimes disorienting character of Reformation controversy is captured by Richard Popkin, who notes that Catholic and Protestant controversialists turned their dialectical subtleties on one another, "each side trying to sap the foundations of the other, and each trying to show that the other was faced with an insoluble form of the classical sceptical problem of the criterion" (*The History of Skepticism from Erasmus to Descartes* [1964; reprint, New York: Harper and Row, 1968], p. 14), and by Stephen Greenblatt: "Throughout the sixteenth century, Protestant and Catholic polemicists demonstrated brilliantly how each other's religion—the very anchor of reality for millions of souls—was a cunning theatrical illusion, a demonic fantasy, a piece of poetry" ("Marlowe and Renaissance Self-Fashioning," in *Two Renaissance Mythmakers*, ed. Alvin B. Kernan [Baltimore: Johns Hopkins Press, 1977], p. 62).

26. E. M. W. Tillyard, *Shakespeare's History Plays* (London: Chatto and Windus, 1944), p. 90.

27. Wolfgang Clemen, *English Tragedy Before Shakespeare*, trans. T. S. Dorsch (London: Methuen, 1961), p. 58.

28. See especially Altman, *Tudor Play of Mind*, pp. 249–59, and Franco Moretti, "'A Huge Eclipse': Tragic Form and the Deconsecration of Sovereignty," *Genre* 15 (1982): 7–40.

29. Willard Farnham, *The Medieval Heritage of Elizabethan Tragedy* (Berkeley and Los Angeles: University of California Press, 1936), pp. 263ff.; Ribner, *English History Play*, pp. 51–55.

30. See Spivack, *Shakespeare and the Allegory of Evil*, p. 313. S. L. Bethell compares Ambidexter to Groucho Marx in *Shakespeare and the Popular Dramatic Tradition* (1944; reprint, New York: Staples Press, 1948), p. 97.

31. For other instances of Ambidexter's abrupt parodies of the play's ostensible direction, see Patricia Russell, "Romantic Narrative

Plays: 1570–1590," *Stratford-upon-Avon Studies* 9, ed. John Russell Brown and Bernard Harris (1966; reprint, London: Edward Arnold, 1974), pp. 110–11, 122.

32. "Politique Discourses on Trueth and Lying," in *Elizabethan Critical Essays*, ed. G. Gregory Smith (Oxford: Clarendon Press, 1904), pp. 341–44.

33. Stephen Gosson, *Playes Confuted in Fiue Actions*, quoted in Chambers, *The Elizabethan Stage*, 4: 216. For a general discussion of contemporary attitudes toward history's relationship to poetry, see Campbell, *Shakespeare's "Histories,"* chapter 9.

34. The unorthodox implications of apparently orthodox Renaissance plays have often been noted, for example by Rossiter in his preface to *Woodstock* and in *Angel with Horns*, ed. Graham Storey (London: Longmans, Green, 1961), and, more recently, by Alvin B. Kernan, *The Playwright as Magician* (New Haven: Yale University Press, 1979), pp. 90–91; Stephen Greenblatt, "Invisible Bullets: Renaissance Authority and Its Subversion," *Glyph* 8 (1981): 40–61; and Stephen Orgel, "Making Greatness Familiar," *Genre* 15 (1982): 41–48.

35. These readings may be found, respectively, in Fredson Thayler Bowers, *Elizabethan Revenge Tragedy, 1587–1642* (Princeton: Princeton University Press, 1940), pp. 8off.; G. K. Hunter, "Ironies of Justice in *The Spanish Tragedy*," *Renaissance Drama* 8 (1965): 89–104; and Philip Edwards, introduction to the Revels edition of *The Spanish Tragedy* (London: Methuen, 1959), pp. li–lii.

36. The controversy over Marlowe's tragedies of the imagination continues unabated. For recent treatments, compare Altman, *Tudor Play of Mind*, chapter 10, which traces a "growing anxiety about the capacity of wit, in its fullest sense, to master reality" and a discovery "that all invention is essentially self-referential" (p. 322), and Lawrence Danson, "Christopher Marlowe: The Questioner," *English Literary Renaissance* 12 (1982), which argues that Marlowe's plays retain a "coherent moral vision" through all such difficulties (p. 11).

10. THE FIRST TETRALOGY

1. Sigurd Burckhardt, *Shakespearean Meanings* (Princeton: Princeton University Press, 1968), p. 112.

2. Ibid., p. 93.

3. The disintegration of ceremony and social coherence in the world of these plays is discussed in J. P. Brockbank's important essay,

"The Frame of Disorder—'Henry VI,'" *Stratford-upon-Avon Studies* 3, ed. John Russell Brown and Bernard Harris (1961; reprint London: Edward Arnold, 1967), 73–99. See also Edward I. Berry, *Patterns of Decay: Shakespeare's Early Histories* (Charlottesville: University Press of Virginia, 1975).

4. *Pierce Pennilesse His Supplication to the Devil*, in *The Works of Thomas Nashe*, ed. Ronald B. McKerrow, rev. F. P. Wilson (Oxford: Basil Blackwell, 1958), 1: 212.

5. Shakespeare, furthermore, attributes to the French what the chronicles of Hall and Holinshed describe as a tactic used by English supporters; see *Narrative and Dramatic Sources of Shakespeare*, ed. Geoffrey Bullough (New York: Columbia University Press, 1960), 3: 69, and *Shakespeare's Holinshed*, ed. R. Hosley (New York: G. P. Putnam's Sons, 1968), p. 164.

6. Brockbank rightly points out the challenge Joan presents to Talbot's heroic consolation, despite her exaggeration of his decay ("Frame of Disorder," p. 76). For further discussion of Joan's parodies, see David Riggs, *Shakespeare's Heroical Histories: "Henry VI" and Its Literary Tradition* (Cambridge, Mass.: Harvard University Press, 1971), pp. 104–8.

7. Compare Burgundy's desertion of the English in Part I, 3.3, one scene after vowing to enshrine Talbot in his heart and erect there "thy noble deeds as valour's monuments" (3.2.119–20).

8. York's ambiguous morality is discussed by Berry, *Patterns of Decay*, pp. 43–46.

9. Irving Ribner, *The English History Play in the Age of Shakespeare* (London: Methuen, 1965), pp. 106ff., and M. M. Reese, *The Cease of Majesty* (London: Edward Arnold, 1961), p. 197.

10. Brockbank, "Frame of Disorder," pp. 86–87. See also A. C. Hamilton on the trilogy's inversions of didactic expectations and moral patterns, *The Early Shakespeare* (San Marino, Calif.: Huntington Library, 1967), especially pp. 28, 39.

11. See especially Clarence Valentine Boyer, *The Villain as Hero in Elizabethan Tragedy* (New York: Dutton, 1914); Sidney Thomas, *The Antic Hamlet and Richard III* (New York: King's Crown, 1943); and Bernard Spivack, *Shakespeare and the Allegory of Evil* (New York: Columbia University Press, 1958).

12. Charles Lamb, "G. F. Cooke in 'Richard the Third,'" in *The Works of Charles Lamb*, ed. Thomas Hutchinson (London: Oxford University Press, 1940), p. 48.

13. A. P. Rossiter, *Angel with Horns*, ed. Graham Storey (London: Longmans, Green, 1961), p. 21.

14. Richard G. Moulton calls Richard "an artist in villainy" in *Shakespeare as a Dramatic Artist*, 3rd ed., rev. (Oxford: Clarendon Press, 1892), pp. 93, 95, and there are many similar characterizations. See especially Rossiter on Richard's appeal as the "appeal of the actor" whose function is "not merely 'the acting of drama,' but also 'the drama of consummate acting,'" offering "the false as more attractive than the true (the actor's function)" (*Angel with Horns*, pp. 16–20).

15. Wilbur Sanders, *The Dramatist and the Received Idea: Studies in the Plays of Marlowe and Shakespeare* (Cambridge: Cambridge University Press, 1968), p. 78.

16. Moulton, *Shakespeare as a Dramatic Artist*, p. 113. Contrast the practice of earlier moral histories, which places the forces of illusion and misrule (*King Johan*'s Catholics; *Respublica*'s Reformation) on one side and opposes to them stability on the other.

17. The Scrivener's commentary may have been borrowed from Thomas More's account of Richard's staged acceptance of the crown. For discussion, see Stephen Greenblatt, *Renaissance Self-Fashioning* (Chicago: University of Chicago Press, 1980), pp. 13–14. See also Greenblatt's use of the Machiavelli quotation cited below as a counterpoint, pp. 14–15.

18. I quote the translation of Ralphe Robynson (1551), from *Three Renaissance Classics*, ed. Burton A. Milligan (New York: Charles Scribner's Sons, 1952), p. 57.

19. John L. Palmer, *Political Characters of Shakespeare* (London: Macmillan, 1945), p. 104.

20. Robert Ornstein, *A Kingdom for a Stage* (Cambridge, Mass.: Harvard University Press, 1972), p. 79.

21. See Wolfgang Clemen, "Anticipation and Foreboding in Shakespeare's Early Histories," *Shakespeare Survey* 6 (1953): 25–35.

22. *Angel with Horns*, p. 59.

23. Ibid., pp. 21–22.

24. Sanders, *The Dramatist and the Received Idea*, pp. 89–90.

25. Henry Ansgar Kelly argues that Tillyard's objective providentialism is an "ex post facto Platonic form" imposed on the plays by critics, but admits that *Richard III* seems to be an exception (*Divine Providence in the England of Shakespeare's Histories* [Cambridge: Cambridge University Press, 1970], pp. 276–95). The unappealing, even "repulsive," character of the retributive scheme is discussed by Nicholas Brooke, *Shakespeare's Early Tragedies* (London: Methuen, 1968), especially pp. 76–79. See also Robert G. Hunter, *Shakespeare and the Mystery of God's Judgments* (Athens, Ga.: University of Georgia Press, 1976), chapter 4.

26. Max M. Reese, *The Cease of Majesty: A Study of Shakespeare's History Plays* (London: Edward Arnold, 1961), p. 212.

27. Travis Bogard, "Shakespeare's Second Richard," *PMLA* 70 (1955): 193.

28. Reese, *Cease of Majesty*, p. 98.

11. THE SUBSTANCE OF
RICHARD II

1. For helpful notation, see *The Life and Death of King Richard the Second*, new variorum edition, ed. Matthew W. Black (Philadelphia: Lippincott, 1955), pp. 136–38, and *King Richard II*, Arden edition, ed. Peter Ure (London: Methuen, 1966), pp. 70–72. Ernest B. Gilman describes the effect of the speech, and of much of the play, in terms of perspectivism and anamorphosis, in *The Curious Perspective: Literary and Pictorial Wit in the Seventeenth Century* (New Haven: Yale University Press, 1978).

2. *Richard II*, ed. J. Dover Wilson (Cambridge: Cambridge University Press, 1939), p. 171.

3. E. A. Abbott, *A Shakespearian Grammar* (London: Macmillan, 1883), pp. 167–68.

4. Derek Traversi, *Shakespeare from Richard II to Henry V* (Stanford: Stanford University Press, 1957), p. 16.

5. John Palmer, *The Political Characters of Shakespeare* (1945; reprint, London: Macmillan, 1957), p. 123.

6. E. M. W. Tillyard, *Shakespeare's History Plays* (London: Chatto and Windus, 1944), p. 252.

7. M. M. Mahood, *Shakespeare's Wordplay* (London: Methuen, 1957), p. 80.

8. See Donald M. Friedman, "John of Gaunt and the Rhetoric of Frustration," *ELH* 43 (1976): "It is as if the heroic suspension of grammar is meant to figure the sheer effort of will" (p. 287). This essay considers the speech's dramatic context and Gaunt's political motives in order to question the traditional view of the speech as a "set-piece of patriotic fervor."

9. The dramatic "refurbishing" of Richard has long been recognized. Hazlitt attributes it to his sufferings, which "make us forget that he ever was a king" (*Characters of Shakespeare's Plays* [1817; reprint, London: Oxford University Press, 1966], p. 141). For a full and subtle reading of "imaginative" themes dominating political issues, see James Winny, *The Player King: A Theme of Shakespeare's Histories*

(London: Chatto and Windus, 1968), pp. 46–47 and chapter 2. Imaginative themes, however, are inseparable from the political in this play, for it is only through the protracted disintegration of Richard's political power that his mind comes to seem so extraordinary.

10. Richard's fantastic confidence is another instance of Shakespeare's habit of placing the "Elizabethan world picture" in the most ironic contexts.

11. Ernst Kantorowicz, *The King's Two Bodies* (Princeton: Princeton University Press, 1957), p. 20.

12. Edward Dowden, *Shakspere: A Critical Study of His Mind and Art*, 10th ed. (London: Kegan Paul, 1892), pp. 194–95, 201.

13. Tillyard, *Shakespeare's History Plays*, p. 256.

14. For Richard as actor, and for theatricality as a metaphor for the state in general, see Leonard F. Dean, "*Richard II*: The State and the Image of the Theater," *PMLA* 67 (1952): 211–18, and Thomas F. Van Laan, *Role-Playing in Shakespeare* (Toronto: University of Toronto Press, 1978), pp. 117–30. Also useful is George A. Bonnard, "The Actor in *Richard II*," *Shakespeare Jahrbuch* 87 (1952): 87–101. Peter Ure objects to this line of argument in his Arden preface (pp. lxxviii–lxxix) but I cannot agree with him.

15. The notion of Richard as a poet, whether admirable or fantastical, underlies an enormous amount of criticism of the play. See Mark Van Doren, Wolfgang Clemen, James Calderwood, et al. Pushed to Van Doren's "Richard is a poet, not a king," the argument appears a little thin, but it points, I think, to an essential aspect of the play (*Shakespeare* [New York: Henry Holt and Company, 1939], p. 89). An early, fanciful version of the claim, but powerful nonetheless, is G. Wilson Knight's: Richard in prison is "exactly analogous to the creative consciousness which gives birth to poetry"; Knight also finds Richard to be on the brink of mysticism, but believes he falls short because "he remains an individualist to the last" (*The Imperial Theme* [London: Oxford University Press, 1931], pp. 351, 366).

16. Richard Altick notes that the play's images render "the physical act of speech, the sheer act of language, so conspicuous, they call attention to its illusory nature" ("Symphonic Imagery in *Richard II*," *PMLA* 62 [1947]: 350). See also James L. Calderwood's "metadramatic" reading of the play as embodying a crisis of poetic language in the transition from Richard to Bolingbroke: "The whole thrust of the play implies the poet's awareness that he now writes not within and in imitation of a world order but toward an order of his own making" (*Shakespearean Metadrama* [Minneapolis: University of Minnesota Press, 1971], p. 181).

17. For the "problem of the criterion," see Richard H. Popkin, *The History of Scepticism from Erasmus to Descartes* (New York: Harper and Row, 1964), chapter 1, and A. J. Ayer, *The Problem of Knowledge* (Baltimore: Penguin, 1956), pp. 31–35.

18. A. P. Rossiter, *Angel with Horns*, ed. Graham Storey (London: Longmans, Green, 1961), pp. 30–37. Shakespeare makes a point of Bolingbroke's performances, perhaps the most adroit of which is the cunning mixture of exaggerated loyalty and self-assertion before Flint Castle, where he offers at one moment "on both his knees" to "kiss King Richard's hand," and at the next directs a dumb show presaging insurrection: "Let's march without the noise of threat'ning drum, / That from this castle's tottered battlements / Our fair appointments may be well perus'd" (3.3.35ff.). See also Dean, "*Richard II*," cited in note 14 above.

19. On "privative terms," see Sister Miriam Joseph, *Shakespeare's Use of the Arts of Language* (1947; reprint, New York: Hafner, 1966), p. 134.

20. Karl Thompson, "Richard II, Martyr," *Shakespeare Quarterly* 8 (1957): 165–66.

21. S. K. Heninger, "The Sun-King Analogy in *Richard II*," *Shakespeare Quarterly* 11 (1960): 325.

22. Both Richard and Bolingbroke discover the "endless mutability" and "restlessness" of the self, Alvin B. Kernan argues: "Man has broken into a strange, new existence where he is free to slide back and forth along the vast scale of being, coming to rest momentarily at various points, but never knowing for certain just who and what he is" ("The Henriad: Shakespeare's Major History Plays," *Yale Review* 59 [Autumn 1969]: 8–9).

23. Fred Leeman, *Hidden Images: Games of Perception, Anamorphic Art, Illusion* (New York: Abrams, 1976), p. 48.

12. "KING OF INFINITE SPACE": HAMLET AND HIS FICTIONS

1. For Hamlet's political dilemma, see John Dover Wilson, *What Happens in "Hamlet,"* 3rd ed. (Cambridge: Cambridge University Press, 1951), pp. 30–38. See also Francis Fergusson, *The Idea of a Theater* (Princeton: Princeton University Press, 1949), p. 101: "Hamlet has lost a throne, and has lost thereby a social, publicly acceptable *persona* . . . he haunts the stage like the dispossessed of classical drama." The

phrase "boundary situation" is discussed by Richard B. Sewall, *The Vision of Tragedy* (New Haven: Yale University Press, 1959), p. 5 and p. 151, n. 10.

2. C. S. Lewis, "Hamlet: The Prince or the Poem?" in *Proceedings of the British Academy*, vol. 28 (London: Oxford University Press, 1942), p. 11.

3. Among the many discussions of Hamlet's quibbles and verbal parodies see M. M. Mahood, *Shakespeare's Wordplay* (London: Methuen, 1957), chapter 5; Maurice Charney, *Style in Hamlet* (Princeton: Princeton University Press, 1969), pp. 259ff.; and Lawrence Danson, *Tragic Alphabet* (New Haven: Yale University Press, 1974), chapter 2.

4. The fullest reading of the speech and its references is in Harry Levin, *The Question of Hamlet* (New York: Oxford University Press, 1959), pp. 138–64.

5. *Aeneid* quotations from *The Aeneid of Virgil: A Verse Translation*, trans. Allen Mandelbaum (Berkeley and Los Angeles: University of California Press, 1971); line numbers refer to this edition and to the Loeb Latin respectively.

6. Wendell Claussen, "An Interpretation of the *Aeneid*," in *Virgil: A Collection of Critical Essays*, ed. Steele Commager (Englewood Cliffs, N.J.: Prentice-Hall, 1966), p. 77.

7. Maynard Mack, "The World of Hamlet," in *Tragic Themes in Western Literature*, ed. Cleanth Brooks (New Haven: Yale University Press, 1955), p. 33. For medieval and Renaissance understanding of Aeneas's struggle through darkness and illusion, see Michael Murrin, *The Allegorical Epic: Essays in Its Rise and Decline* (Chicago: University of Chicago Press, 1980), chapter 2.

8. Brooks Otis, *Virgil: A Study in Civilized Poetry* (Oxford: Clarendon Press, 1964); see index entries under "death and resurrection."

9. See G. Wilson Knight, *The Wheel of Fire: Interpretations of Shakespearean Tragedy* (London: Oxford University Press, 1930), chapter 2.

10. For a discussion of the importance, and implicit ironies, of Hamlet's theatrical awareness in relation to contemporary critical controversy, see William A. Ringler, Jr., "Hamlet's Defense of the Players," in *Essays on Shakespeare and Elizabethan Drama in Honor of Hardin Craig*, ed. Richard Hosley (Columbia, Mo.: University of Missouri Press, 1962), pp. 201–12.

11. Leon Battista Alberti, *On Painting*, trans. John R. Spencer, rev. ed. (New Haven: Yale University Press, 1966), p. 56 and pp. 109–10, n. 44.

12. Dover Wilson, *What Happens in "Hamlet,"* pp. 138, 140.

13. Harley Granville-Barker, *Prefaces to Shakespeare* (Princeton: Princeton University Press, 1946), 1: 89–91.

14. Leslie Fiedler suggests furthermore that *The Mousetrap* teases us with a potential infinite regress: "Had Claudius not interrupted with his terror, his ironic cry of 'Give me some light!' a Hamlet-character, some melancholy sniffer out of evil, would inevitably have had to come upon the scene to contrive another play to catch the conscience of Gonzago [family name of Lucianus] and in that play another Hamlet, and so on" ("The Defense of Illusion and the Creation of Myth," in *English Institute Studies, 1948,* ed. D. A. Robertson, Jr. [New York: Columbia University Press, 1949], p. 88).

15. I am not suggesting that Horatio is an opportunist; his suicidal gesture in the final scene, that more of "an antique Roman than a Dane," bespeaks his loyalty to Hamlet. But he makes it before hearing of Fortinbras's arrival and Hamlet's endorsement of the new order. Horatio is the only major character who prospers under the three regimes—Old Hamlet's, Claudius's, and Fortinbras's—and is, with Stanley in *Richard III* and York in *Richard II*, one of Shakespeare's political "survivors."

16. Dover Wilson's argument that Lucianus's lines are the "some dozen or sixteen" written by Hamlet complements my reading here, although I do not think that we can do better in the case of *The Mousetrap* than to regard the entire play as psychologically, if not literally, Hamlet's own.

17. William Hazlitt, *Characters of Shakespeare's Plays* (1817; reprint, London: Oxford University Press, 1966), p. 83.

18. For the problem of "other minds" in *Hamlet,* see Harold Skulsky, *Spirits Finely Touched* (Athens, Ga.: University of Georgia Press, 1976), chapter 1.

19. Hardin Craig, *An Interpretation of Shakespeare* (New York: Dryden Press, 1948), p. 186.

20. Levin, *The Question of Hamlet,* pp. 41–42.

21. Hamlet's "meditation" is suggested by Louis L. Martz, *The Poetry of Meditation* (New Haven: Yale University Press, 1954), pp. 137–38, and developed at greater length by Eleanor Prosser, *Hamlet and Revenge,* 2nd ed. (Stanford: Stanford University Press, 1971), pp. 221ff. Prosser discerns a "positively sunny" disposition in Hamlet (p. 221) by sifting for symbols and using the final scene's providentialism as a conclusion for the meditation. Her assumption seems to be that if a symbol is traditional, it is the sign of good cheer rather than of merely "modern anxieties." For a different view of late-medieval and

Renaissance preoccupations with death, see Lynn White, Jr., "Death and the Devil," in *The Darker Side of the Renaissance: Beyond the Fields of Reason*, ed. Robert S. Kinsman (Berkeley and Los Angeles: University of California Press, 1974), pp. 25–46.

22. An intriguing discussion of the general topic appears in Alan Paskow, "The Meaning of My Own Death," *International Philosophical Quarterly* 14 (March 1974): 51–69. Paskow's warning about the illusion of rectitude after confronting death has important implications for *Hamlet* (pp. 67–69).

23. Prosser, *Hamlet and Revenge*, p. 221.

24. St. Augustine, *Confessions*, trans. R. S. Pine-Coffin (Baltimore: Penguin, 1961), p. 262 (11.11).

25. Michael Goldman, *Shakespeare and the Energies of Drama* (Princeton: Princeton University Press, 1972), chapter 6. For recent discussions of *Hamlet*'s challenges to its audience's comprehension, see in addition to Goldman, Robert Hapgood, "Hamlet Nearly Absurd: The Dramaturgy of Delay," *Tulane Drama Review* 9 (1965): 132–45; Norman Rabkin, *Shakespeare and the Common Understanding* (New York: Free Press, 1967), pp. 1–13; Stephen Booth, "On the Value of *Hamlet*," in *Reinterpretations of Elizabethan Drama*, ed. Norman Rabkin (New York: Columbia University Press, 1969); and Brent M. Cohen, " 'What Is It You Would See?': *Hamlet* and the Conscience of the Theatre," *English Literary History* 44 (1977): 222–47.

AFTERWORD

1. Francis Fergusson, *The Idea of the Theater* (Princeton: Princeton University Press, 1949), pp. 102–4, 140.

2. Rosemond Tuve, *Allegorical Imagery: Some Mediaeval Books and Their Posterity* (Princeton: Princeton University Press, 1966), p. 127.

3. Fergusson, *Idea of the Theater*, p. 146.

4. I quote from Douglas Bush, *The Renaissance and English Humanism* (1939; reprint, Toronto: University of Toronto Press, 1968), pp. 24, 33; and Lynn White, Jr., "Death and the Devil," in *The Darker Side of the Renaissance: Beyond the Fields of Reason*, ed. Robert S. Kinsman (Berkeley and Los Angeles: University of California Press, 1974), p. 26.

5. This issue has recently been discussed by David Quint in *Origin and Originality in Renaissance Literature: Versions of the Source* (New Haven: Yale University Press, 1983), pp. 8–21.

6. Much of this paragraph is indebted to Sydney J. Freedberg,

Parmigianino: His Works in Painting (Cambridge, Mass.: Harvard University Press, 1950), pp. 104–6.

7. John Ashbery, "Self-Portrait in a Convex Mirror," in *Self-Portrait in a Convex Mirror* (New York: Viking Press, 1975), p. 70.

8. See Norman Rabkin, "Rabbits, Ducks, and Henry V," *Shakespeare Quarterly* 28 (1977): 279–96.

INDEX

446 · Index

Wenck, Johannes, *continued*
48, 54, 60, 66, 88, 279, 379–
80n55, 392–93n30
Wetherbee, Winthrop, 374n20,
395n2
White, Lynn, Jr., 435n4, 435n21
Whitney, Lois, 420n24
Whittaker, T., 379–80n55
Wickham, Glynne, 423n5,
424n14
William of Ockham, 59–61, 64,
387n42
Willis, Richard, 404n4
Wilson, John Dover, 307, 347,
432n1, 434n16
Wilson, Thomas, 151, 405n7
Wimsatt, William, 147, 404n2

Wind, Edgar, 391n14, 392n25
Winny, James, 430n9
Winters, Yvor, 417n6
Wittgenstein, Ludwig, 54
Wolff, Samuel Lee, 419n18
Wonder (*admiratio*), 19, 86, 122

Xenophanes, 79

Yates, Frances, 394n4, 418n14
Yeats, William Butler, 51
Young, Richard B., 174, 176,
410n15
Young, Karl, 423n3

Zandvoort, R. W., 412n4, 419n18,
421n31

Compositor:	Wilsted and Taylor
Text:	10/12 Bembo
Display:	Bembo
Printer:	Thomson-Shore, Inc.
Binder:	John H. Dekker & Sons